VIZ GRAPHIC NOVEL

SILENT MÖBIUS ™

VOL. 4

1999 A.D.

On a visit to Japan for work on a shadowy project, the hermetic magician Gigelf Liqueur becomes involved in a disaster. A gate is opened to another world—the world of Nemesis, home of evil entities known as Lucifer Hawks who visited our Earth in ancient times. Soon afterward, Gigelf Liqueur is never seen again.

2023 A.D.

Tokyo has become a gigantic 21st-century metropolis, but it is haunted by supernatural danger. In response to the growing attacks on citizens by the mysterious Lucifer Hawks, Rally Cheyenne forms a special section of the Tokyo Police known as the A.M.P.—Attacked Mystification Police Department. With the help of second-in-command Lebia Maverick, Shinto priestess Nami Yamigumo, and cyborg "megadyne" Kiddy Phenil, the A.M.P. monitors and combats the infestation. For Rally Cheyenne, the matter is personal; for she is the child of a Lucifer Hawk and a human mother, and her sister, Rosa, willingly vanished long ago into her father's dark world.

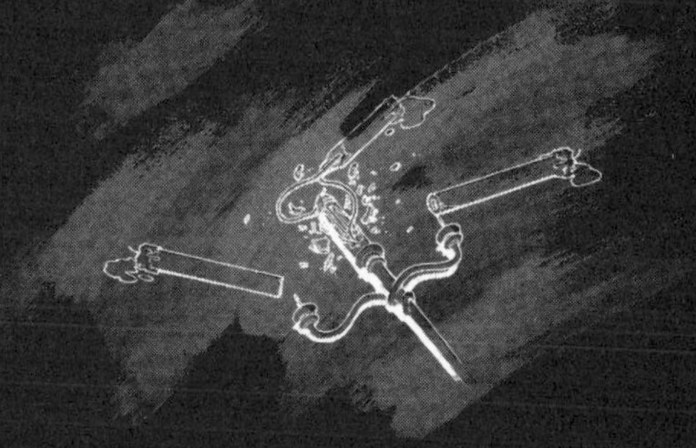

2026 A.D.

Two new members join the A.M.P.: Yuki Saiko, an inexperienced psychic, and Katsumi Liqueur, who is blessed or cursed with her father's magical powers. Finding herself an especial target of the Lucifer Hawks, Katsumi gradually discovers more about her father's legacy, and inherits his mightiest magical weapon—Grospoliner, the sentient king of swords. Even Katsumi's boyfriend, policeman Robert DeVice, is drawn into the battles that center around her. But for every block that is destroyed or citizen who is killed by the Lucifer Hawks' growing powers, the A.M.P. must try harder to discover the origins and goals of their foes.

2028 A.D.

The present day...

VIZ GRAPHIC NOVEL

SILENT MÖBIUS ™

VOL. 4

STORY AND ART BY
KIA ASAMIYA

This volume contains the monthly comics
SILENT MÖBIUS: INTO THE LABYRINTH #1
through #6 in their entirety.

STORY AND ART BY KIA ASAMIYA

ENGLISH ADAPTATION BY
FRED BURKE & TOSHIFUMI YOSHIDA

Touch-Up Art & Lettering/Wayne Truman
(Ch. 9, 10, 12) & Dan Nakrosis (Ch. 11)
Cover Design/Hidemi Sahara
Layout Design/Sean Lee
Editor/Jason Thompson

Editor-in-Chief/Hyoe Narita
Publisher/Seiji Horibuchi
Director of Sales & Marketing/Oliver Chin

Printed in Canada

Published by Viz Communications, Inc.
P.O. Box 77010 ▪ San Francisco, CA
94107

10 9 8 7 6 5 4 3 2 1
First printing, March 2000

Vizit our web sites at www.viz.com,
www.pulp-mag.com, www.j-pop.com
and www.animerica-mag.com!

CONTENTS

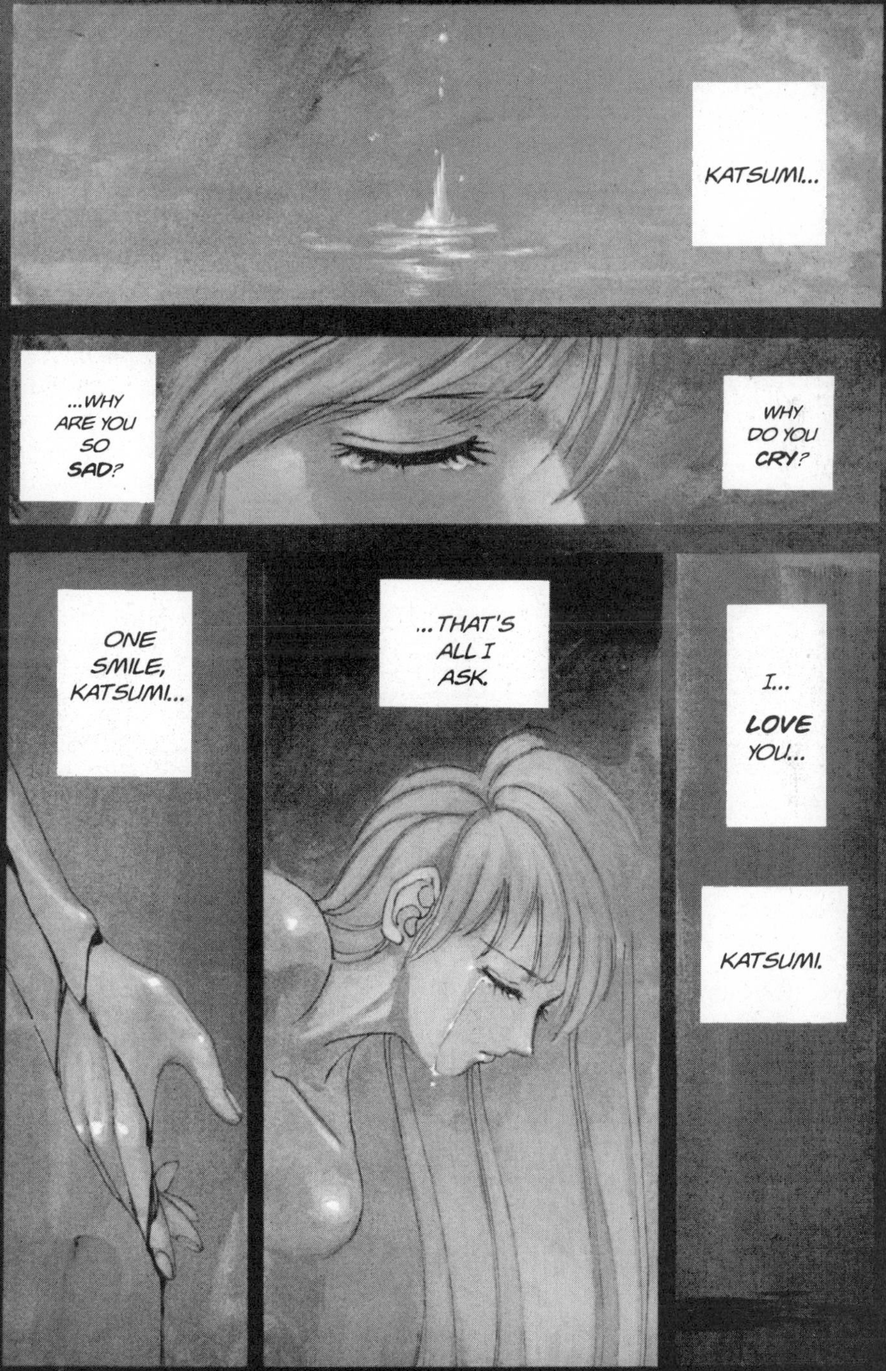
KATSUMI...
...WHY ARE YOU SO SAD?
WHY DO YOU CRY?
ONE SMILE, KATSUMI...
...THAT'S ALL I ASK.
I... LOVE YOU...
KATSUMI.

CHAPTER 09:

PREMONITION

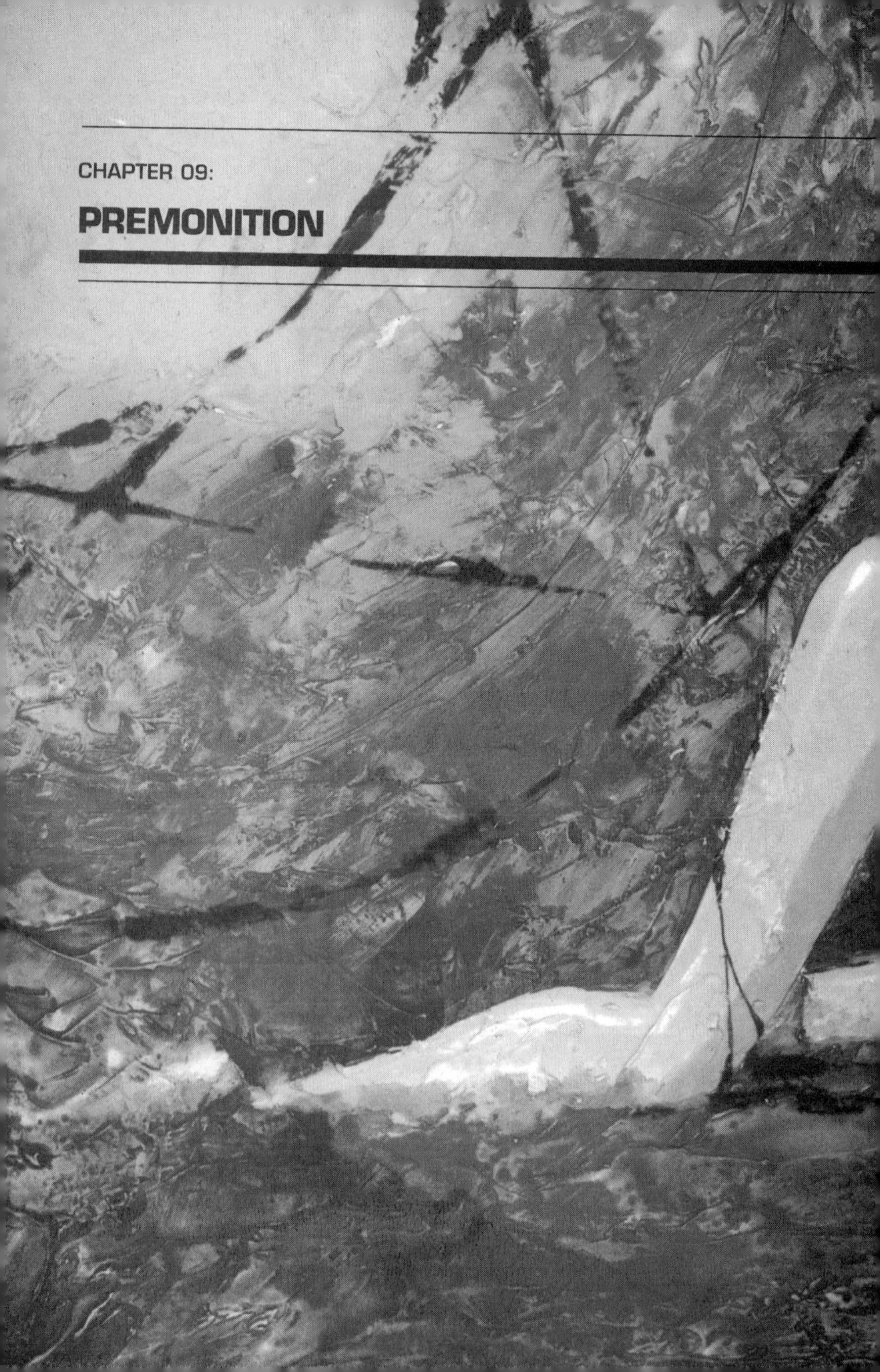

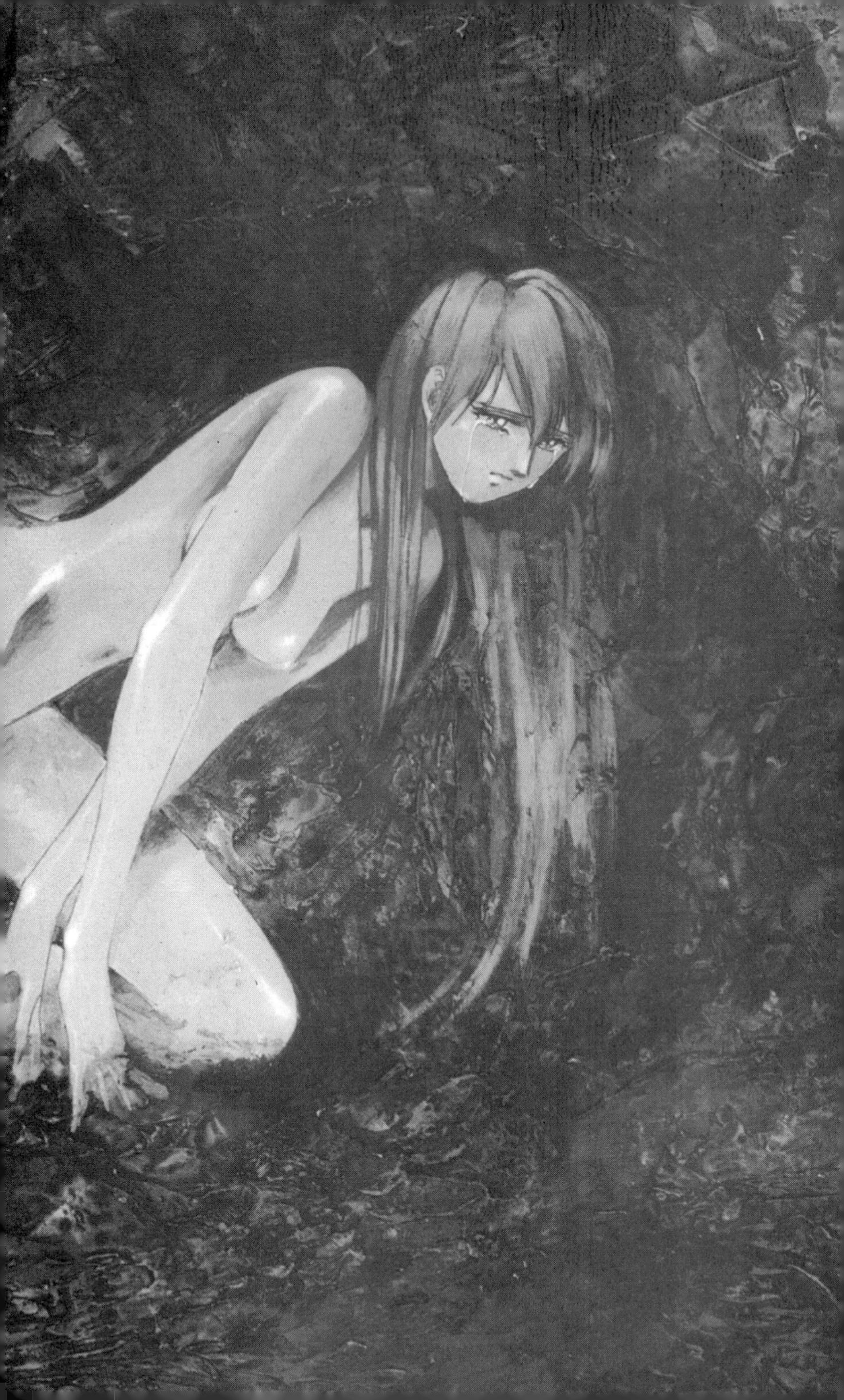

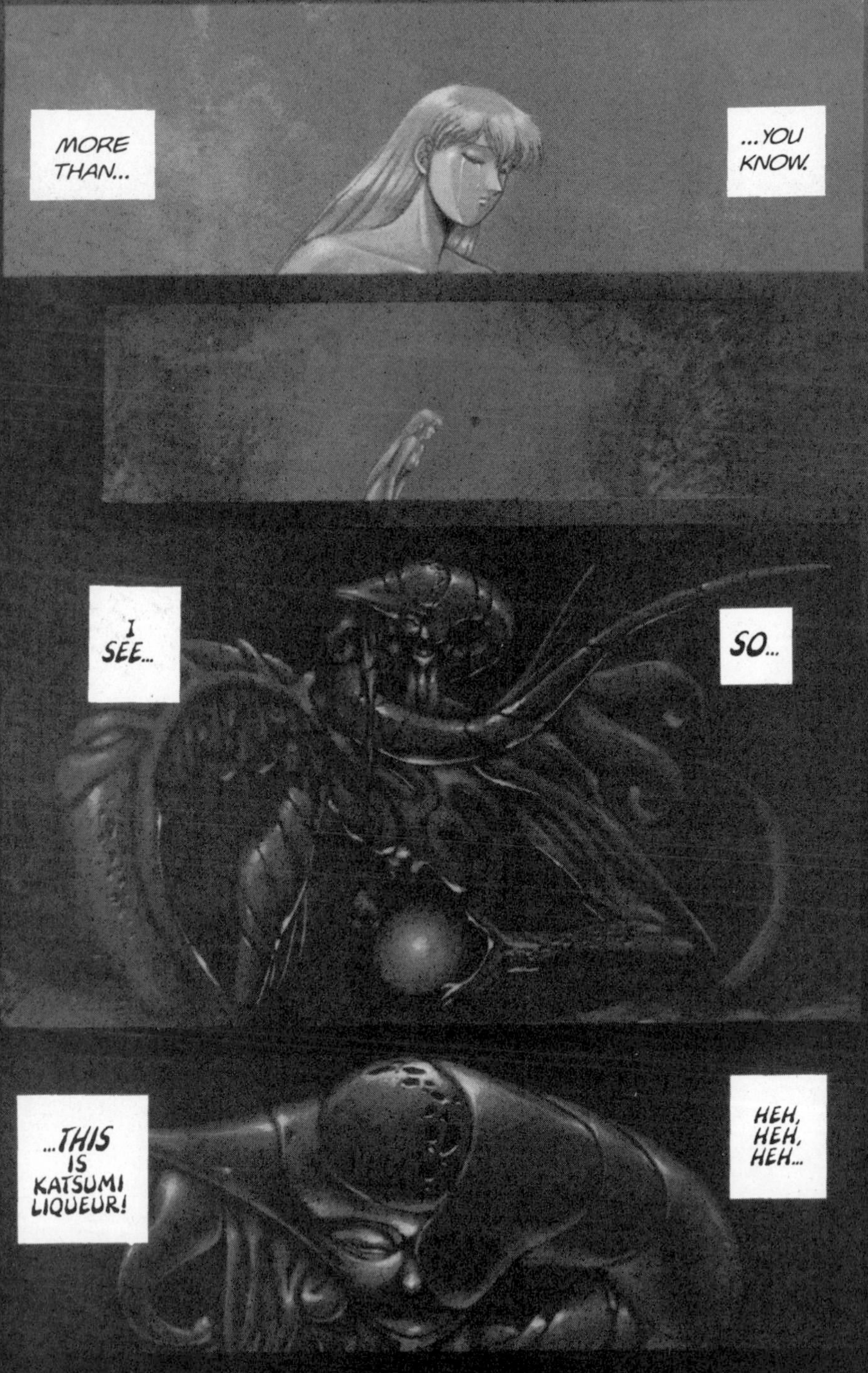
MORE THAN...
...YOU KNOW.
I SEE...
SO...
...THIS IS KATSUMI LIQUEUR!
HEH, HEH, HEH...

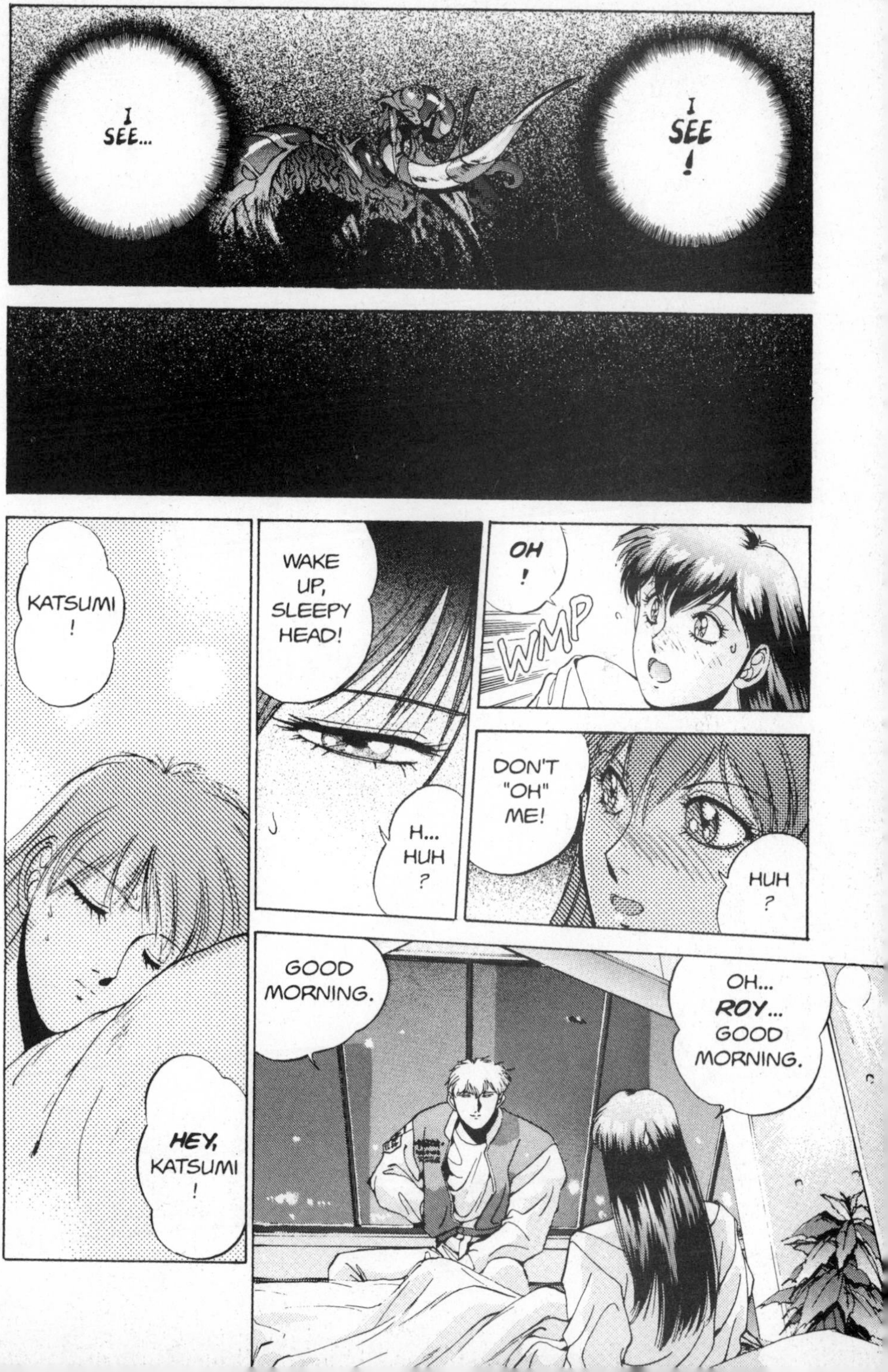
I SEE...
I SEE !
KATSUMI !
HEY, KATSUMI !
WAKE UP, SLEEPY HEAD!
H... HUH ?
OH !
WMP
DON'T "OH" ME!
HUH ?
GOOD MORNING.
OH... ROY... GOOD MORNING.

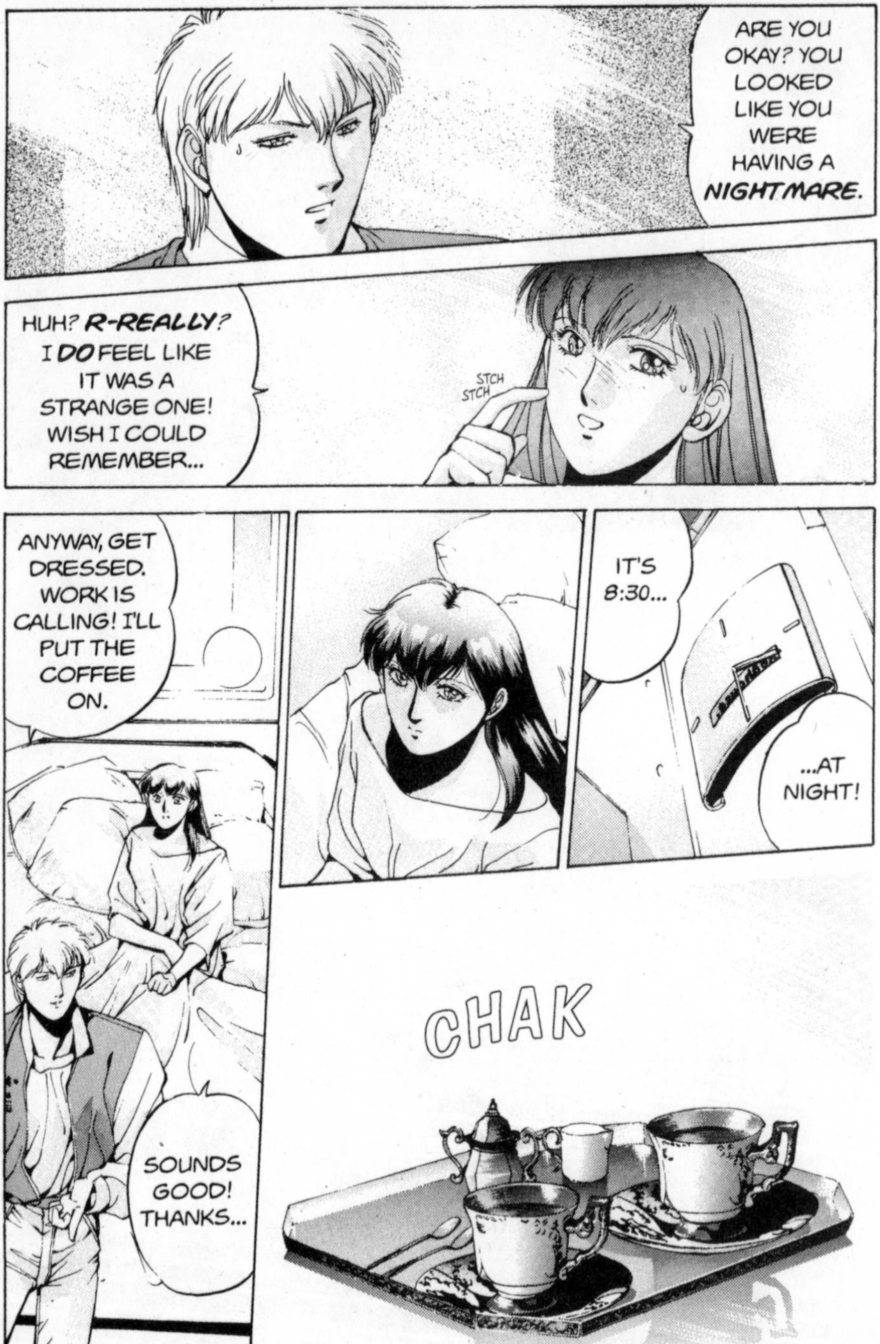
ARE YOU OKAY? YOU LOOKED LIKE YOU WERE HAVING A NIGHTMARE.
HUH? R-REALLY? I DO FEEL LIKE IT WAS A STRANGE ONE! WISH I COULD REMEMBER...
STCH STCH
ANYWAY, GET DRESSED. WORK IS CALLING! I'LL PUT THE COFFEE ON.
SOUNDS GOOD! THANKS...
IT'S 8:30...
...AT NIGHT!
CHAK

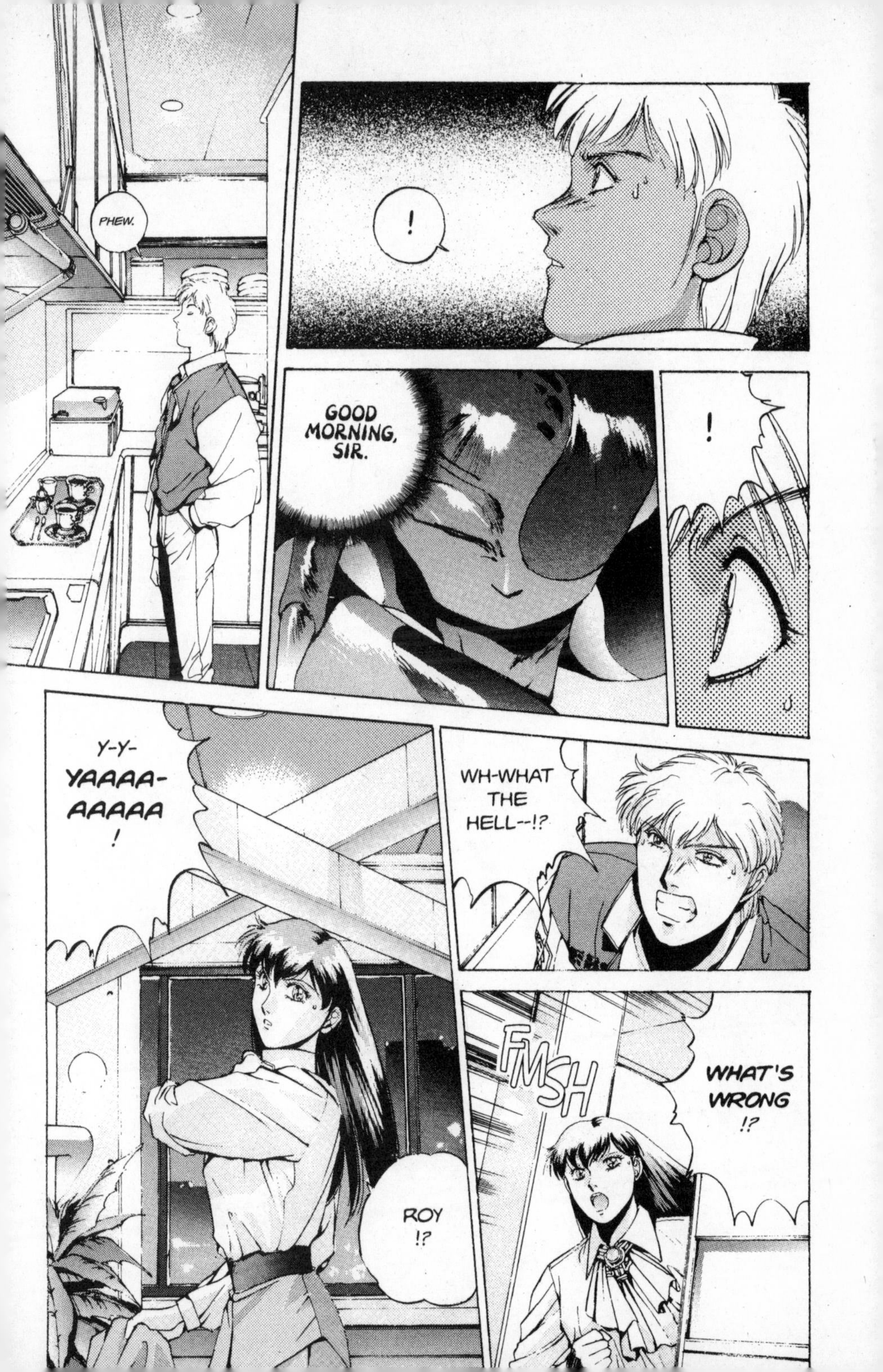
PHEW.
!
GOOD MORNING, SIR.
!
Y-Y- YAAAA-AAAAA !
WH-WHAT THE HELL--!?
ROY !?
FMSH
WHAT'S WRONG !?

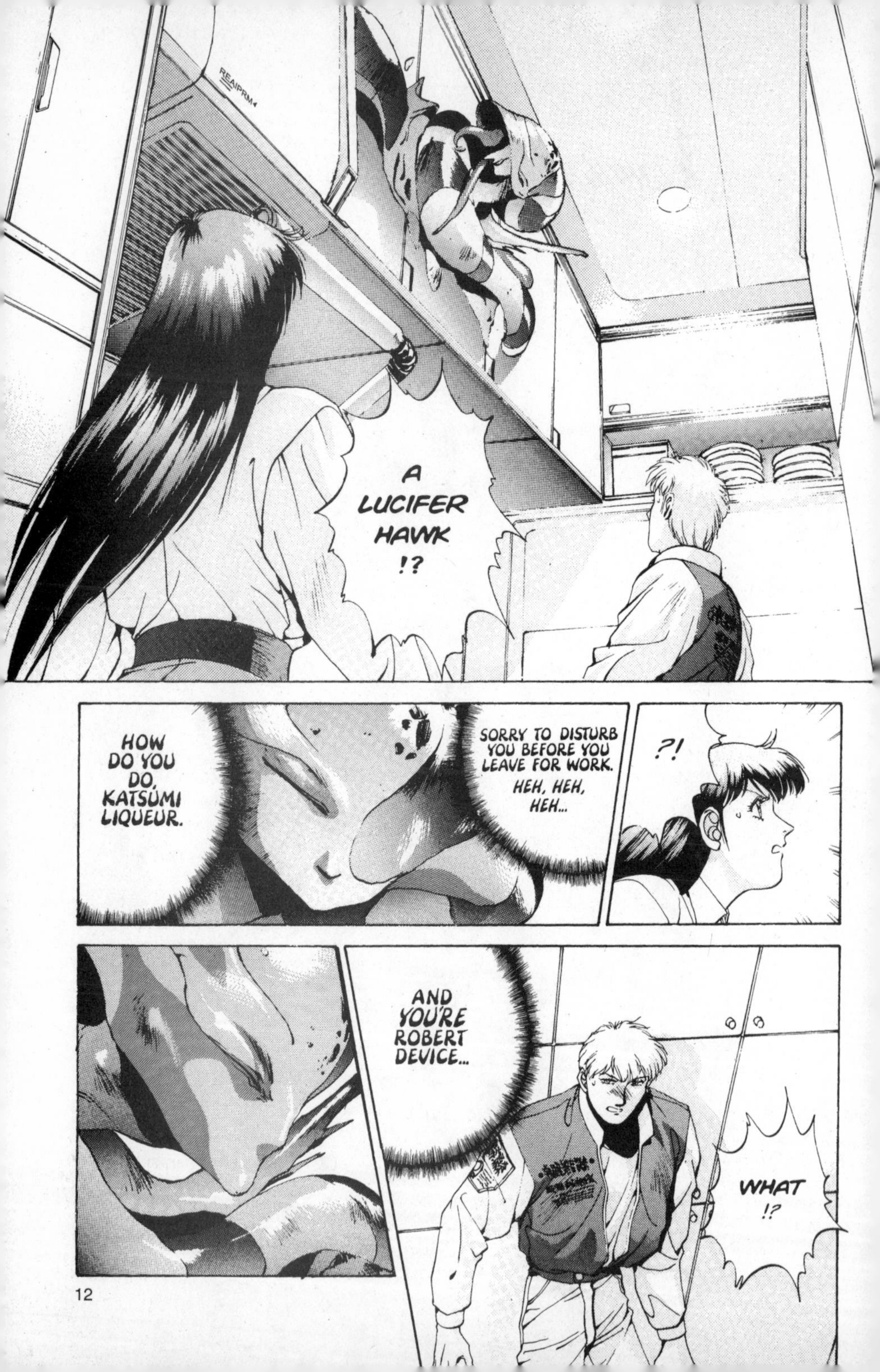
A LUCIFER HAWK !?
HOW DO YOU DO, KATSUMI LIQUEUR.
SORRY TO DISTURB YOU BEFORE YOU LEAVE FOR WORK. HEH, HEH, HEH...
?!
AND YOU'RE ROBERT DEVICE...
WHAT !?

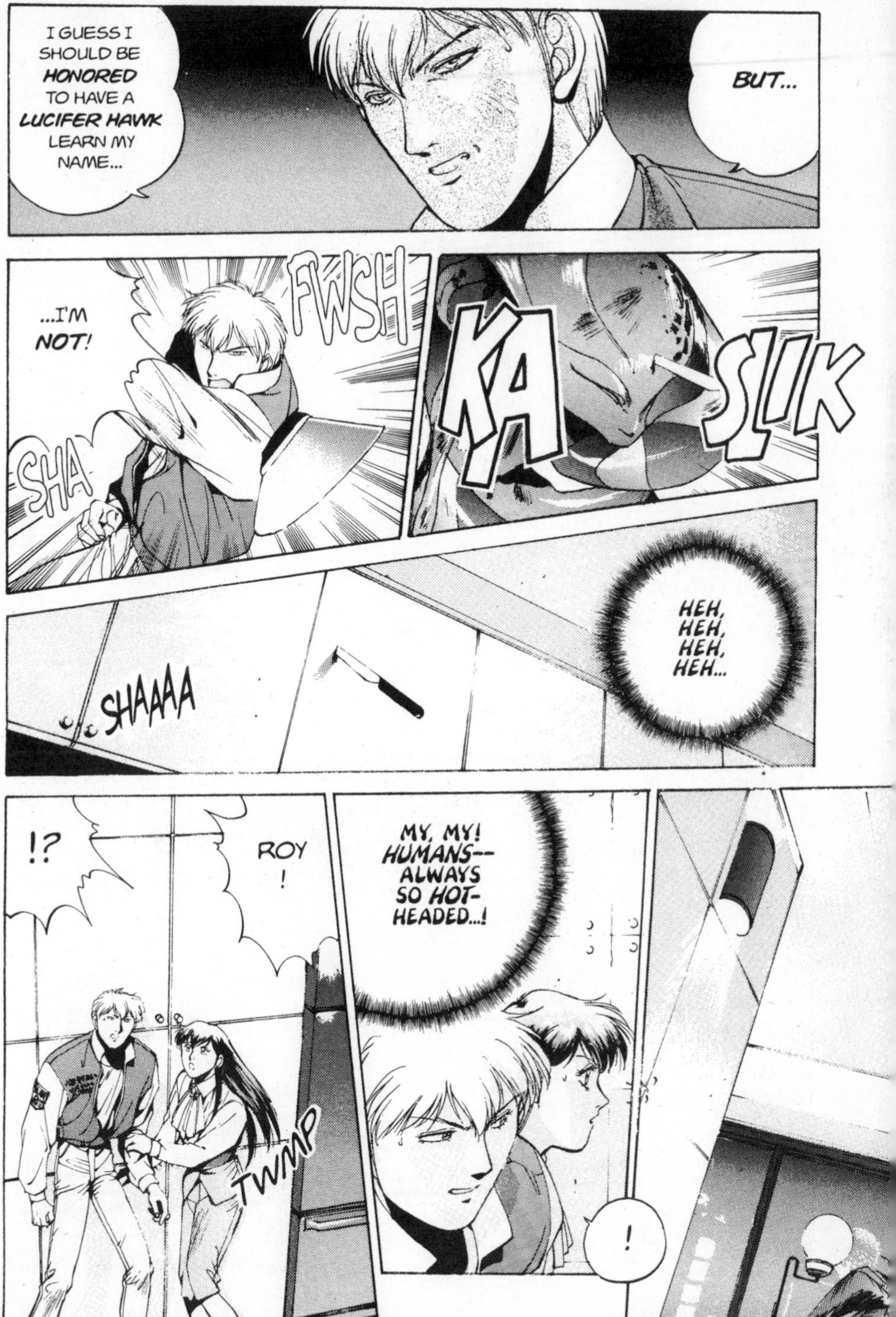
I GUESS I SHOULD BE HONORED TO HAVE A LUCIFER HAWK LEARN MY NAME...
BUT...
...I'M NOT!
FWSH
SHA
KA
SLIK
SHAAAA
HEH, HEH, HEH, HEH...
!?
ROY!
TWMP
MY, MY! HUMANS-- ALWAYS SO HOT-HEADED...!
!

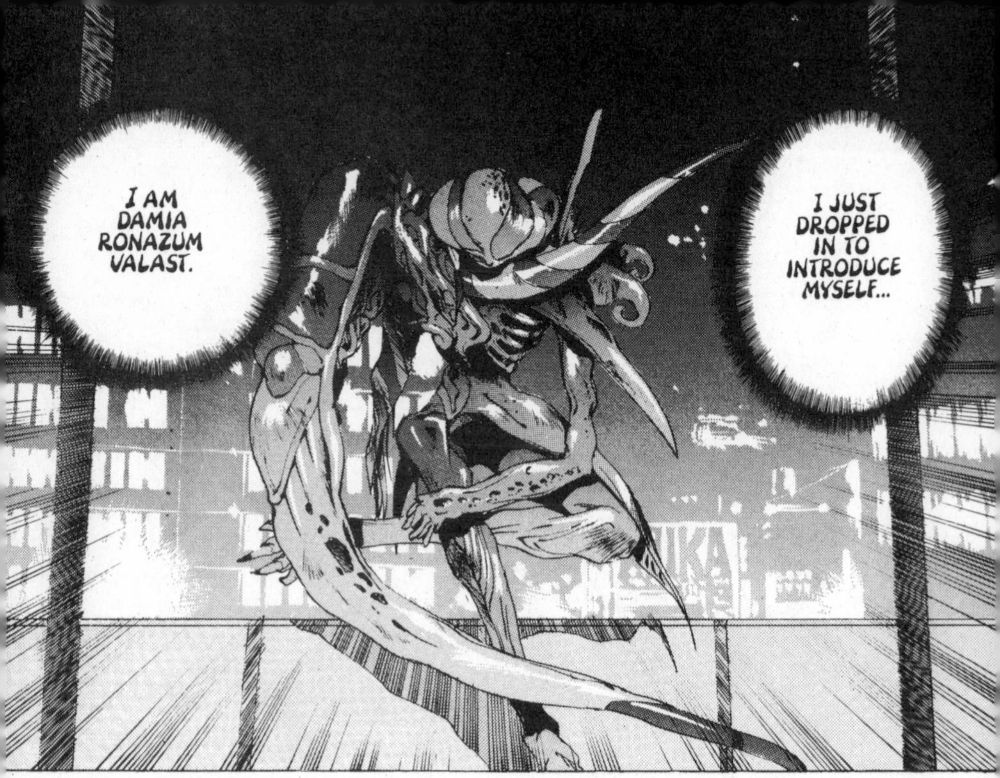
I AM DAMIA RONAZUM VALAST.
I JUST DROPPED IN TO INTRODUCE MYSELF...

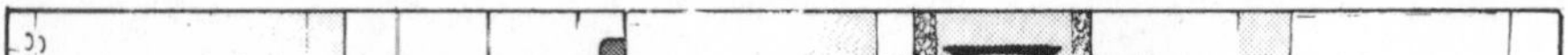
OH...

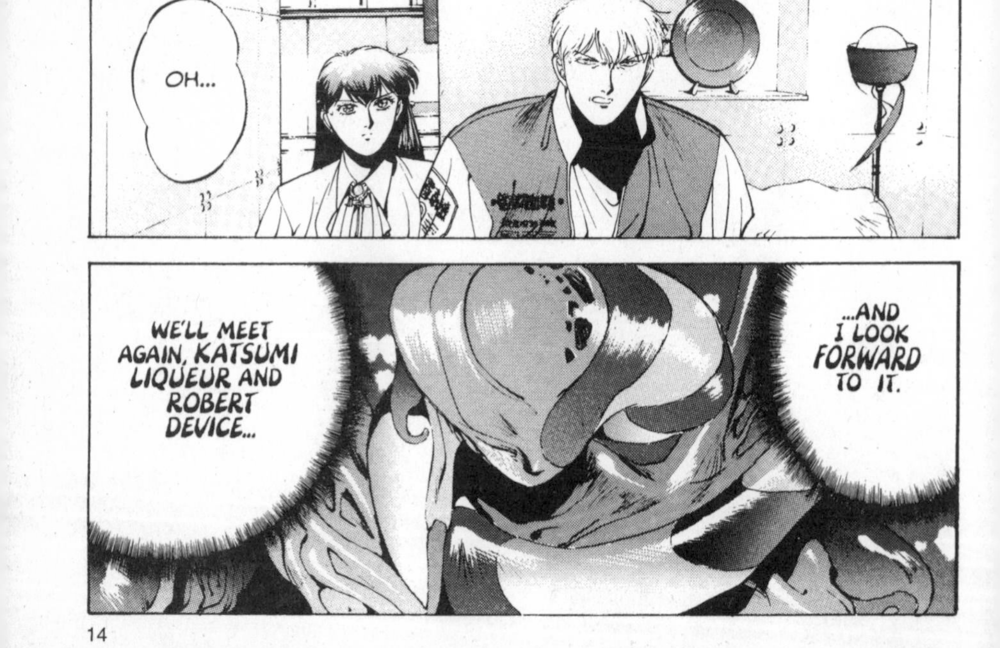
WE'LL MEET AGAIN, KATSUMI LIQUEUR AND ROBERT DEVICE...
...AND I LOOK FORWARD TO IT.

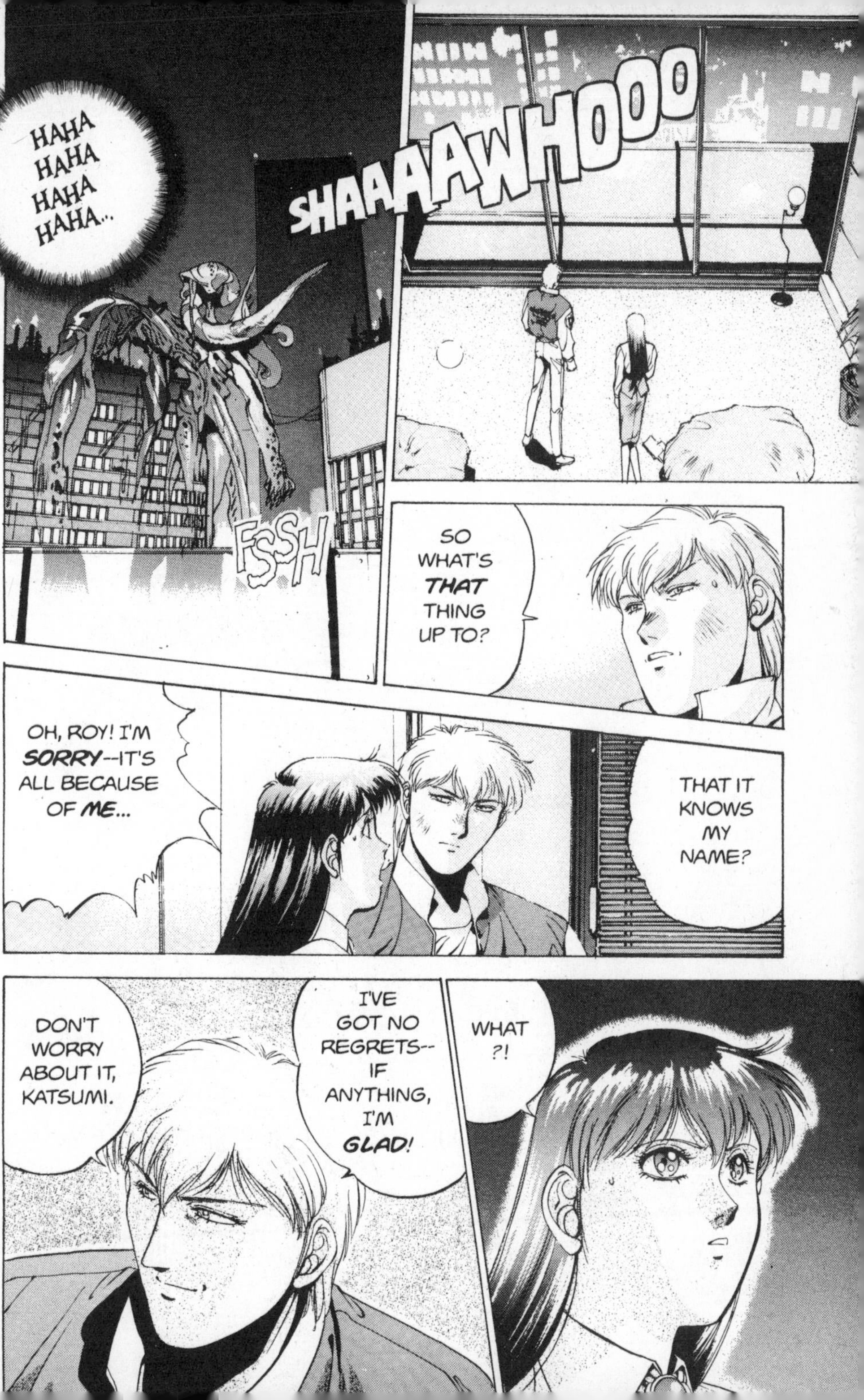
HAHA HAHA HAHA HAHA...
SHAAAAWHOOO
FSSH
SO WHAT'S **THAT** THING UP TO?
OH, ROY! I'M **SORRY**--IT'S ALL BECAUSE OF **ME**...
THAT IT KNOWS MY NAME?
DON'T WORRY ABOUT IT, KATSUMI.
I'VE GOT NO REGRETS-- IF ANYTHING, I'M **GLAD**!
WHAT ?!

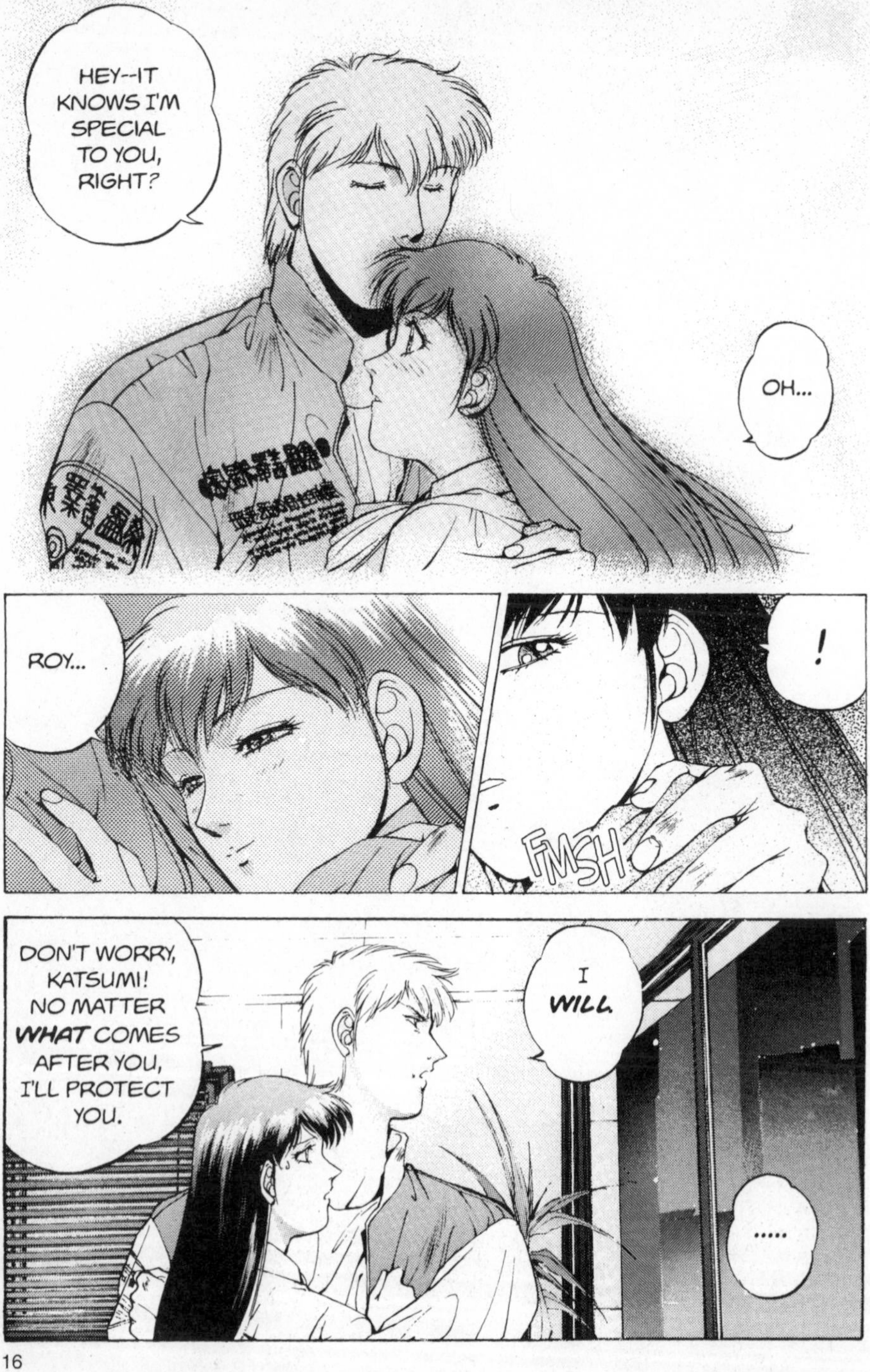
HEY--IT KNOWS I'M SPECIAL TO YOU, RIGHT?
OH...
ROY...
!
FMSH
DON'T WORRY, KATSUMI! NO MATTER WHAT COMES AFTER YOU, I'LL PROTECT YOU.
I WILL.
.....

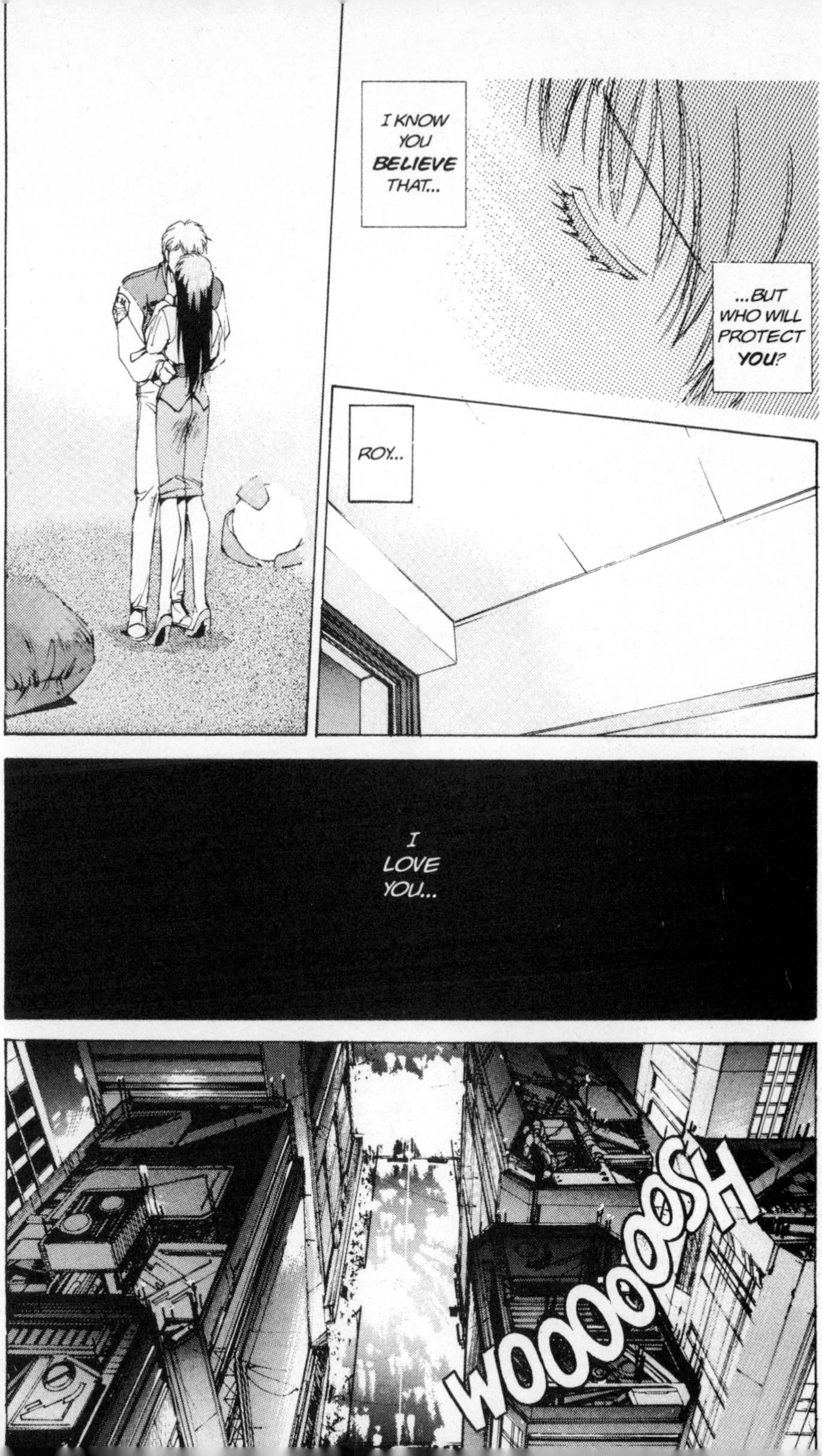
I KNOW YOU BELIEVE THAT...
...BUT WHO WILL PROTECT YOU?
ROY...
I LOVE YOU...
WOOOOOOSH

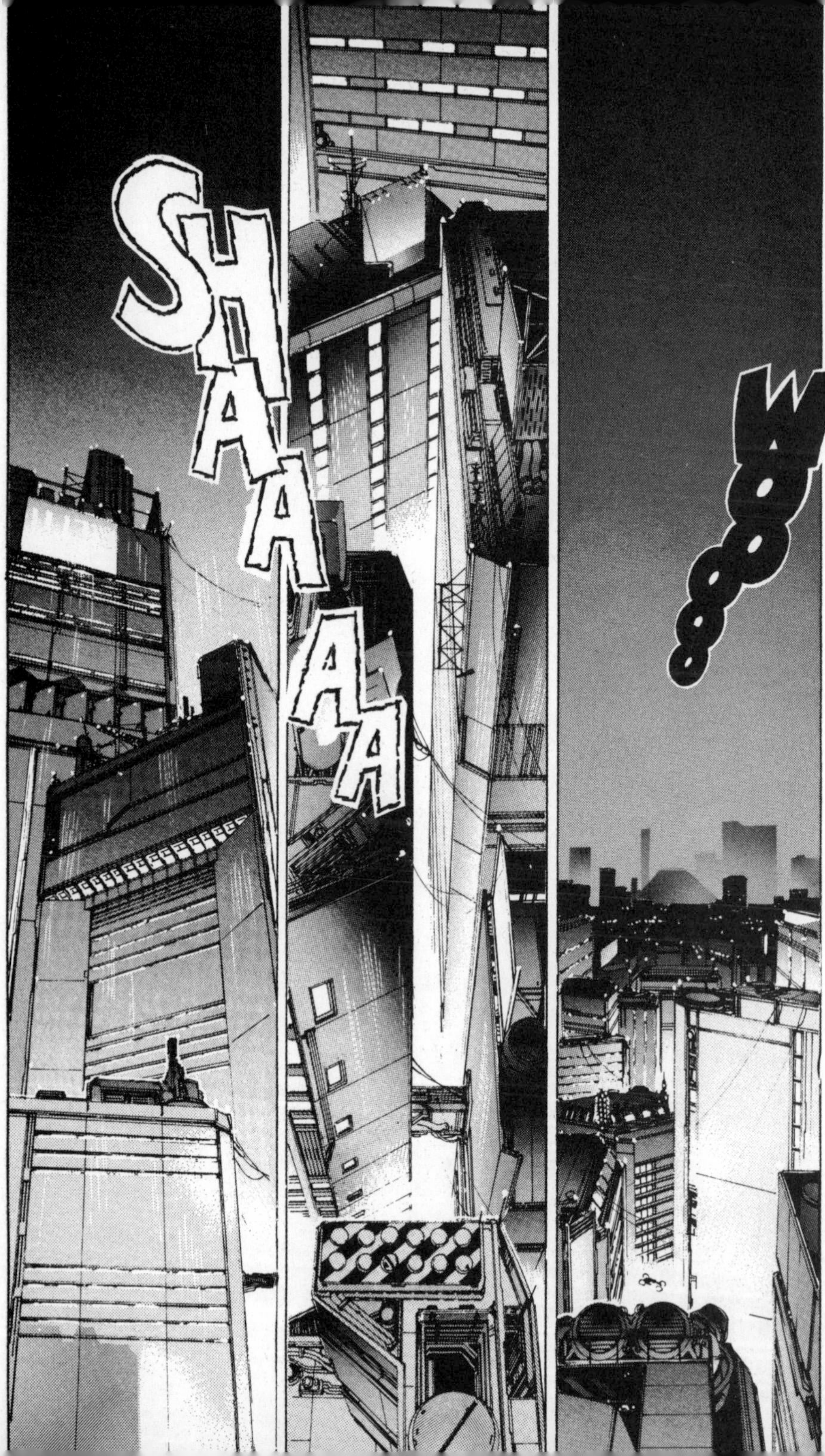
SHAAAA
WOOOOO

VRRRMMM

KATSUMI! COME IN!

THIS IS KATSUMI! WHAT'S UP LEBIA? I'M ON MY WAY TO THE STATION NOW. I'M NOT LATE, AM I?

THAT'S NOT IT, I'M AFRAID. WE'VE CORNERED A LUCIFER HAWK IN AREA G.

WHAT!? ALREADY!?

PROCEED TO THE SITE DIRECTLY.

SORRY TO RUSH YOU...

KIDDY AND THE GROUP ARE ALREADY THERE. YOU KNOW THE PROCEDURES, RIGHT?

ISN'T THAT KINDA FAST?

VMMMSH

SKREEE

I KNOW, I KNOW...

BE THERE IN A SEC!

SKRRK

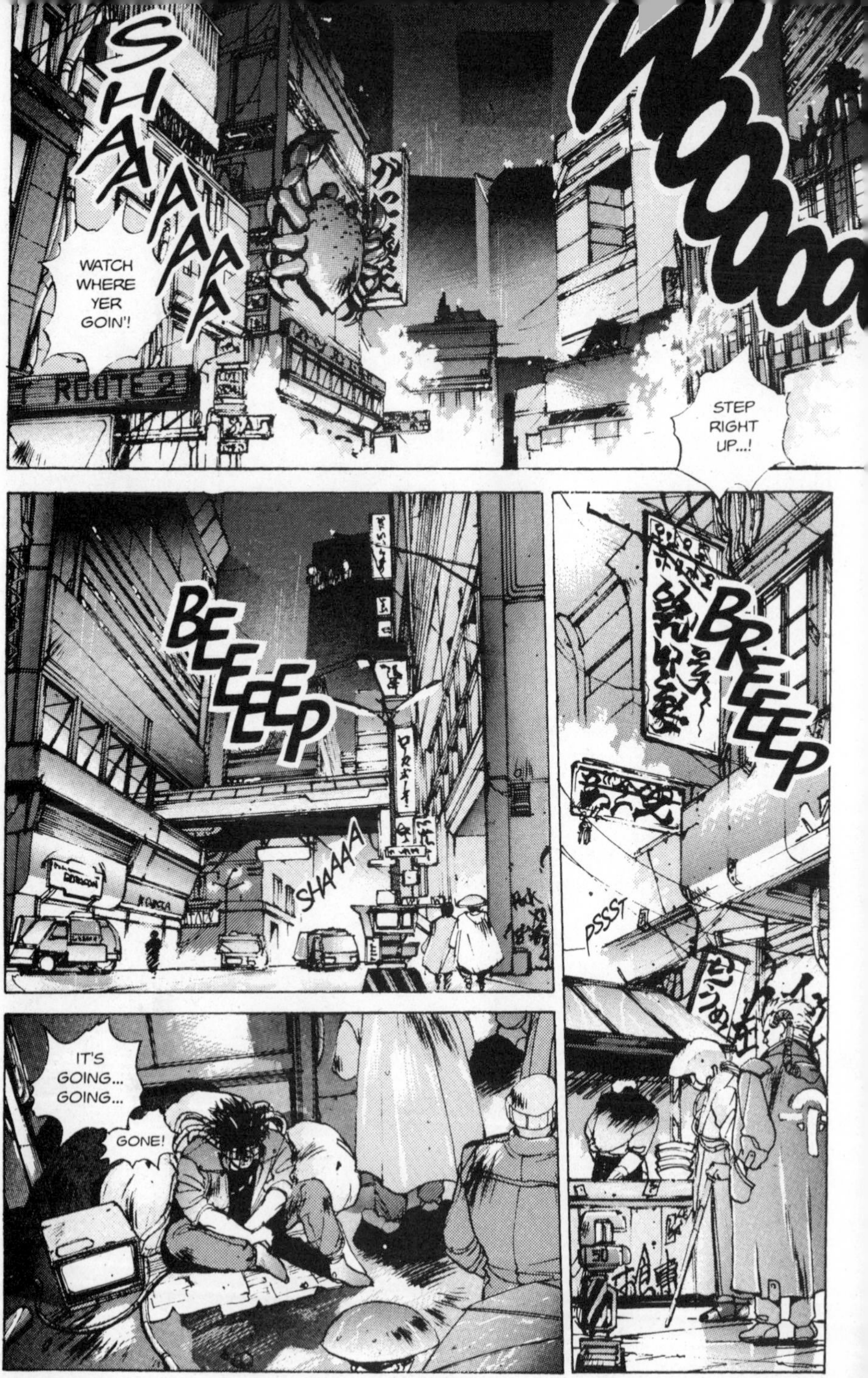
SHAAAAAAA
WATCH WHERE YER GOIN'!
ROUTE 2
STEP RIGHT UP...!
BEEEEEP
SHAAAA
IT'S GOING... GOING...
GONE!
BREEEEEP
PSSST

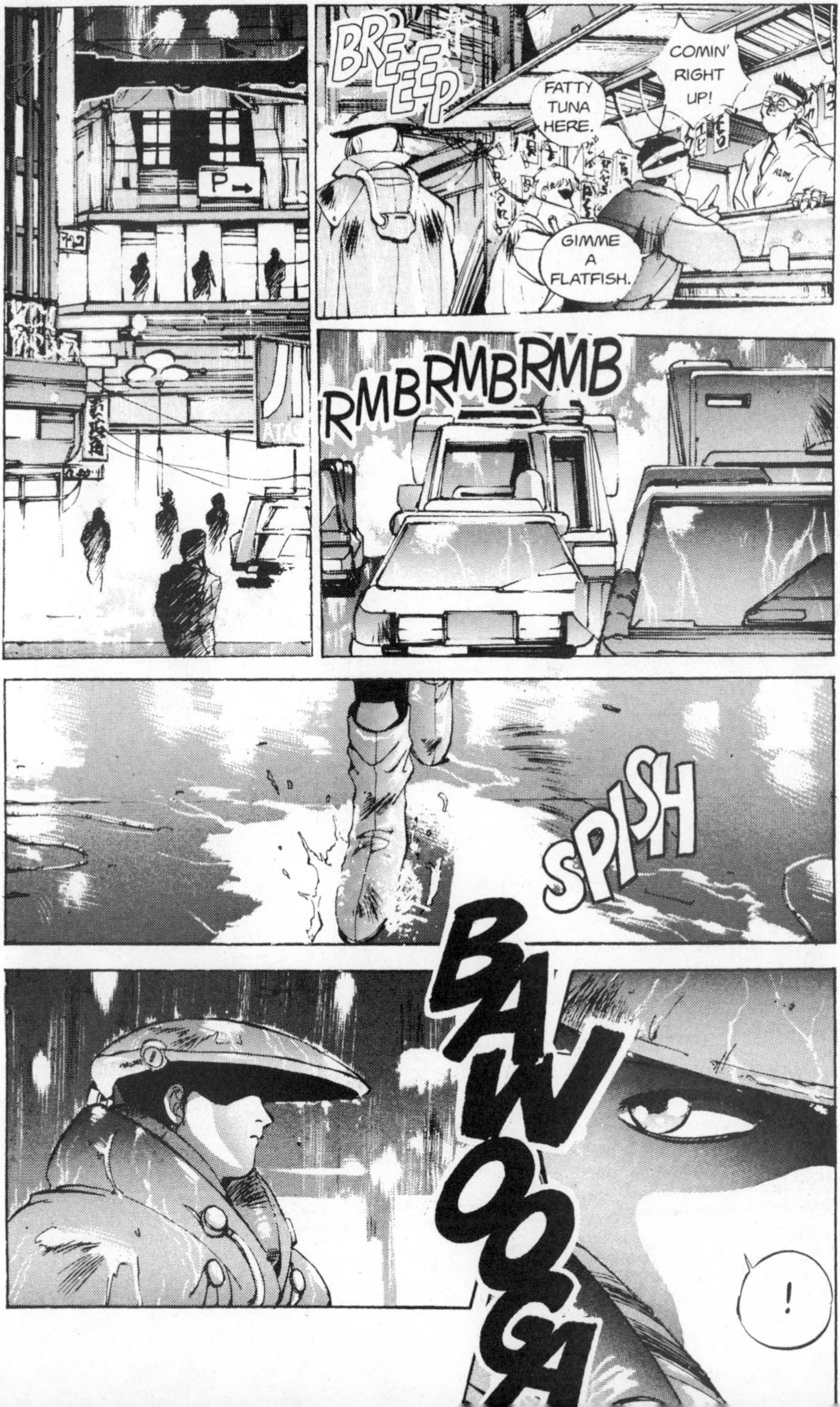
BREEEEP
FATTY TUNA HERE.
COMIN' RIGHT UP!
GIMME A FLATFISH.
RMBRMBRMB
SPISH
BAWOOGA
!

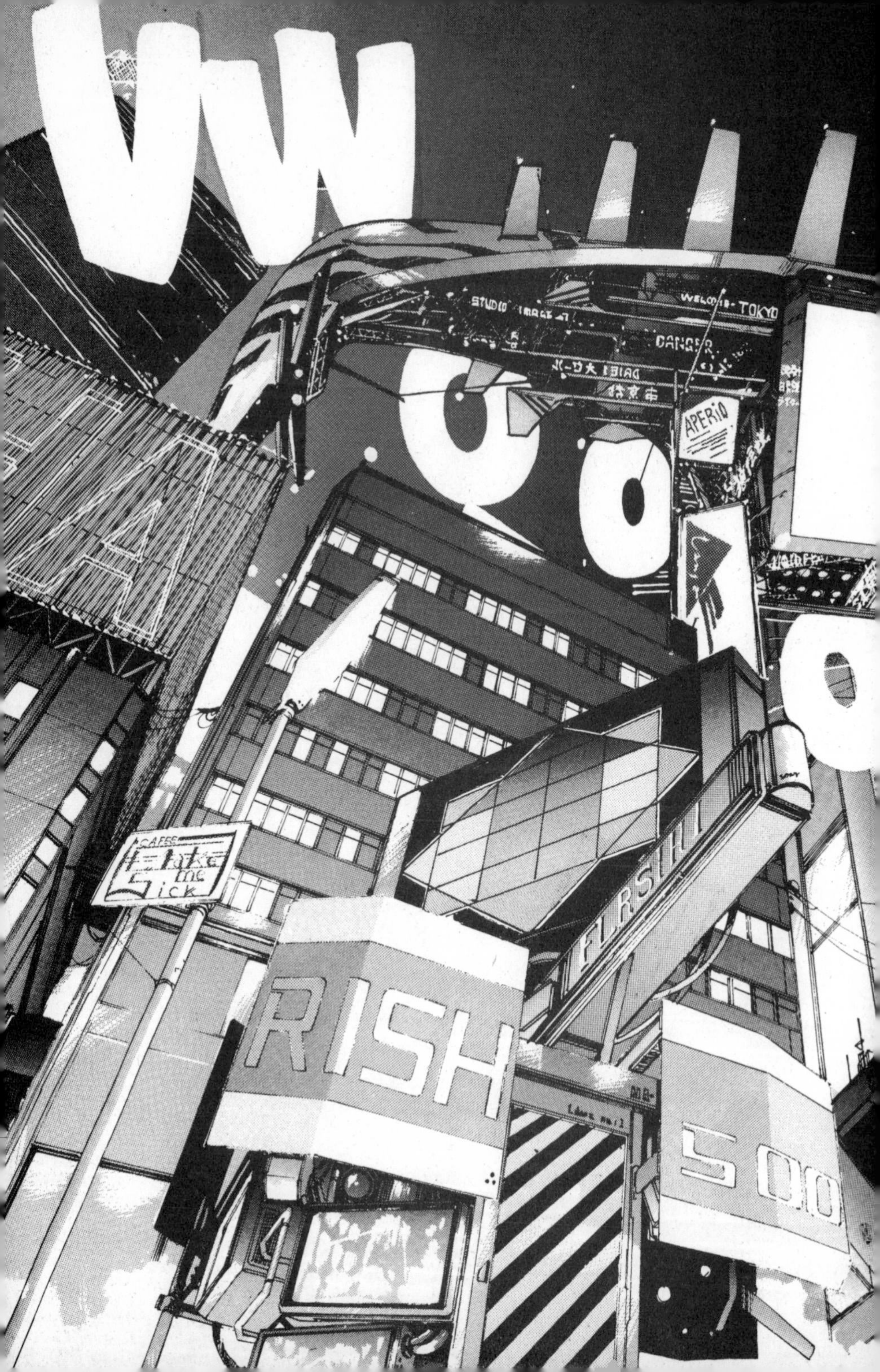
STUDIO
TOKYO
DANGER
DAIEI
APERIQ
CAFFE
FLRSHI
RISH
500

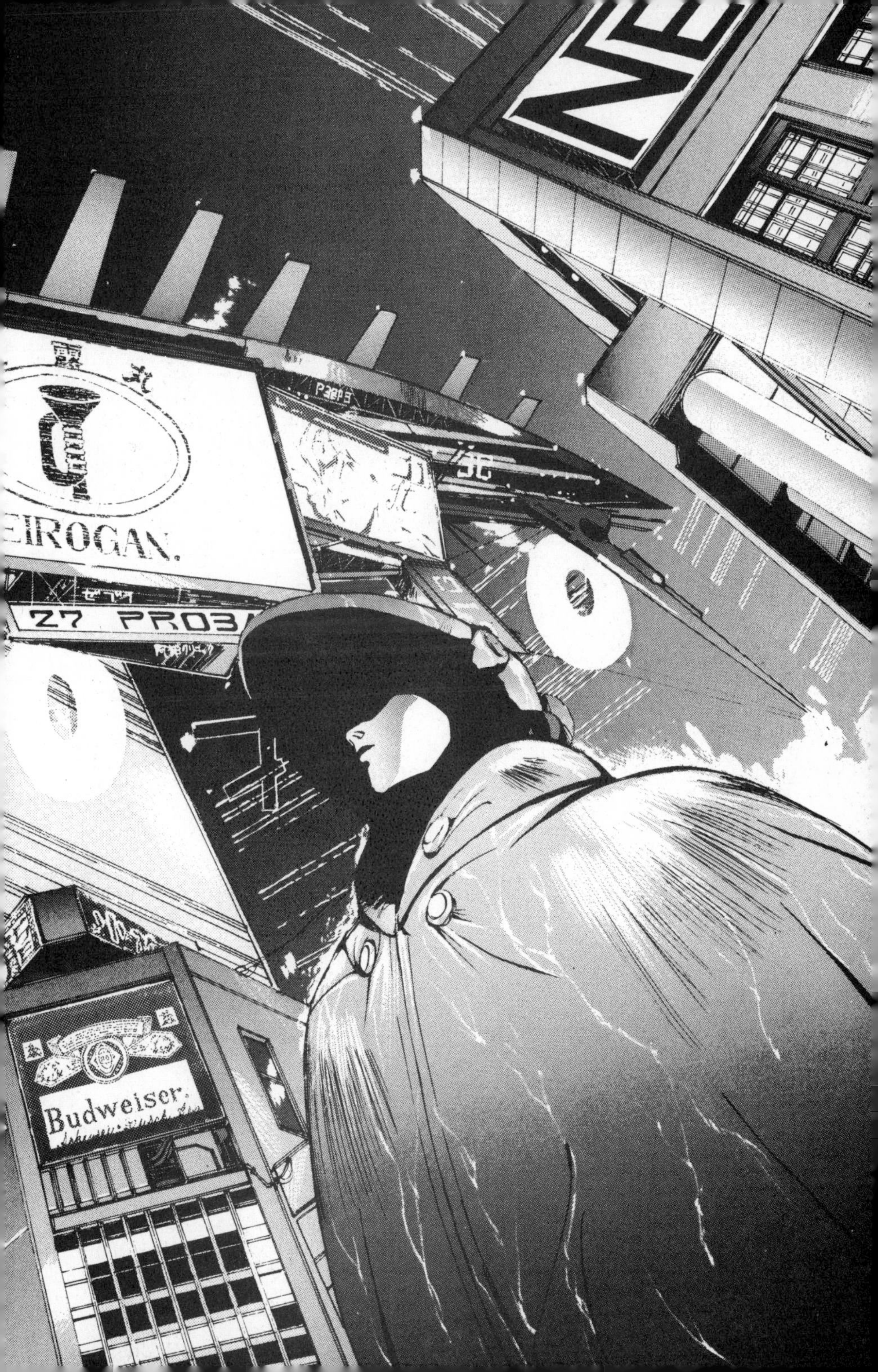
NE
EIROGAN.
27 PROB
Budweiser.

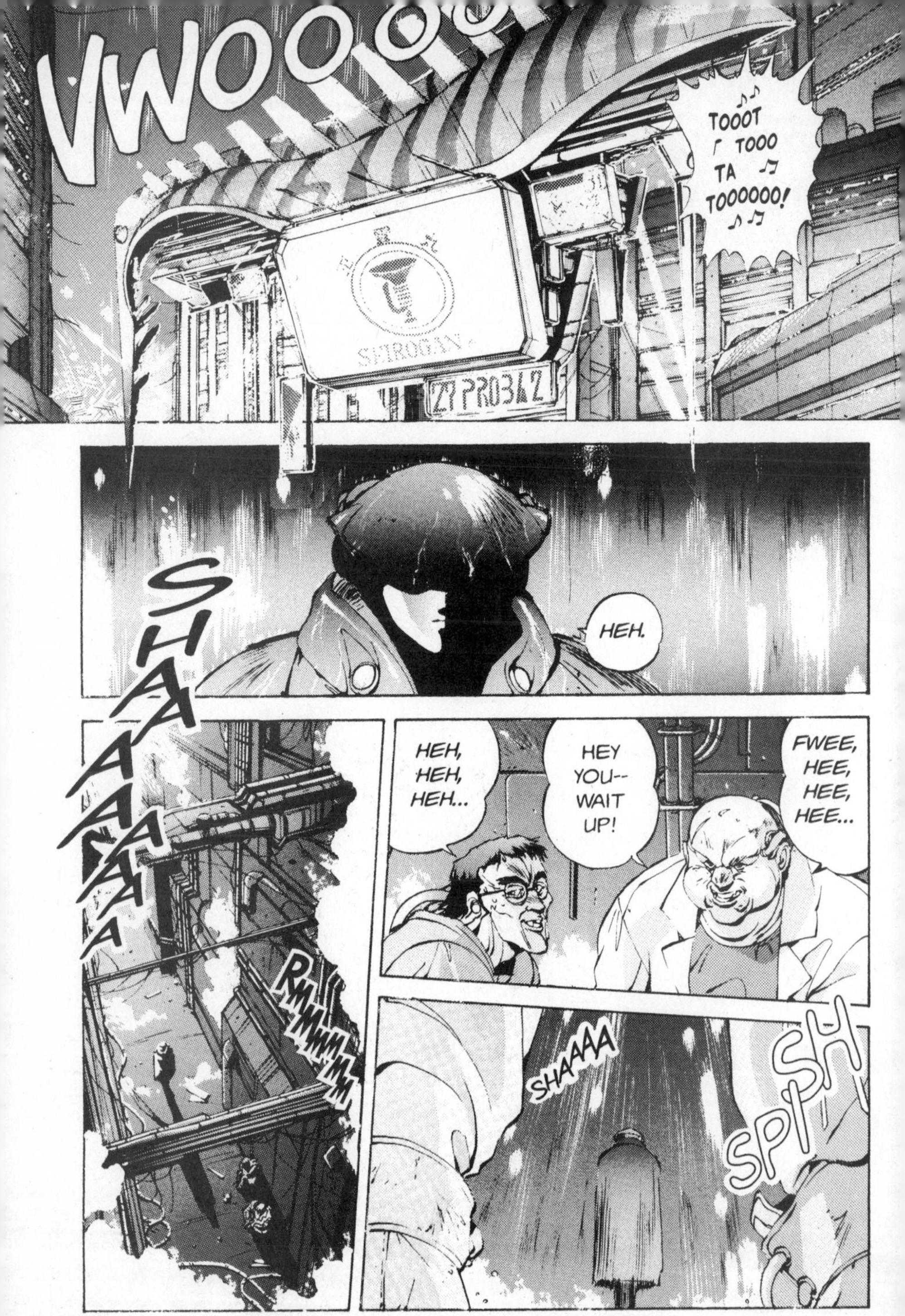
VWOOOO
SEIROGAN
TOOOT TOOO TA TOOOOOO!
SHAAAAAAAAAA
HEH.
RMMMMMMM
HEH, HEH, HEH...
HEY YOU-- WAIT UP!
FWEE, HEE, HEE, HEE...
SHAAAA
SPISH

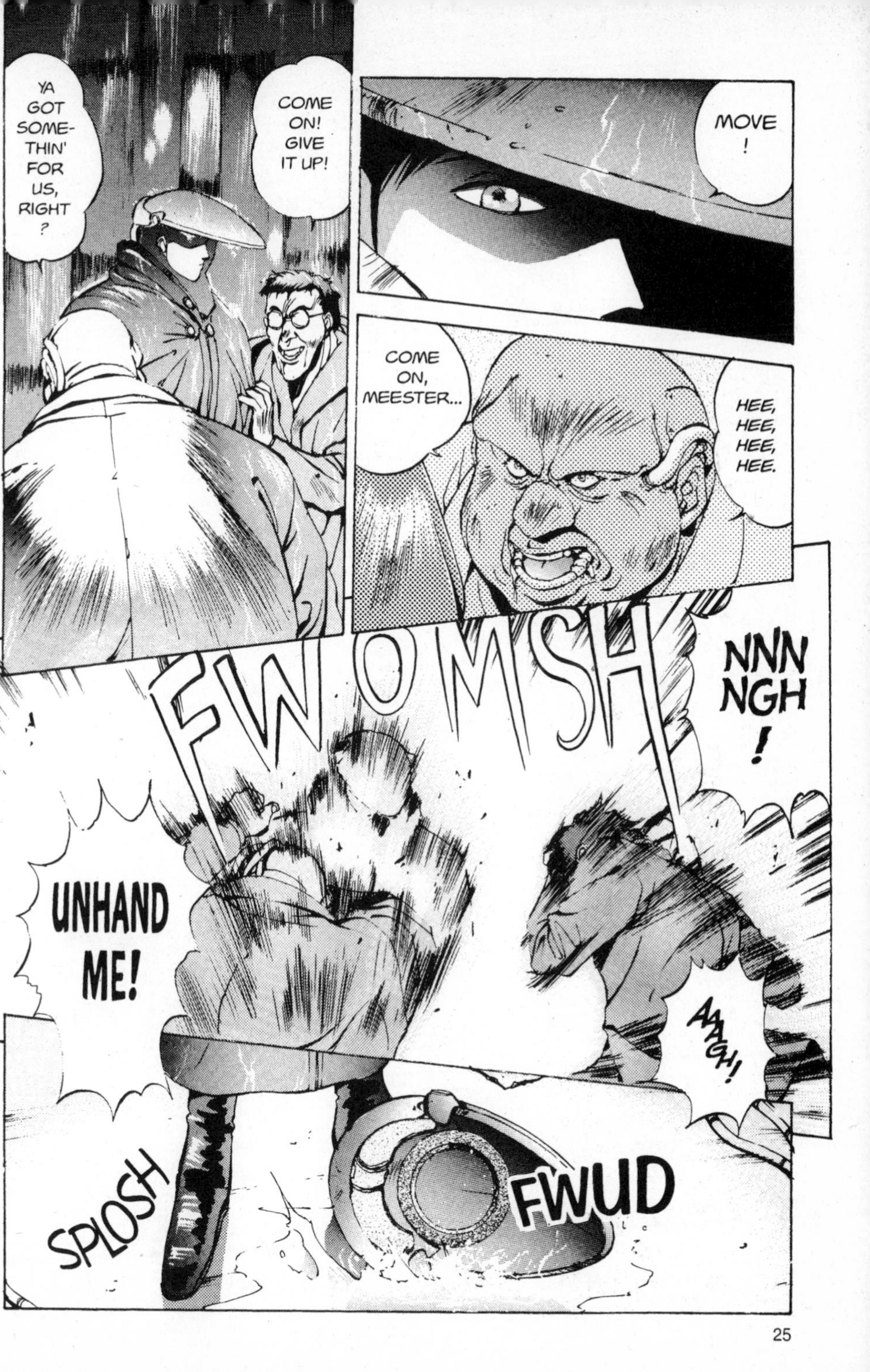
YA GOT SOME-THIN' FOR US, RIGHT ?
COME ON! GIVE IT UP!
MOVE !
COME ON, MEESTER...
HEE, HEE, HEE, HEE.
FWOMSH
NNNNGH !
UNHAND ME!
AAAGH!
SPLOSH
FWUD

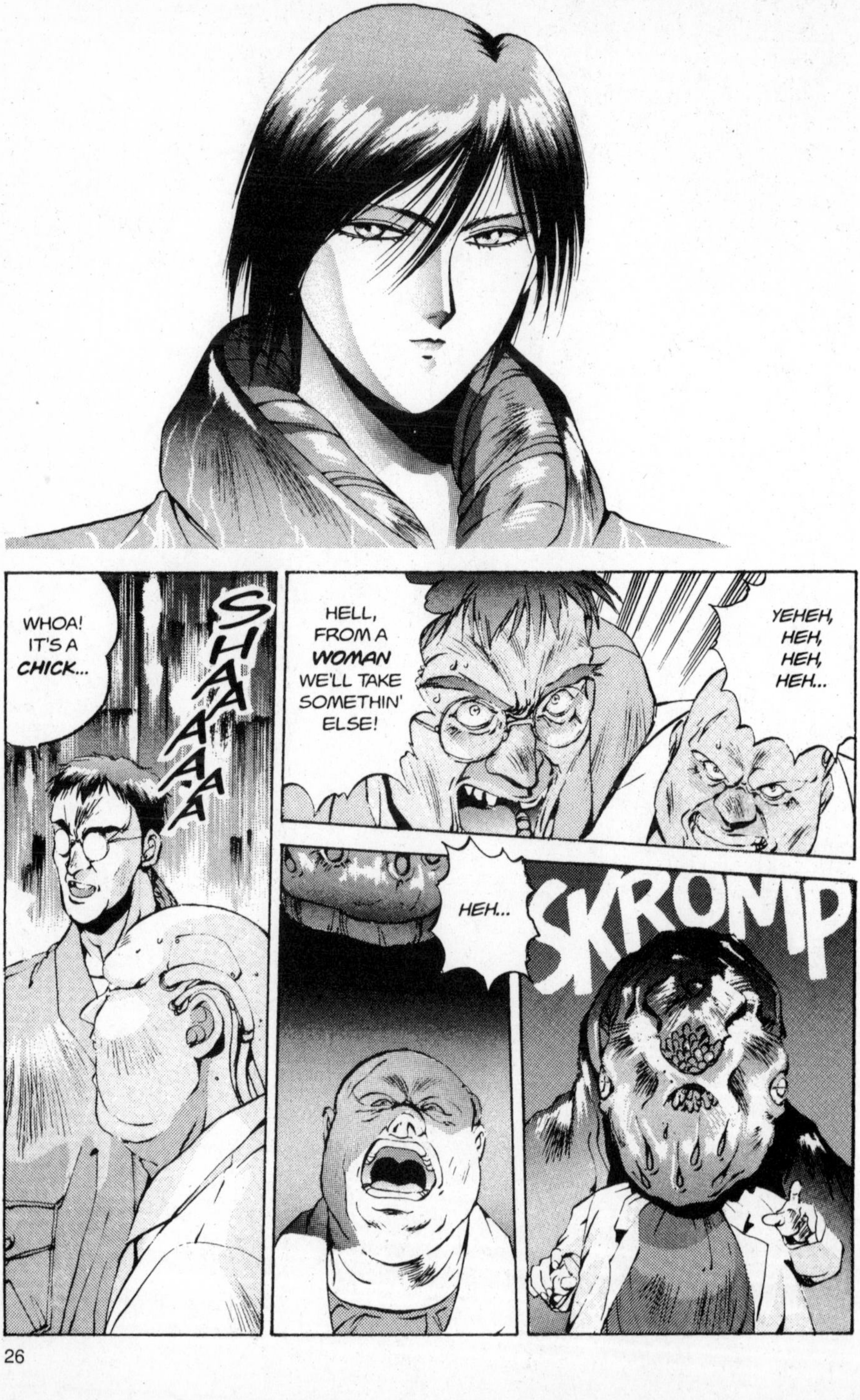
WHOA! IT'S A CHICK...
SHAAAAA
HELL, FROM A WOMAN WE'LL TAKE SOMETHIN' ELSE!
YEHEH, HEH, HEH, HEH...
HEH...
SKROMP

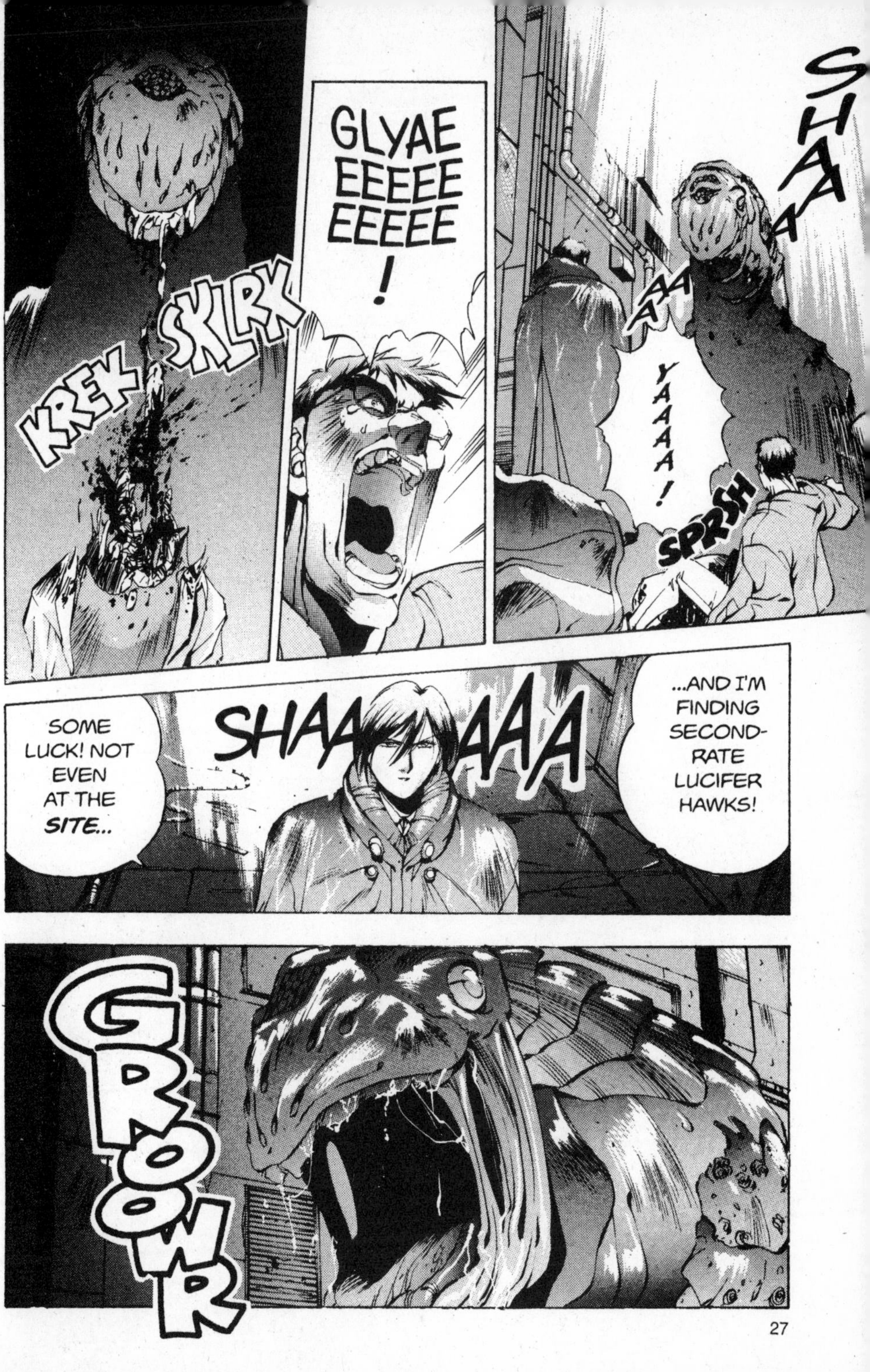
KREK
SKLRK
GLYAE EEEEE EEEEE !
SHAAAA
AAA
YAAAAA!
SPRSH
SOME LUCK! NOT EVEN AT THE SITE...
SHAAAAAA
...AND I'M FINDING SECOND-RATE LUCIFER HAWKS!
GROOWR

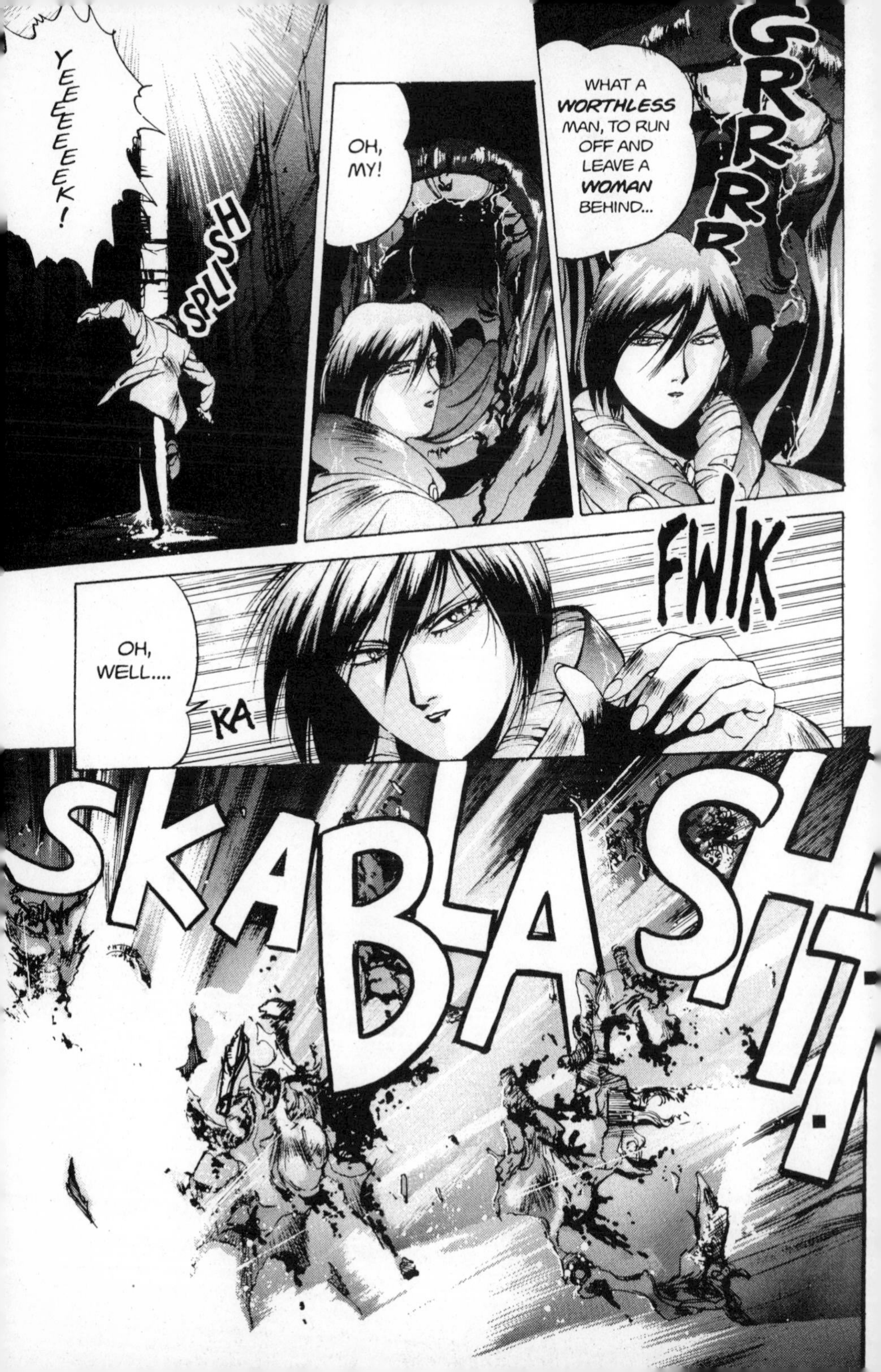
YEEEEEEEK!
SPLISH
OH, MY!
WHAT A **WORTHLESS** MAN, TO RUN OFF AND LEAVE A **WOMAN** BEHIND...
GRRRR
OH, WELL....
KA
FWIK
SKABLASH!!

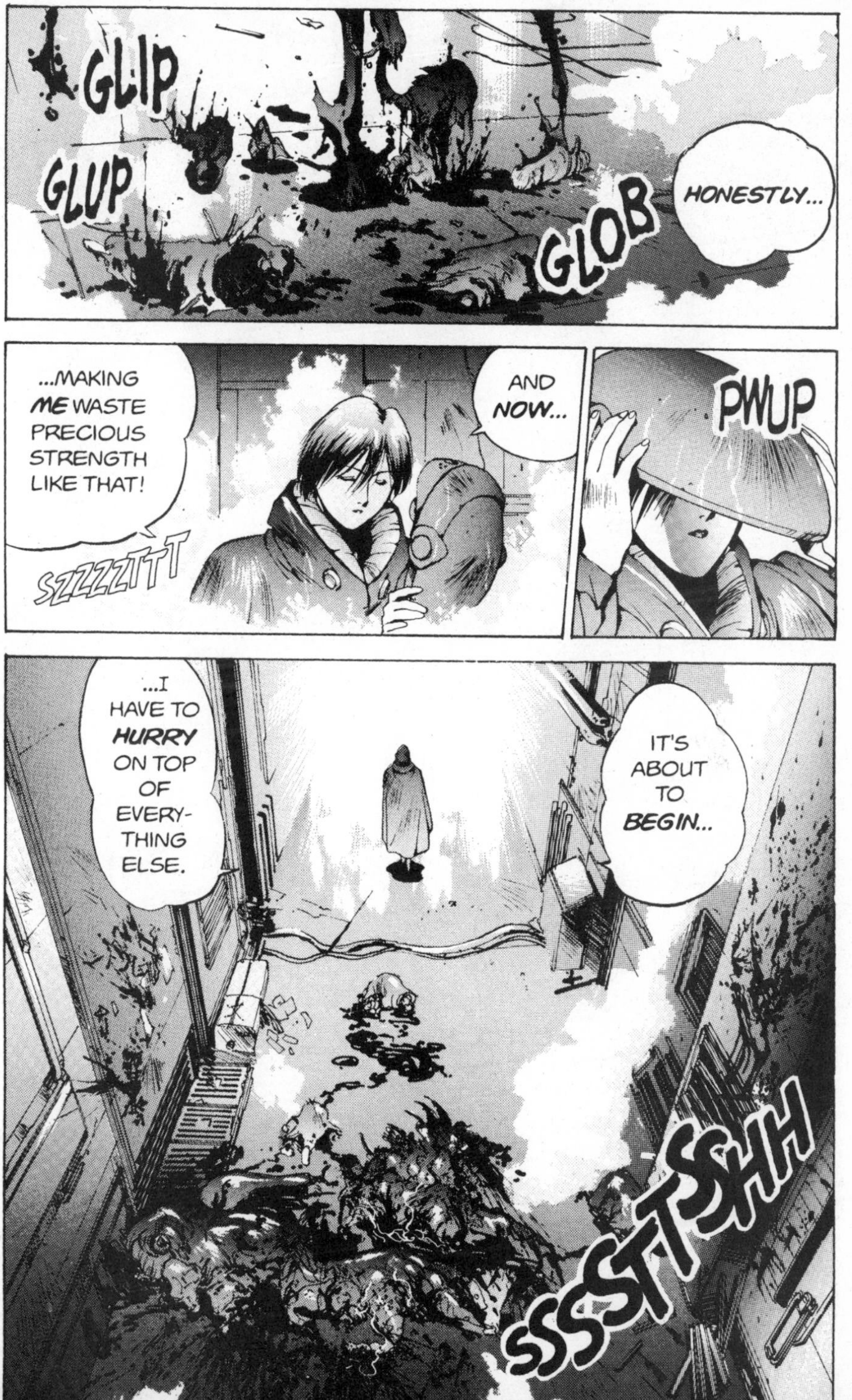
GLIP
GLUP
GLOB
HONESTLY...
...MAKING ME WASTE PRECIOUS STRENGTH LIKE THAT!
SZZZZTTT
AND NOW...
PWUP
...I HAVE TO HURRY ON TOP OF EVERY-THING ELSE.
IT'S ABOUT TO BEGIN...
SSSSTTSSHH

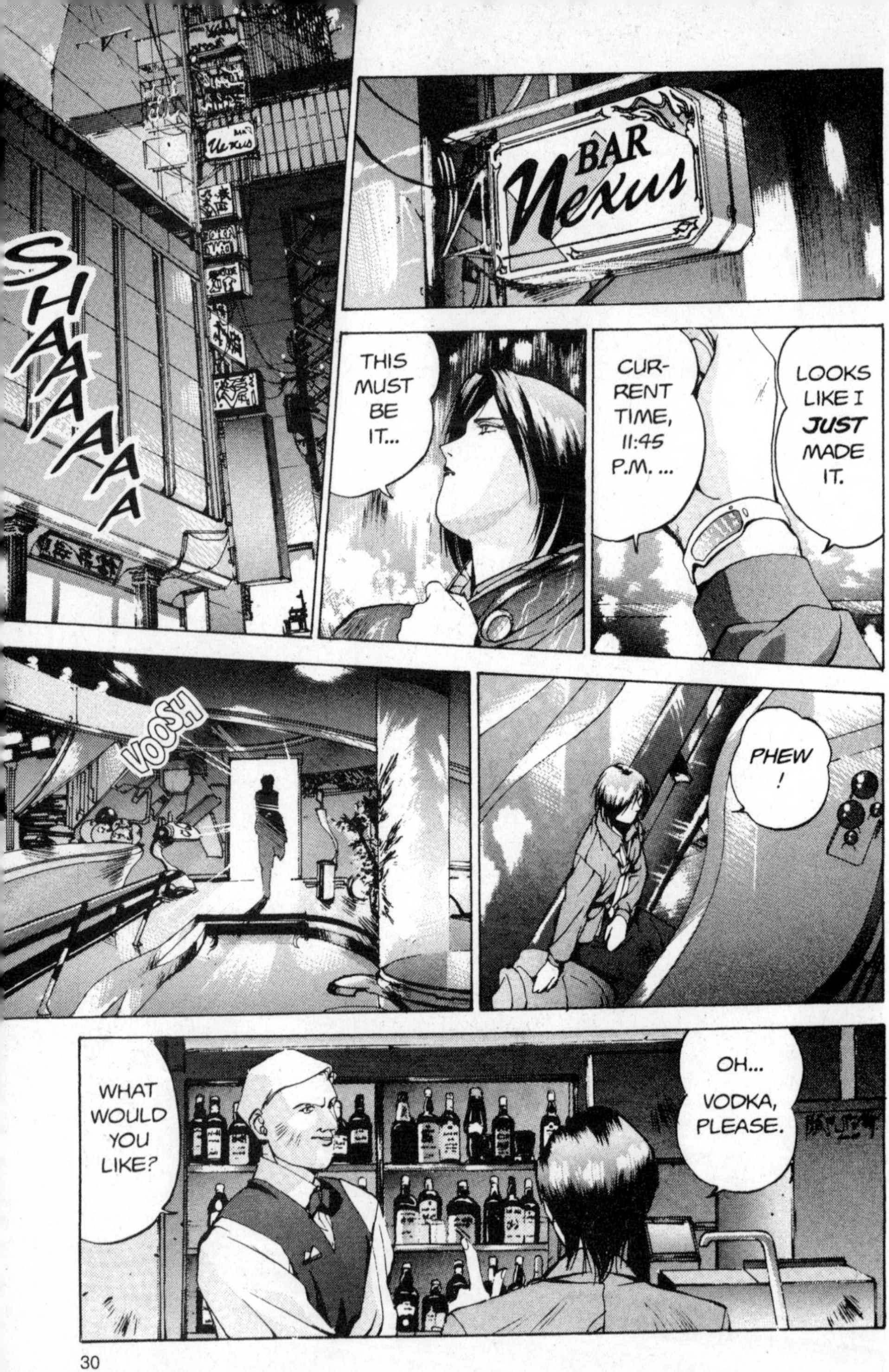
SHAAAAAA
BAR Nexus
THIS MUST BE IT...
CUR-RENT TIME, 11:45 P.M. ...
LOOKS LIKE I **JUST** MADE IT.
VOOSH
PHEW!
WHAT WOULD YOU LIKE?
OH...
VODKA, PLEASE.

KLNK

NOW...

...LET'S HAVE A *FIRST-HAND* LOOK....

...AT THE A.M.P. !

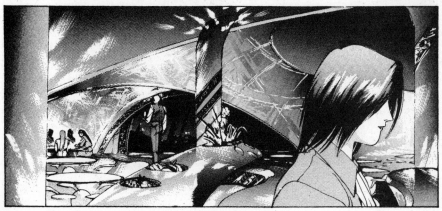

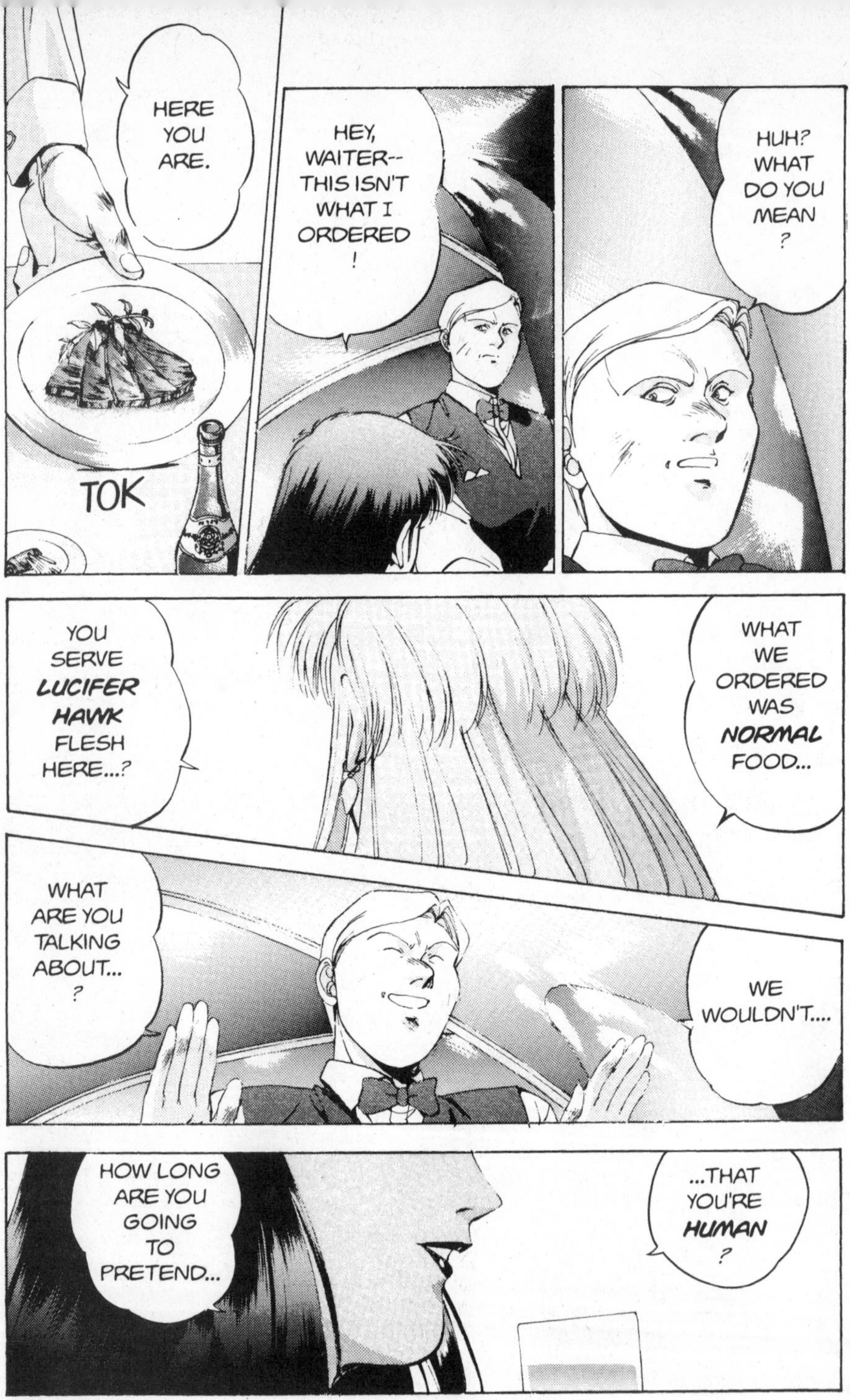
HERE YOU ARE.
TOK
HEY, WAITER-- THIS ISN'T WHAT I ORDERED!
HUH? WHAT DO YOU MEAN?
YOU SERVE *LUCIFER HAWK* FLESH HERE...?
WHAT WE ORDERED WAS *NORMAL* FOOD...
WHAT ARE YOU TALKING ABOUT...?
WE WOULDN'T....
HOW LONG ARE YOU GOING TO PRETEND...
...THAT YOU'RE *HUMAN*?

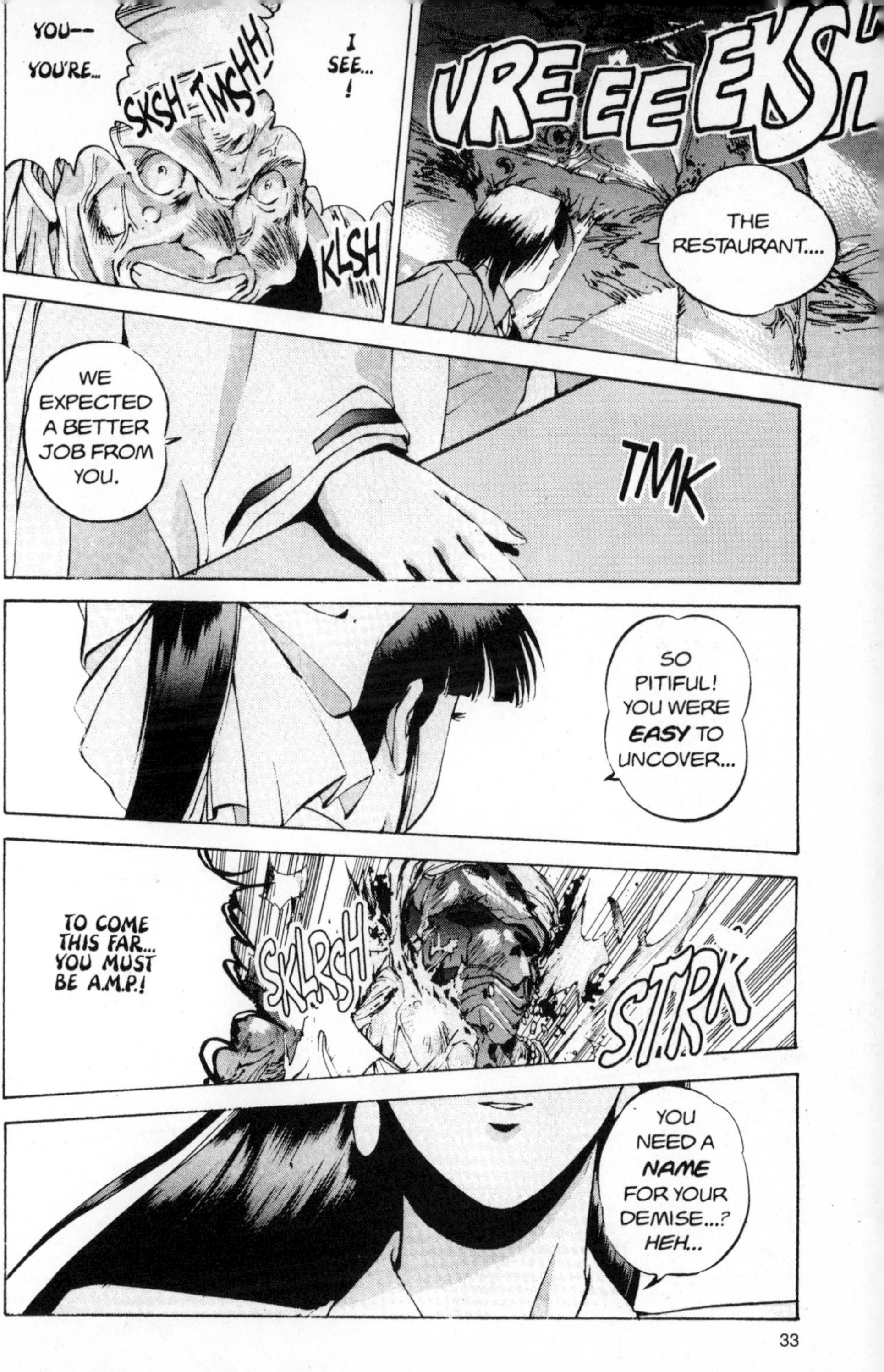
YOU-- YOU'RE...
SKSH TMSHH!
I SEE... !
KLSH
VREEEEKSH
THE RESTAURANT....
WE EXPECTED A BETTER JOB FROM YOU.
TMK
SO PITIFUL! YOU WERE EASY TO UNCOVER...
TO COME THIS FAR... YOU MUST BE A.M.P.!
SKLRSH
STRK
YOU NEED A NAME FOR YOUR DEMISE...? HEH...

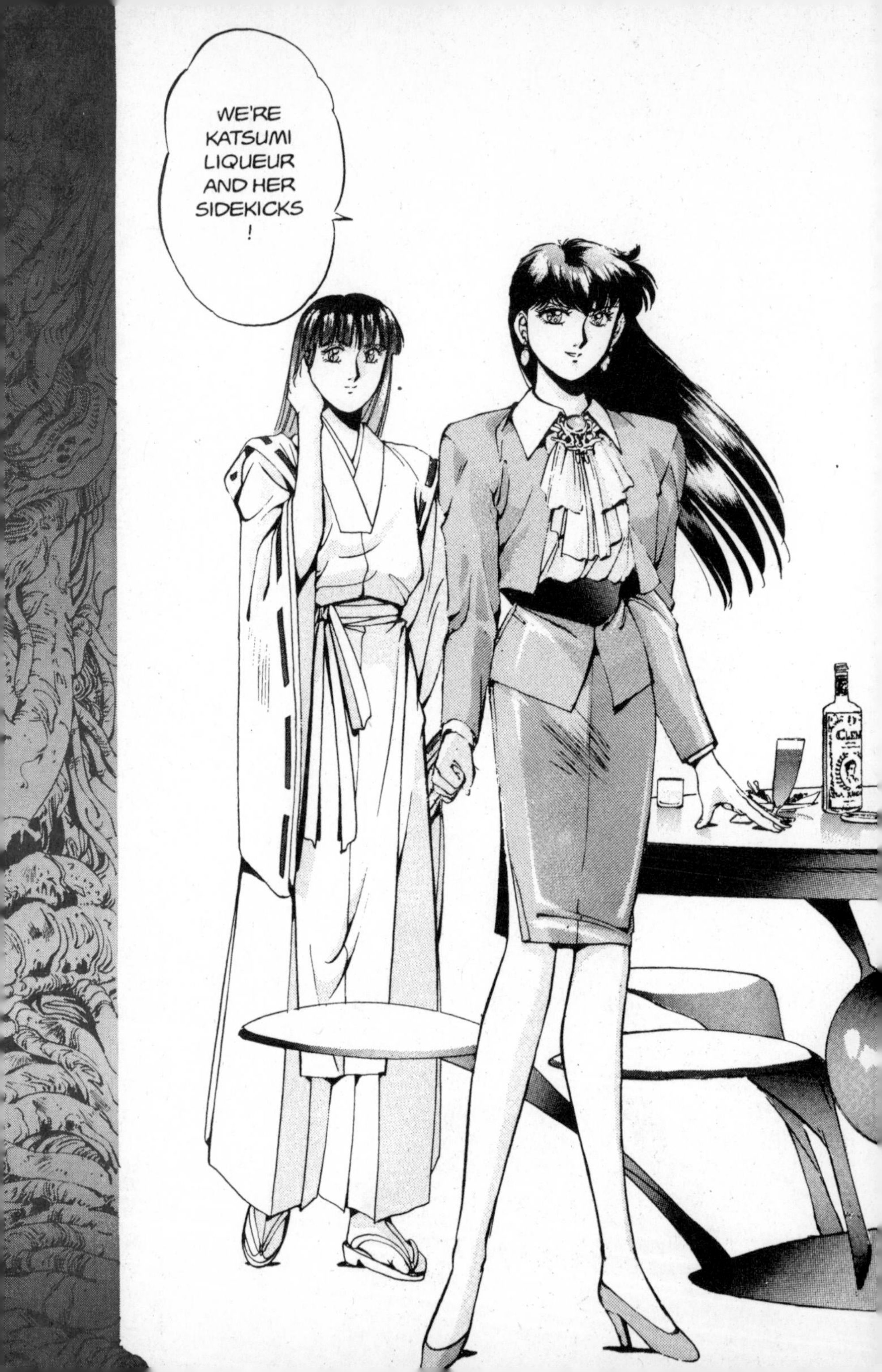
WE'RE KATSUMI LIQUEUR AND HER SIDEKICKS !

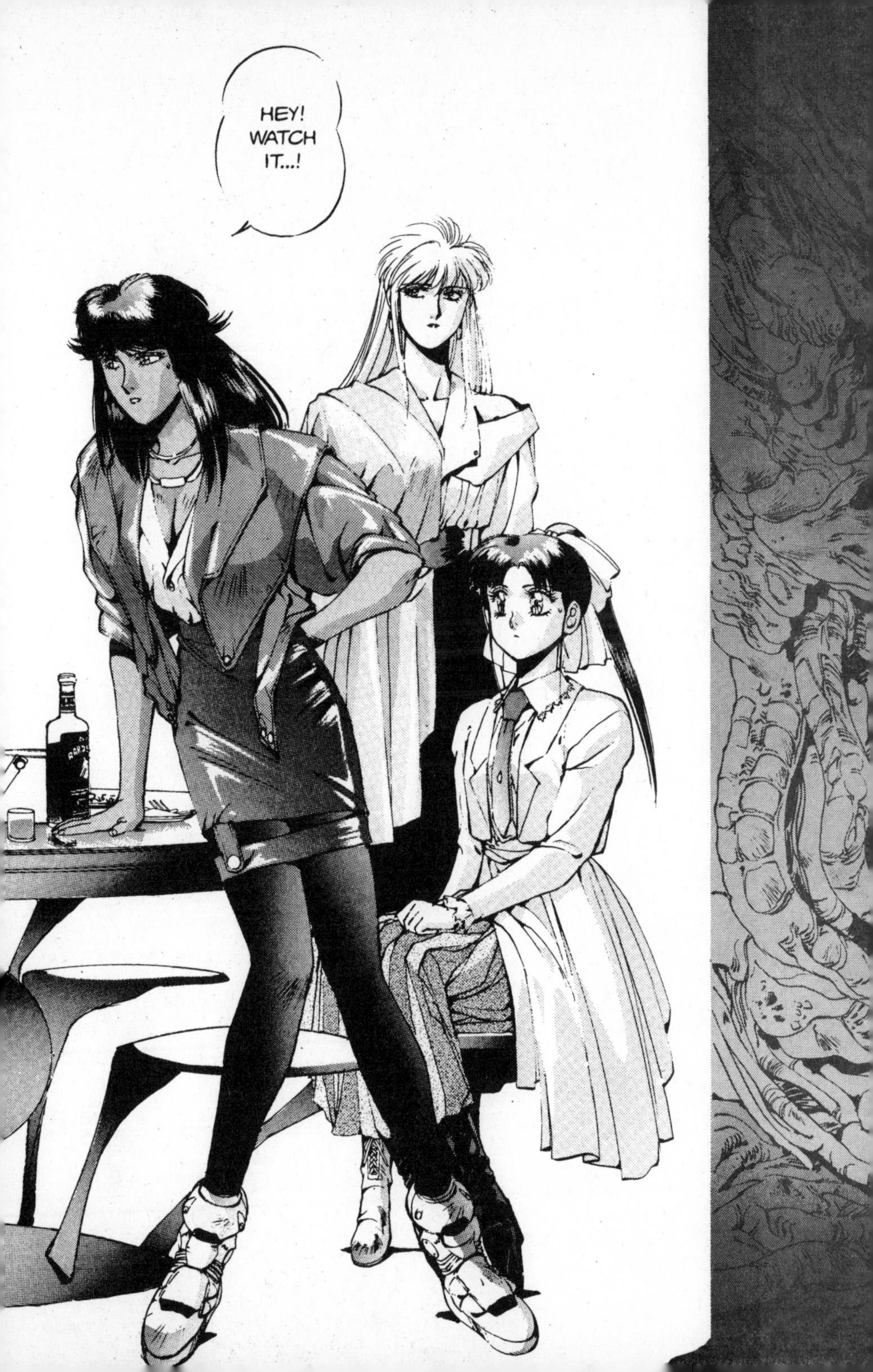
HEY! WATCH IT...!

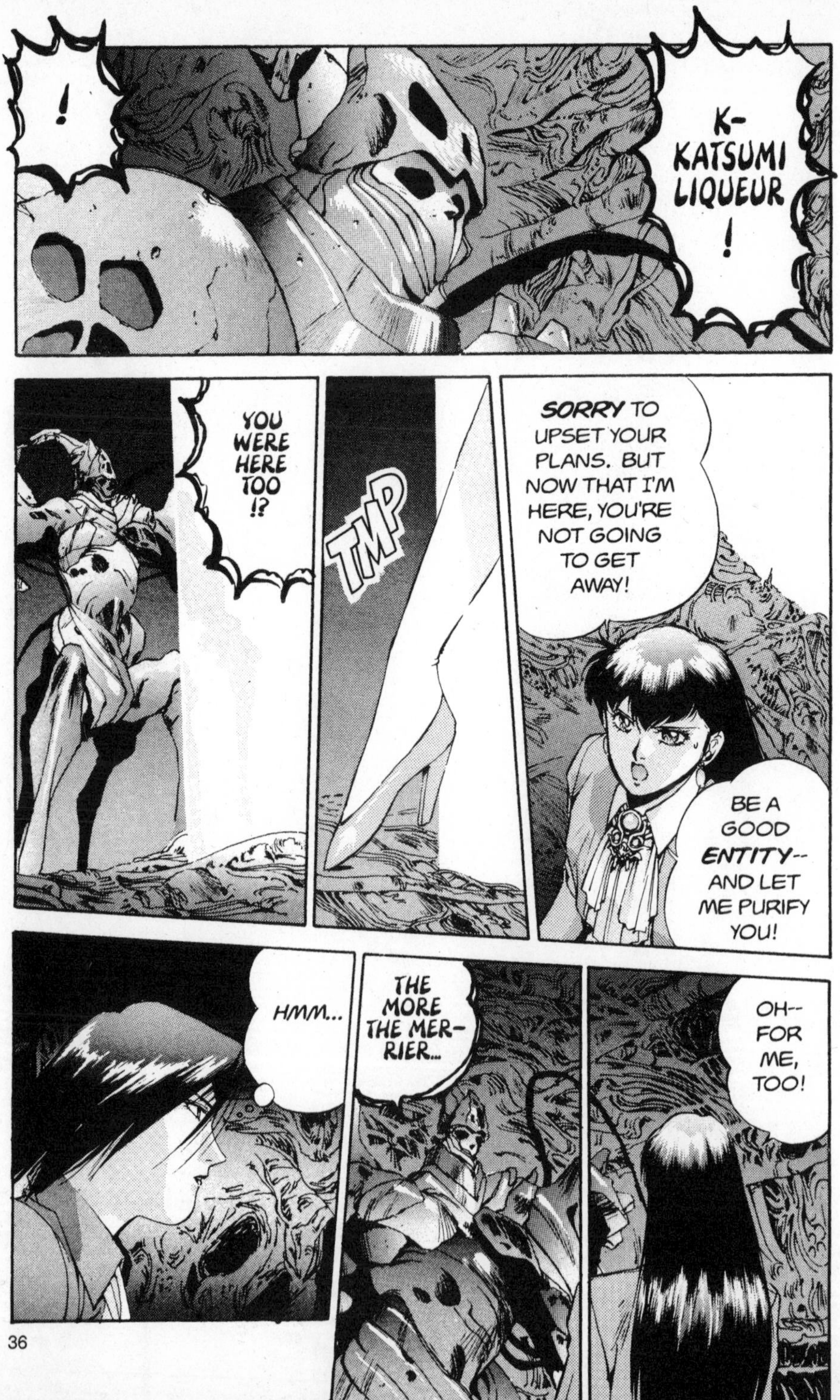
!
K-
KATSUMI
LIQUEUR
!
YOU WERE HERE TOO !?
TMP
SORRY TO UPSET YOUR PLANS. BUT NOW THAT I'M HERE, YOU'RE NOT GOING TO GET AWAY!
BE A GOOD ENTITY-- AND LET ME PURIFY YOU!
HMM...
THE MORE THE MER-RIER...
OH-- FOR ME, TOO!

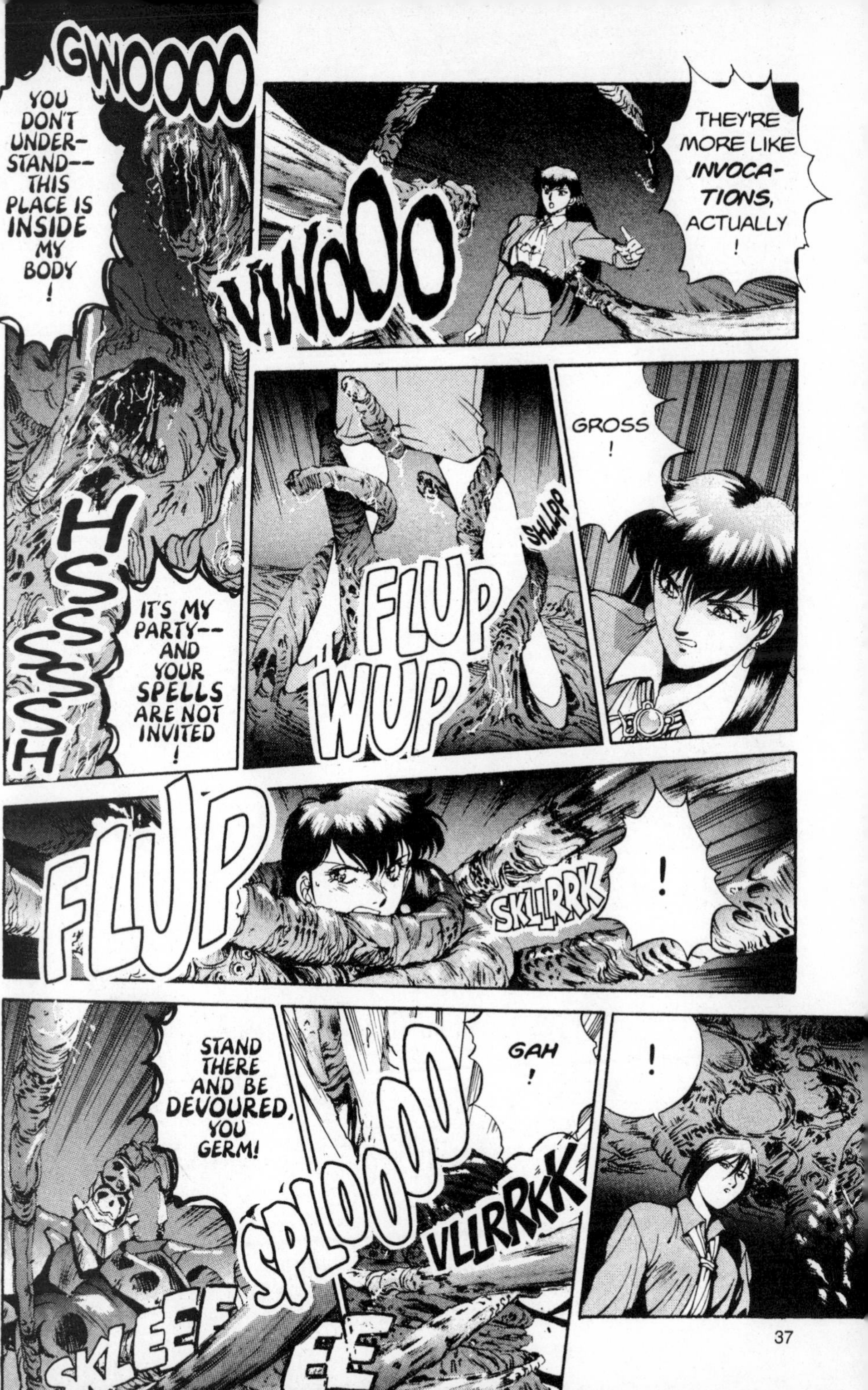
GWOOOO
YOU DON'T UNDER-STAND-- THIS PLACE IS INSIDE MY BODY!
HSSSSSH
IT'S MY PARTY-- AND YOUR SPELLS ARE NOT INVITED!
VWOOO
THEY'RE MORE LIKE INVOCA-TIONS, ACTUALLY!
FLUP WUP
SHLUPP
GROSS!
FLUP
SKLIRRK
!
STAND THERE AND BE DEVOURED, YOU GERM!
SKLEEEE
SPLOOOOO
VLIRRKK
GAH!
!

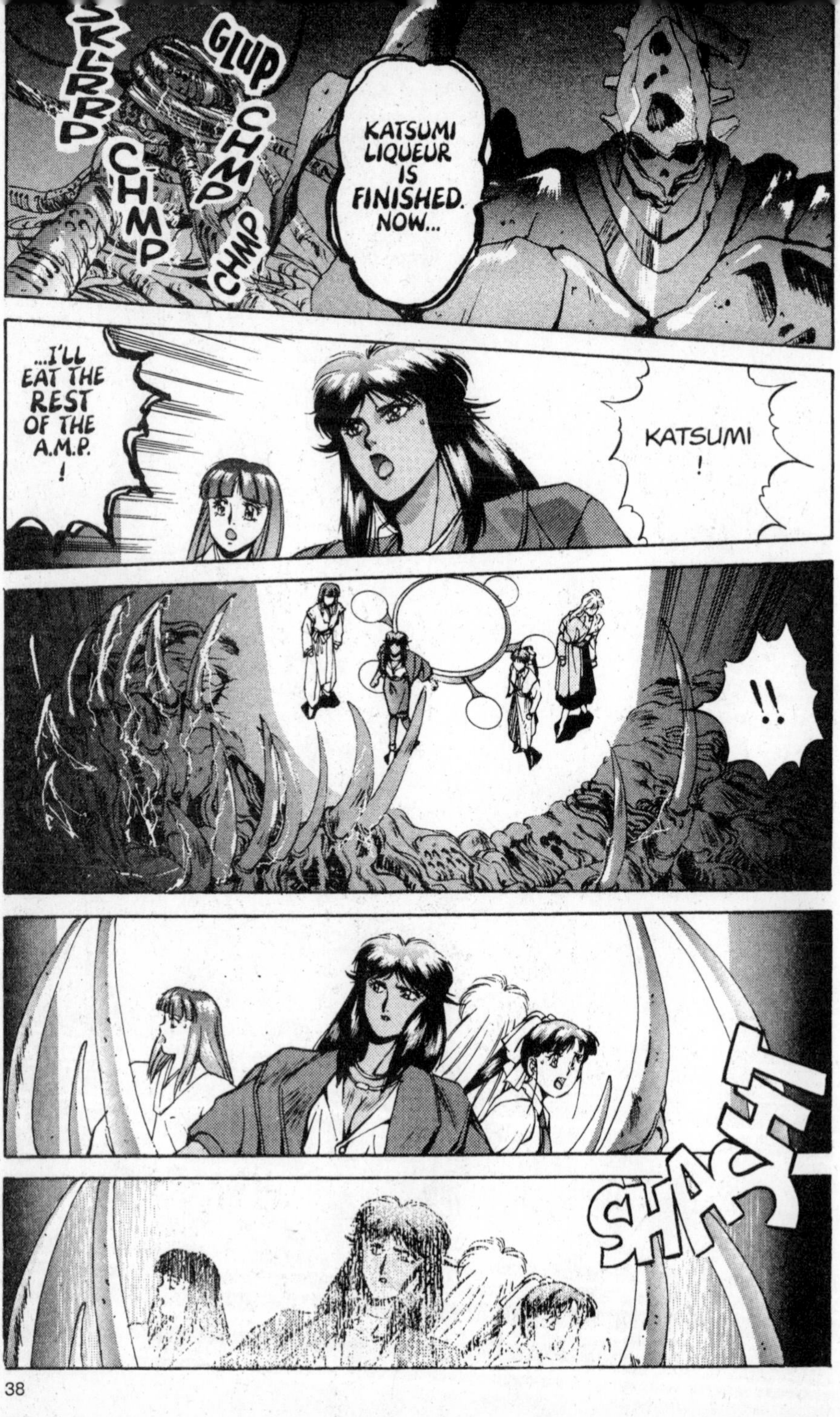

SKLRRP
GLUP
CHMP
CHMP
CHMP
KATSUMI LIQUEUR IS FINISHED. NOW...
...I'LL EAT THE REST OF THE A.M.P. !
KATSUMI !
!!
SHACHT

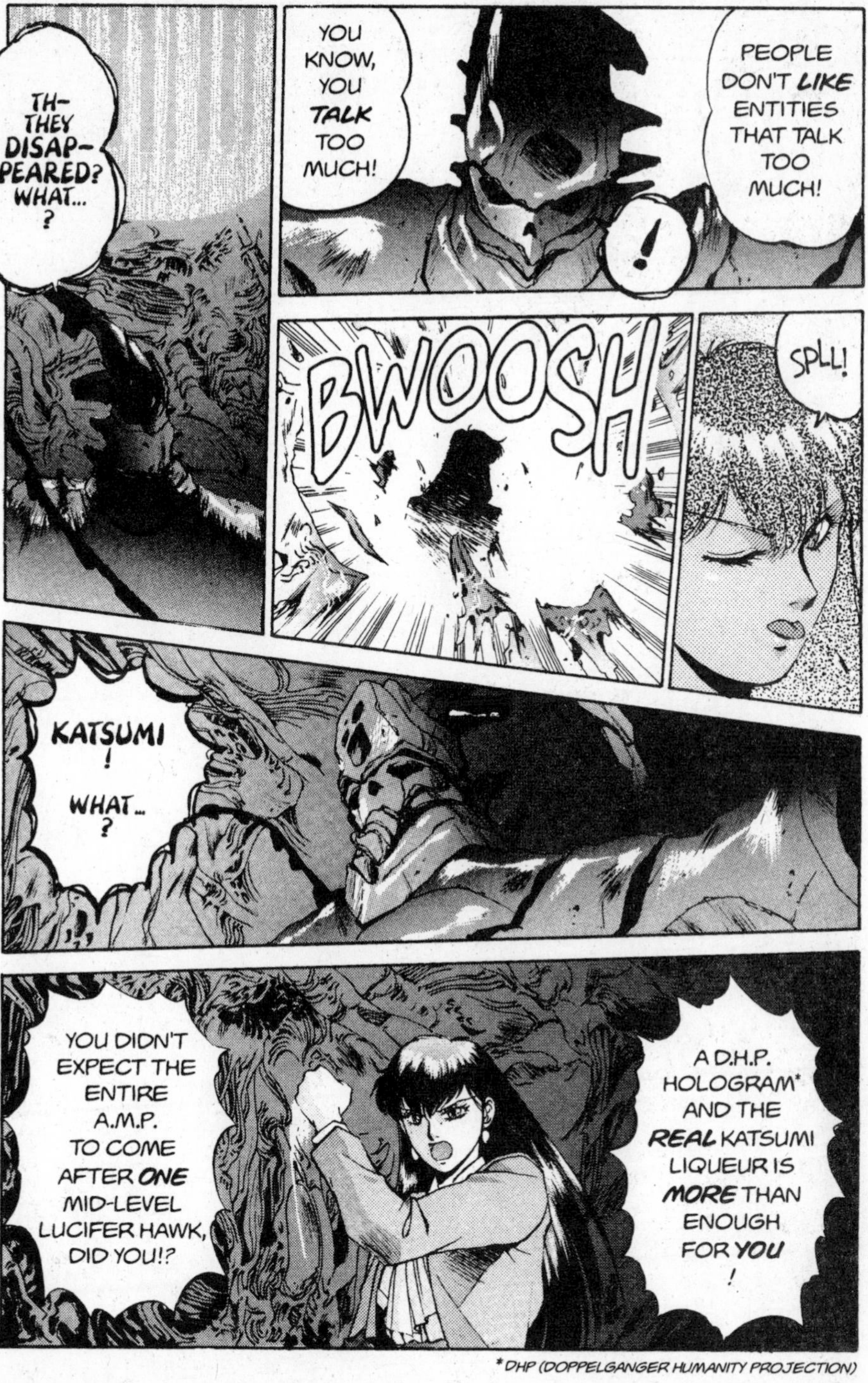
TH-THEY DISAPPEARED? WHAT... ?
YOU KNOW, YOU TALK TOO MUCH!
PEOPLE DON'T LIKE ENTITIES THAT TALK TOO MUCH!
!
BWOOSH
SPLL!
KATSUMI! WHAT... ?
YOU DIDN'T EXPECT THE ENTIRE A.M.P. TO COME AFTER ONE MID-LEVEL LUCIFER HAWK, DID YOU!?
A D.H.P. HOLOGRAM* AND THE REAL KATSUMI LIQUEUR IS MORE THAN ENOUGH FOR YOU!

* DHP (DOPPELGANGER HUMANITY PROJECTION)

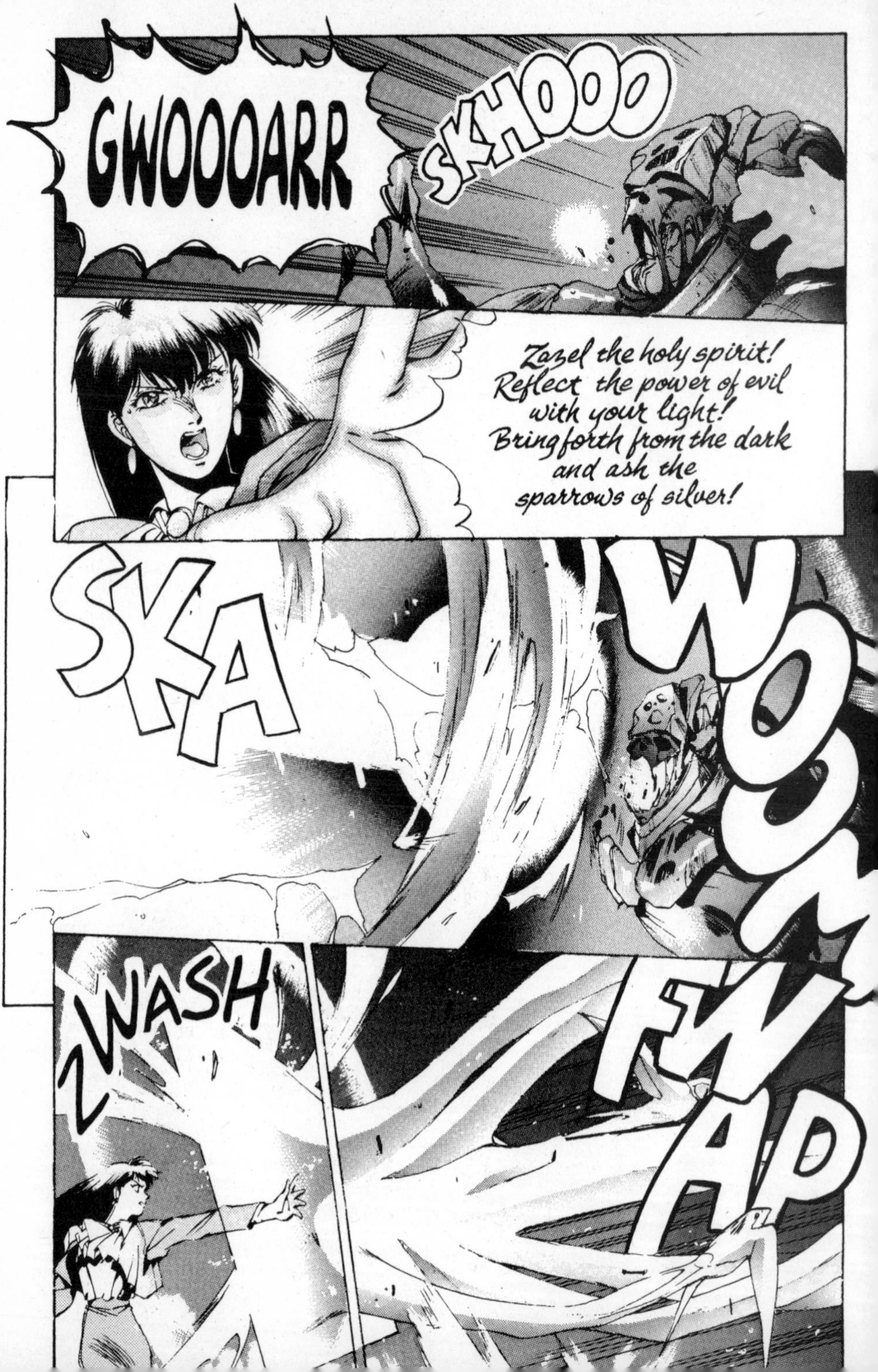
GWOOOARR
SKHOOO
Zazel the holy spirit! Reflect the power of evil with your light! Bringforth from the dark and ash the sparrows of silver!
SKA
WO
ZWASH
FWAP

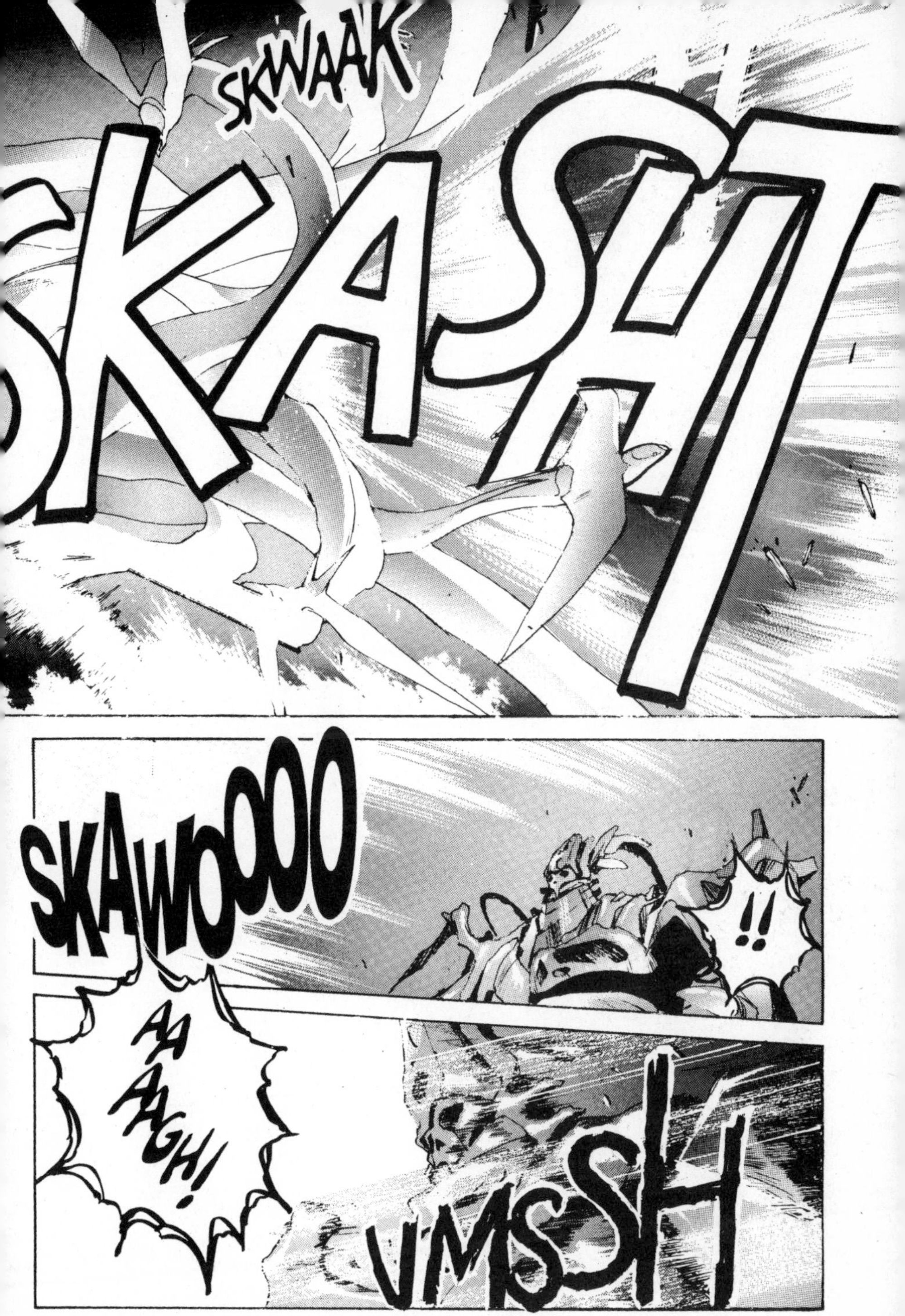
SKWAAK
SKASH
SKAWOOOO
!!
AAAAGH!
VMSSH

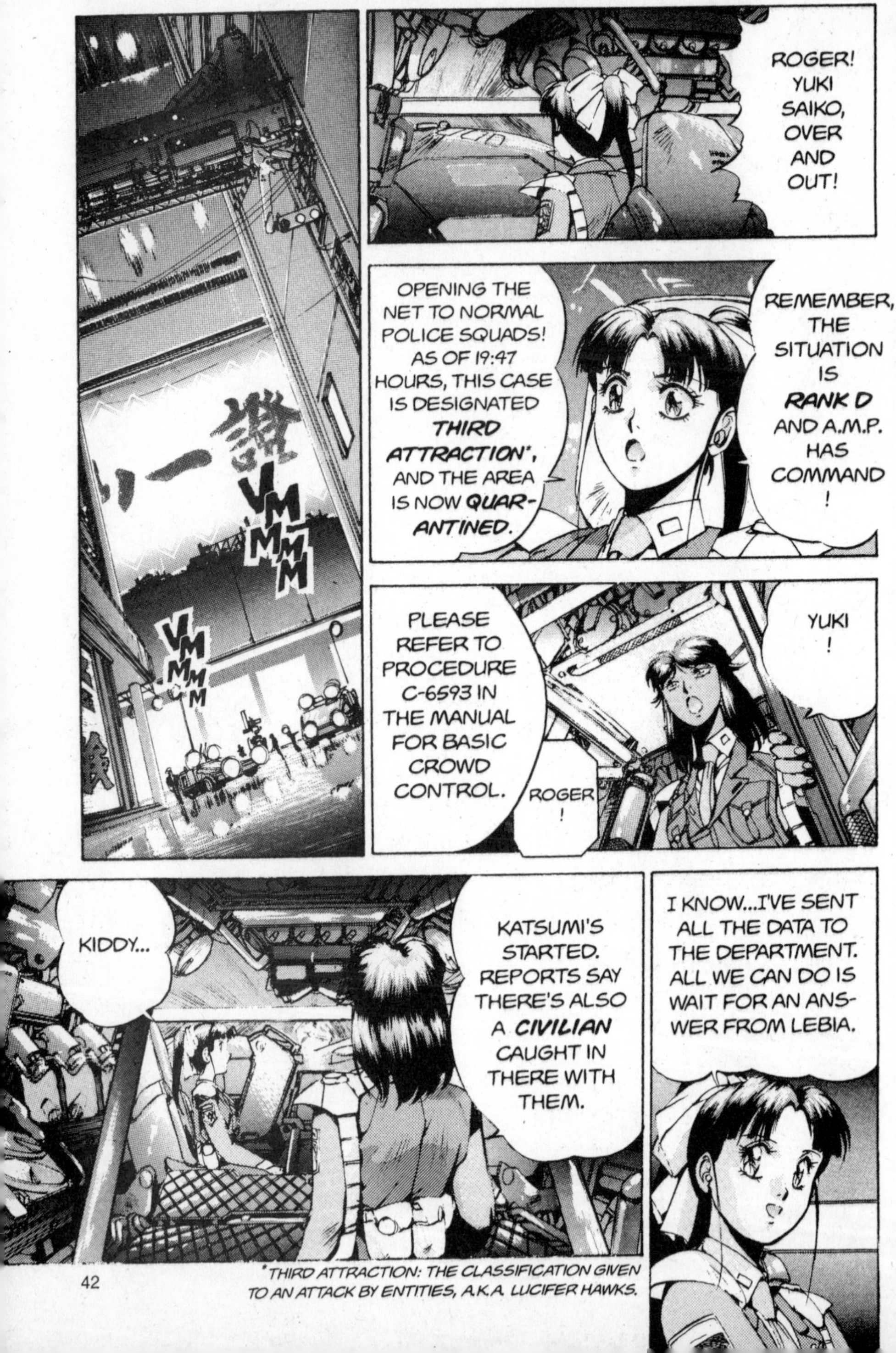
VMMMM
VMMMM
ROGER! YUKI SAIKO, OVER AND OUT!
OPENING THE NET TO NORMAL POLICE SQUADS! AS OF 19:47 HOURS, THIS CASE IS DESIGNATED THIRD ATTRACTION*, AND THE AREA IS NOW QUARANTINED.
REMEMBER, THE SITUATION IS RANK D AND A.M.P. HAS COMMAND!
PLEASE REFER TO PROCEDURE C-6593 IN THE MANUAL FOR BASIC CROWD CONTROL.
ROGER!
YUKI!
KIDDY...
KATSUMI'S STARTED. REPORTS SAY THERE'S ALSO A CIVILIAN CAUGHT IN THERE WITH THEM.
I KNOW...I'VE SENT ALL THE DATA TO THE DEPARTMENT. ALL WE CAN DO IS WAIT FOR AN ANSWER FROM LEBIA.

*THIRD ATTRACTION: THE CLASSIFICATION GIVEN TO AN ATTACK BY ENTITIES, A.K.A. LUCIFER HAWKS.

IF THE LUCIFER HAWK ESCAPES THAT RESTAURANT...

WE *MAY* HAVE TO TAKE THIS BABY INTO BATTLE ON THE VERY DAY WE GOT IT!

BUT THIS ISN'T A COMBAT VEHICLE.

HEH... I KNOW THAT.

BUT I REALLY WANT TO SEE WHAT IT CAN DO...

SHAAAAOOOO

A.M.P.'S BRAND NEW "SIMURGH"!

YOU SEEM REALLY FOND OF IT, KIDDY.

SSSTSSSSST

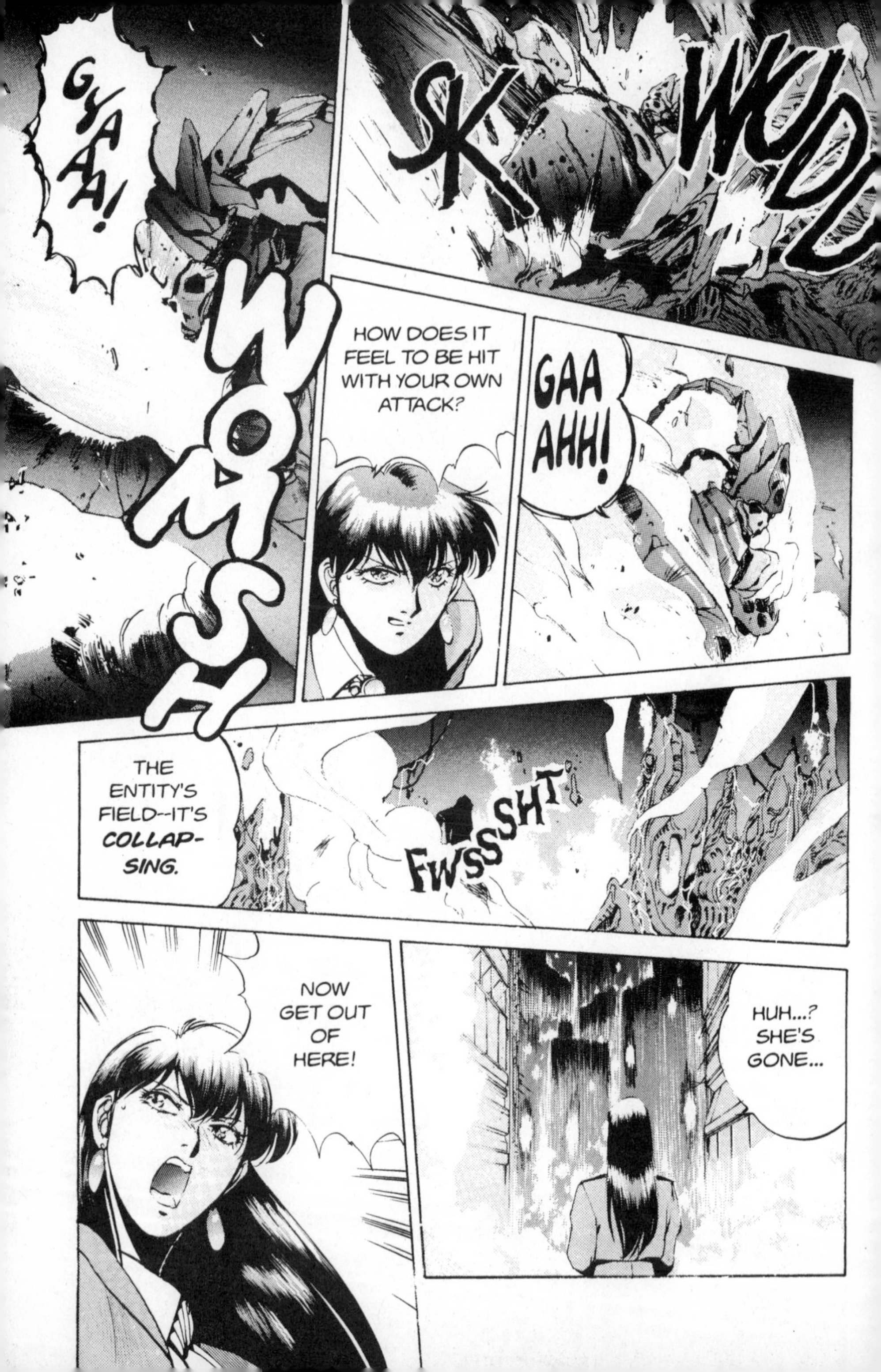
GYAAA!
SK-WUDU
WOMSH
HOW DOES IT FEEL TO BE HIT WITH YOUR OWN ATTACK?
GAA AHH!
THE ENTITY'S FIELD--IT'S COLLAP-SING.
FWSSSHT
NOW GET OUT OF HERE!
HUH...? SHE'S GONE...

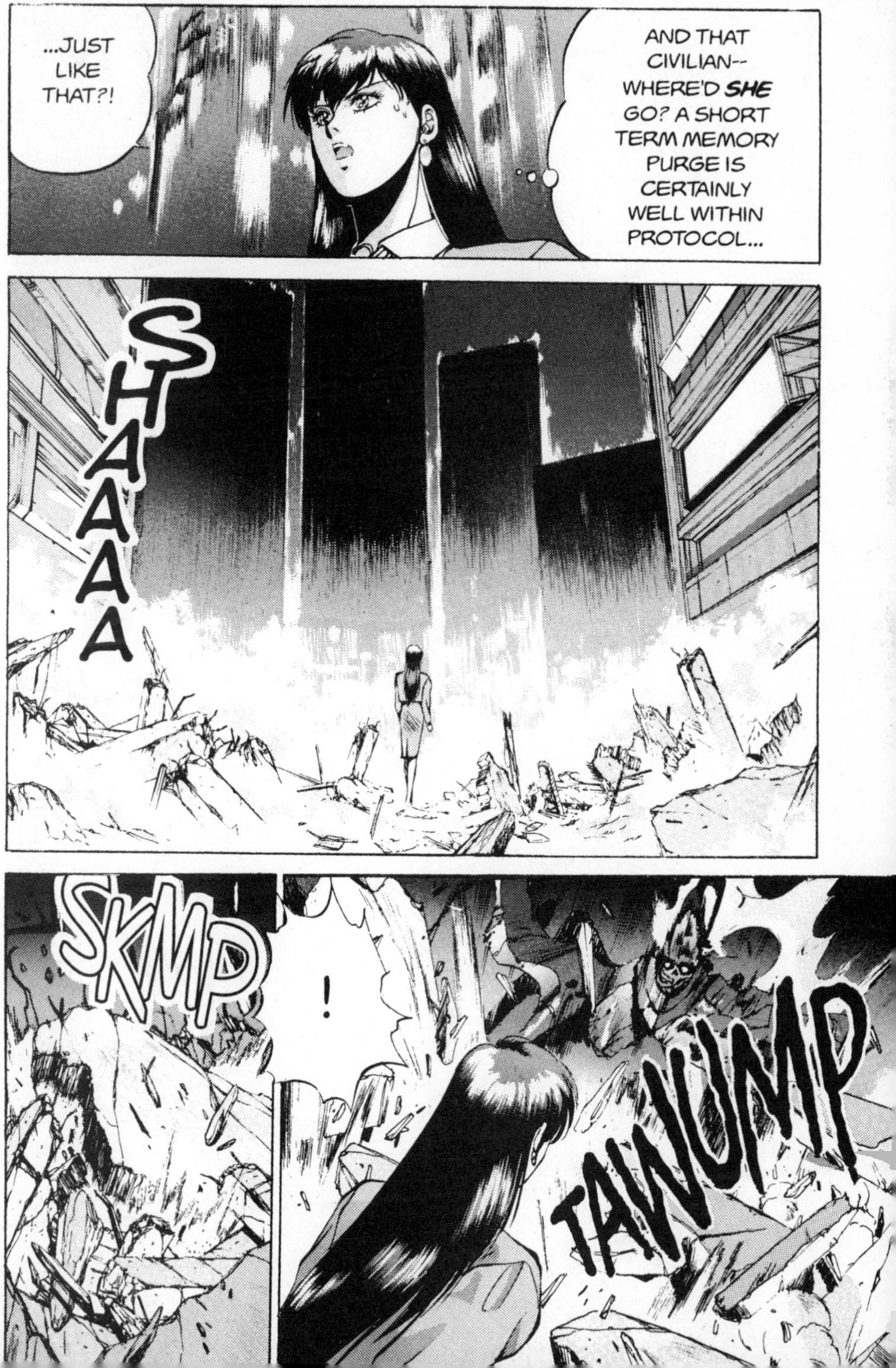
...JUST LIKE THAT?!
AND THAT CIVILIAN-- WHERE'D SHE GO? A SHORT TERM MEMORY PURGE IS CERTAINLY WELL WITHIN PROTOCOL...
SHAAAAA
SKMP
!
TAWUMP

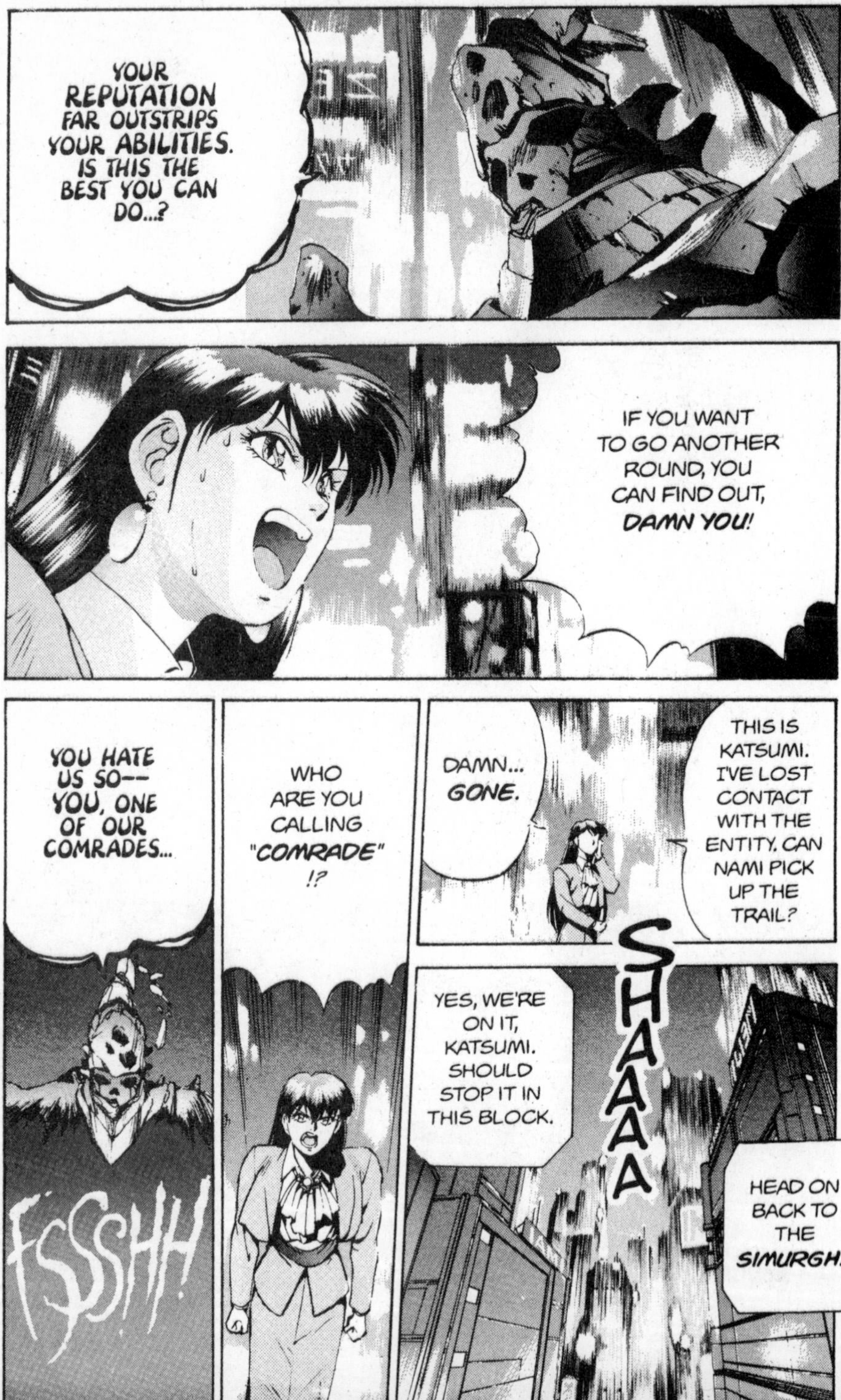
YOUR REPUTATION FAR OUTSTRIPS YOUR ABILITIES. IS THIS THE BEST YOU CAN DO...?
IF YOU WANT TO GO ANOTHER ROUND, YOU CAN FIND OUT, DAMN YOU!
YOU HATE US SO-- YOU, ONE OF OUR COMRADES...
FSSHH!
WHO ARE YOU CALLING "COMRADE" !?
DAMN... GONE.
THIS IS KATSUMI. I'VE LOST CONTACT WITH THE ENTITY. CAN NAMI PICK UP THE TRAIL?
YES, WE'RE ON IT, KATSUMI. SHOULD STOP IT IN THIS BLOCK.
SHAAAA
HEAD ON BACK TO THE SIMURGH...

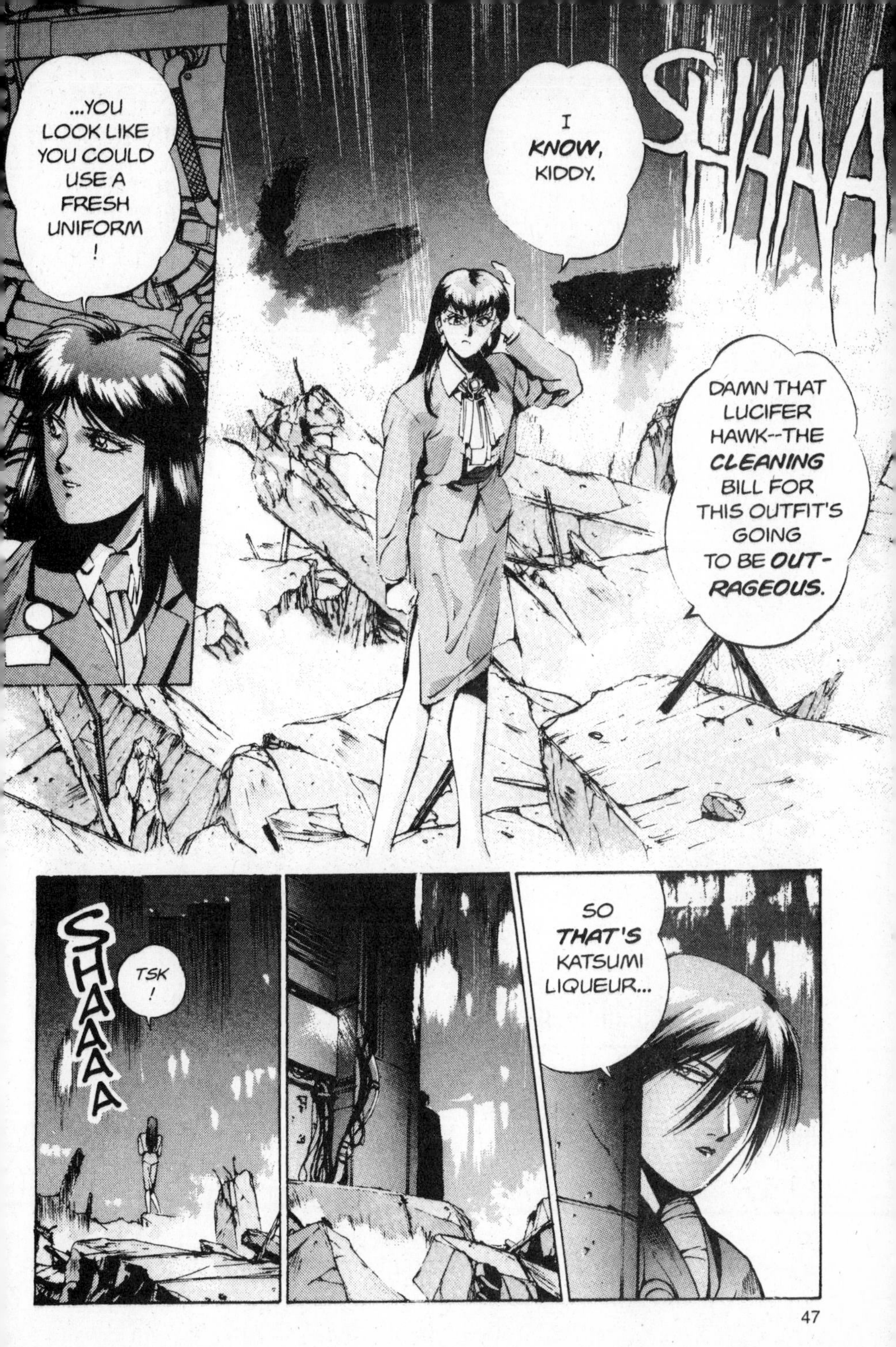
...YOU LOOK LIKE YOU COULD USE A FRESH UNIFORM !
I KNOW, KIDDY.
SHAAA
DAMN THAT LUCIFER HAWK--THE CLEANING BILL FOR THIS OUTFIT'S GOING TO BE OUT-RAGEOUS.
SHAAAA
TSK !
SO THAT'S KATSUMI LIQUEUR...

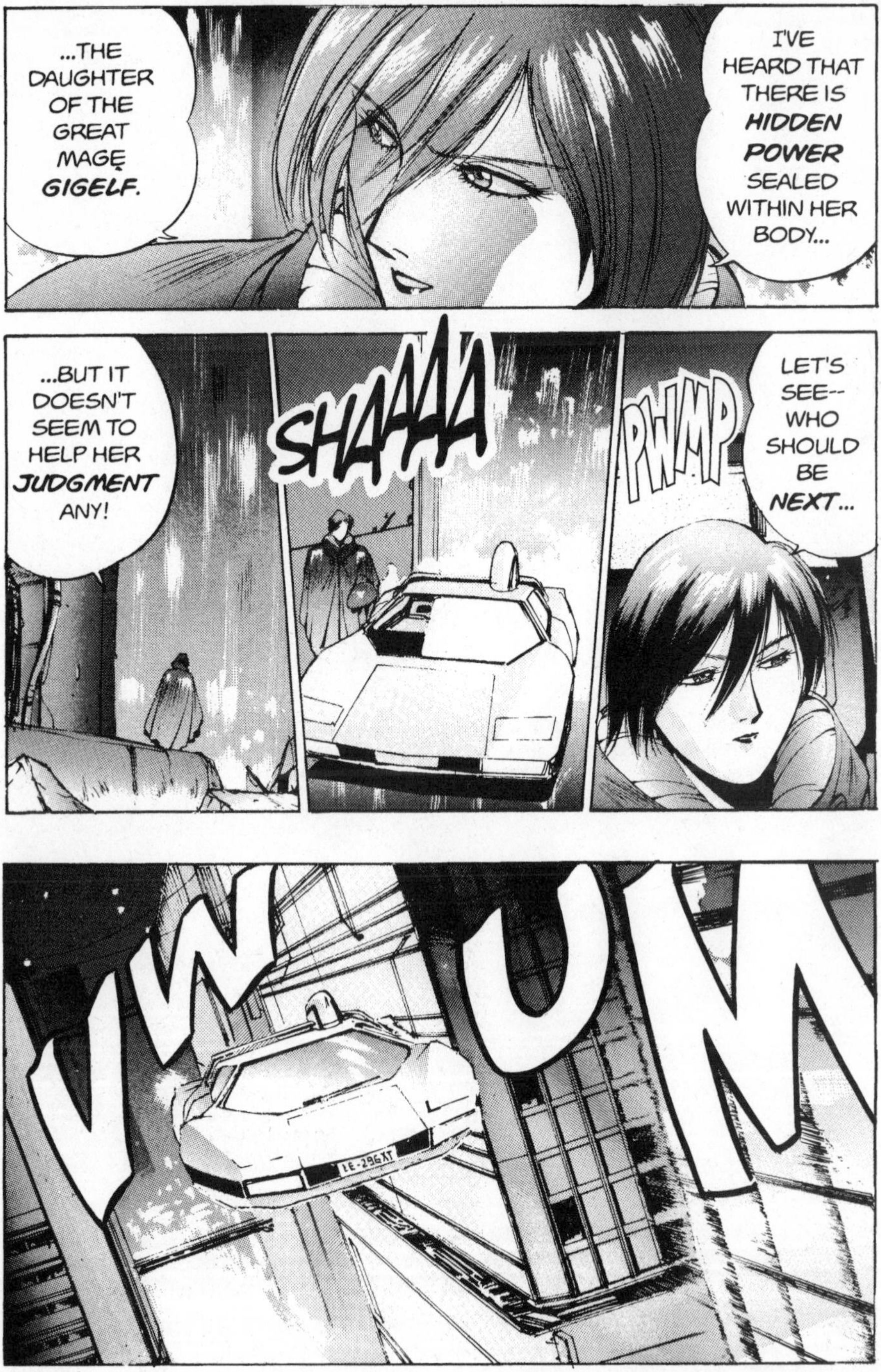

...THE DAUGHTER OF THE GREAT MAGE GIGELF.
I'VE HEARD THAT THERE IS HIDDEN POWER SEALED WITHIN HER BODY...
...BUT IT DOESN'T SEEM TO HELP HER JUDGMENT ANY!
SHAAAA
PWMP
LET'S SEE-- WHO SHOULD BE NEXT...
VWUM

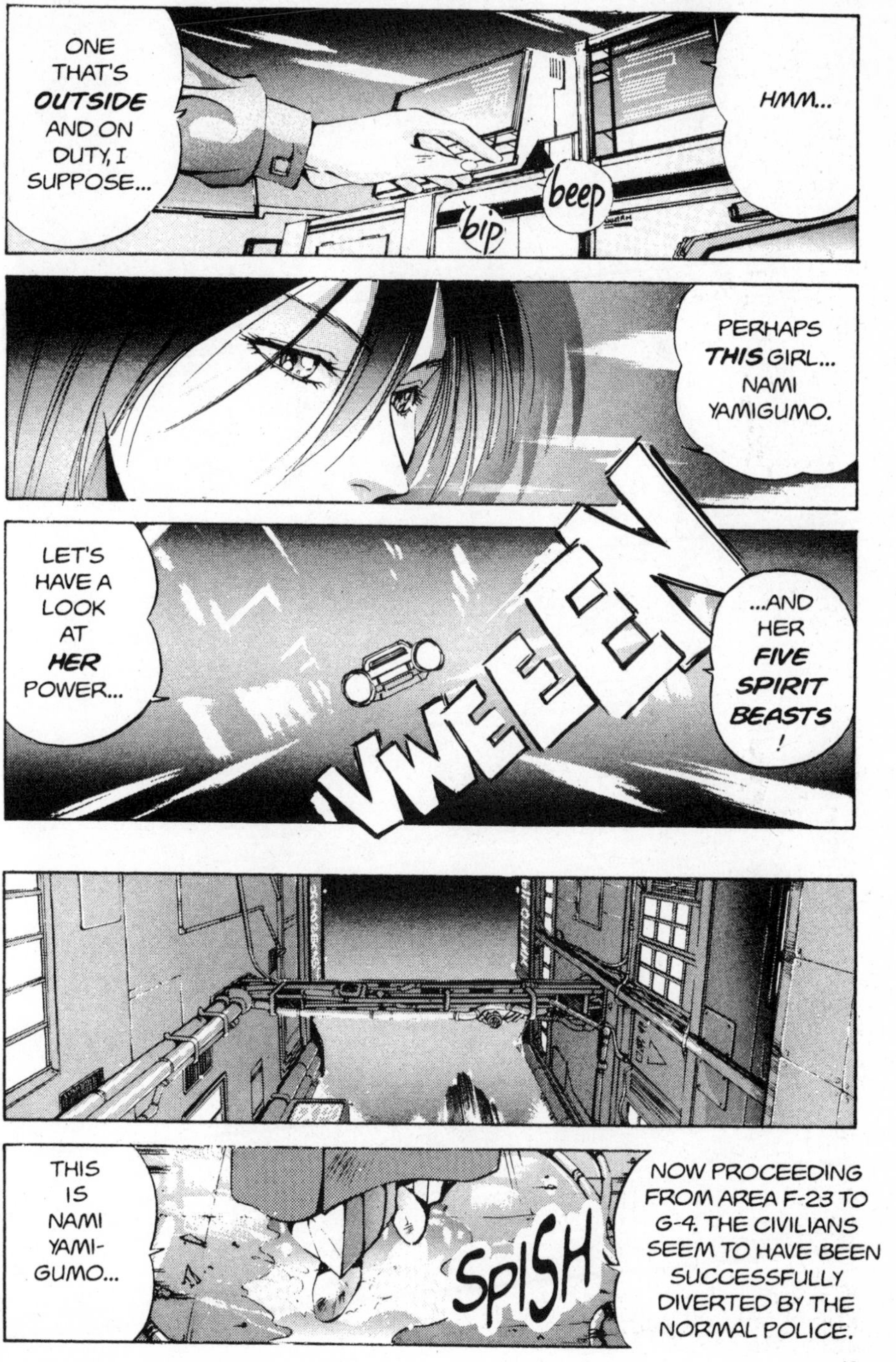
ONE THAT'S OUTSIDE AND ON DUTY, I SUPPOSE...
HMM...
beep
bip
PERHAPS THIS GIRL... NAMI YAMIGUMO.
LET'S HAVE A LOOK AT HER POWER...
VWEEEN
...AND HER FIVE SPIRIT BEASTS!
THIS IS NAMI YAMI-GUMO...
SPISH
NOW PROCEEDING FROM AREA F-23 TO G-4. THE CIVILIANS SEEM TO HAVE BEEN SUCCESSFULLY DIVERTED BY THE NORMAL POLICE.

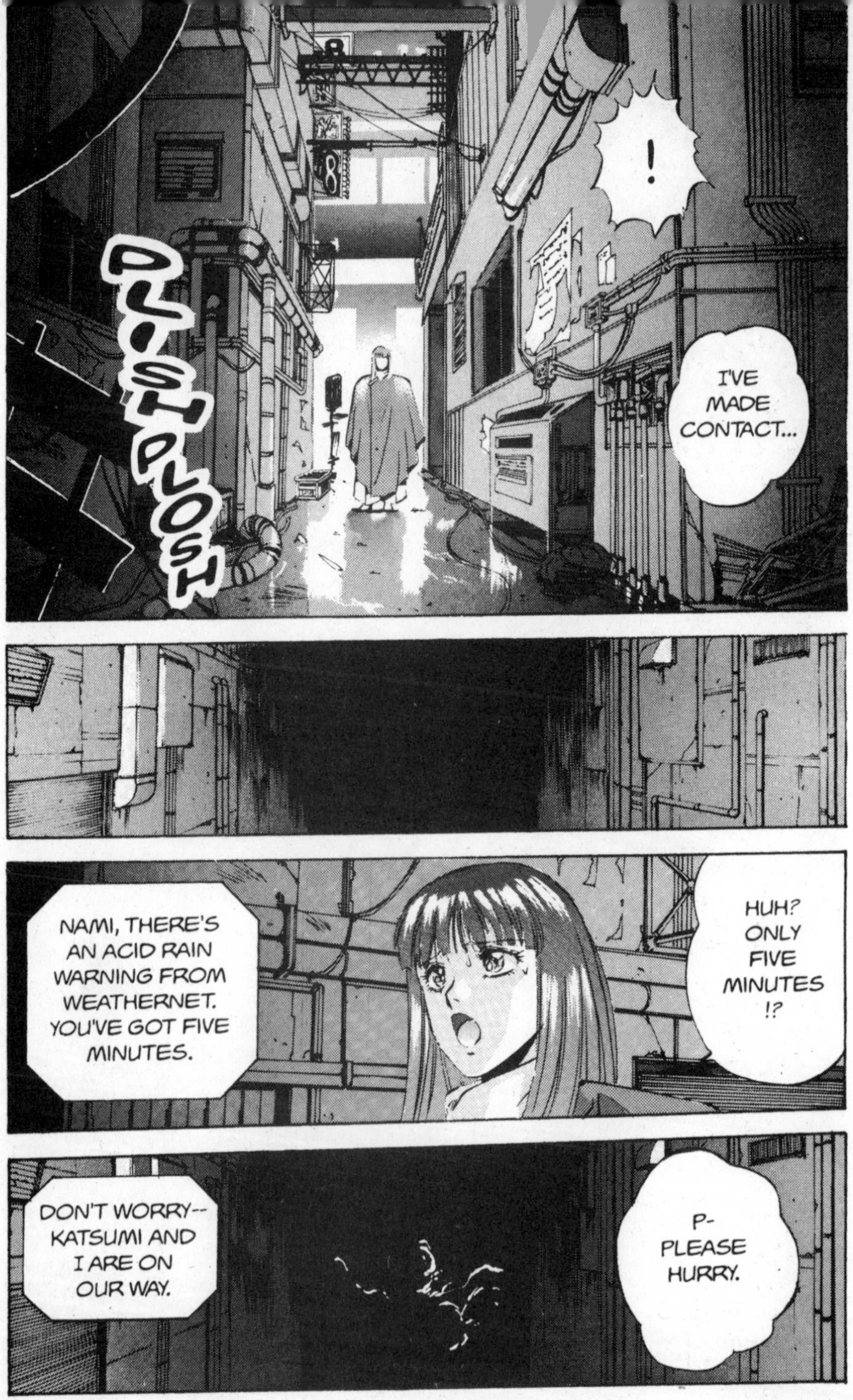
PLISH PLOSH
!
I'VE MADE CONTACT...
NAMI, THERE'S AN ACID RAIN WARNING FROM WEATHERNET. YOU'VE GOT FIVE MINUTES.
HUH? ONLY FIVE MINUTES !?
DON'T WORRY-- KATSUMI AND I ARE ON OUR WAY.
P- PLEASE HURRY.

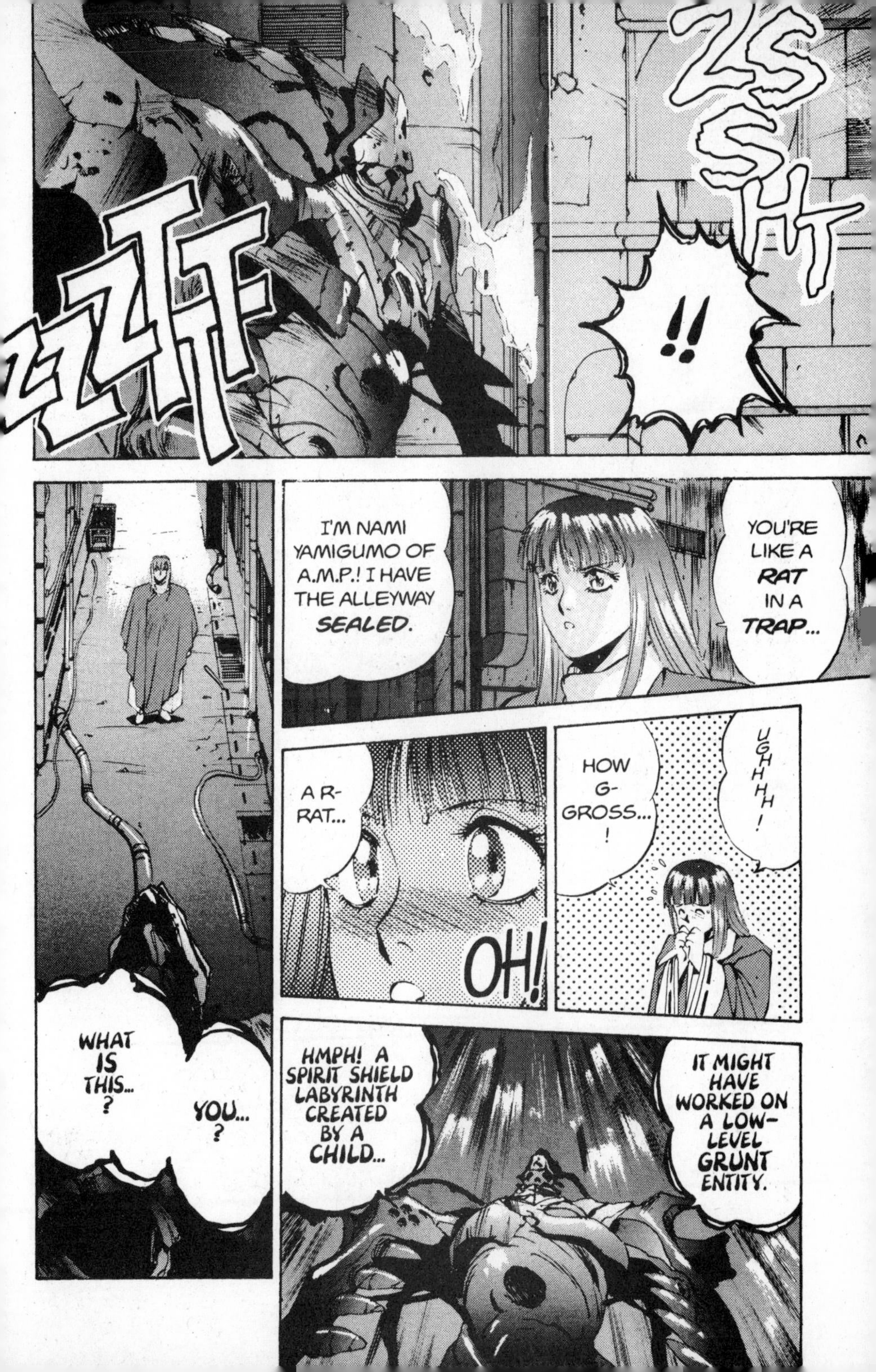
ZZZTTF
ZSSHT
!!
WHAT IS THIS...?
YOU...?
I'M NAMI YAMIGUMO OF A.M.P.! I HAVE THE ALLEYWAY SEALED.
YOU'RE LIKE A RAT IN A TRAP...
A R-RAT...
OH!
HOW G-GROSS...!
UGHHHH!
HMPH! A SPIRIT SHIELD LABYRINTH CREATED BY A CHILD...
IT MIGHT HAVE WORKED ON A LOW-LEVEL GRUNT ENTITY.

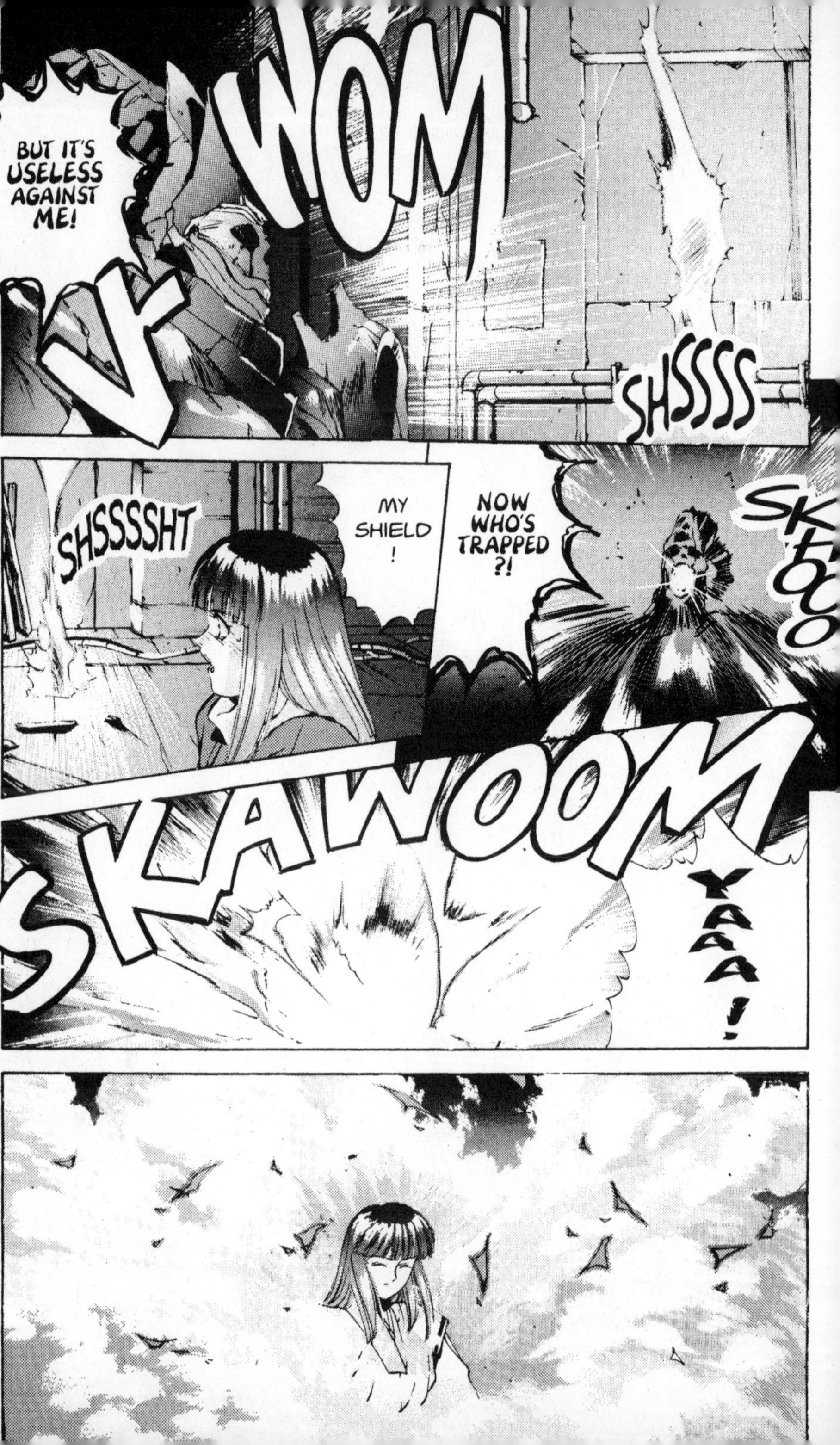
BUT IT'S USELESS AGAINST ME!
VWOM
SHSSSS
SHSSSSHT
MY SHIELD !
NOW WHO'S TRAPPED ?!
SKAWOOM
YAAA!

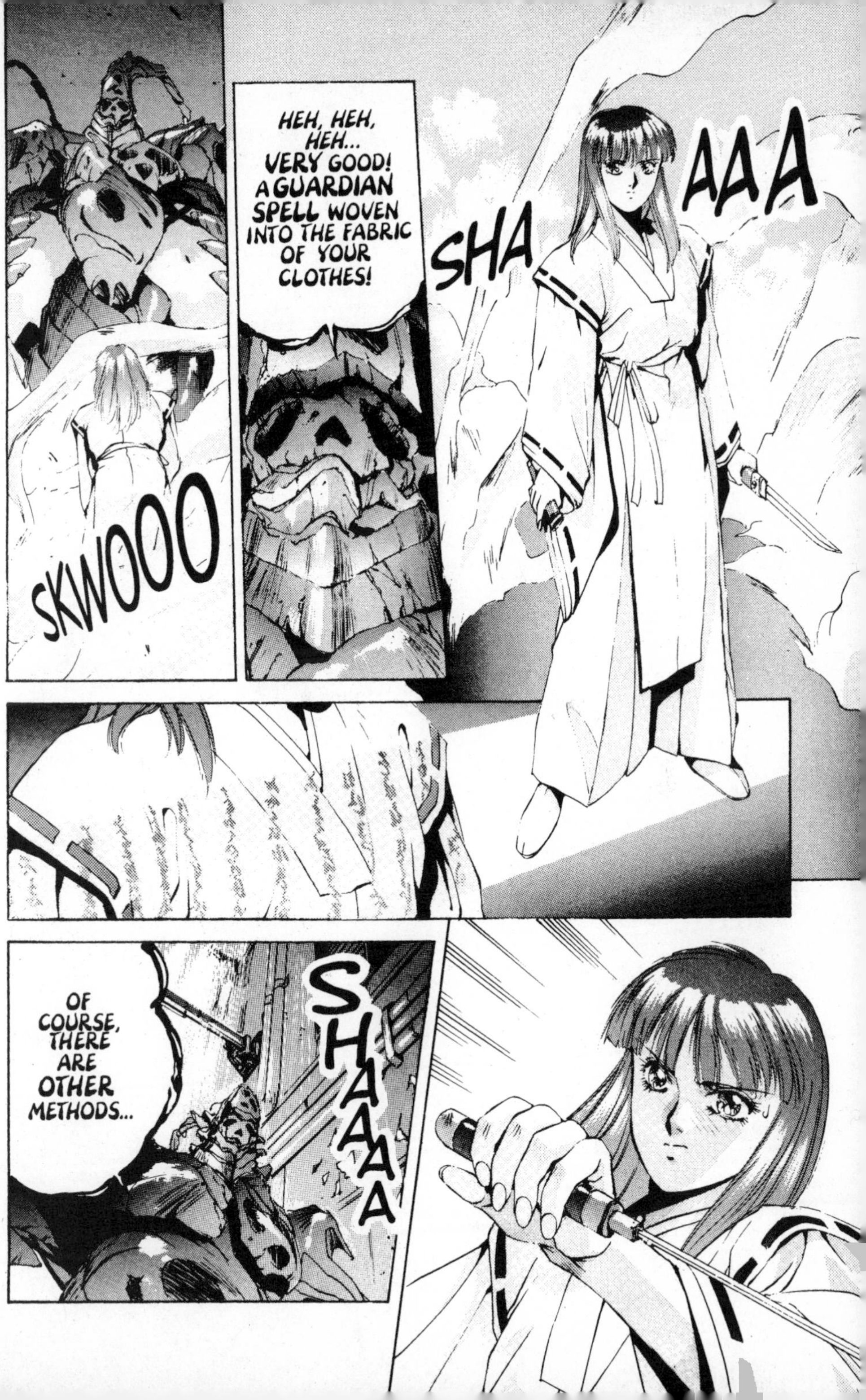
SKWOOO
HEH, HEH, HEH... VERY GOOD! A GUARDIAN SPELL WOVEN INTO THE FABRIC OF YOUR CLOTHES!
SHA AAA
OF COURSE, THERE ARE OTHER METHODS...
SHAAAAA

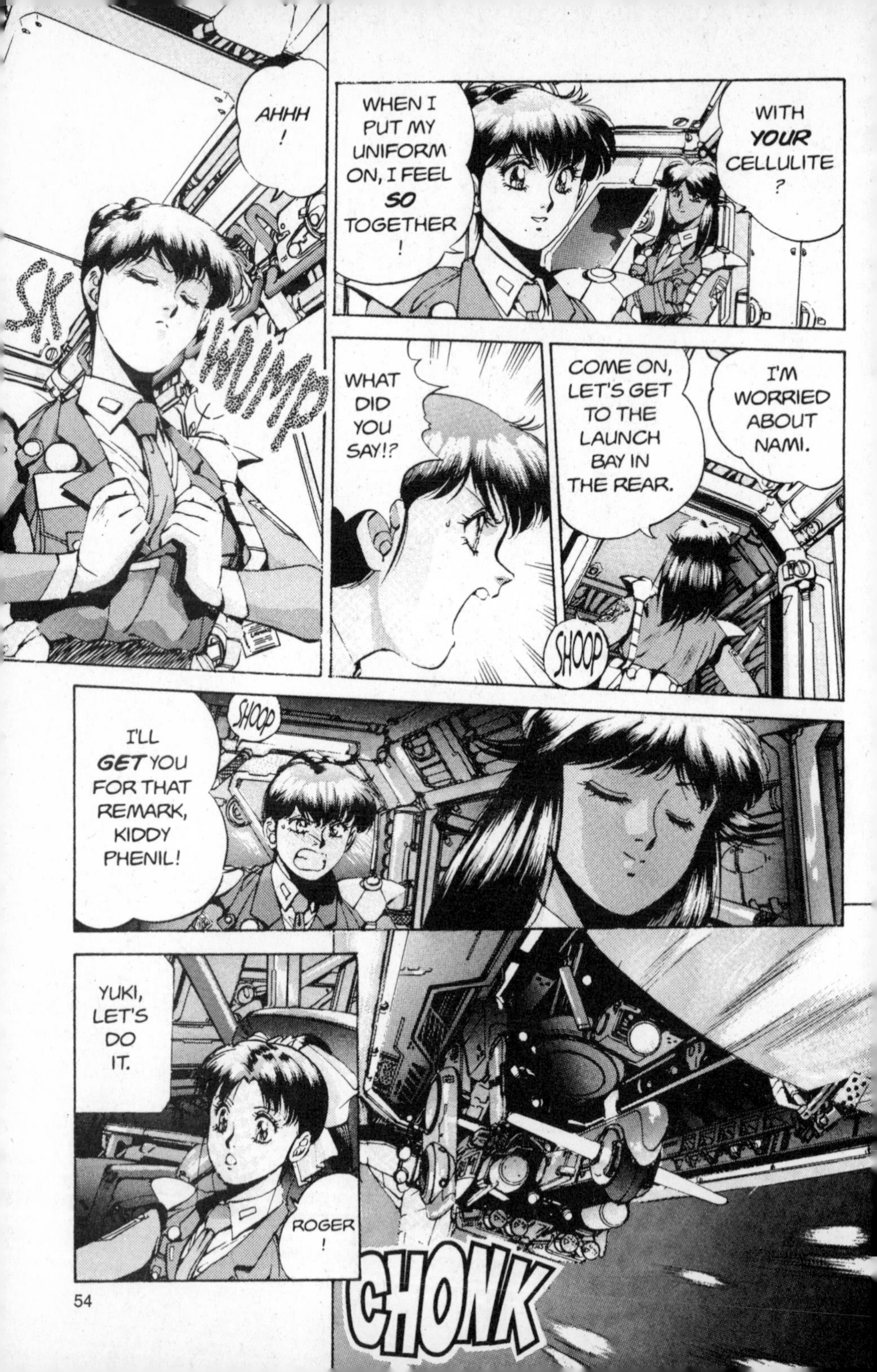
AHHH!
SK
WUMP
WHEN I PUT MY UNIFORM ON, I FEEL **SO** TOGETHER!
WITH **YOUR** CELLULITE?
WHAT DID YOU SAY!?
COME ON, LET'S GET TO THE LAUNCH BAY IN THE REAR.
I'M WORRIED ABOUT NAMI.
SHOOP
SHOOP
I'LL **GET** YOU FOR THAT REMARK, KIDDY PHENIL!
YUKI, LET'S DO IT.
ROGER!
CHONK

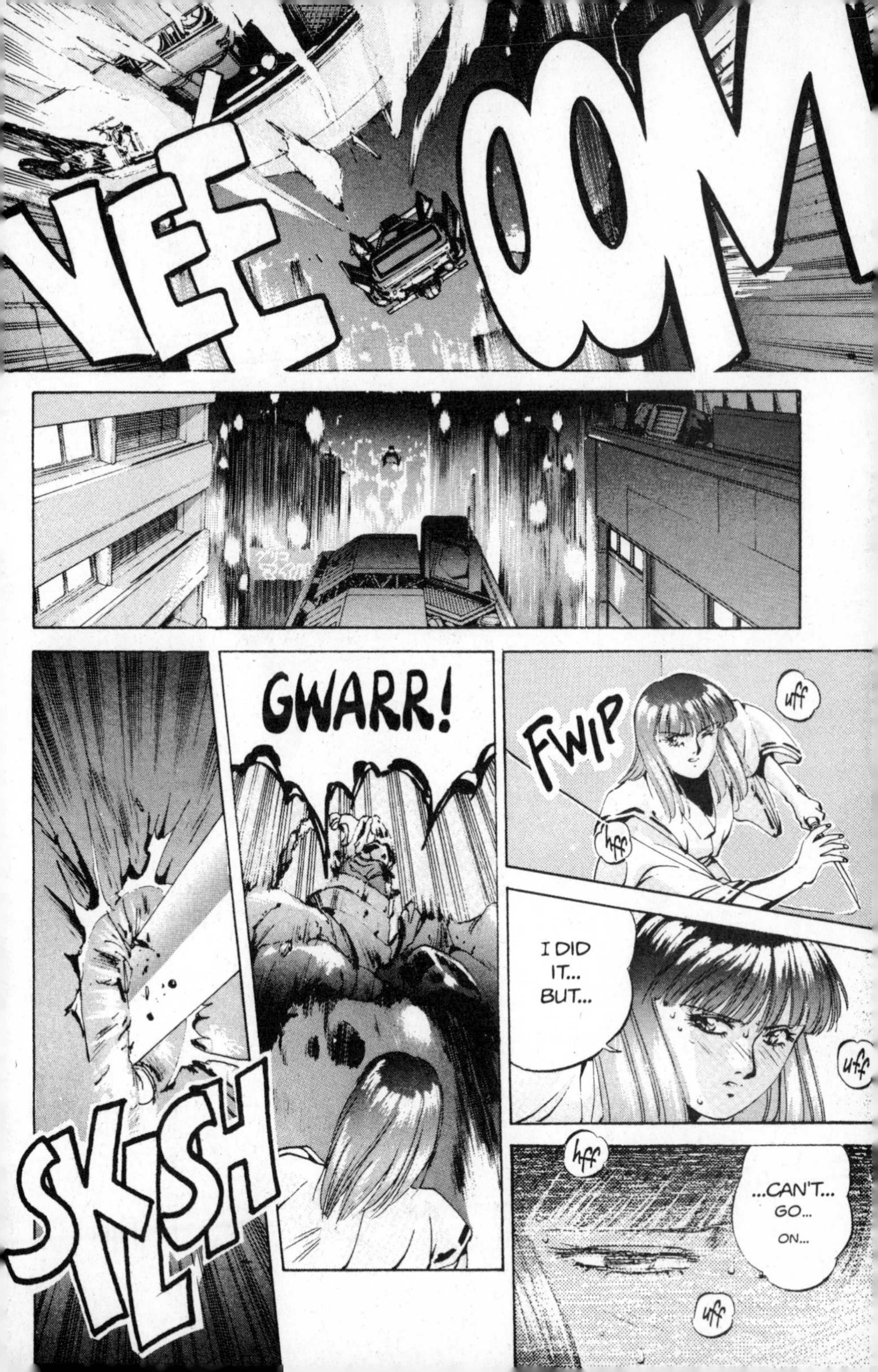
VEEOOM
SKSH
GWARR!
FWIP
uff
hff
I DID IT... BUT...
uff
hff
...CAN'T... GO... ON...
uff

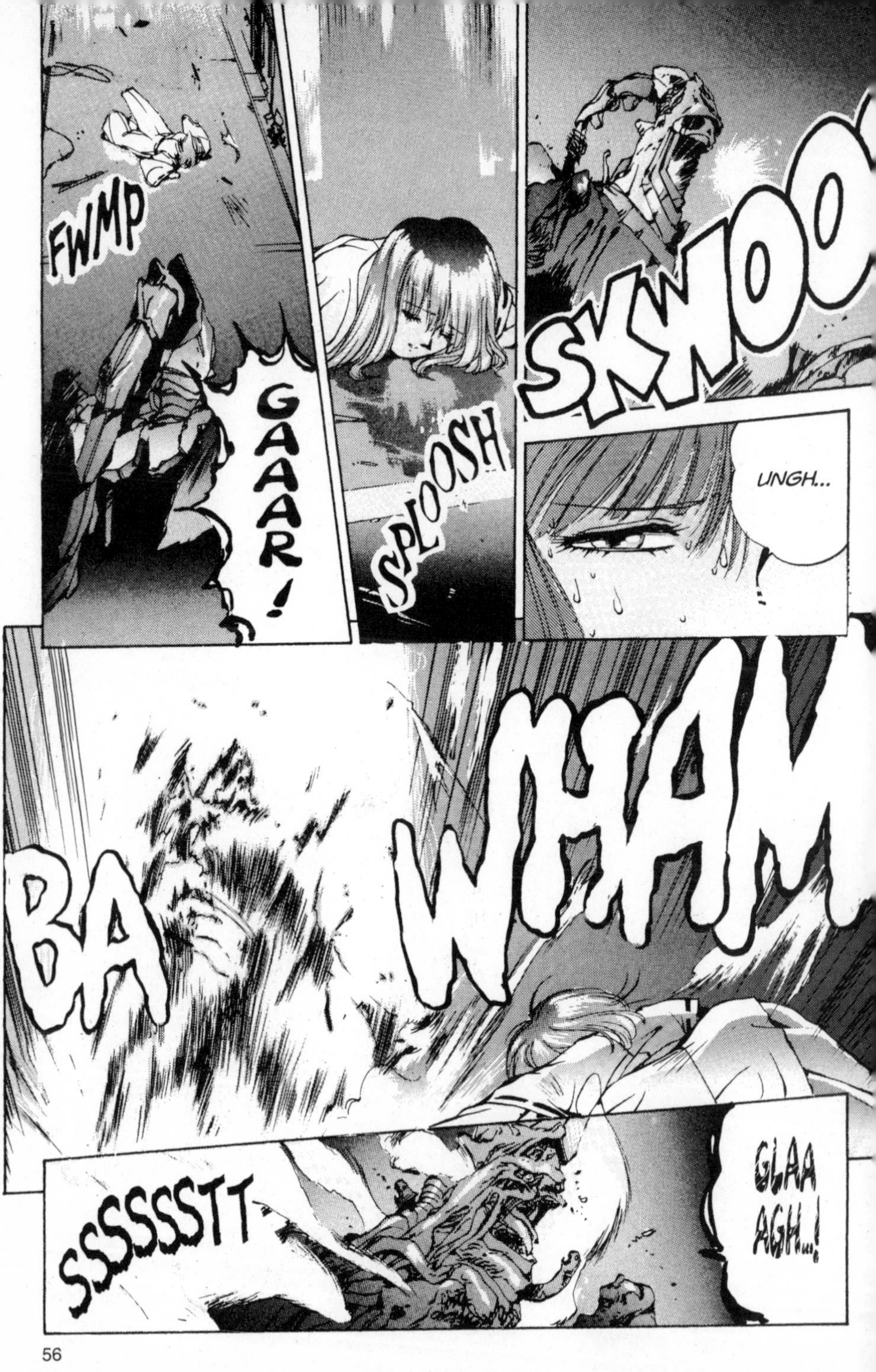
FWMP
GAAAR!
SPLOOSH
SKWOO
UNGH...
BA
WHAM
SSSSSSTT
GLAA AGH...!

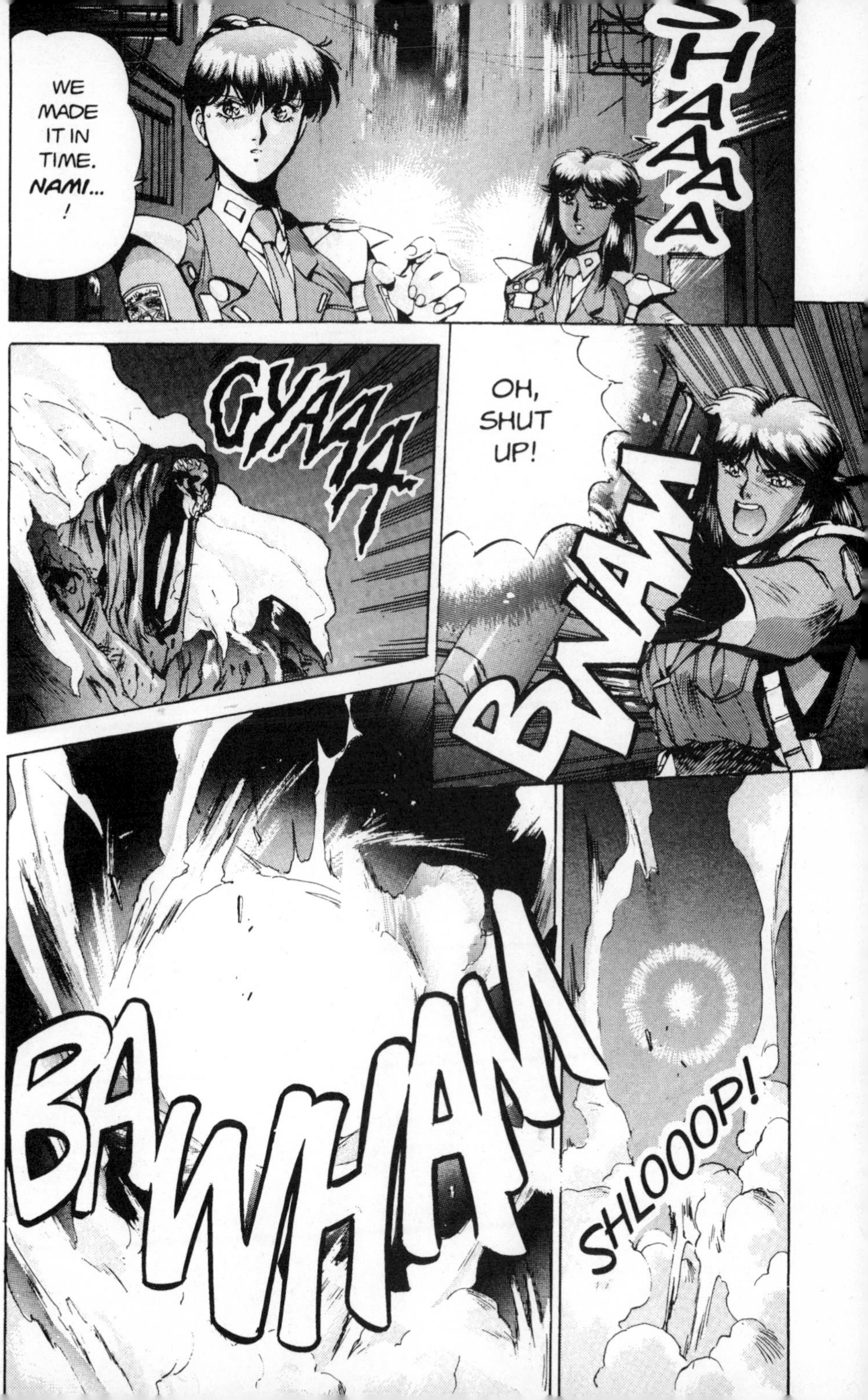
WE MADE IT IN TIME. NAMI...!
SHAAAA
GYAAA
OH, SHUT UP!
BWAM
BAWHAM
SHLOOOP!

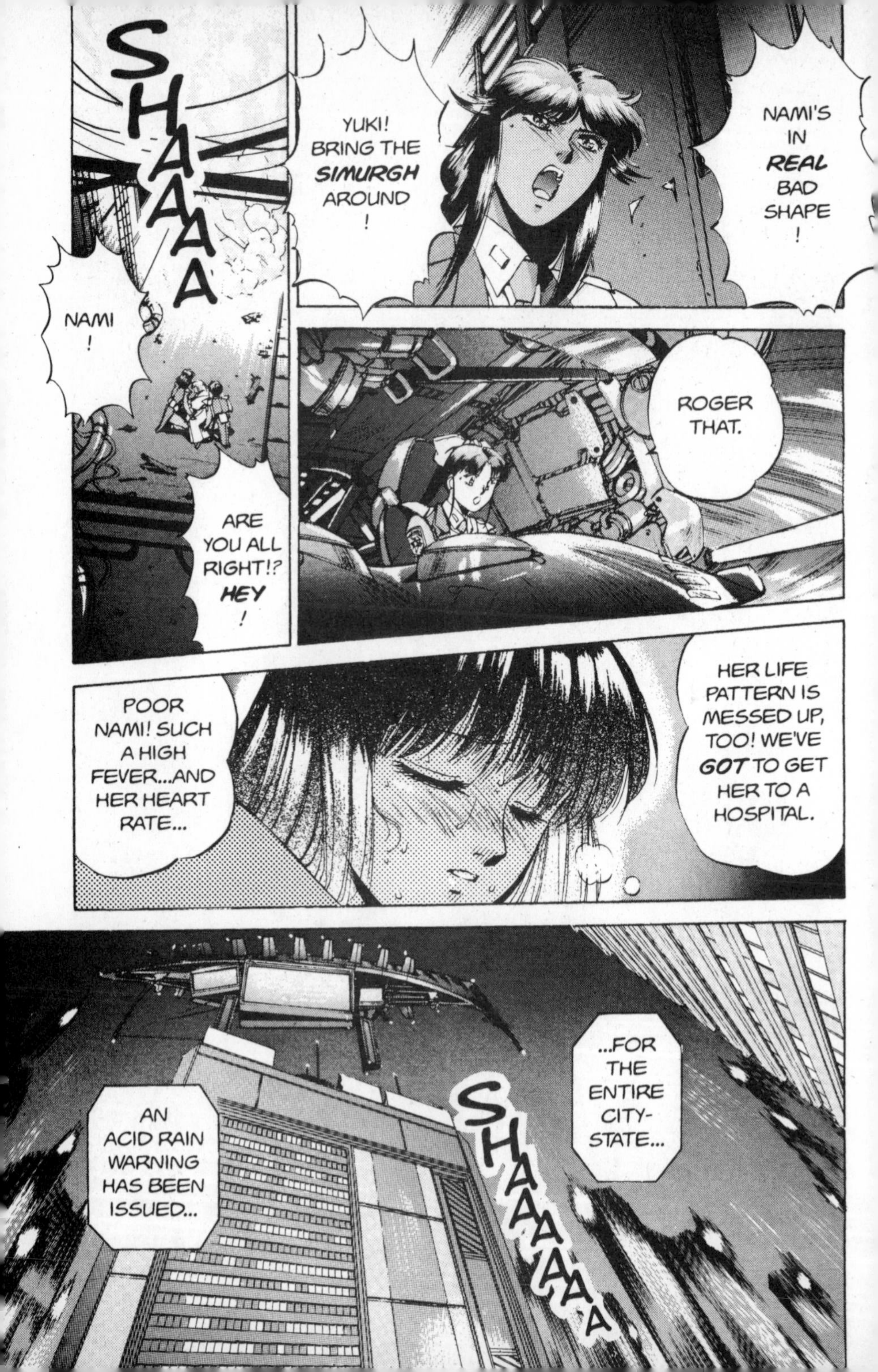
SHAAAA
NAMI!
ARE YOU ALL RIGHT!? HEY!
YUKI! BRING THE SIMURGH AROUND!
NAMI'S IN REAL BAD SHAPE!
ROGER THAT.
POOR NAMI! SUCH A HIGH FEVER...AND HER HEART RATE...
HER LIFE PATTERN IS MESSED UP, TOO! WE'VE GOT TO GET HER TO A HOSPITAL.
AN ACID RAIN WARNING HAS BEEN ISSUED...
...FOR THE ENTIRE CITY-STATE...
SHAAAAAAA

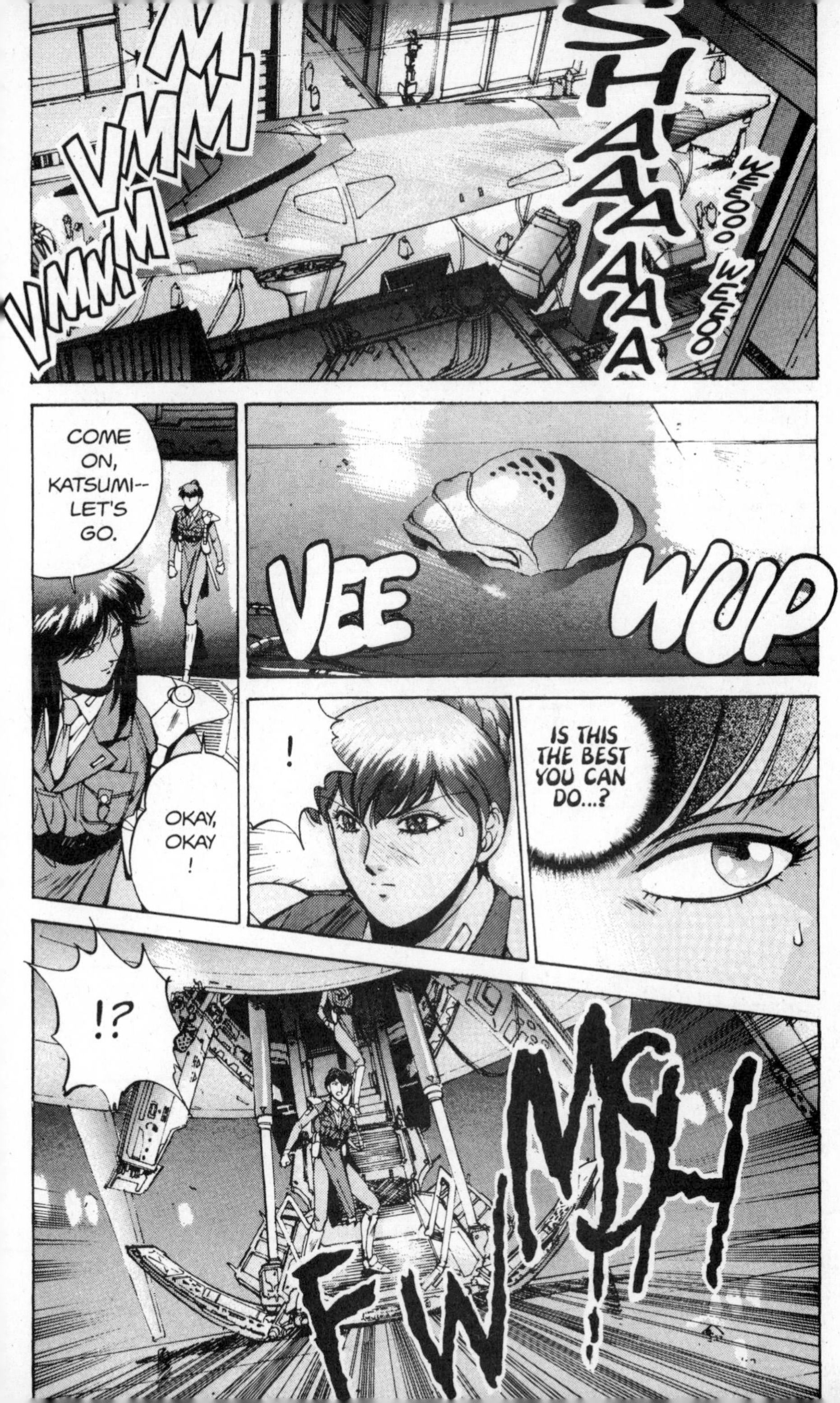

VMMNM VMMM M
SHAAAAA
WEEOOO WEEOO
COME ON, KATSUMI-- LET'S GO.
OKAY, OKAY !
VEE WUP
!
IS THIS THE BEST YOU CAN DO...?
!?
FWMSH!

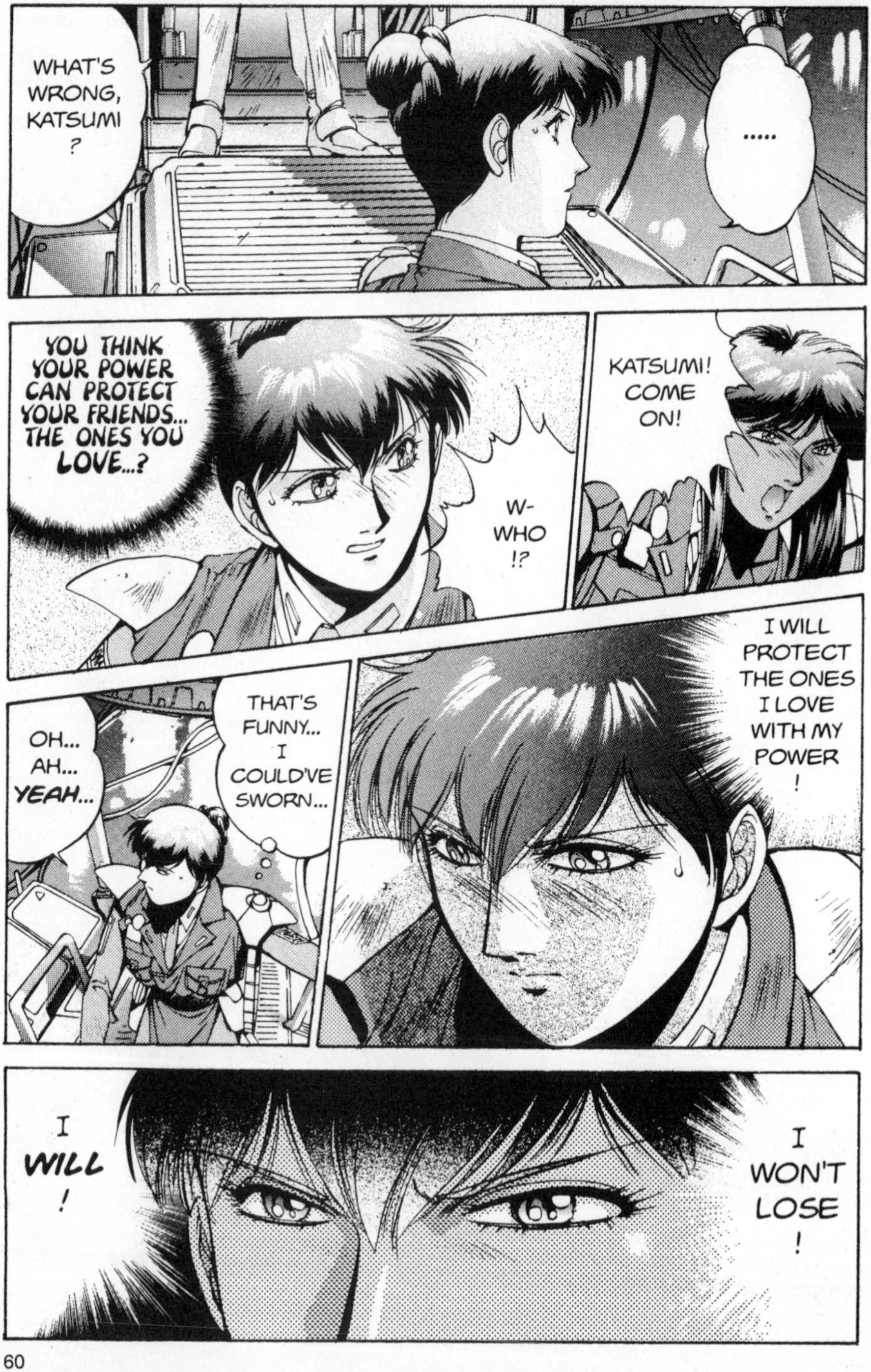
WHAT'S WRONG, KATSUMI ?
.....
YOU THINK YOUR POWER CAN PROTECT YOUR FRIENDS... THE ONES YOU LOVE...?
W- WHO !?
KATSUMI! COME ON!
OH... AH... YEAH...
THAT'S FUNNY... I COULD'VE SWORN...
I WILL PROTECT THE ONES I LOVE WITH MY POWER !
I WILL !
I WON'T LOSE !

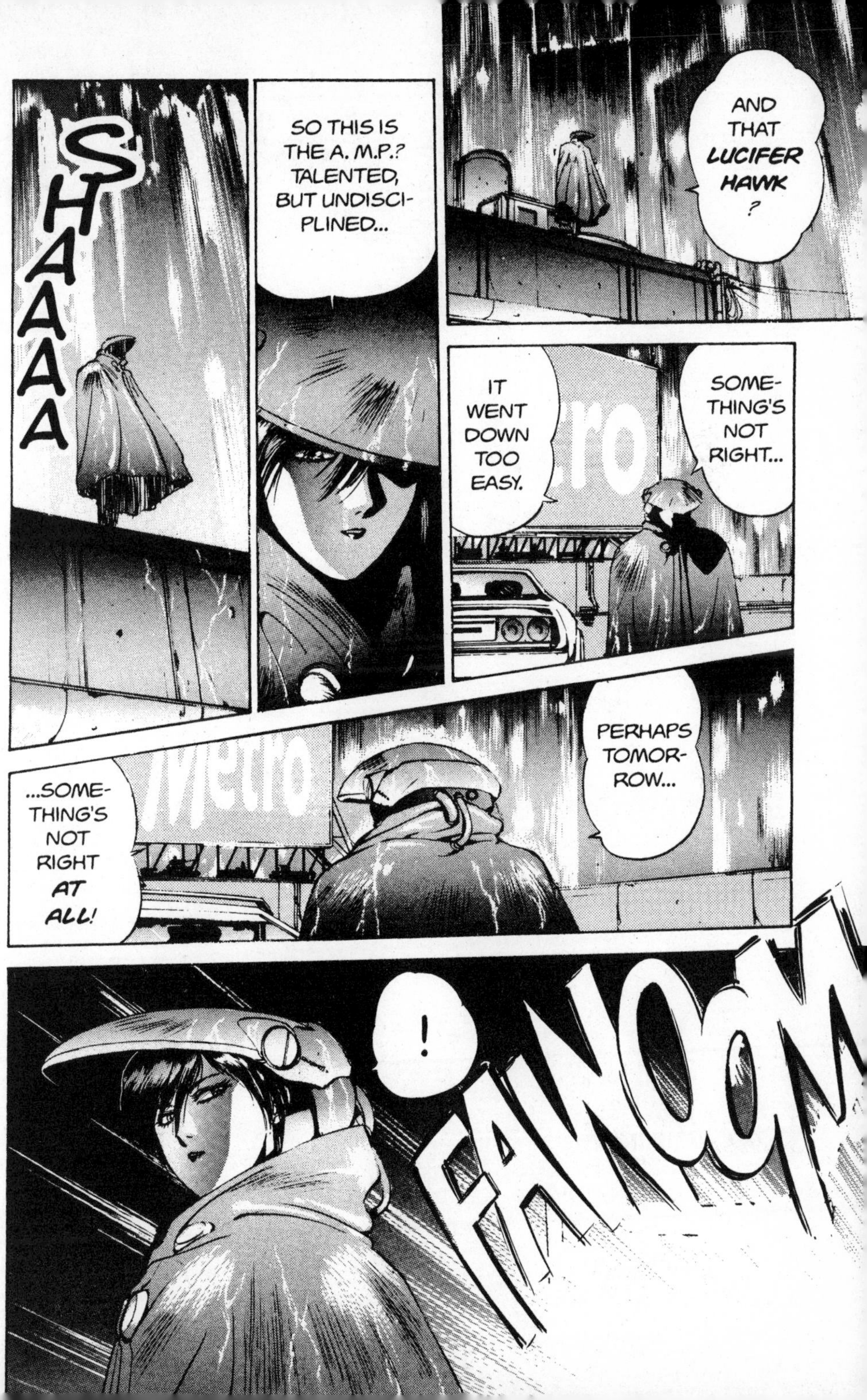
SO THIS IS THE A. M.P.? TALENTED, BUT UNDISCI-PLINED...
AND THAT LUCIFER HAWK?
SOME-THING'S NOT RIGHT...
IT WENT DOWN TOO EASY.
SHAAAAA
PERHAPS TOMOR-ROW...
...SOME-THING'S NOT RIGHT AT ALL!
!
FAWOOM

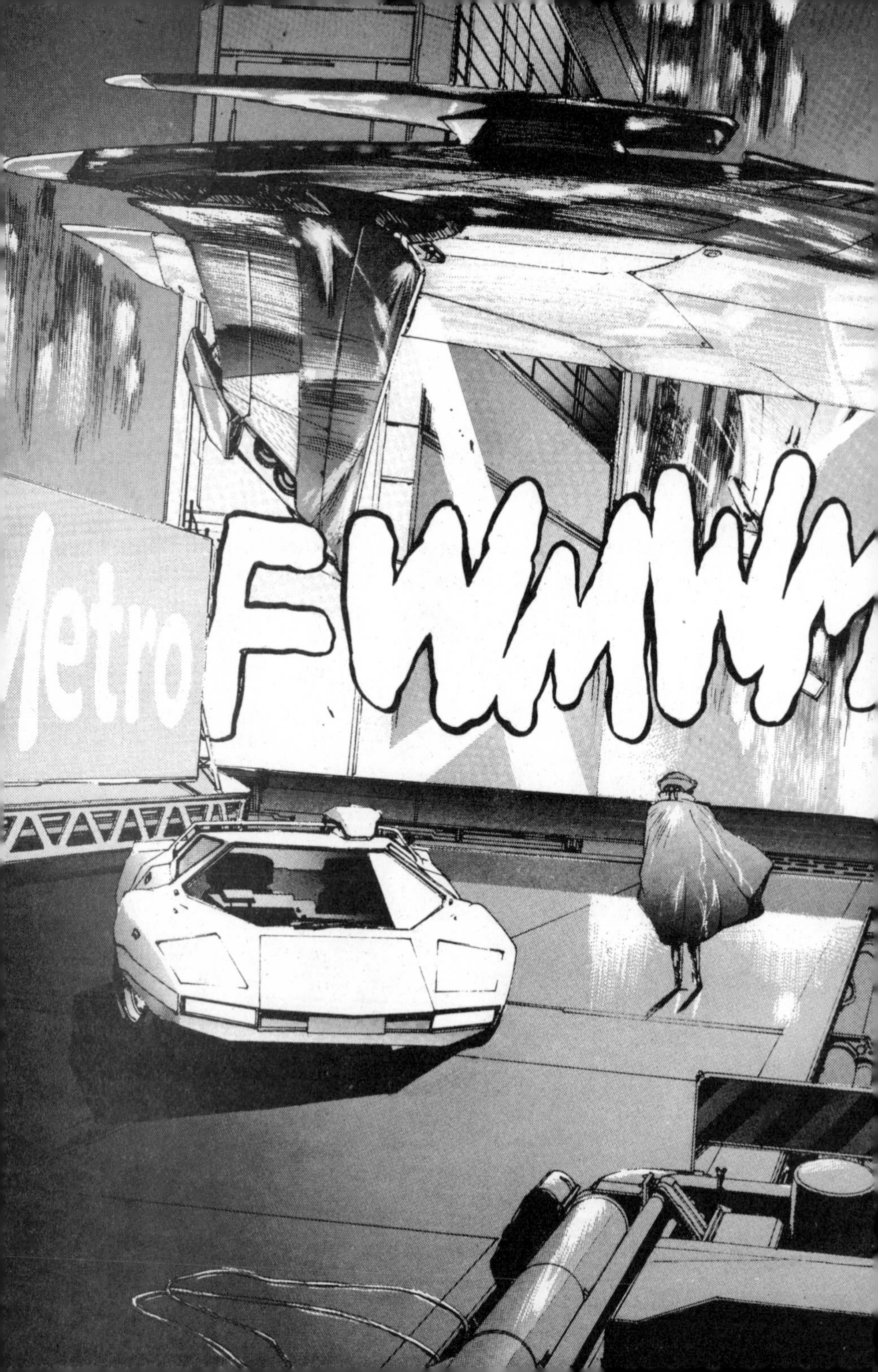
etro

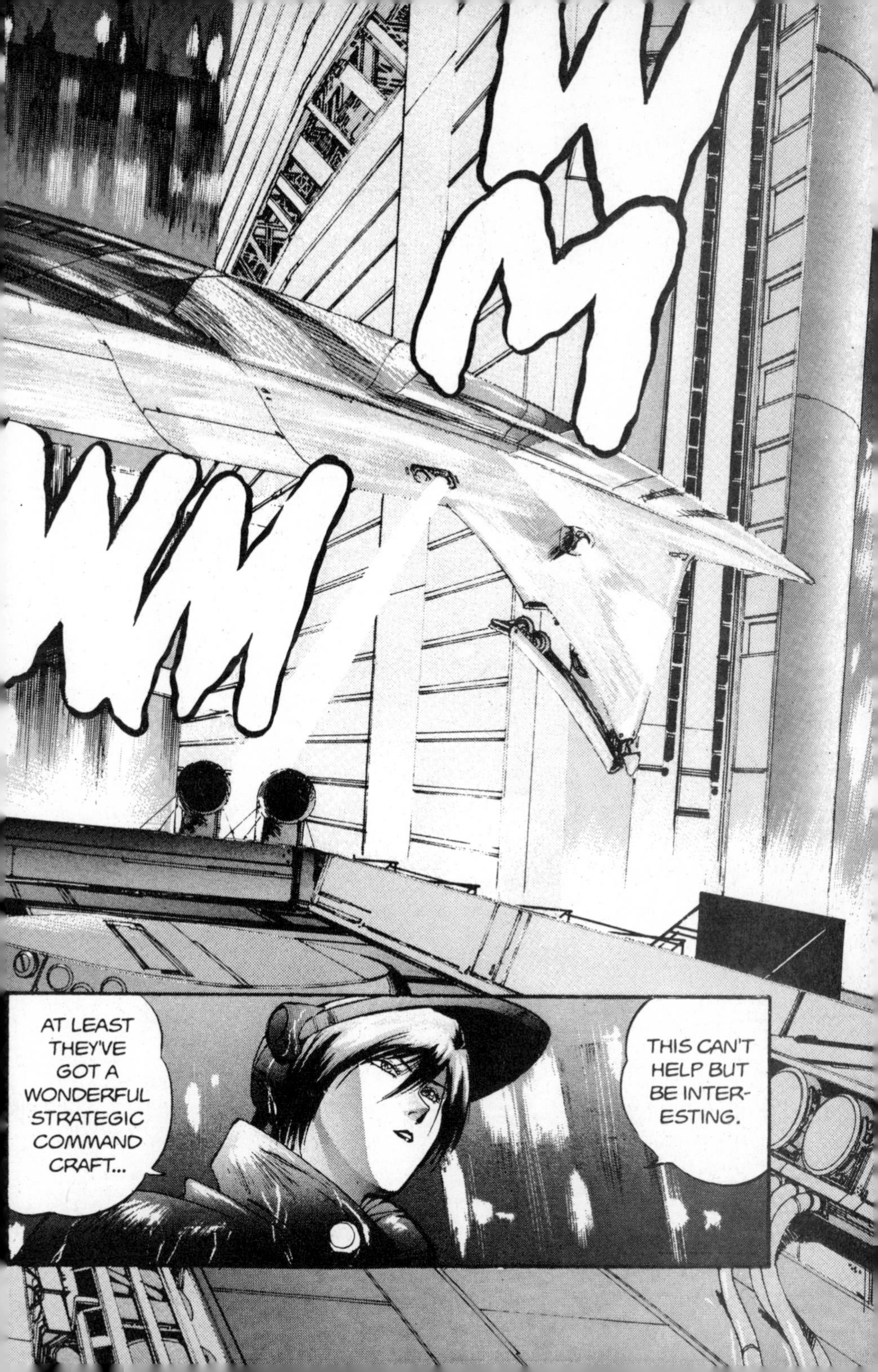
AT LEAST THEY'VE GOT A WONDERFUL STRATEGIC COMMAND CRAFT...
THIS CAN'T HELP BUT BE INTER-ESTING.

SILENT MÖBIUS

CHAPTER 10:

OFFENSE AND DEFENSE

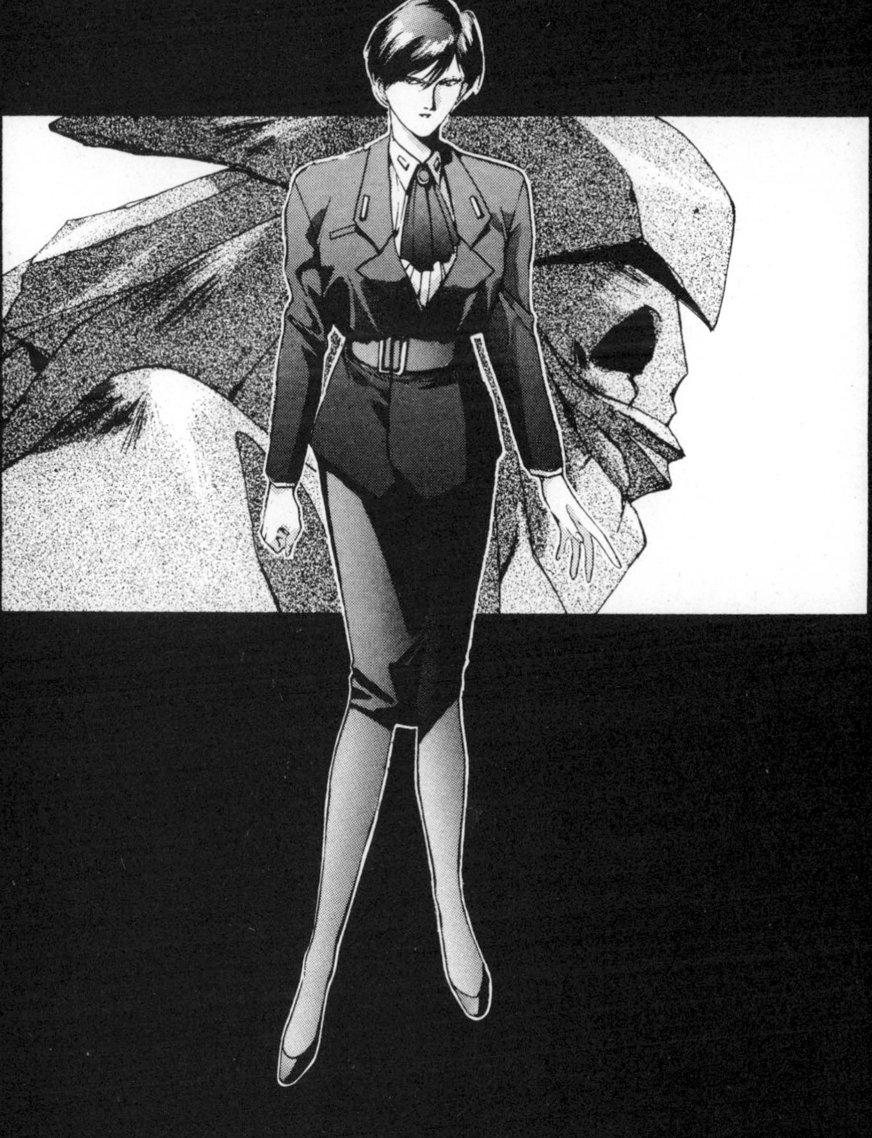

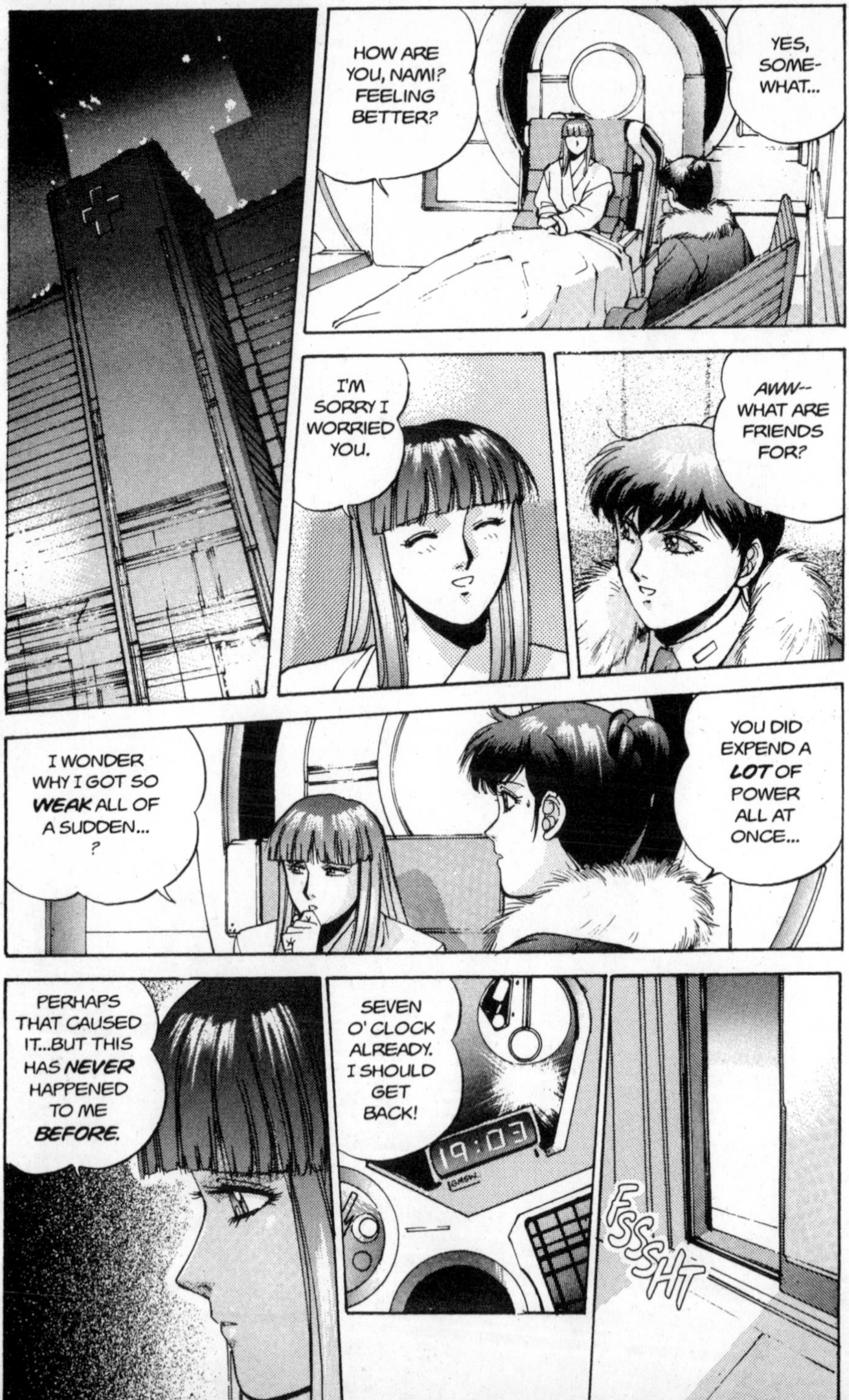
HOW ARE YOU, NAMI? FEELING BETTER?
YES, SOME-WHAT...
I'M SORRY I WORRIED YOU.
AWW-- WHAT ARE FRIENDS FOR?
I WONDER WHY I GOT SO **WEAK** ALL OF A SUDDEN... ?
YOU DID EXPEND A **LOT** OF POWER ALL AT ONCE...
PERHAPS THAT CAUSED IT...BUT THIS HAS **NEVER** HAPPENED TO ME **BEFORE**.
SEVEN O' CLOCK ALREADY. I SHOULD GET BACK!
19:03
FSSSHT

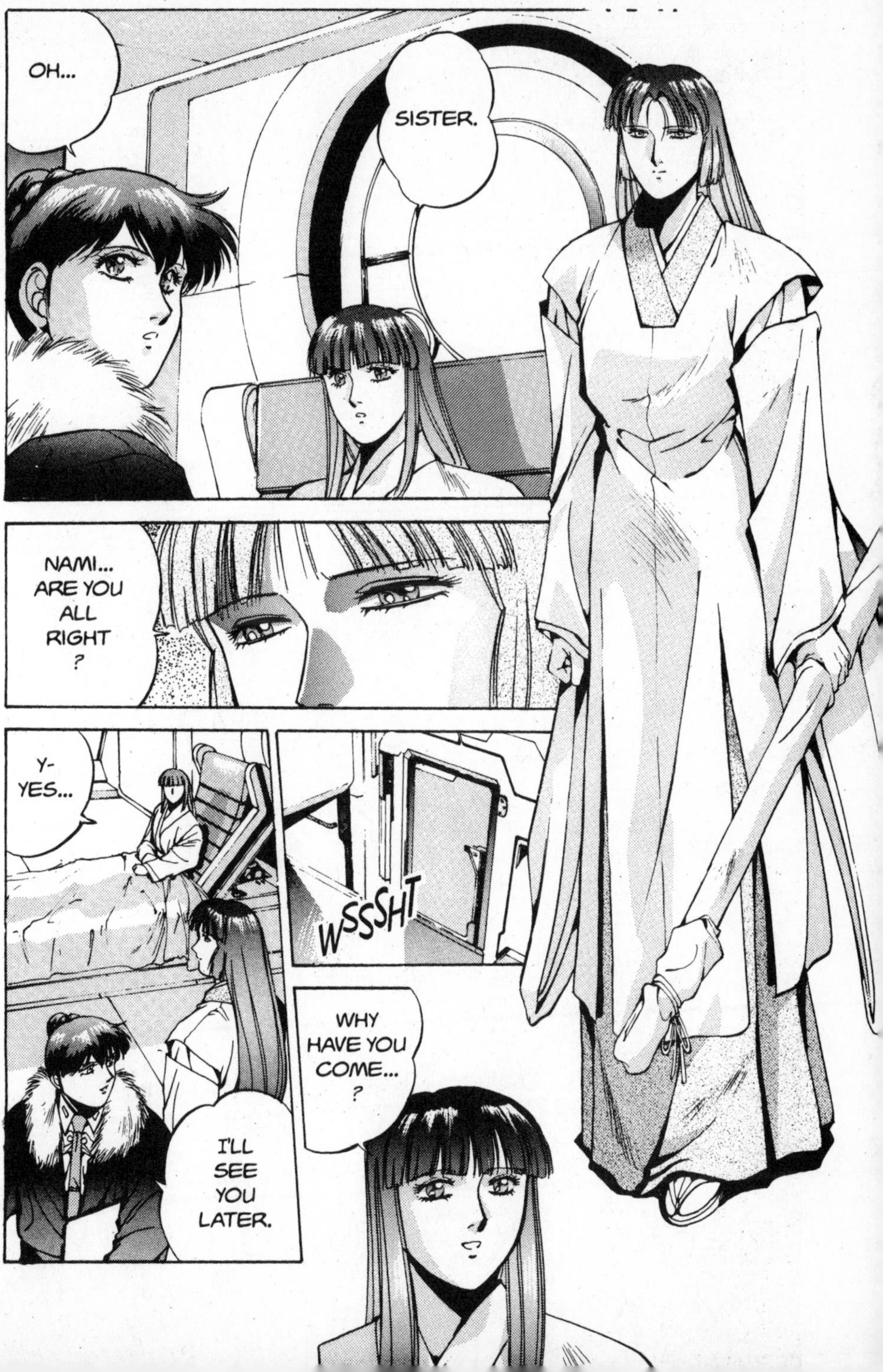
OH...
SISTER.
NAMI... ARE YOU ALL RIGHT ?
Y- YES...
WSSSHT
WHY HAVE YOU COME... ?
I'LL SEE YOU LATER.

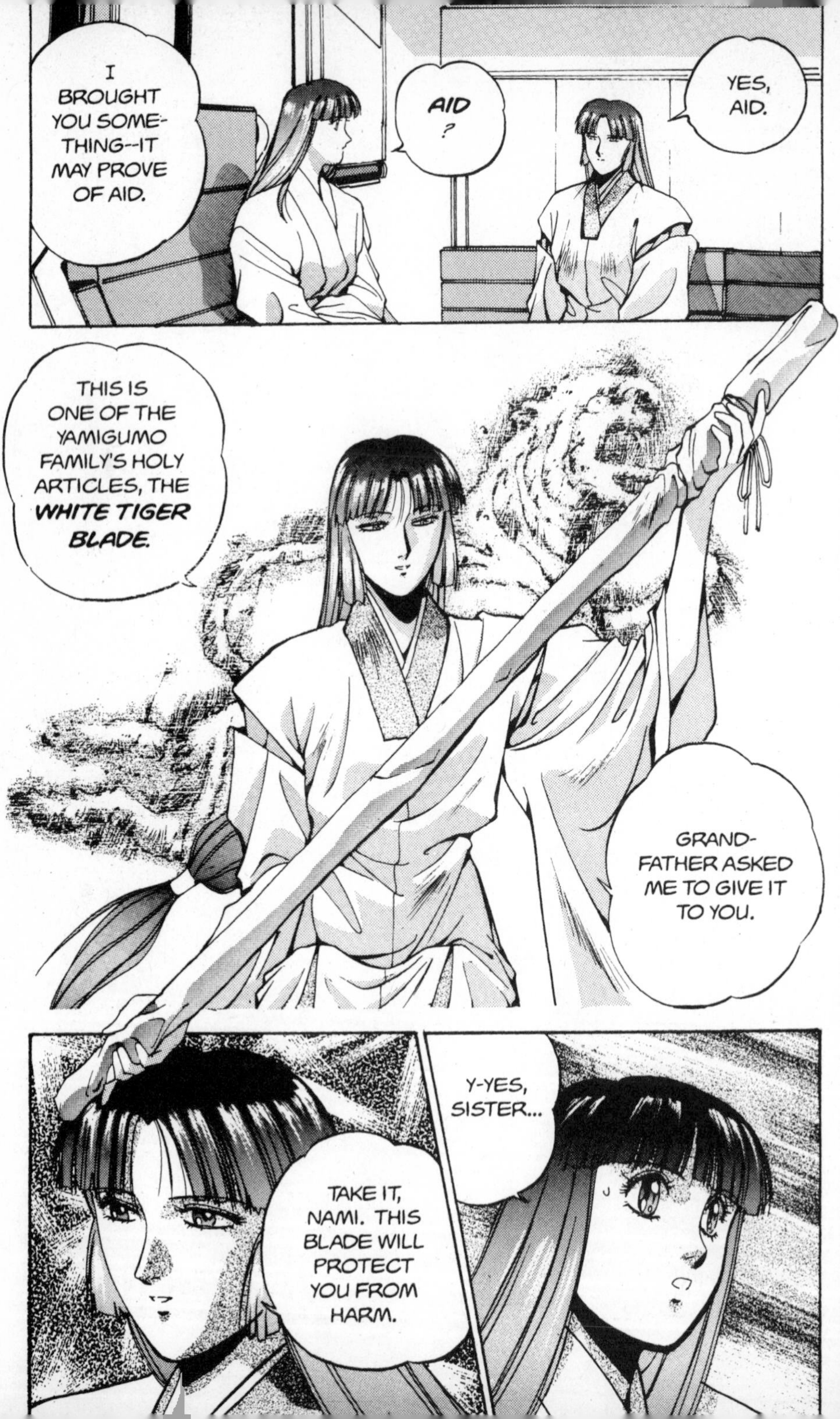
I BROUGHT YOU SOME-THING--IT MAY PROVE OF AID.
AID?
YES, AID.
THIS IS ONE OF THE YAMIGUMO FAMILY'S HOLY ARTICLES, THE WHITE TIGER BLADE.
GRAND-FATHER ASKED ME TO GIVE IT TO YOU.
TAKE IT, NAMI. THIS BLADE WILL PROTECT YOU FROM HARM.
Y-YES, SISTER...

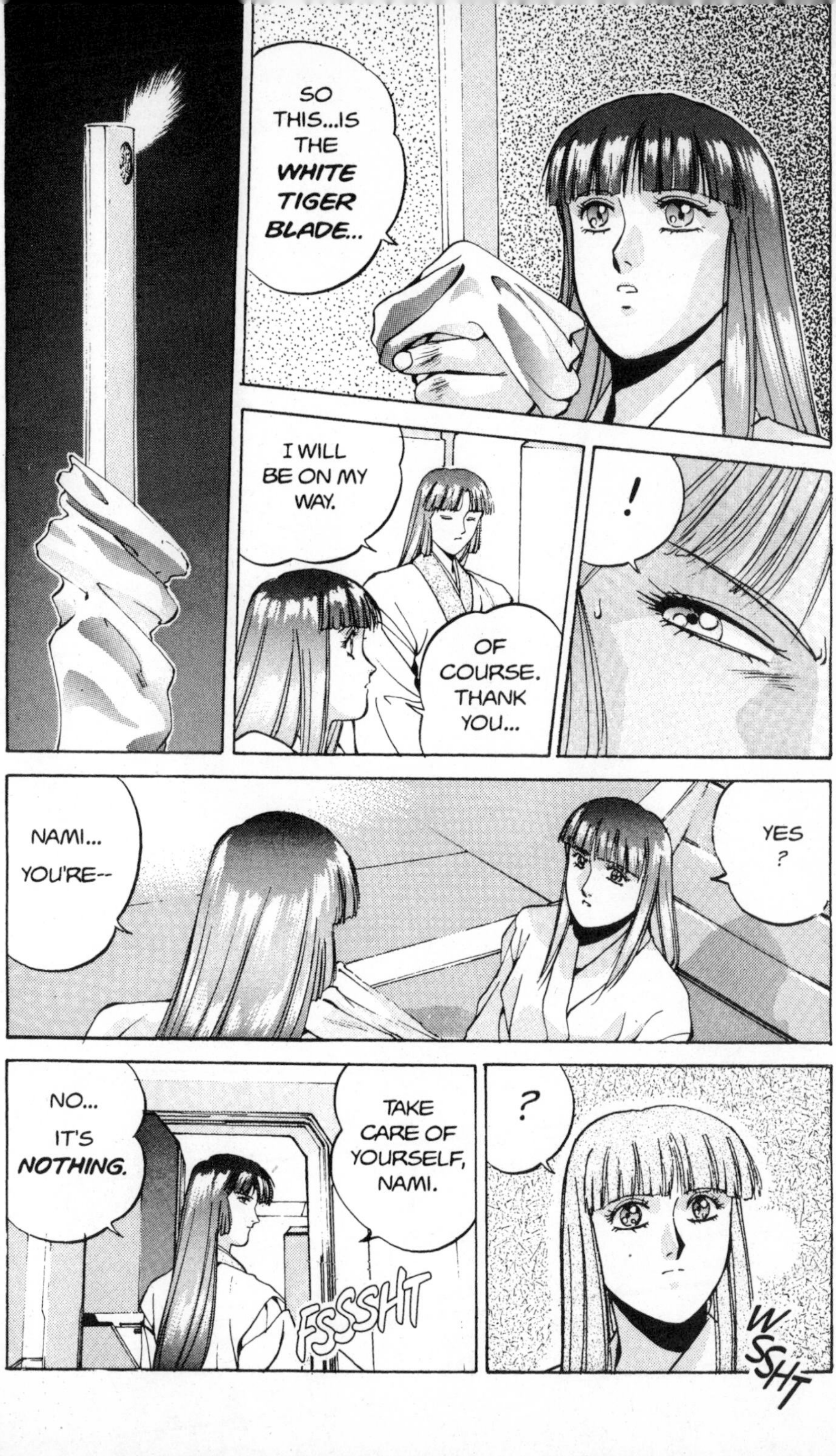
SO THIS...IS THE **WHITE TIGER BLADE...**
I WILL BE ON MY WAY.
OF COURSE. THANK YOU...
!
NAMI... YOU'RE--
YES ?
NO... IT'S **NOTHING.**
TAKE CARE OF YOURSELF, NAMI.
FSSSHT
?
WSSHT

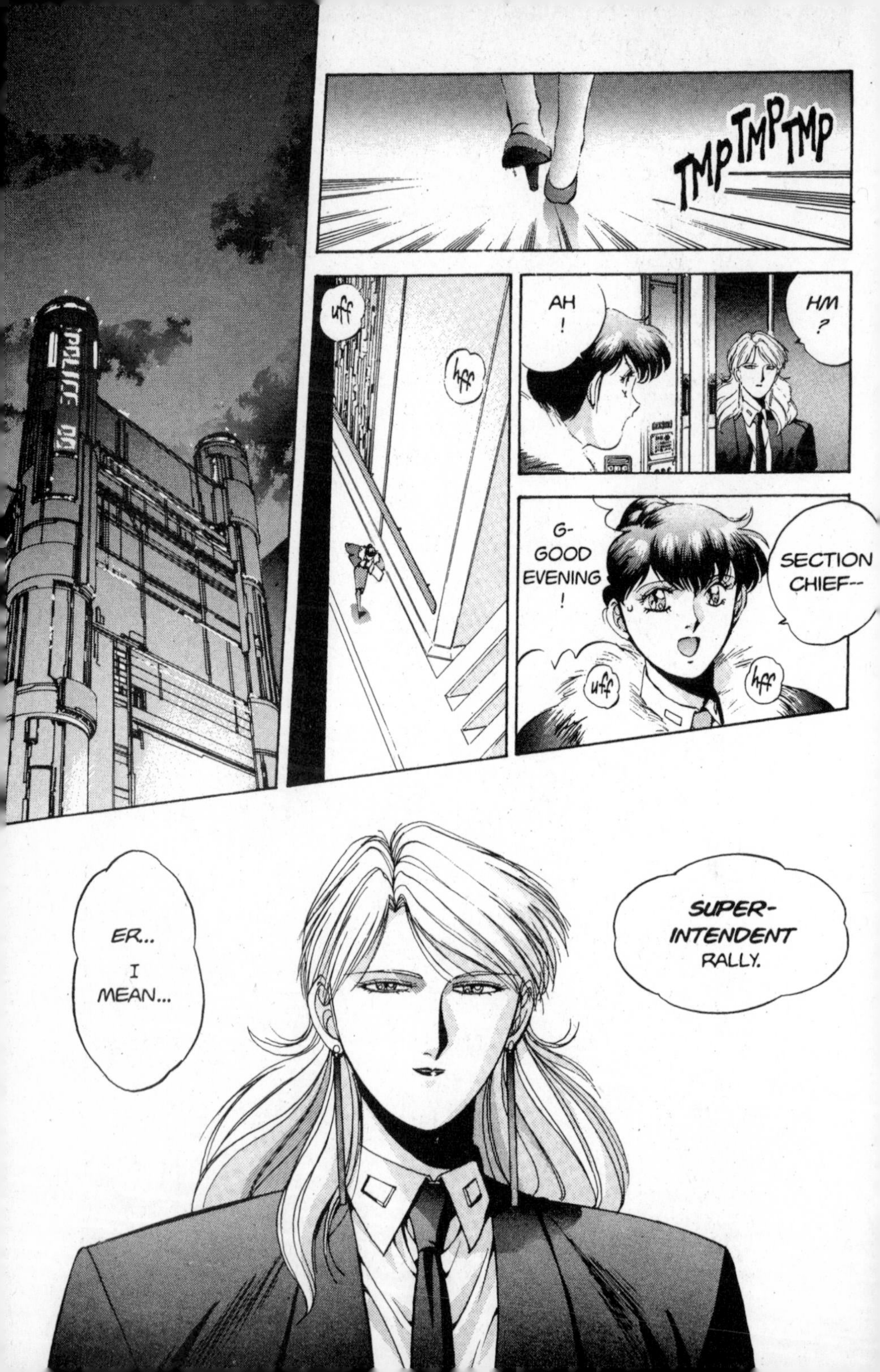
POLICE
TMP TMP TMP
uff
hff
AH!
HM?
G- GOOD EVENING!
SECTION CHIEF--
uff
hff
ER... I MEAN...
SUPER-INTENDENT RALLY.

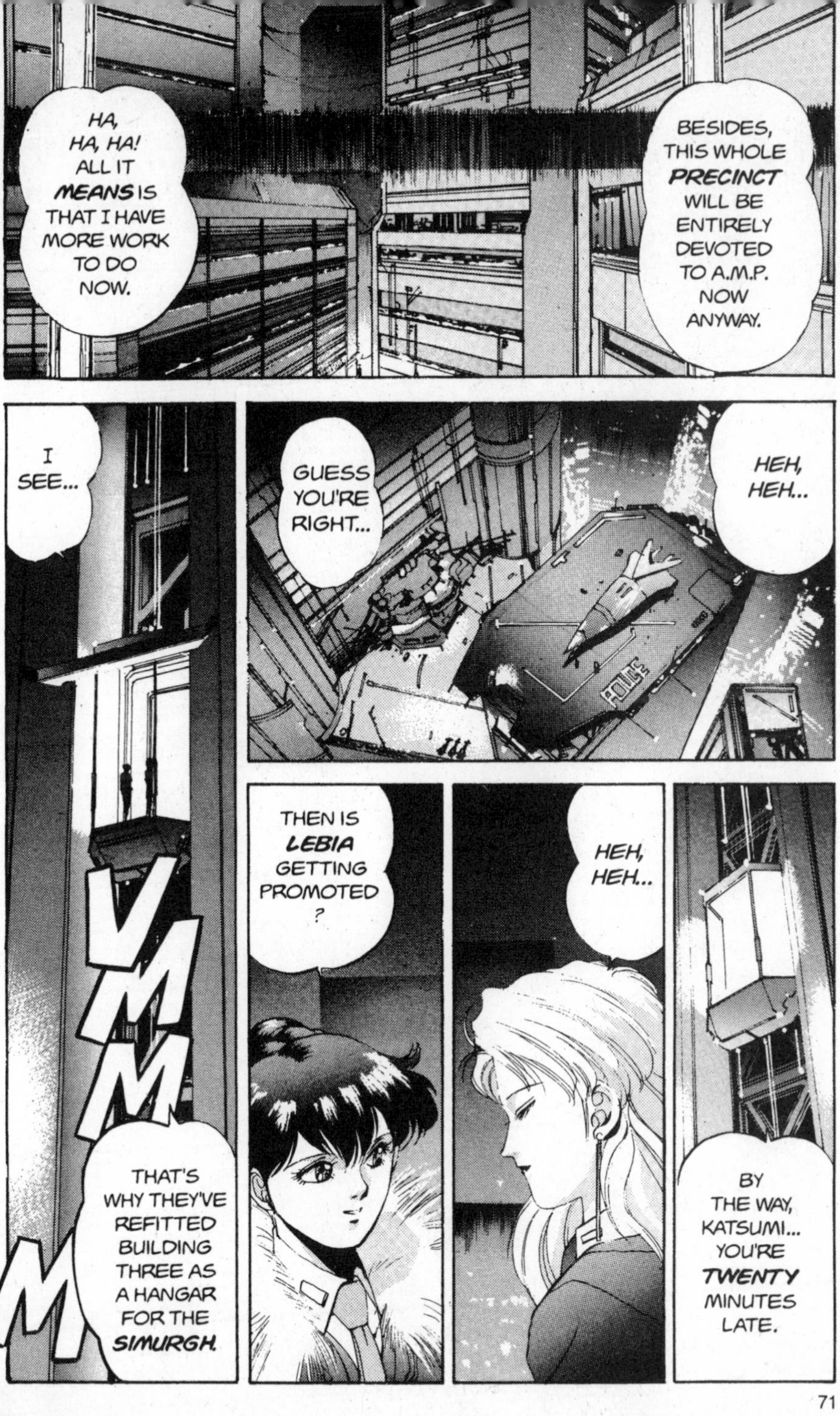
HA, HA, HA! ALL IT MEANS IS THAT I HAVE MORE WORK TO DO NOW.
BESIDES, THIS WHOLE PRECINCT WILL BE ENTIRELY DEVOTED TO A.M.P. NOW ANYWAY.
I SEE...
VMMM
THAT'S WHY THEY'VE REFITTED BUILDING THREE AS A HANGAR FOR THE SIMURGH.
GUESS YOU'RE RIGHT...
HEH, HEH...
THEN IS LEBIA GETTING PROMOTED?
HEH, HEH...
BY THE WAY, KATSUMI... YOU'RE TWENTY MINUTES LATE.

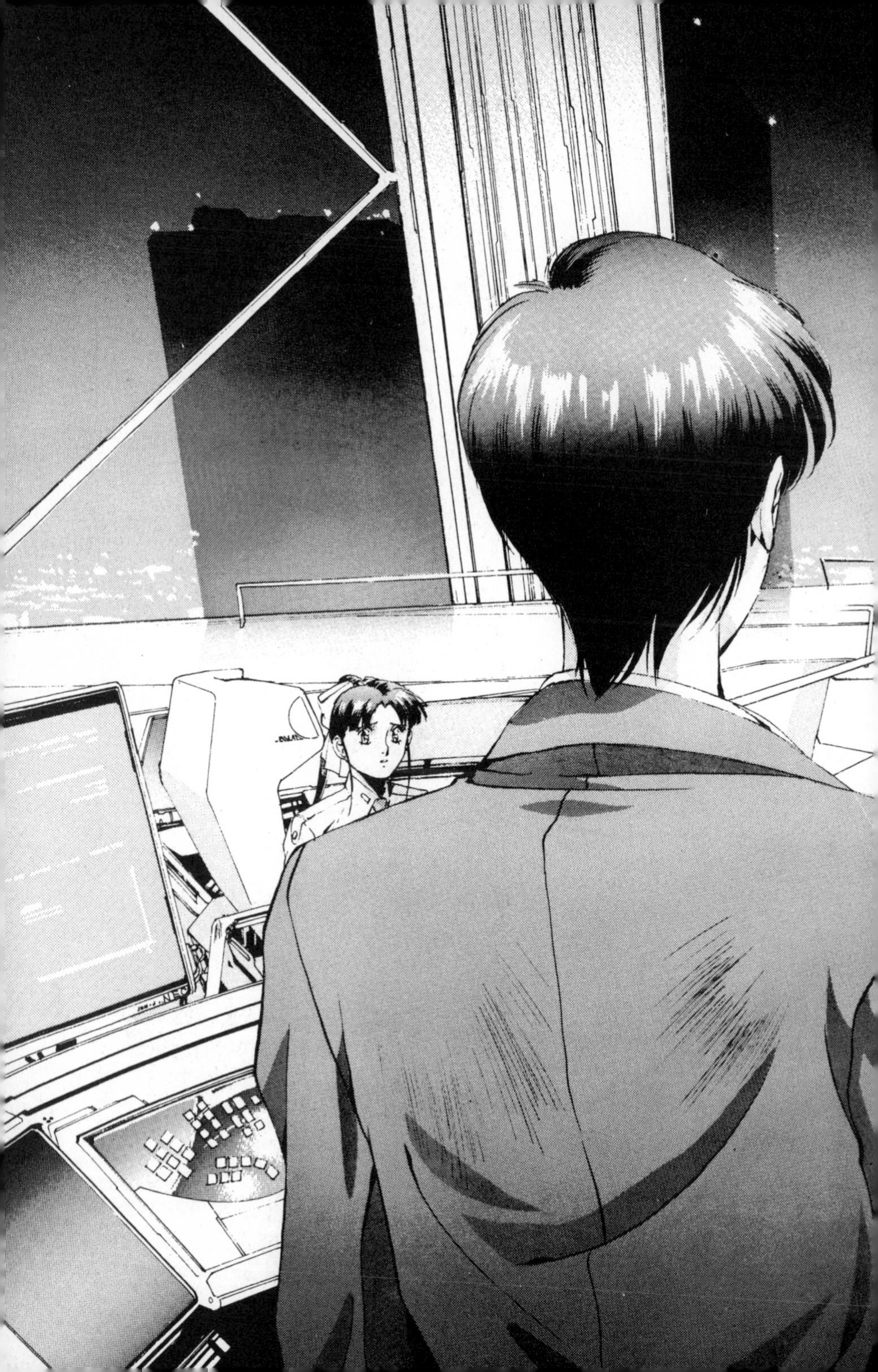

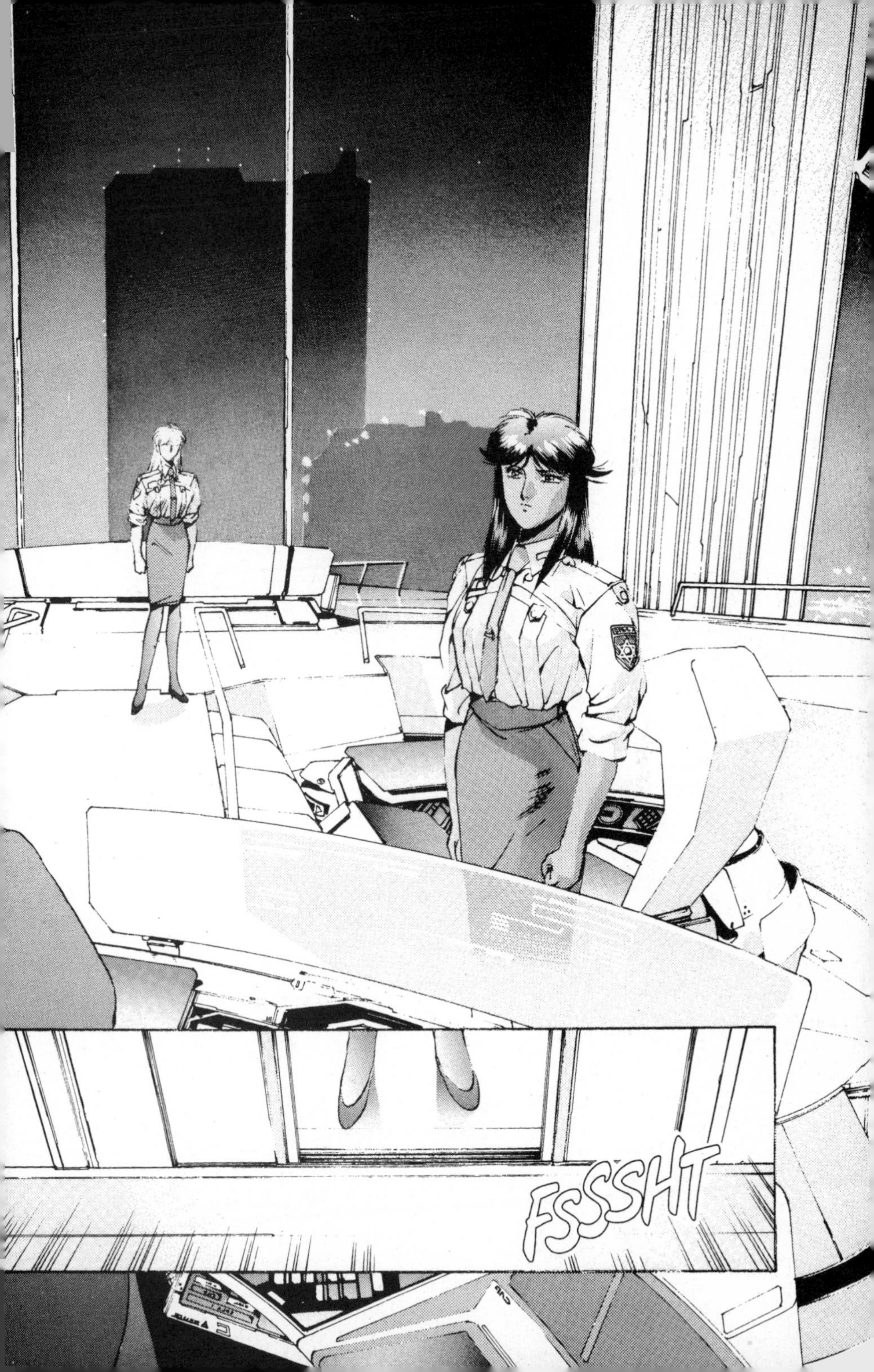
FSSSHT

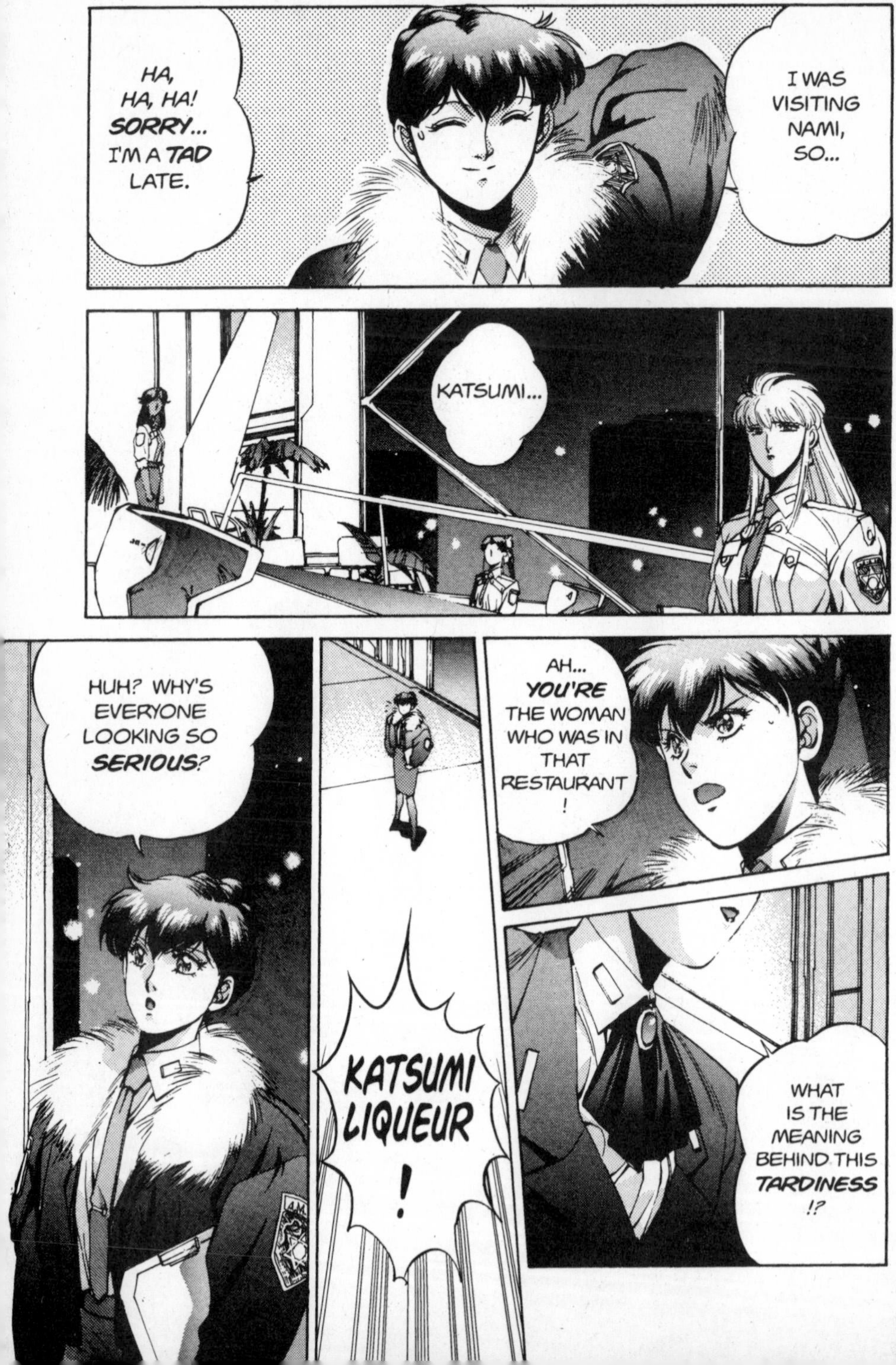
HA, HA, HA! SORRY... I'M A TAD LATE.
I WAS VISITING NAMI, SO...
KATSUMI...
HUH? WHY'S EVERYONE LOOKING SO SERIOUS?
AH... YOU'RE THE WOMAN WHO WAS IN THAT RESTAURANT!
KATSUMI LIQUEUR!
WHAT IS THE MEANING BEHIND THIS TARDINESS!?

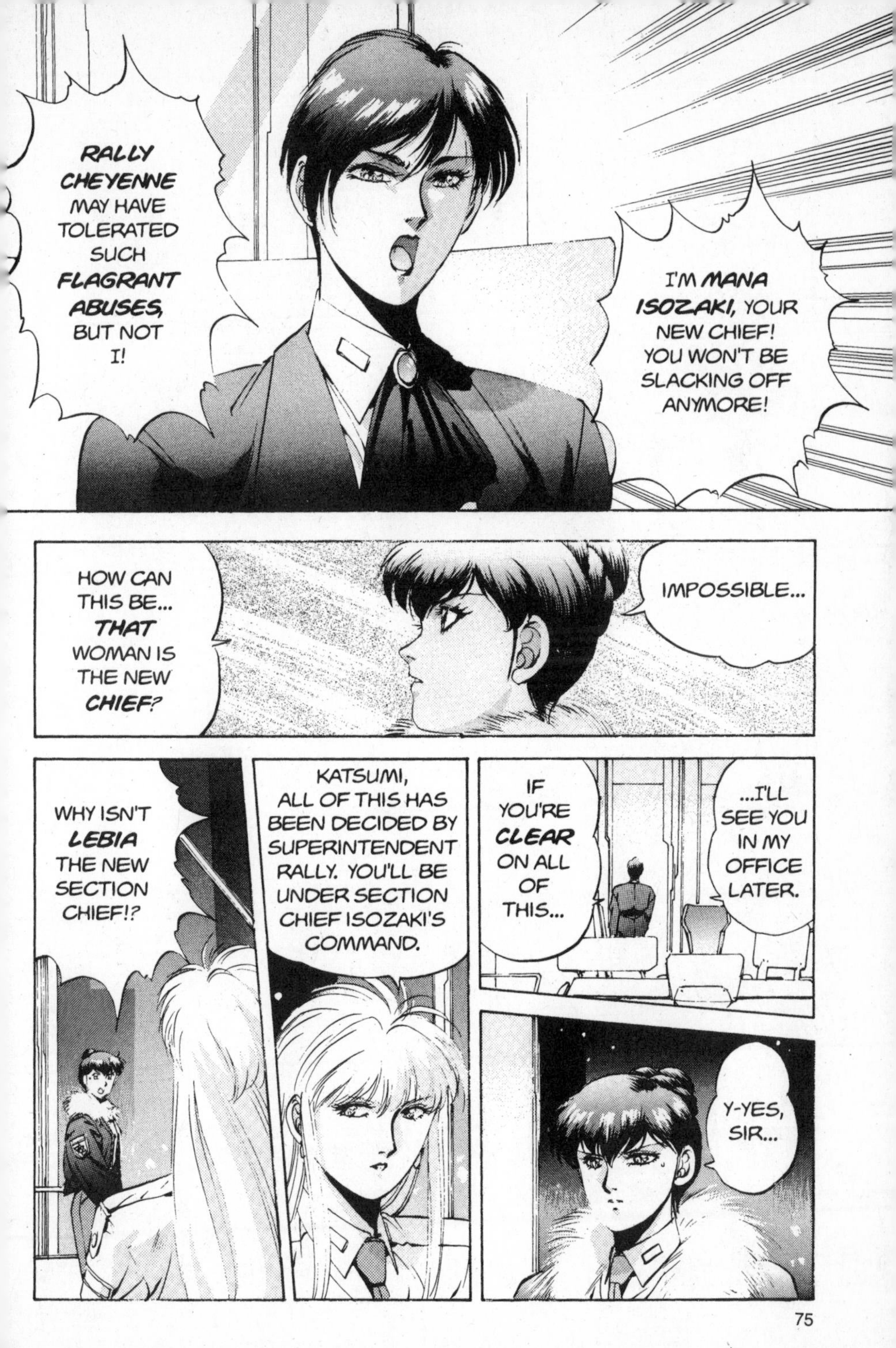
RALLY CHEYENNE MAY HAVE TOLERATED SUCH FLAGRANT ABUSES, BUT NOT I!
I'M MANA ISOZAKI, YOUR NEW CHIEF! YOU WON'T BE SLACKING OFF ANYMORE!
HOW CAN THIS BE... THAT WOMAN IS THE NEW CHIEF?
IMPOSSIBLE...
WHY ISN'T LEBIA THE NEW SECTION CHIEF!?
KATSUMI, ALL OF THIS HAS BEEN DECIDED BY SUPERINTENDENT RALLY. YOU'LL BE UNDER SECTION CHIEF ISOZAKI'S COMMAND.
IF YOU'RE CLEAR ON ALL OF THIS...
...I'LL SEE YOU IN MY OFFICE LATER.
Y-YES, SIR...

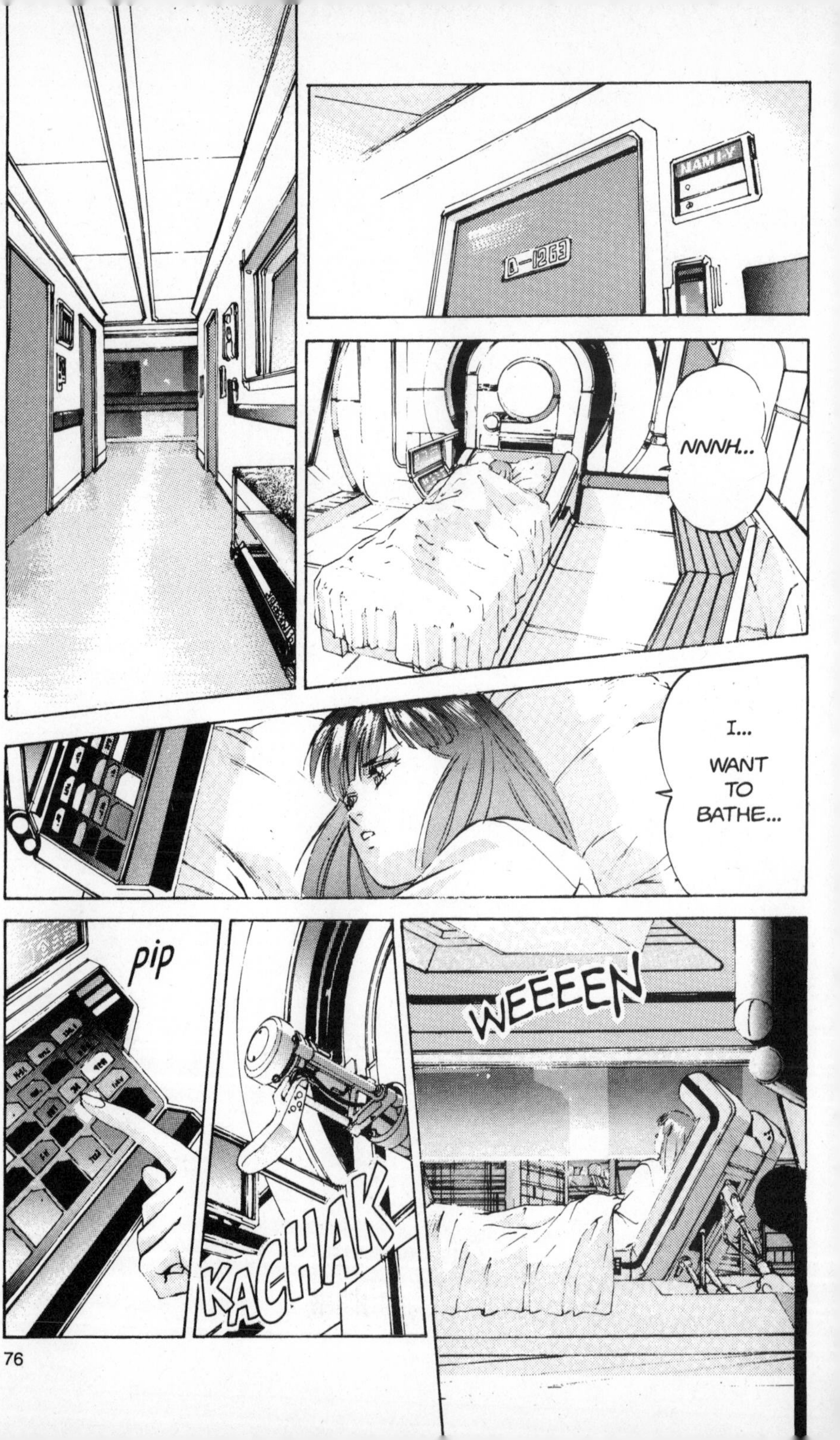
NAMI-Y
NNNH...
I... WANT TO BATHE...
pip
KACHAK
WEEEEN

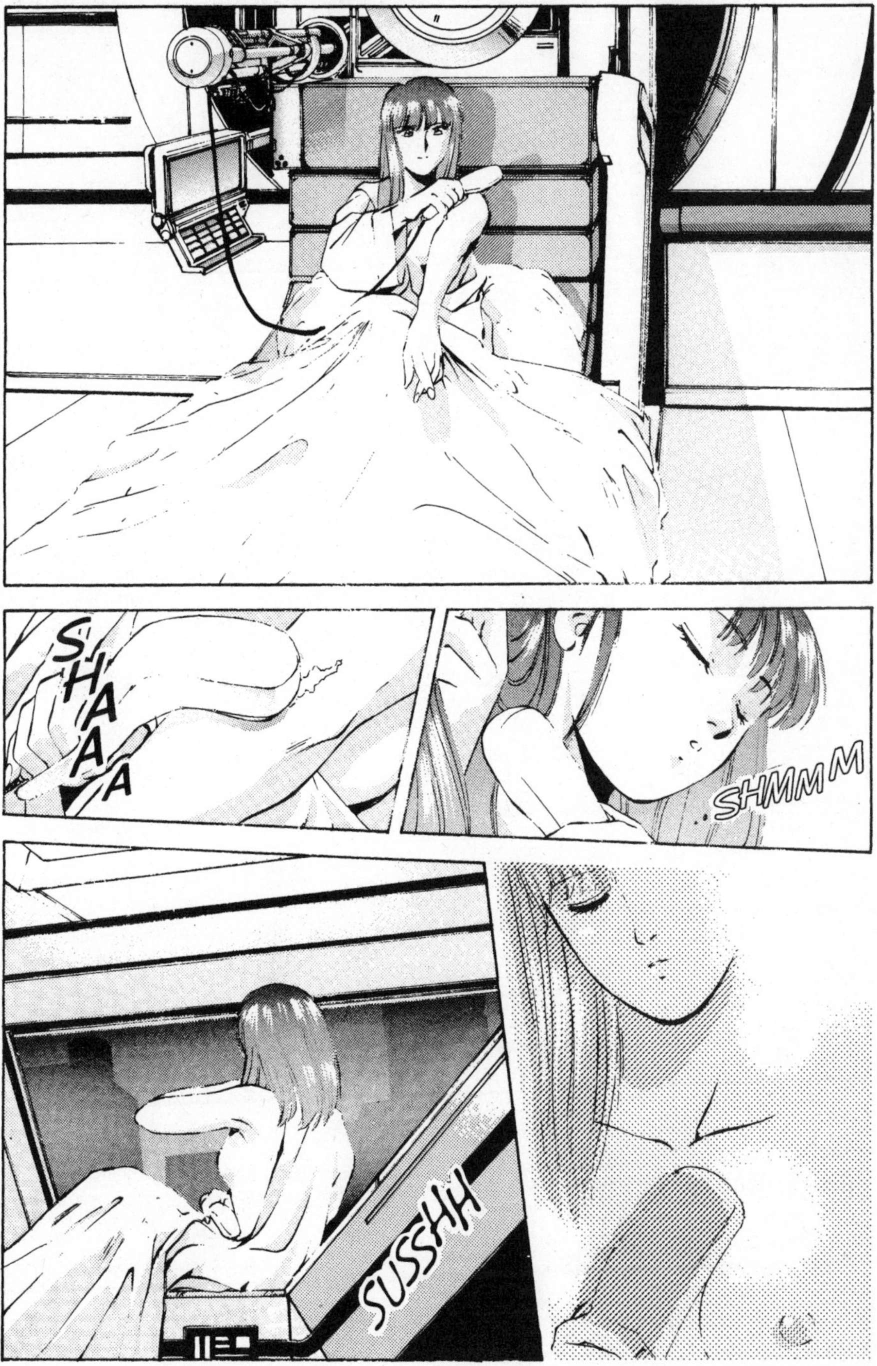
SHAAAA
SHMMM
SUSSHH

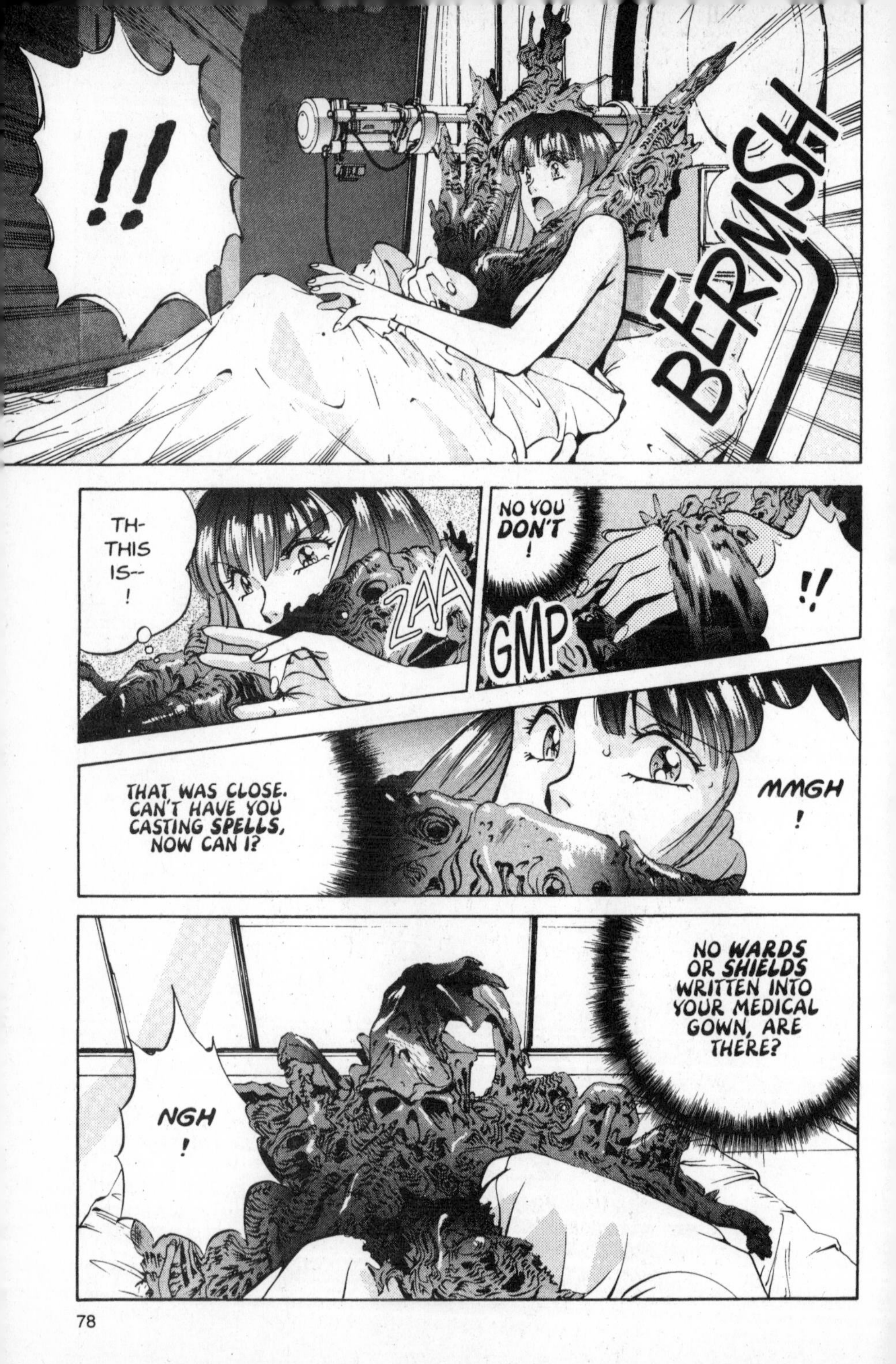
!!
BERMSH
TH-THIS IS--!
ZAA
NO YOU DON'T!
GMP
!!
THAT WAS CLOSE. CAN'T HAVE YOU CASTING SPELLS, NOW CAN I?
MMGH!
NGH!
NO WARDS OR SHIELDS WRITTEN INTO YOUR MEDICAL GOWN, ARE THERE?

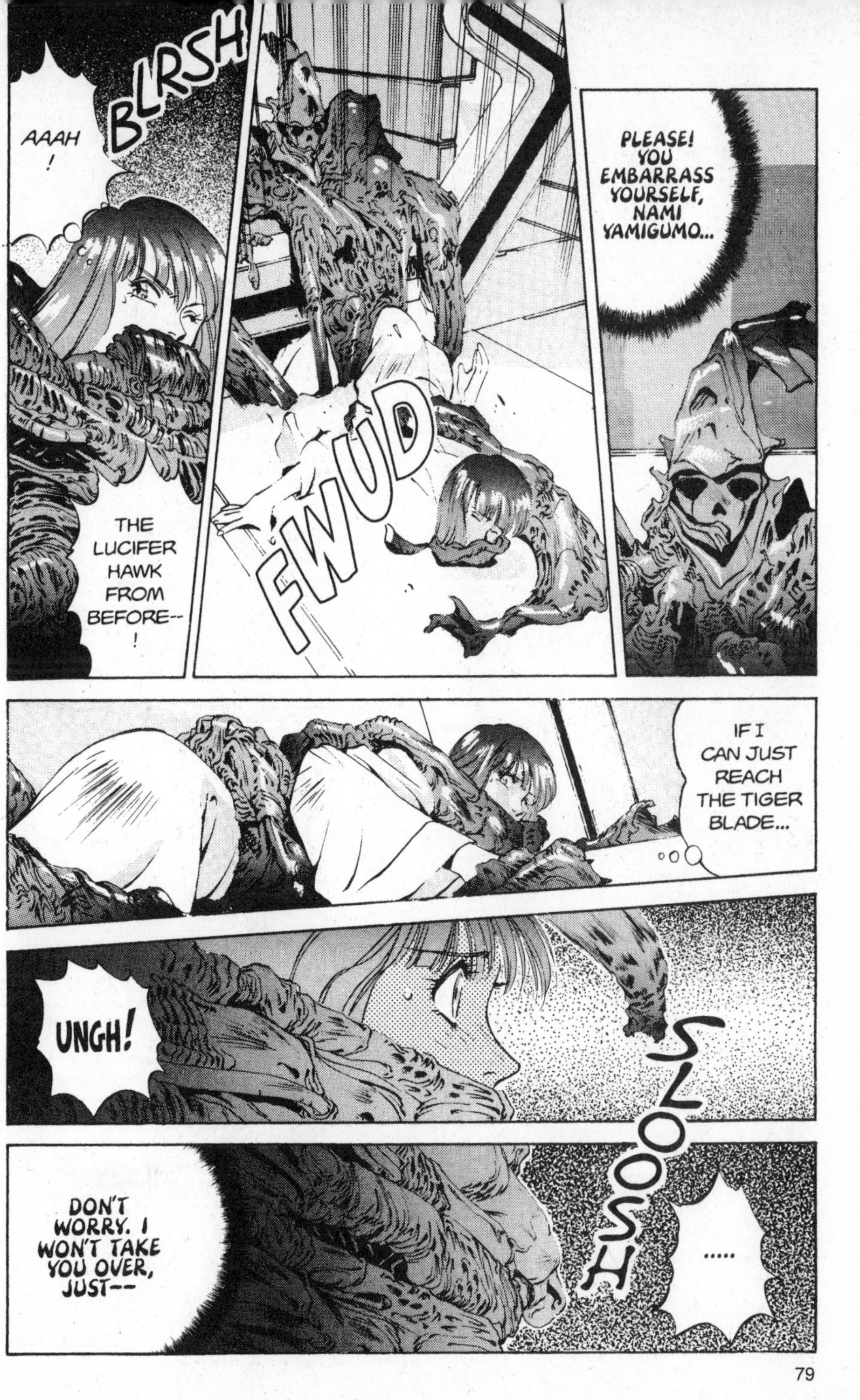
BLRSH
AAAH!
THE LUCIFER HAWK FROM BEFORE--!
FWUD
PLEASE! YOU EMBARRASS YOURSELF, NAMI YAMIGUMO...
IF I CAN JUST REACH THE TIGER BLADE...
UNGH!
SLOOSH
DON'T WORRY. I WON'T TAKE YOU OVER, JUST--
.....

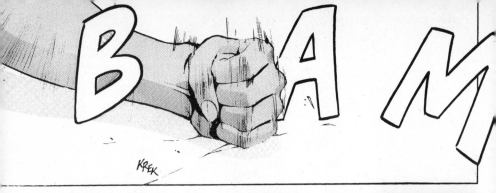

WHO THE **HELL** DOES THAT WOMAN THINK SHE *IS*!?

AND WHY IS **SHE** THE NEW SECTION CHIEF!?

BUT, KIDDY... RALLY DECIDED THAT--

I KNOW, **I KNOW**!

WHAT IS SHE **THINKING** ANYWAY!?

WHO IS THIS **MANA ISOZAKI**!?

WHAT!? NO DATA? **YOU**, LEBIA?

YOU MEAN TO TELL ME THAT THE GREAT LEBIA MAVERICK IS **CLUELESS**!?

KREK

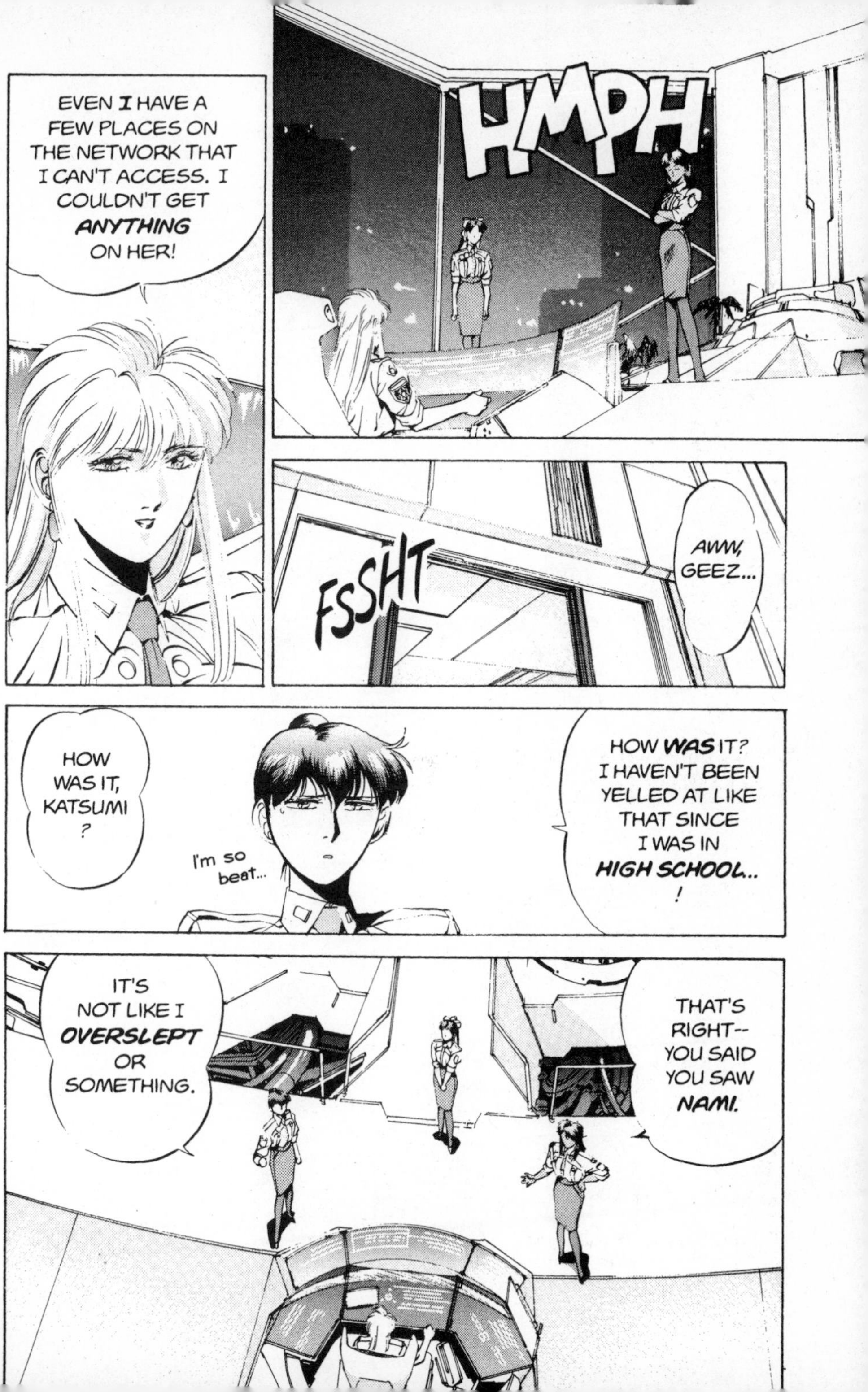
EVEN I HAVE A FEW PLACES ON THE NETWORK THAT I CAN'T ACCESS. I COULDN'T GET ANYTHING ON HER!
HMPH
FSSHT
AWW, GEEZ...
HOW WAS IT, KATSUMI?
I'm so beat...
HOW WAS IT? I HAVEN'T BEEN YELLED AT LIKE THAT SINCE I WAS IN HIGH SCHOOL...!
IT'S NOT LIKE I OVERSLEPT OR SOMETHING.
THAT'S RIGHT-- YOU SAID YOU SAW NAMI.

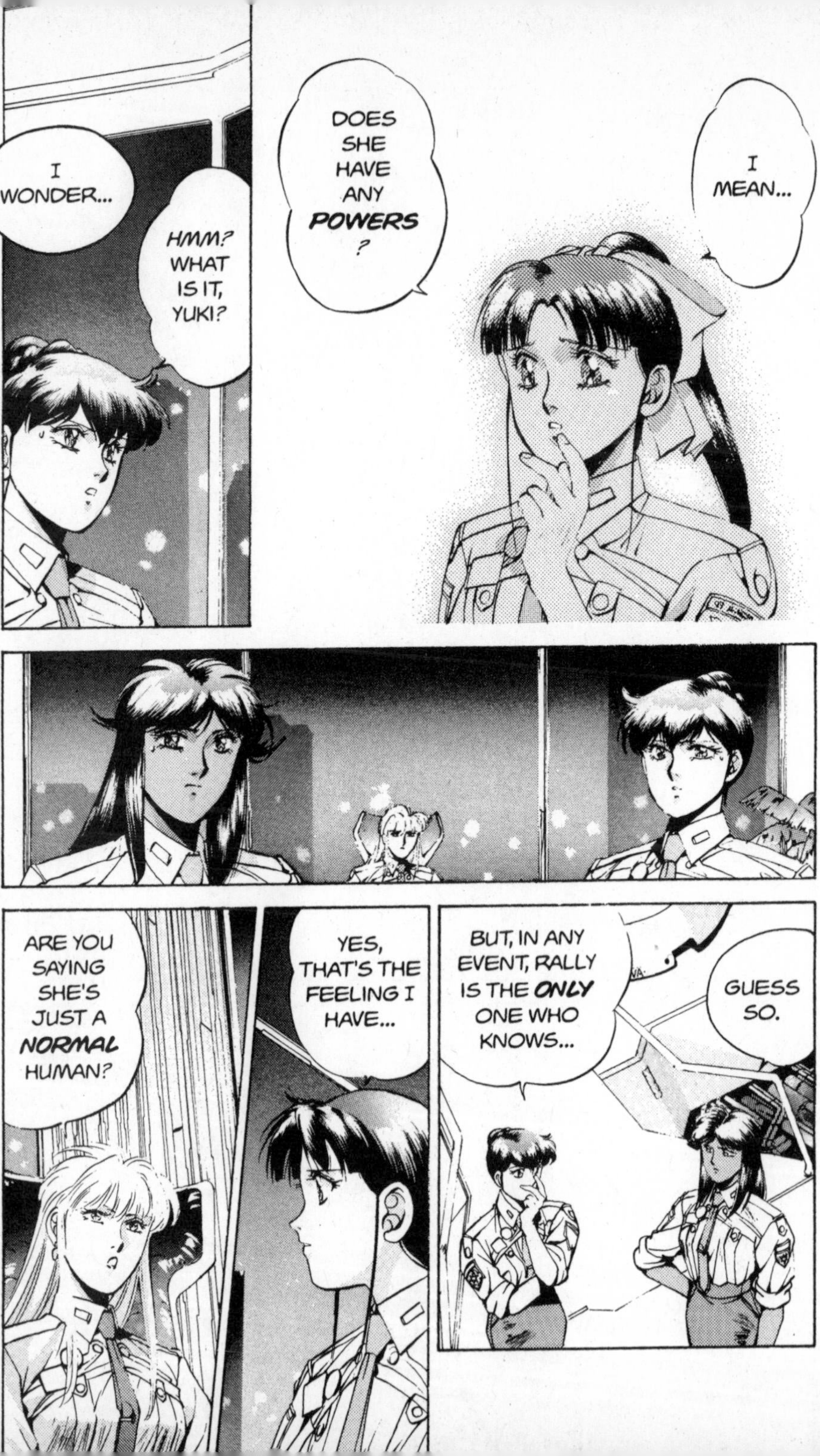
I WONDER...
HMM? WHAT IS IT, YUKI?
DOES SHE HAVE ANY **POWERS** ?
I MEAN...
ARE YOU SAYING SHE'S JUST A **NORMAL** HUMAN?
YES, THAT'S THE FEELING I HAVE...
BUT, IN ANY EVENT, RALLY IS THE **ONLY** ONE WHO KNOWS...
GUESS SO.

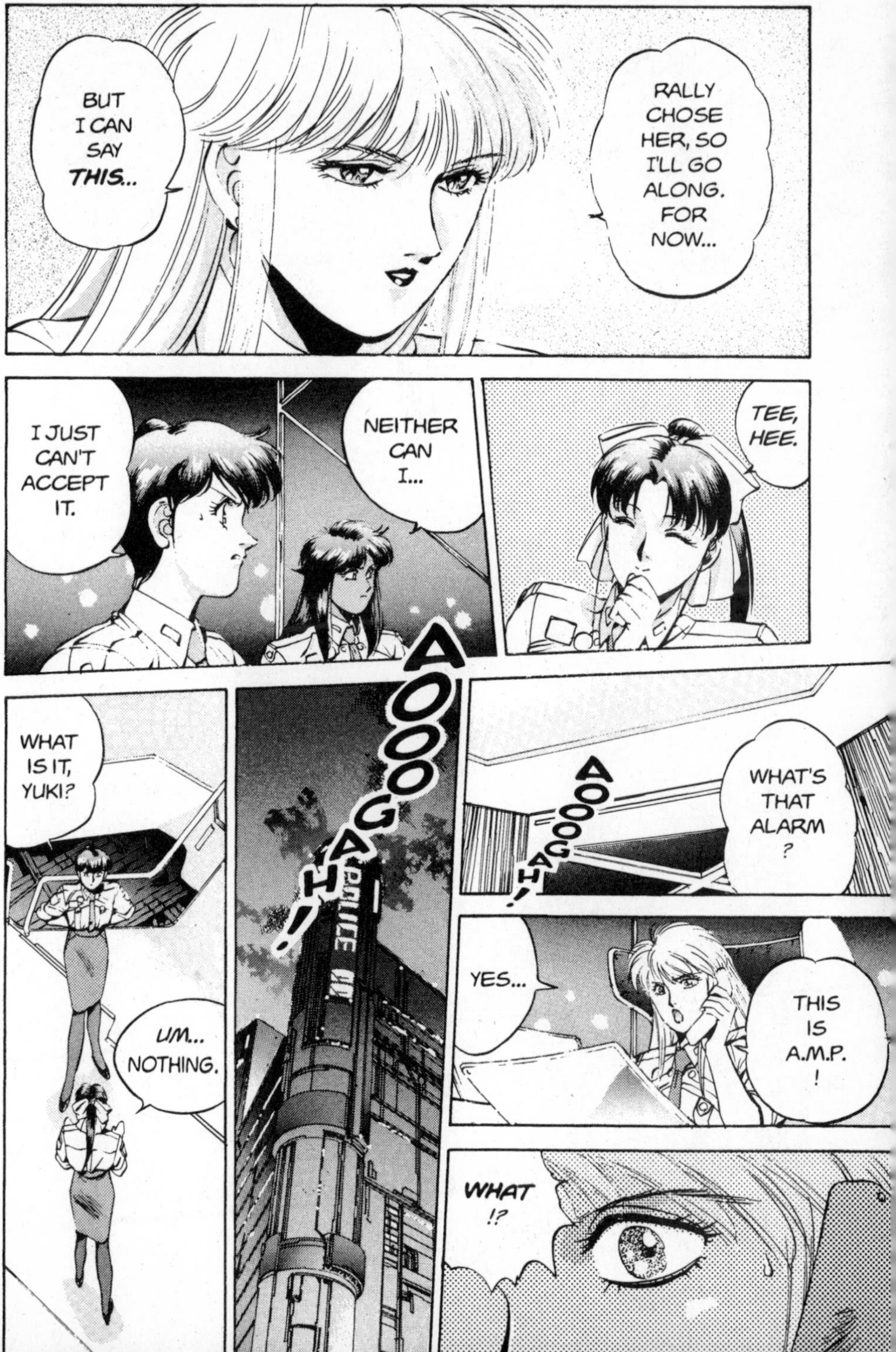
BUT I CAN SAY THIS...
RALLY CHOSE HER, SO I'LL GO ALONG. FOR NOW...
I JUST CAN'T ACCEPT IT.
NEITHER CAN I...
TEE, HEE.
WHAT IS IT, YUKI?
UM... NOTHING.
AOOOOGAH!
AOOOGAH!
WHAT'S THAT ALARM ?
YES...
THIS IS A.M.P. !
WHAT !?

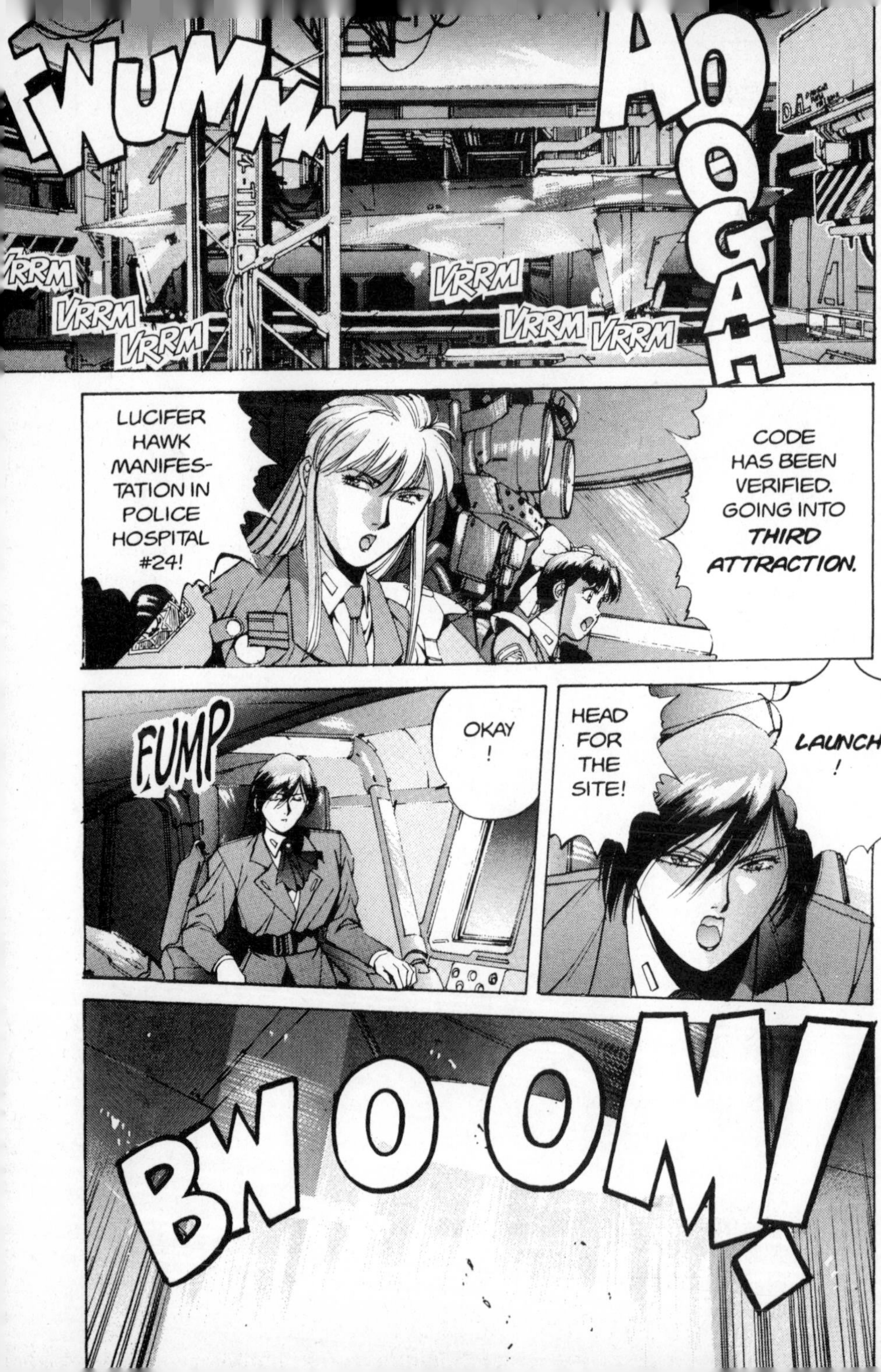
FWUMMM
VRRM
VRRM
VRRM
VRRM
VRRM
VRRM
AOOGAH
LUCIFER HAWK MANIFESTATION IN POLICE HOSPITAL #24!
CODE HAS BEEN VERIFIED. GOING INTO *THIRD ATTRACTION.*
FUMP
OKAY!
HEAD FOR THE SITE!
LAUNCH!
BWOOM!

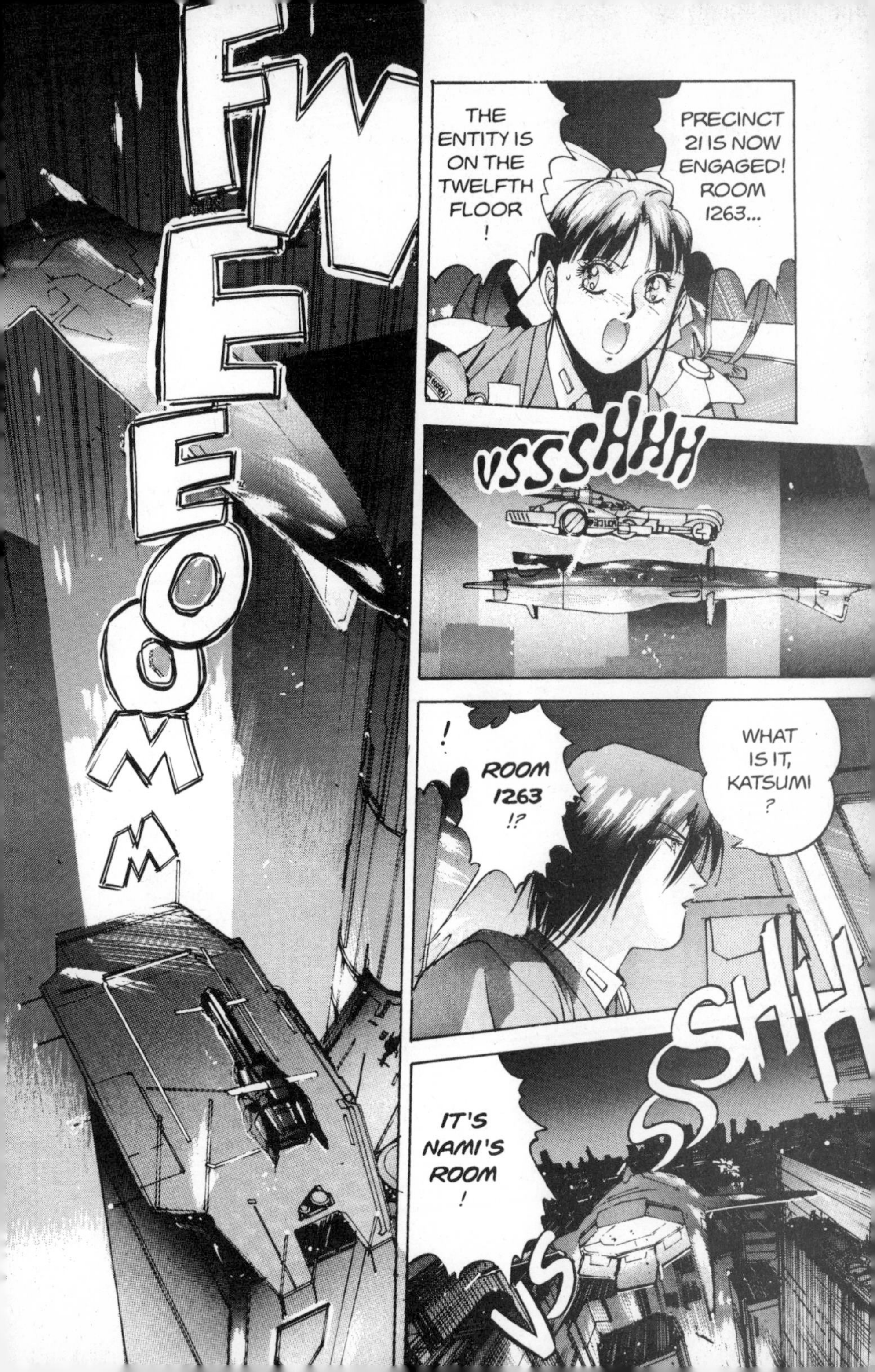
FWEEOOMM
THE ENTITY IS ON THE TWELFTH FLOOR!
PRECINCT 21 IS NOW ENGAGED! ROOM 1263...
VSSSHHH
!
ROOM 1263!?
WHAT IS IT, KATSUMI?
IT'S NAMI'S ROOM!
VSSSHH

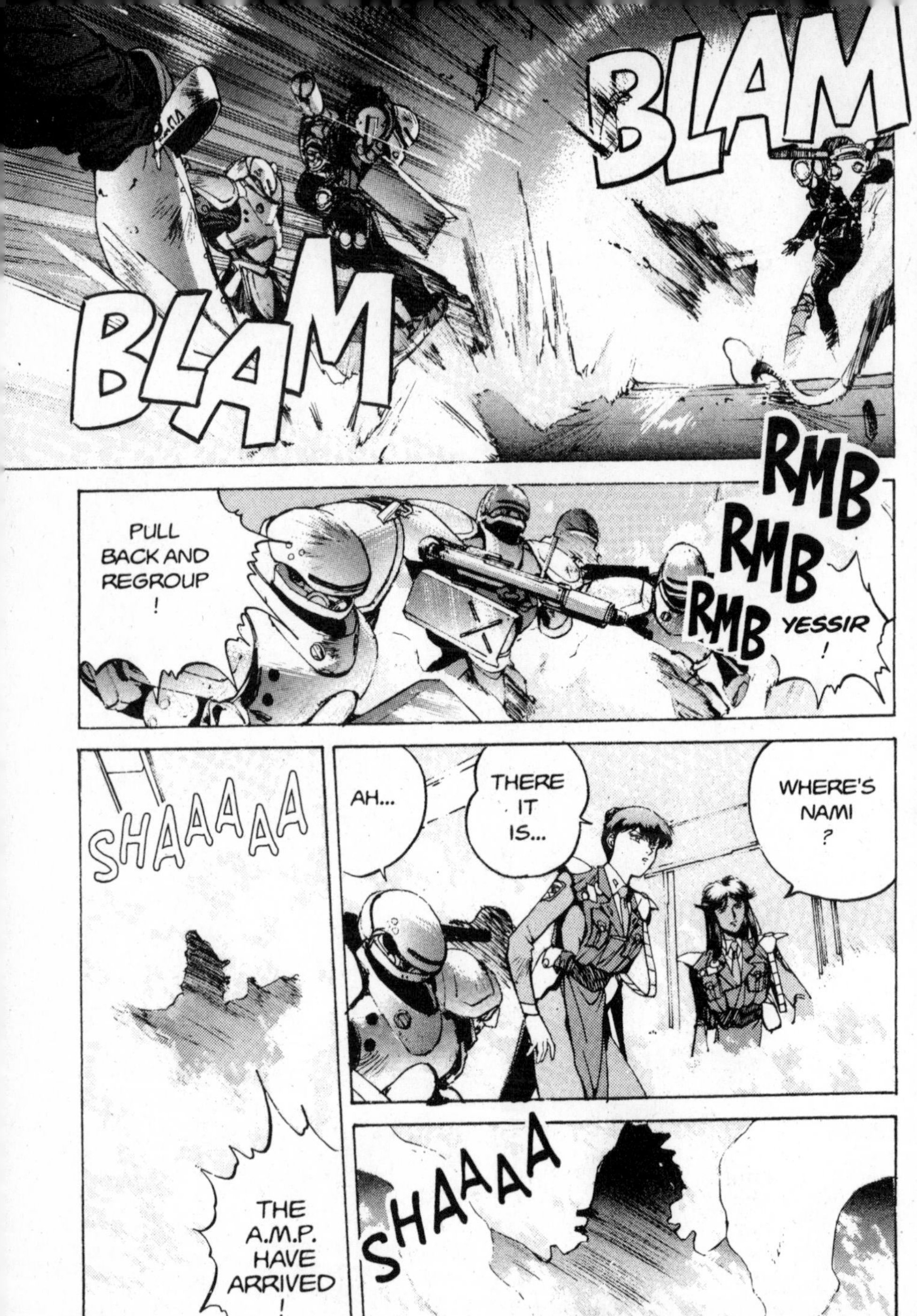
BLAM
BLAM
PULL BACK AND REGROUP !
RMB RMB RMB
YESSIR !
SHAAAAAA
THE A.M.P. HAVE ARRIVED !
AH...
THERE IT IS...
WHERE'S NAMI ?
SHAAAA

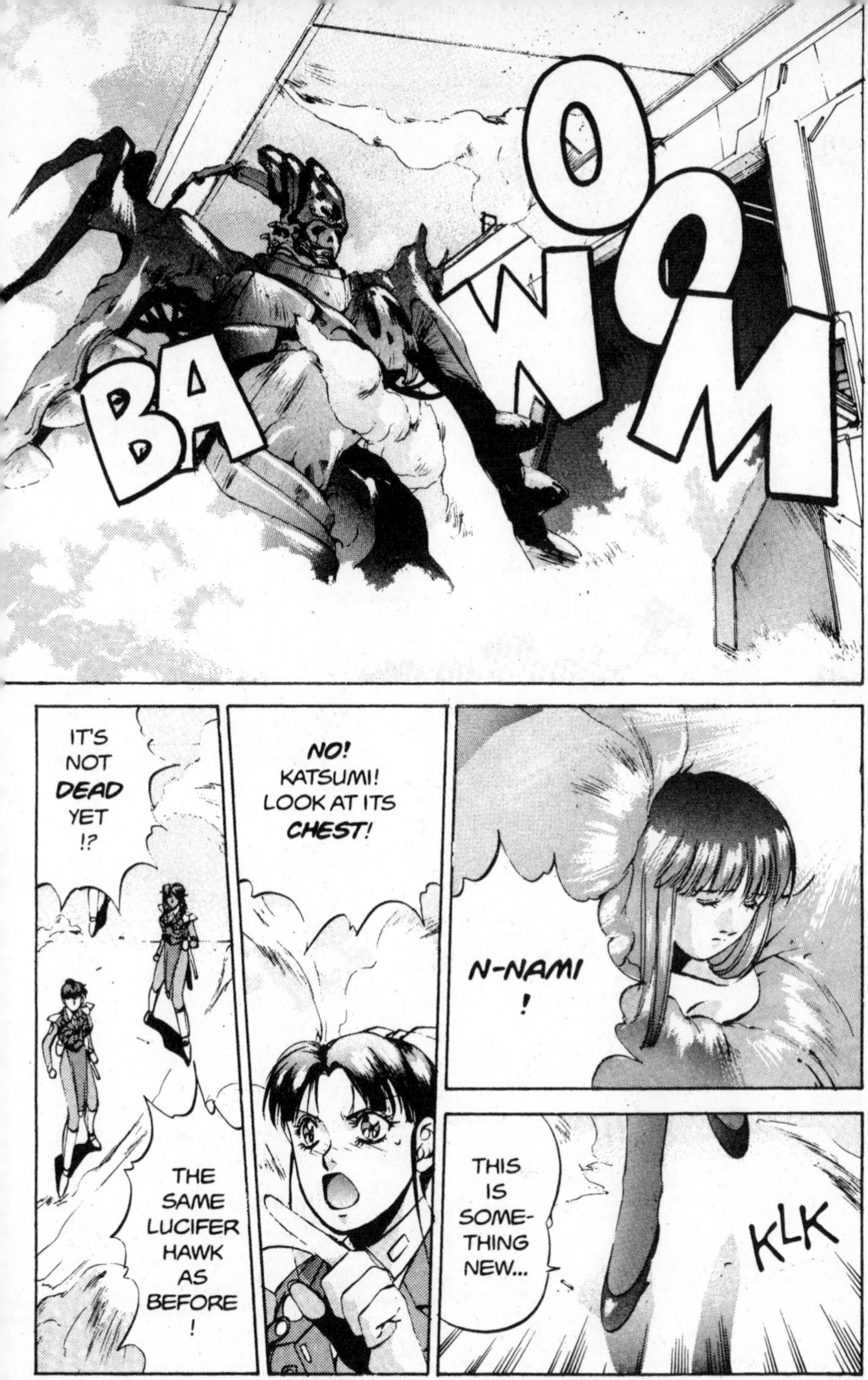
BAWOOM
IT'S NOT DEAD YET !?
THE SAME LUCIFER HAWK AS BEFORE !
NO! KATSUMI! LOOK AT ITS CHEST!
N-NAMI !
THIS IS SOME-THING NEW...
KLK

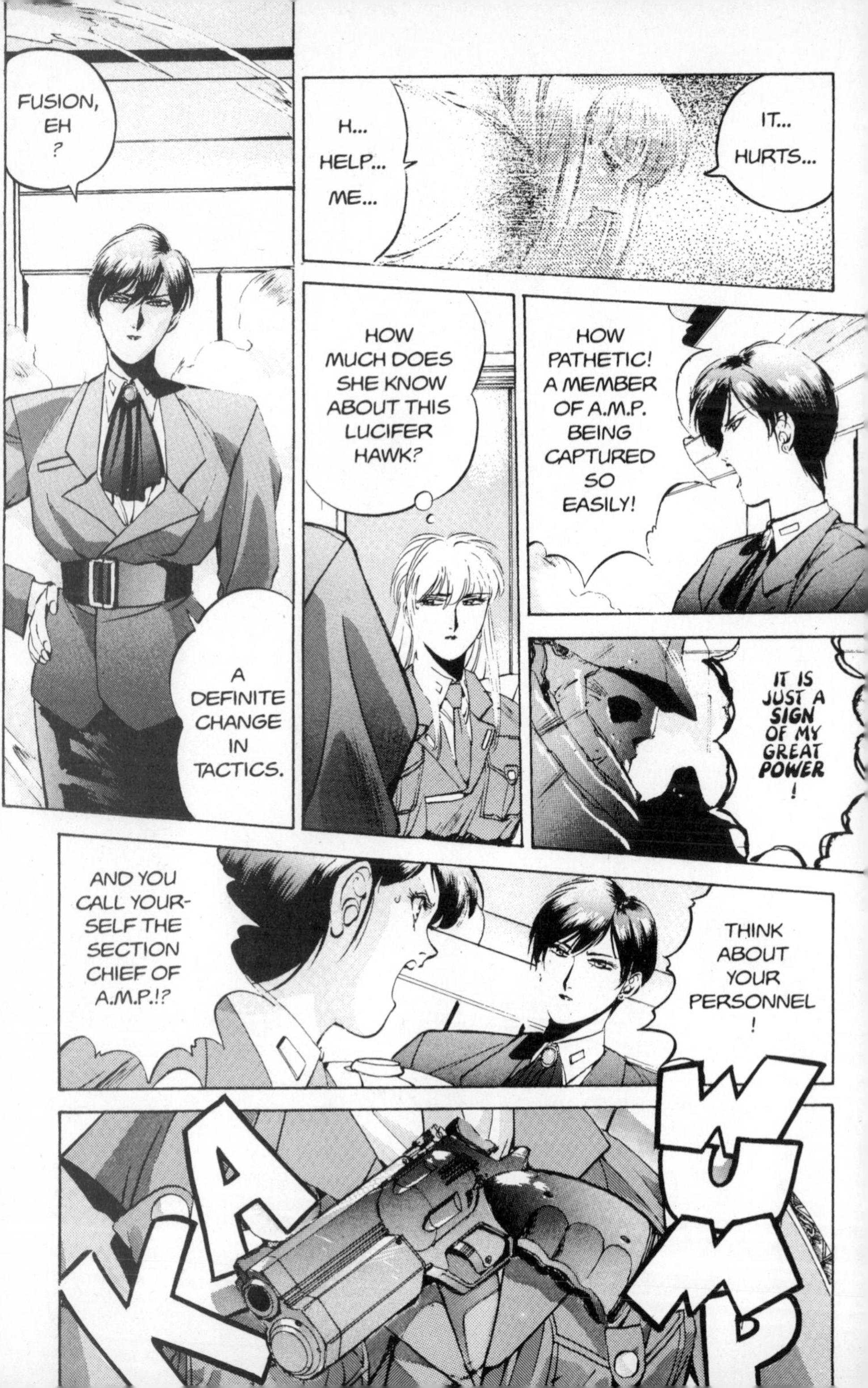
FUSION, EH ?
A DEFINITE CHANGE IN TACTICS.
H... HELP... ME...
IT... HURTS...
HOW MUCH DOES SHE KNOW ABOUT THIS LUCIFER HAWK?
HOW PATHETIC! A MEMBER OF A.M.P. BEING CAPTURED SO EASILY!
IT IS JUST A **SIGN** OF MY GREAT **POWER** !
AND YOU CALL YOURSELF THE SECTION CHIEF OF A.M.P.!?
THINK ABOUT YOUR PERSONNEL !
KA
WUMP

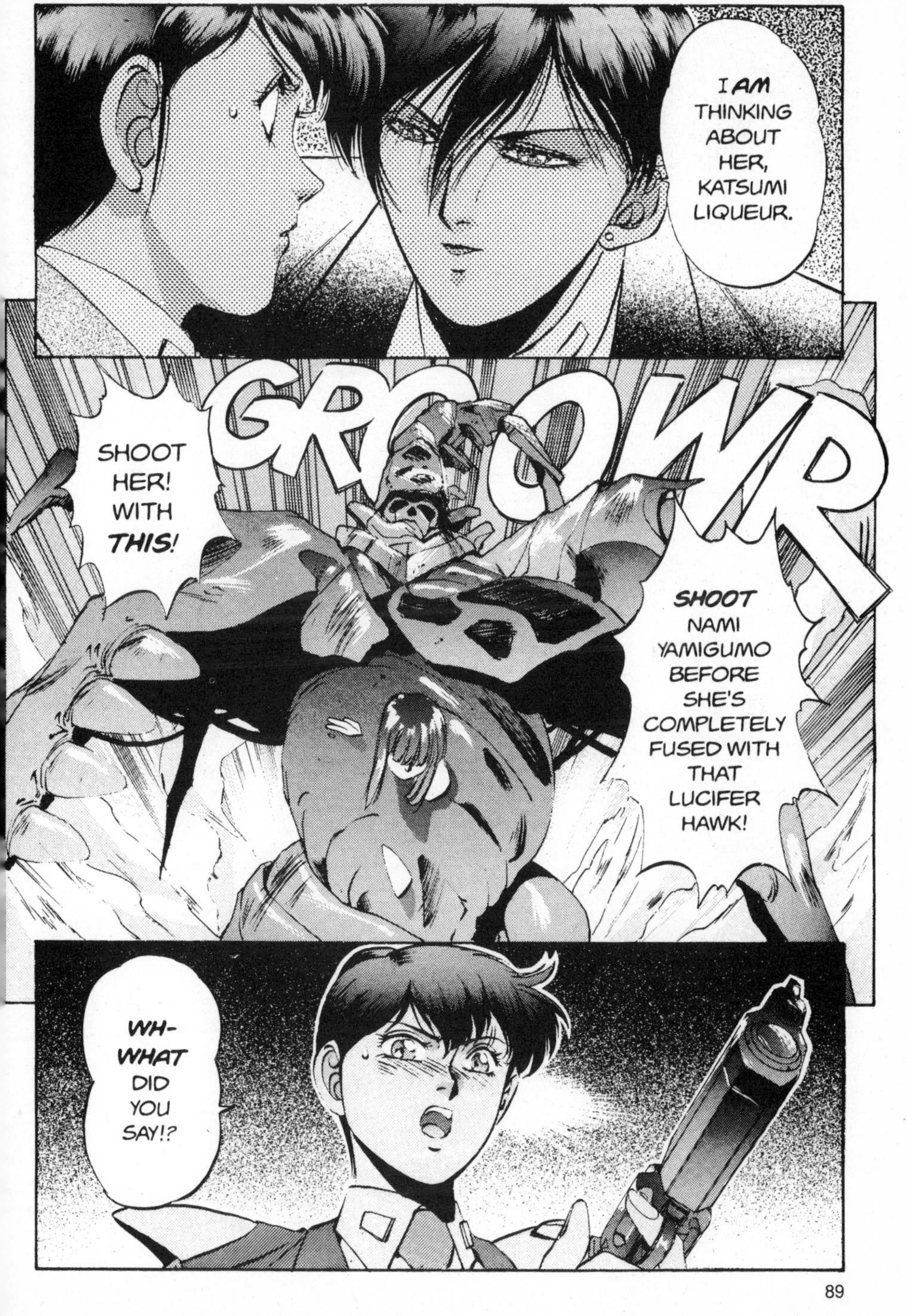

I AM THINKING ABOUT HER, KATSUMI LIQUEUR.
GROOWR
SHOOT HER! WITH THIS!
SHOOT NAMI YAMIGUMO BEFORE SHE'S COMPLETELY FUSED WITH THAT LUCIFER HAWK!
WH- WHAT DID YOU SAY!?

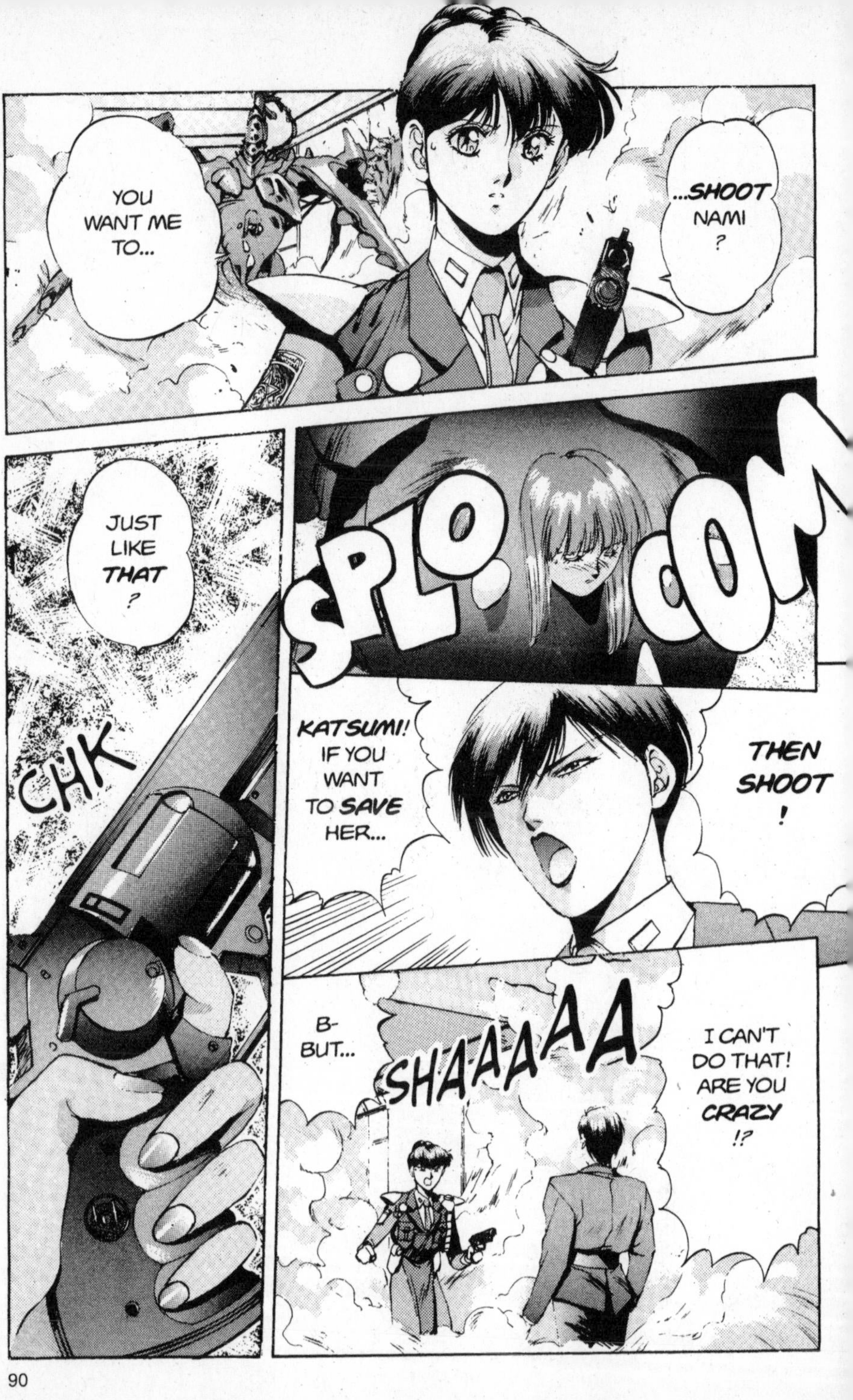

YOU WANT ME TO...
...SHOOT NAMI ?
JUST LIKE THAT ?
CHK
SPLO.COM
KATSUMI! IF YOU WANT TO SAVE HER...
THEN SHOOT !
B- BUT...
SHAAAAAA
I CAN'T DO THAT! ARE YOU CRAZY !?

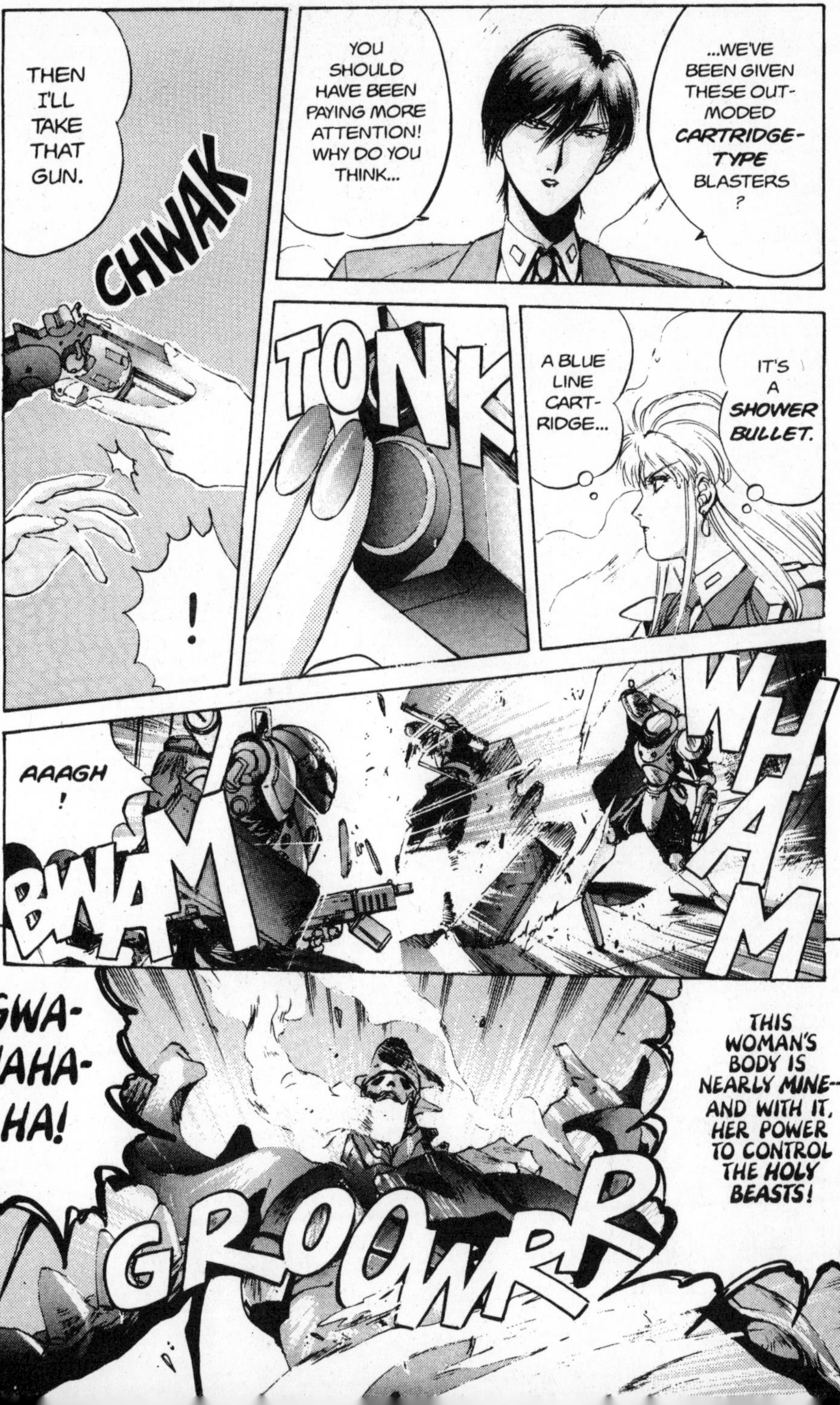
THEN I'LL TAKE THAT GUN.
CHWAK
!
YOU SHOULD HAVE BEEN PAYING MORE ATTENTION! WHY DO YOU THINK...
...WE'VE BEEN GIVEN THESE OUT-MODED **CARTRIDGE-TYPE** BLASTERS ?
TONK
A BLUE LINE CART-RIDGE...
IT'S A **SHOWER BULLET.**
AAAGH !
BWAM
WHAM
GWA-HAHA-HA!
THIS WOMAN'S BODY IS NEARLY MINE-- AND WITH IT, HER POWER TO CONTROL THE HOLY BEASTS!
GROOWRR

ALL...

MY POWER...

N-NO... STOP...

I'LL MAKE THIS BUILDING INTO A **TOMBSTONE** FOR THE A.M.P.!

GWAHAHAHA!

"GWAHAHA," YOURSELF-- *IDIOT.*

!?

I HADN'T **BELIEVED** SUPERINTENDENT RALLY...

...BUT YOU LUCIFER HAWKS REALLY **AR** A BUNCH OF FOOLS

SHAAAAWOOO

FWS SSSHT

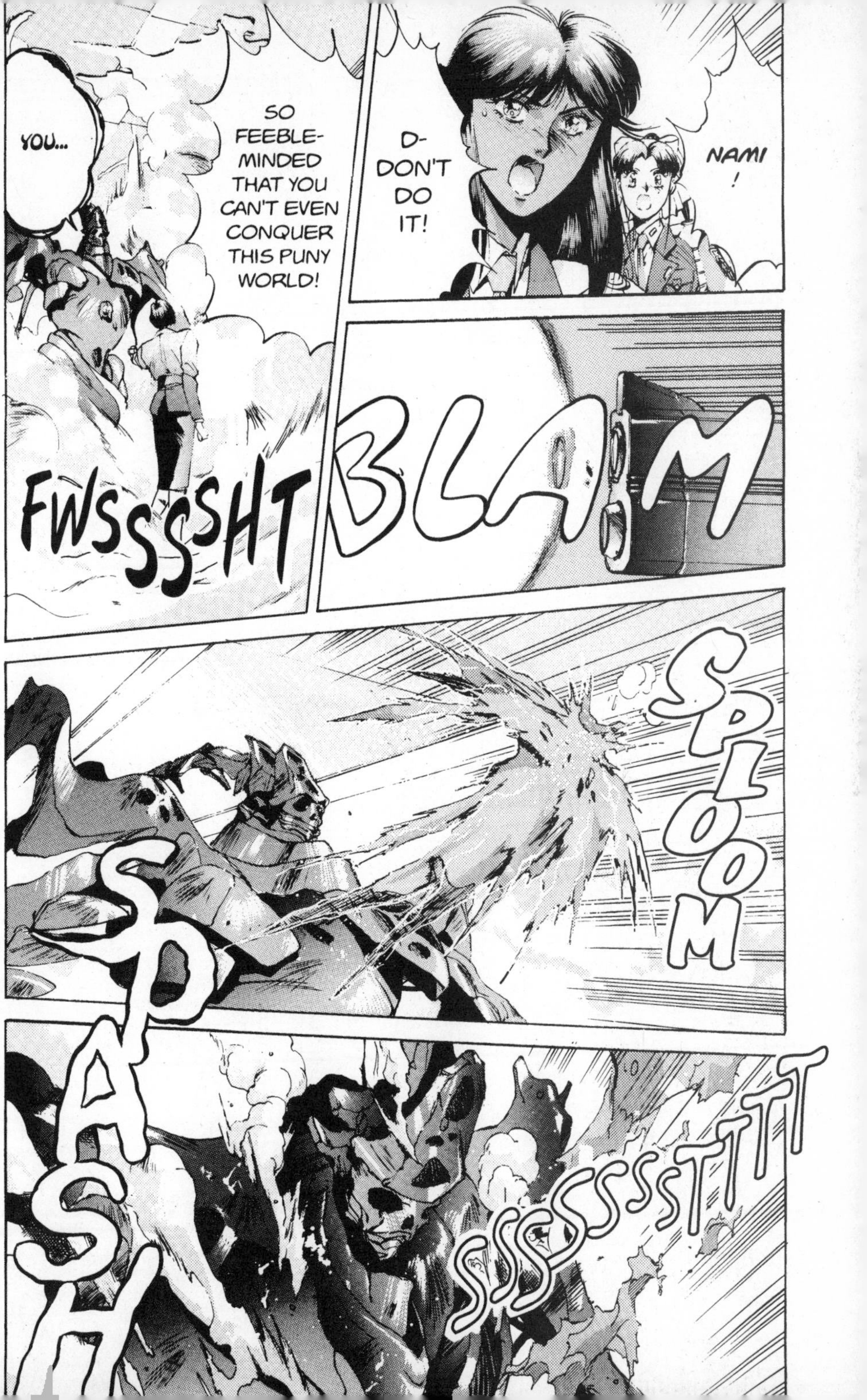
YOU...
SO FEEBLE-MINDED THAT YOU CAN'T EVEN CONQUER THIS PUNY WORLD!
FWSSSSHT
D-DON'T DO IT!
NAMI!
BLAM
SPLOOM
SPLASH
SSSSSSSTTTT

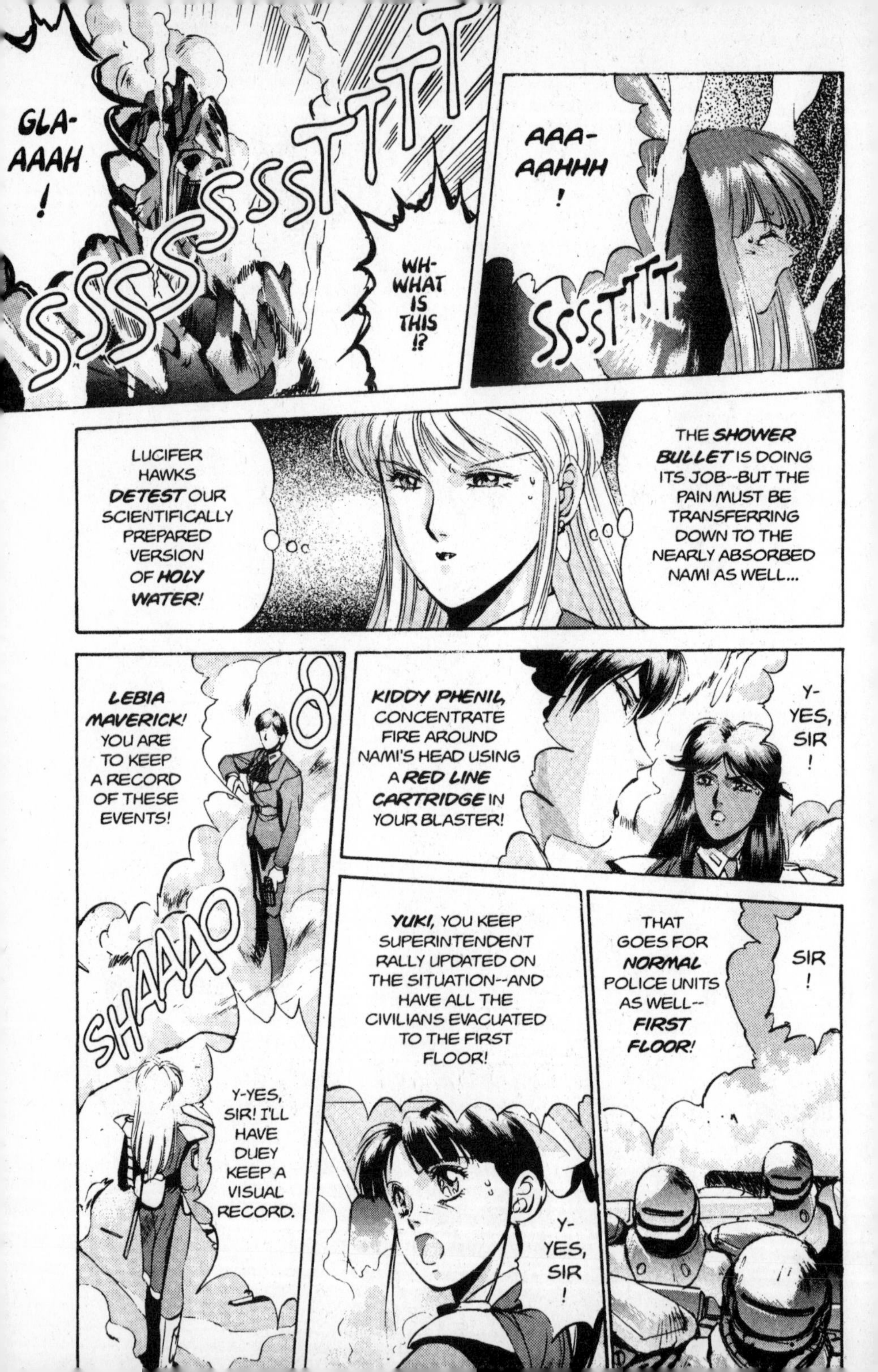
GLA-AAAH!
SSSSSSSSTTTT
WH-WHAT IS THIS!?
AAA-AAHHH!
SSSTTTT
LUCIFER HAWKS **DETEST** OUR SCIENTIFICALLY PREPARED VERSION OF **HOLY WATER**!
THE **SHOWER BULLET** IS DOING ITS JOB--BUT THE PAIN MUST BE TRANSFERRING DOWN TO THE NEARLY ABSORBED NAMI AS WELL...
LEBIA MAVERICK! YOU ARE TO KEEP A RECORD OF THESE EVENTS!
SHAAAO
KIDDY PHENIL, CONCENTRATE FIRE AROUND NAMI'S HEAD USING A **RED LINE CARTRIDGE** IN YOUR BLASTER!
Y-YES, SIR!
Y-YES, SIR! I'LL HAVE DUEY KEEP A VISUAL RECORD.
YUKI, YOU KEEP SUPERINTENDENT RALLY UPDATED ON THE SITUATION--AND HAVE ALL THE CIVILIANS EVACUATED TO THE FIRST FLOOR!
Y-YES, SIR!
THAT GOES FOR **NORMAL** POLICE UNITS AS WELL-- **FIRST FLOOR**!
SIR!

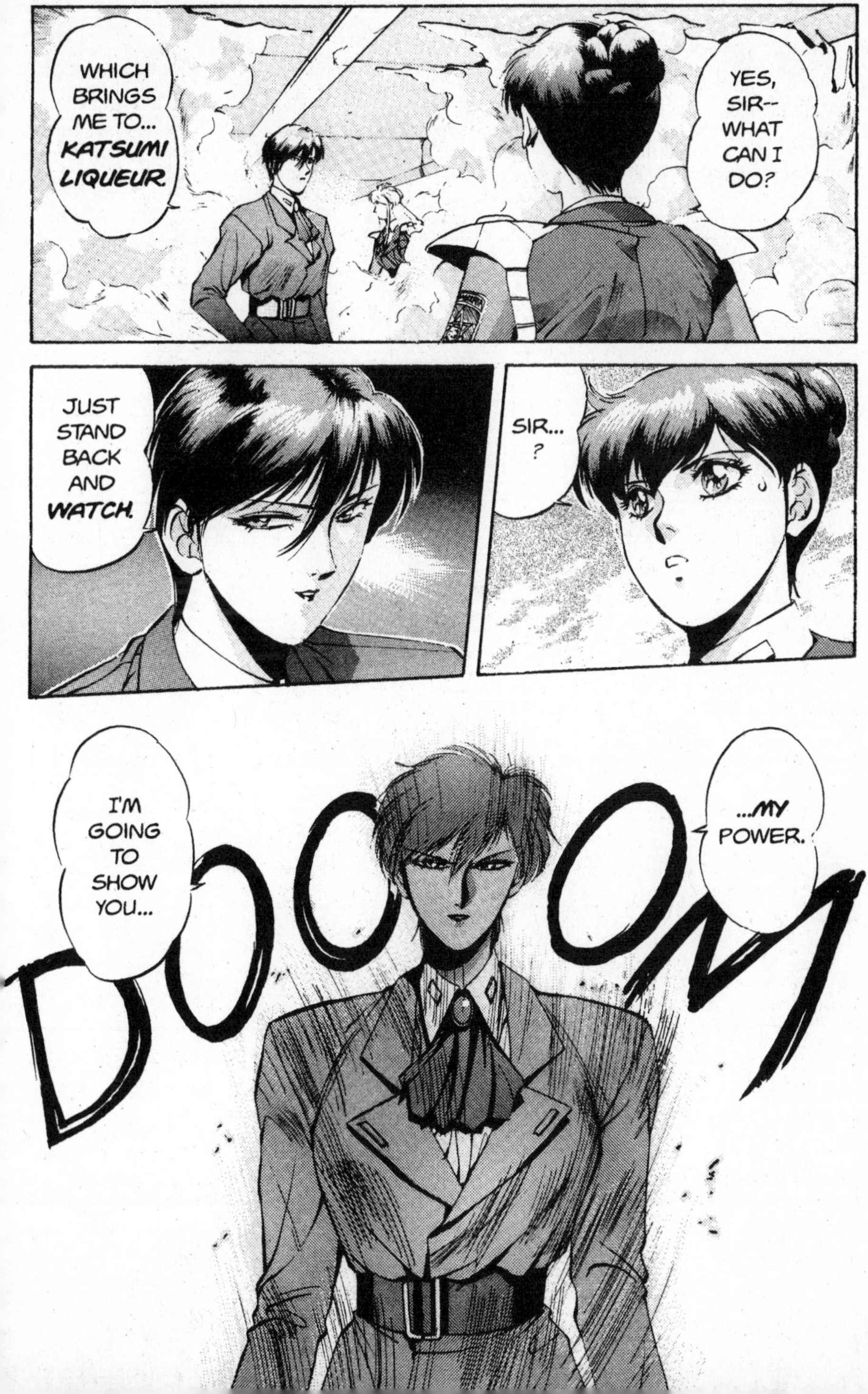
WHICH BRINGS ME TO... KATSUMI LIQUEUR.
YES, SIR-- WHAT CAN I DO?
JUST STAND BACK AND WATCH.
SIR... ?
I'M GOING TO SHOW YOU...
DOOOM
...MY POWER.

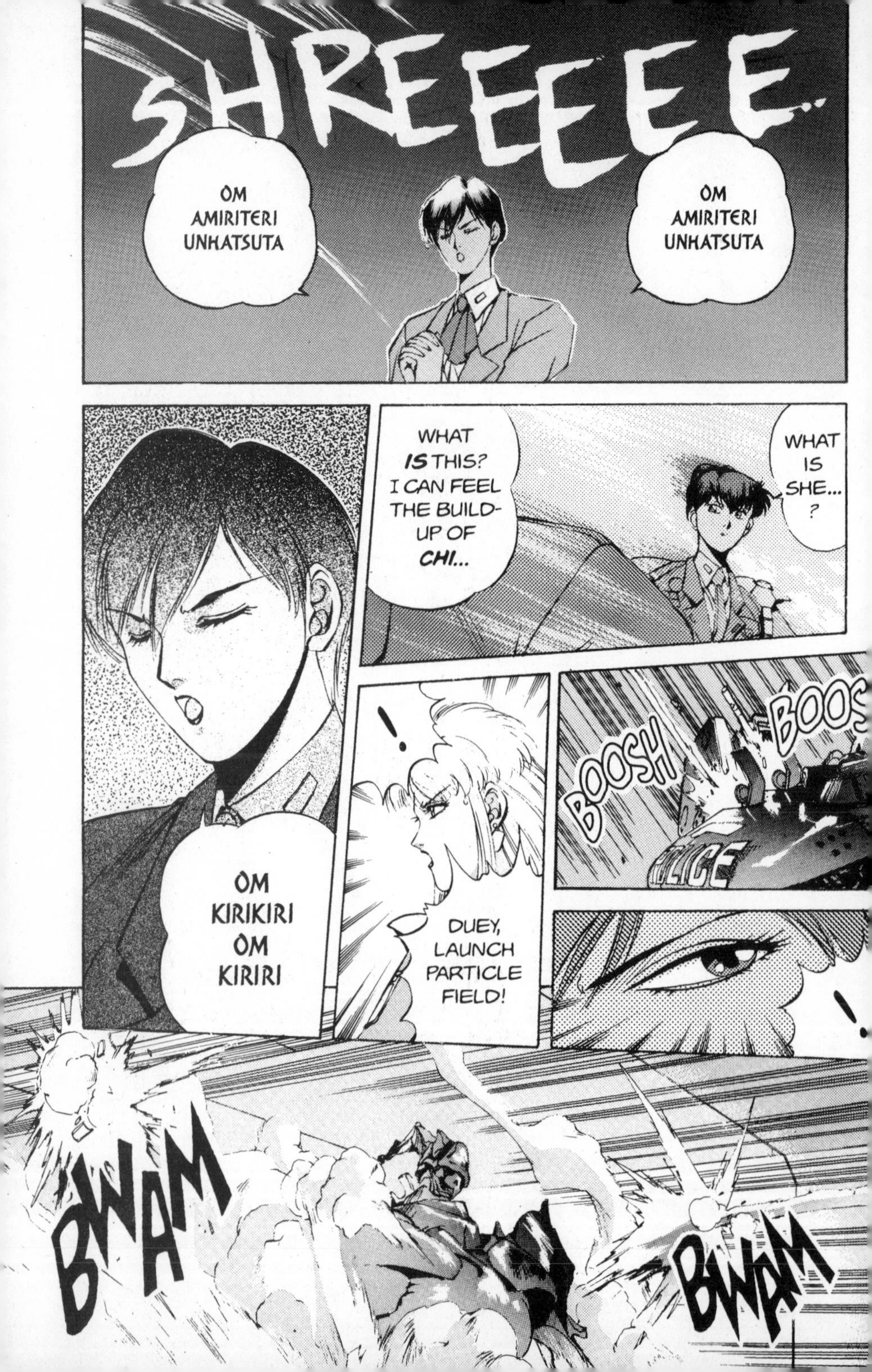
SHREEEEE
OM AMIRITERI UNHATSUTA
OM AMIRITERI UNHATSUTA
OM KIRIKIRI OM KIRIRI
WHAT *IS* THIS? I CAN FEEL THE BUILD-UP OF *CHI*...
WHAT IS SHE...?
!
DUEY, LAUNCH PARTICLE FIELD!
BOOSH
BOOS
!
BWAM
BWAM

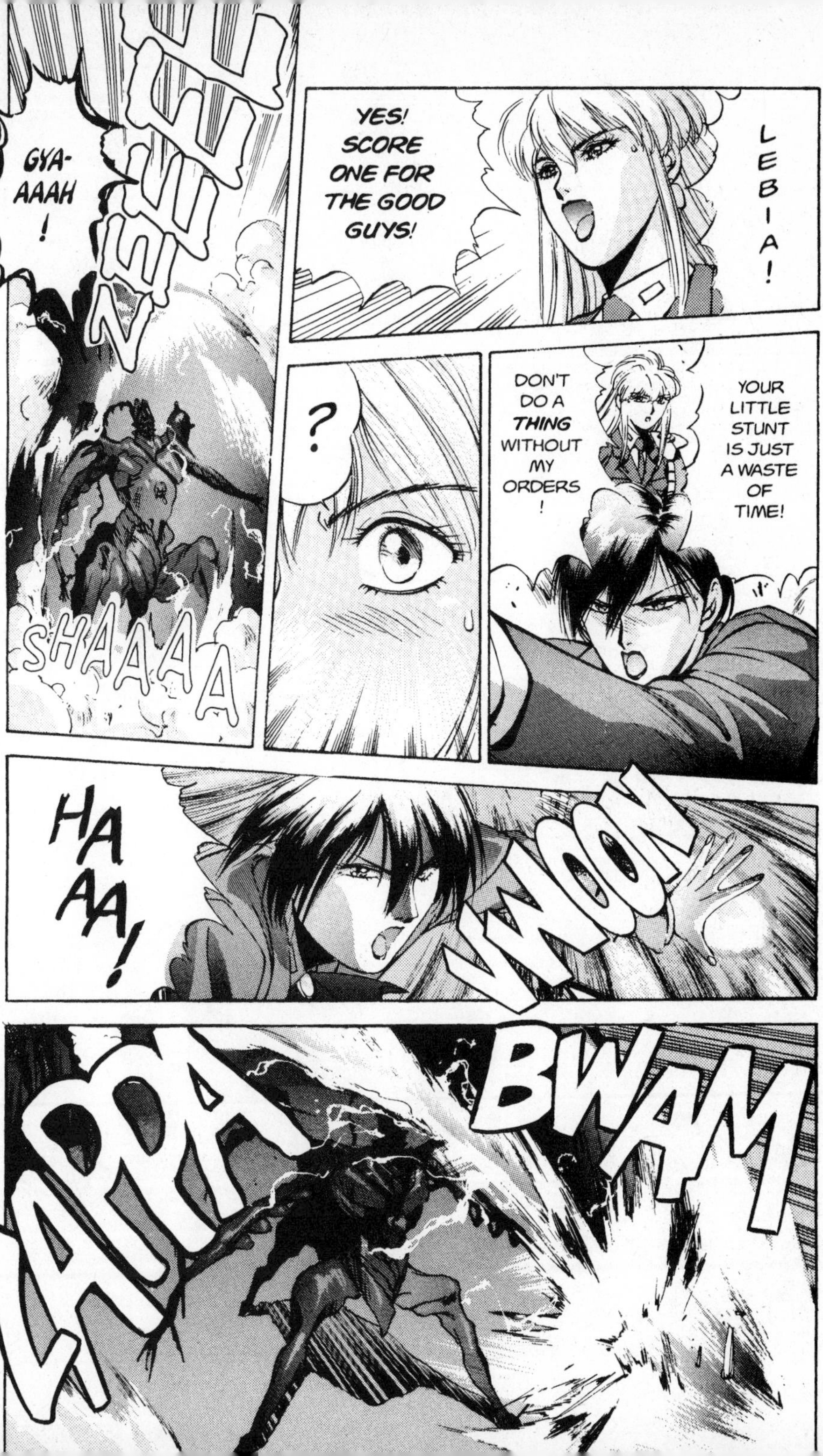
GYA-AAAH!
SHAAAAA
YES! SCORE ONE FOR THE GOOD GUYS!
LEBIA!
?
DON'T DO A THING WITHOUT MY ORDERS!
YOUR LITTLE STUNT IS JUST A WASTE OF TIME!
HAAAA!
VMOON
ZAPPA
BWAM

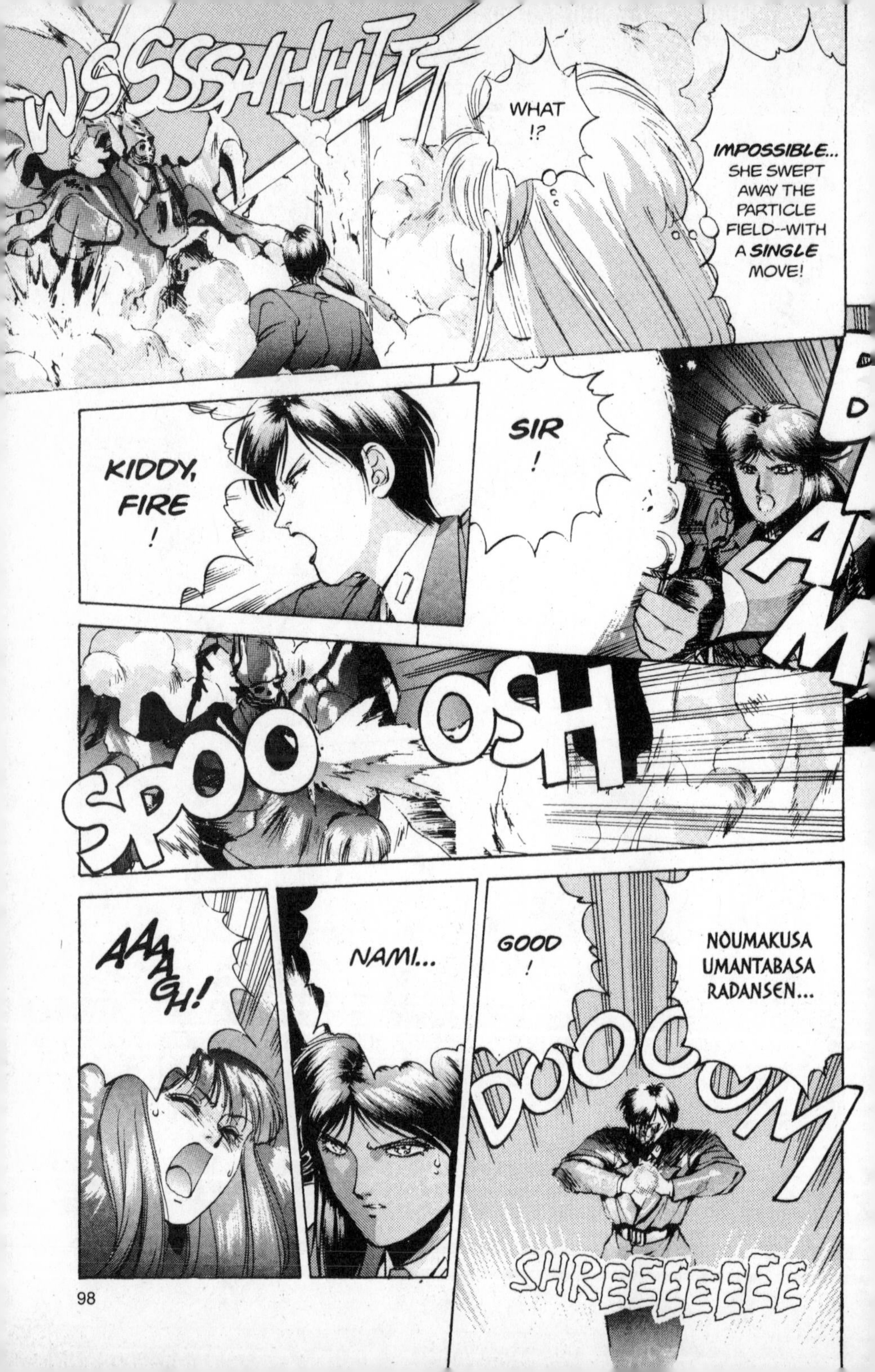
WSSSSHHHTTT
WHAT !?
IMPOSSIBLE... SHE SWEPT AWAY THE PARTICLE FIELD--WITH A SINGLE MOVE!
KIDDY, FIRE !
SIR !
BAM
SPOOOSH
AAAAGH!
NAMI...
GOOD !
NOUMAKUSA UMANTABASA RADANSEN...
DOOOOM
SHREEEEEEEE

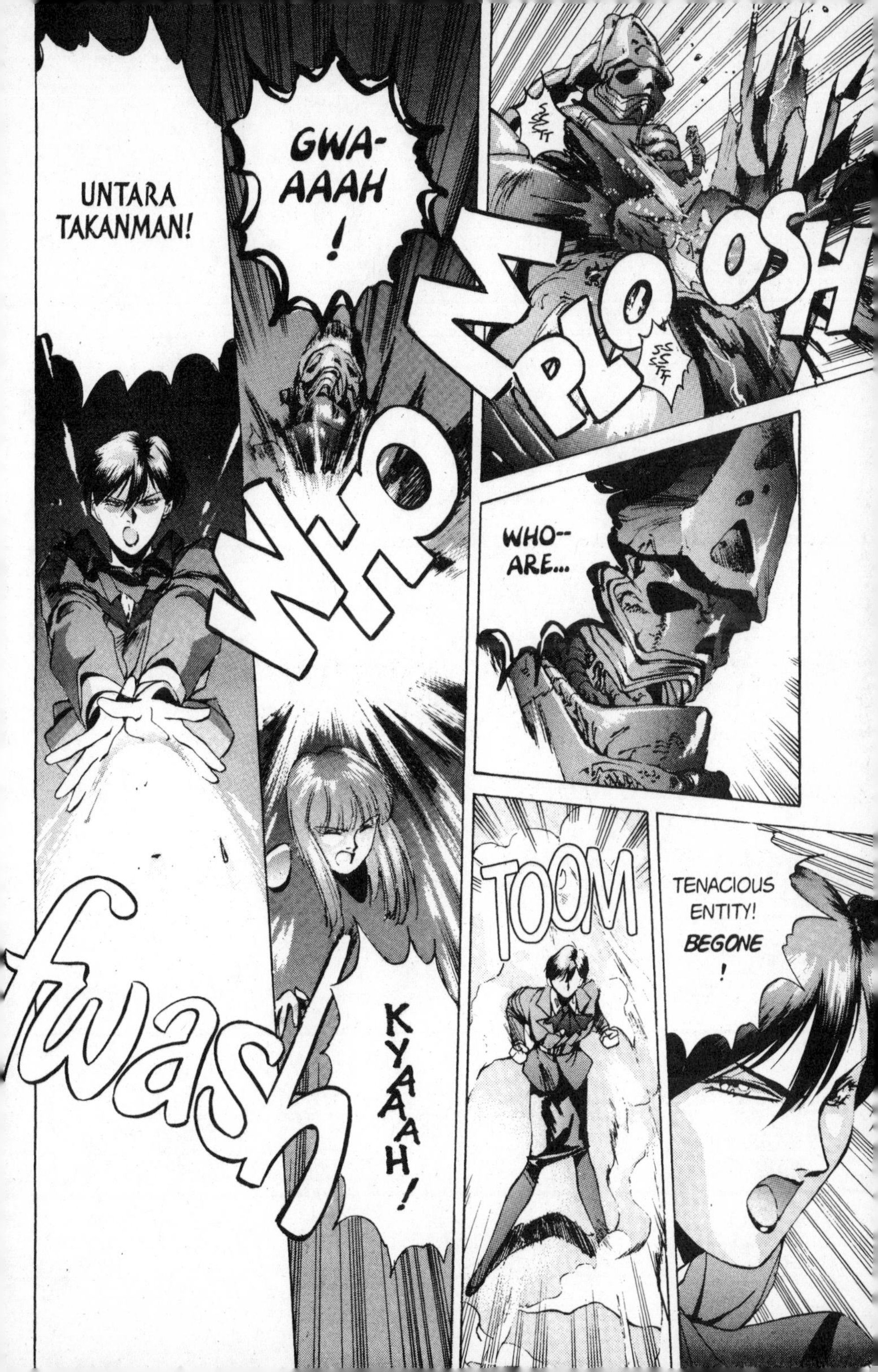
UNTARA TAKANMAN!
fwash
GWA-AAAH!
WHOOM
KYAAAH!
SSSTT
PLOOOSH
SSSTT
WHO-- ARE...
TOOM
TENACIOUS ENTITY! BEGONE!

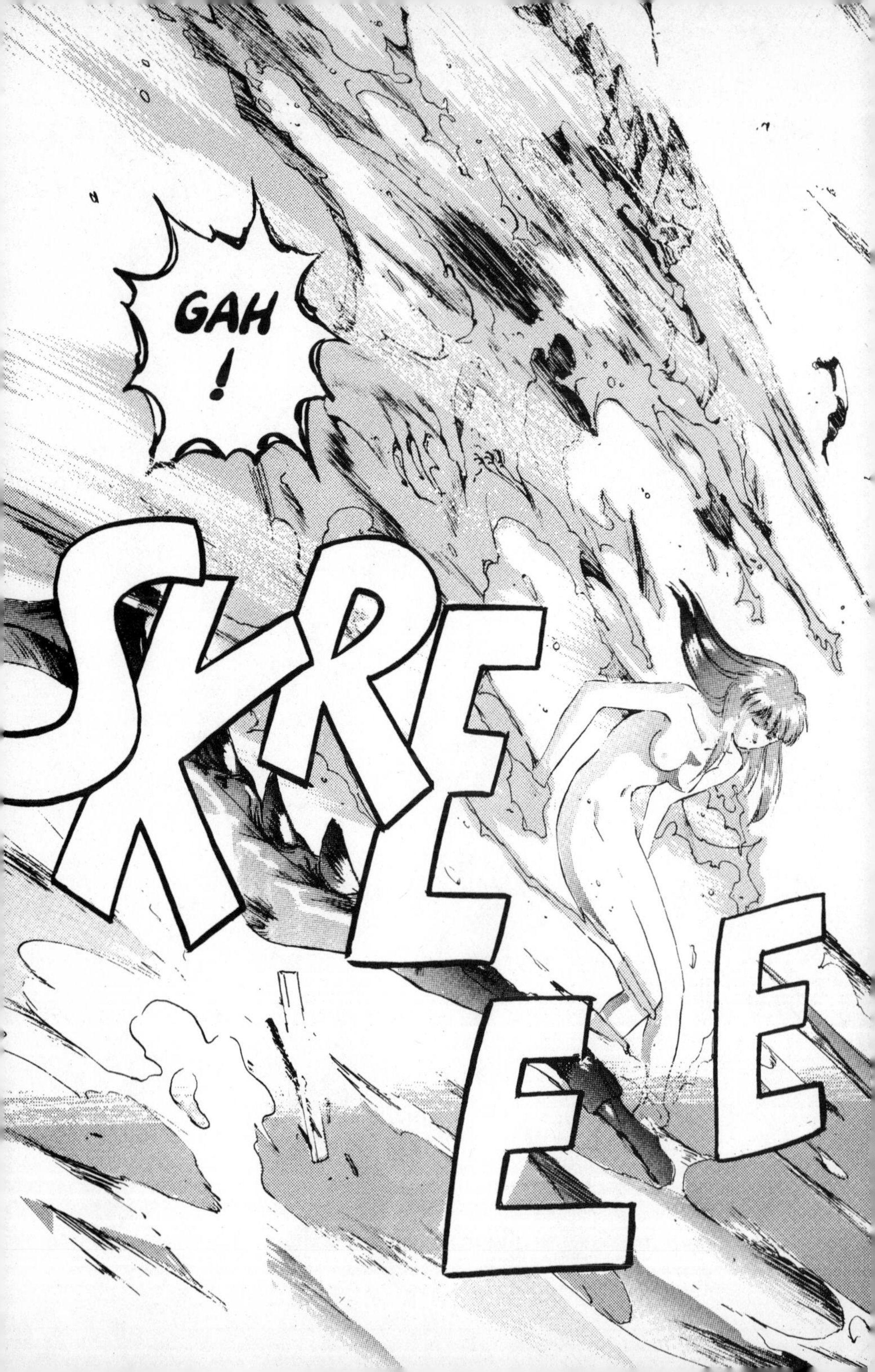
GAH
!
SKREEEE

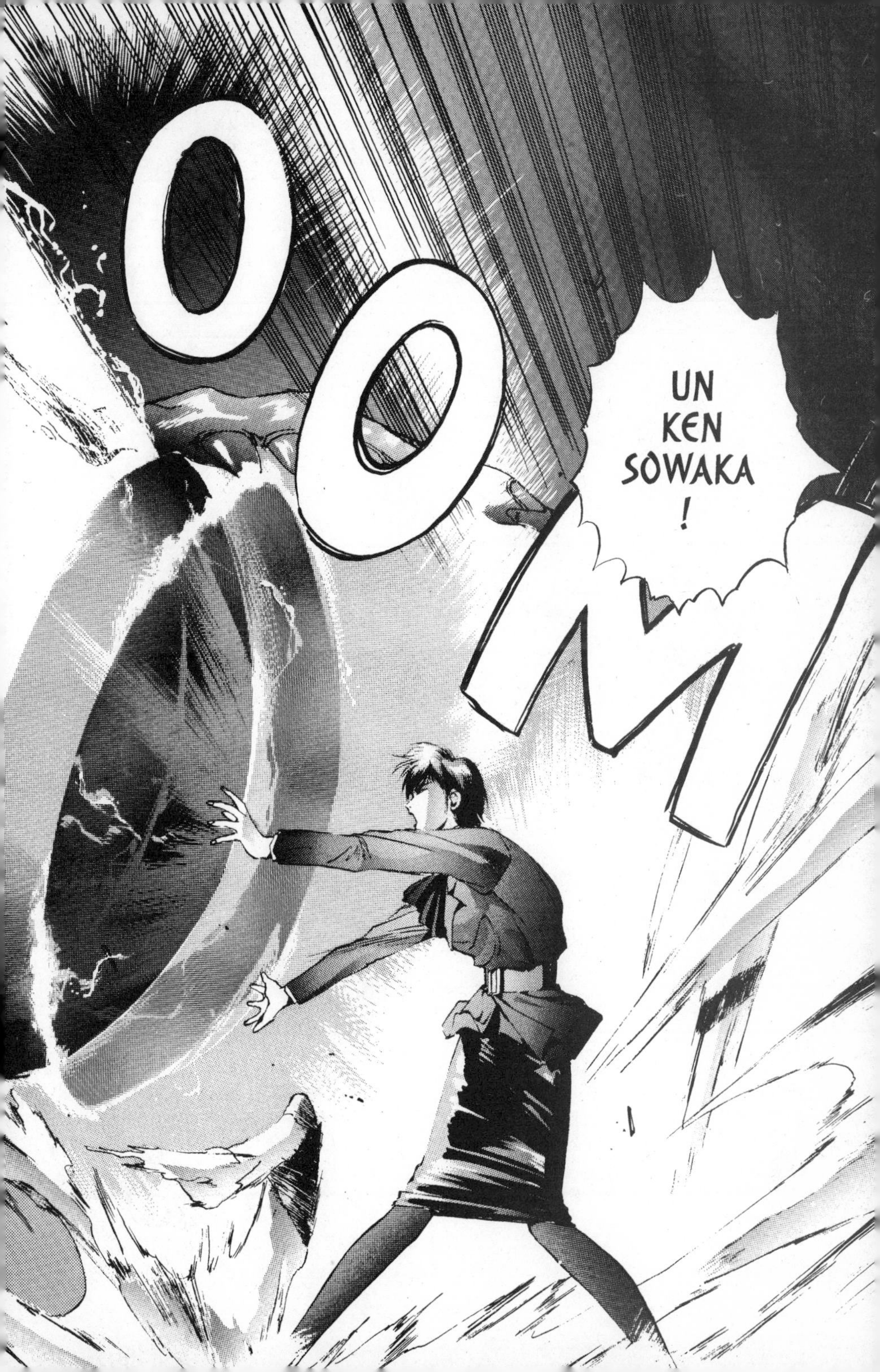
OOM
UN KEN SOWAKA !

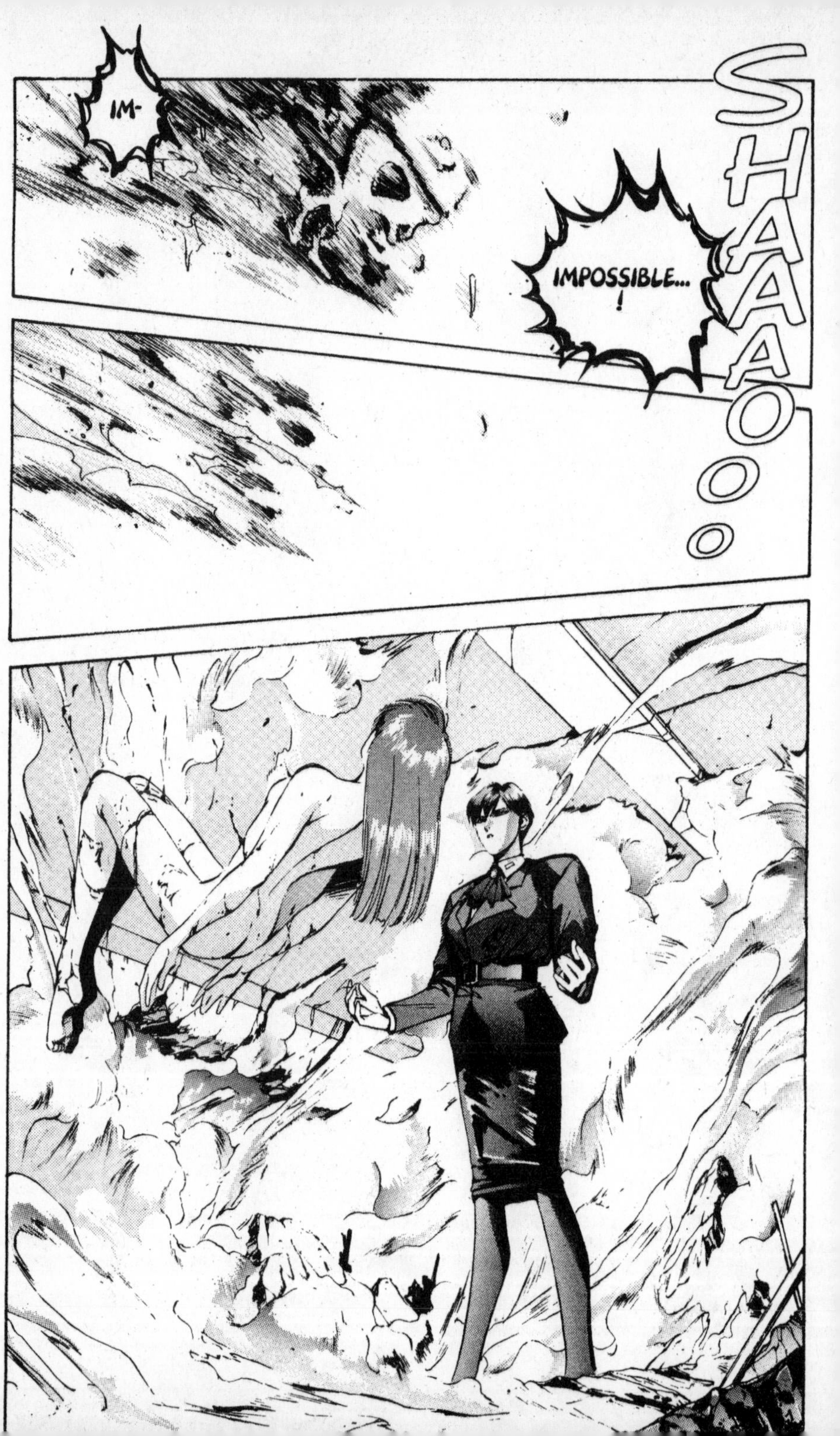
IM-
IMPOSSIBLE... !
SHAAAOOOO

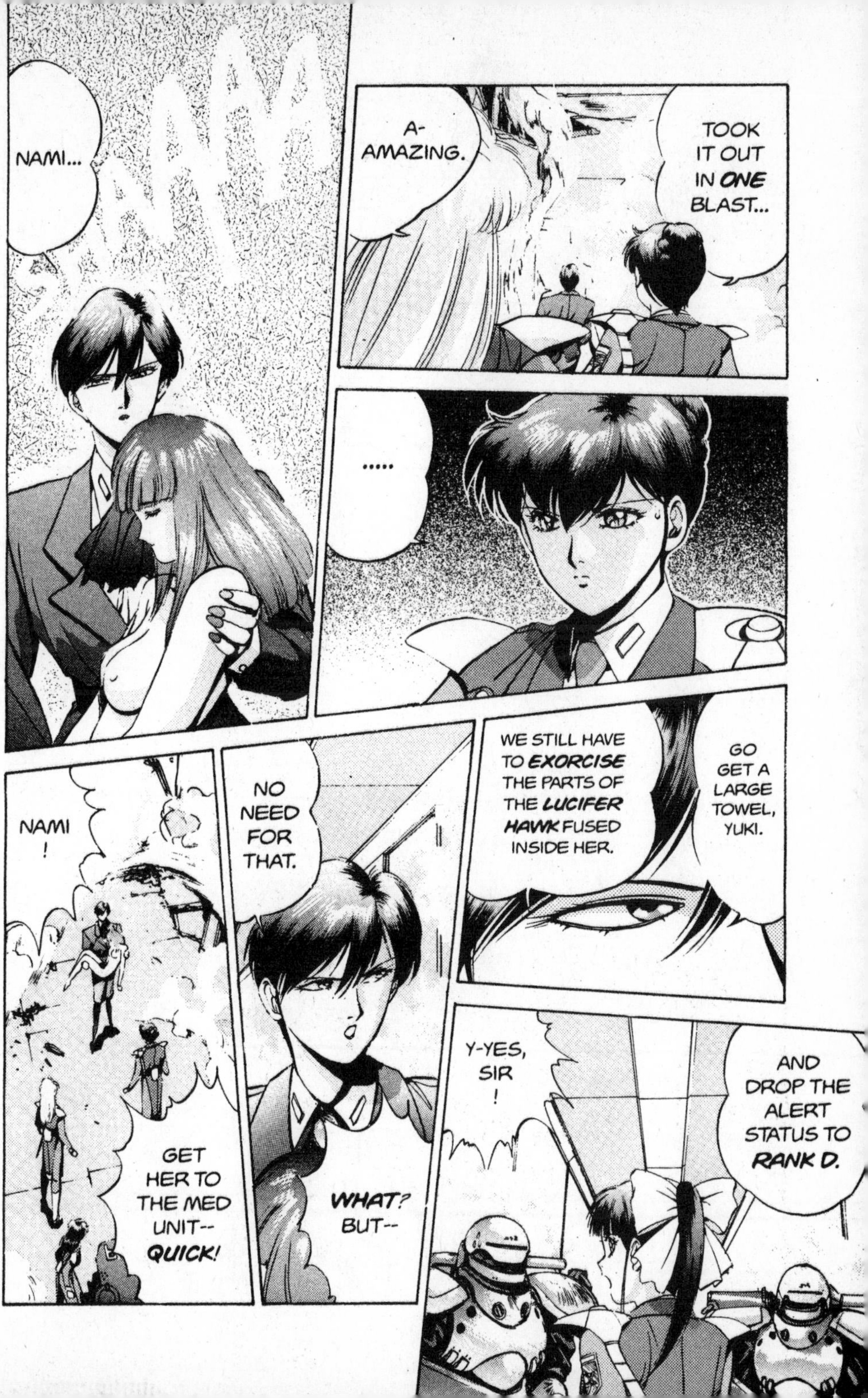
NAMI...
A-AMAZING.
TOOK IT OUT IN ONE BLAST...
.....
NAMI!
GET HER TO THE MED UNIT-- QUICK!
NO NEED FOR THAT.
WHAT? BUT--
WE STILL HAVE TO EXORCISE THE PARTS OF THE LUCIFER HAWK FUSED INSIDE HER.
GO GET A LARGE TOWEL, YUKI.
Y-YES, SIR!
AND DROP THE ALERT STATUS TO RANK D.

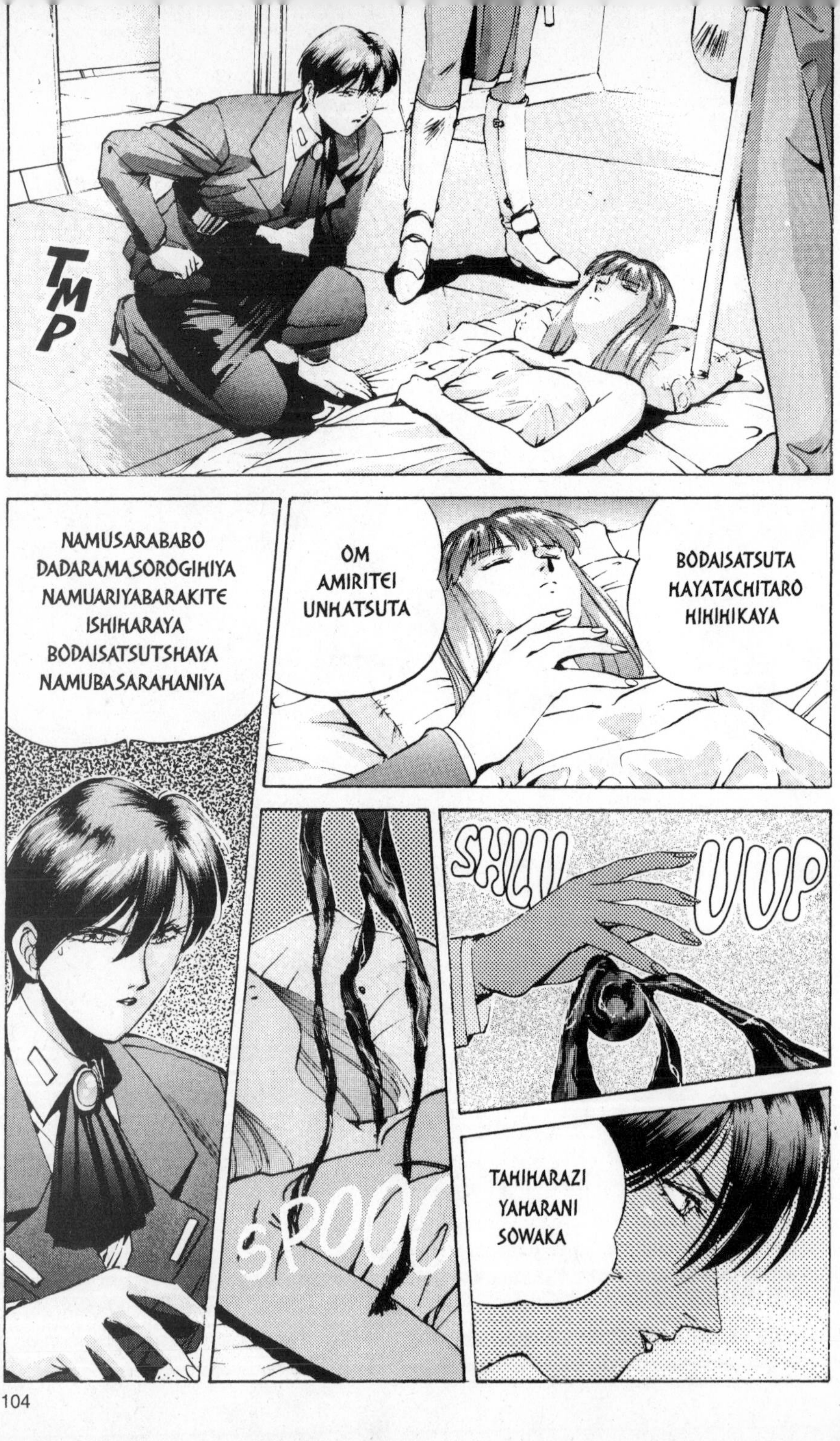
TMP
NAMUSARABABO DADARAMASOROGIHIYA NAMUARIYABARAKITE ISHIHARAYA BODAISATSUTSHAYA NAMUBASARAHANIYA
OM AMIRITEI UNHATSUTA
BODAISATSUTA HAYATACHITARO HIHIHIKAYA
SPOOO
SHUU UUP
TAHIHARAZI YAHARANI SOWAKA

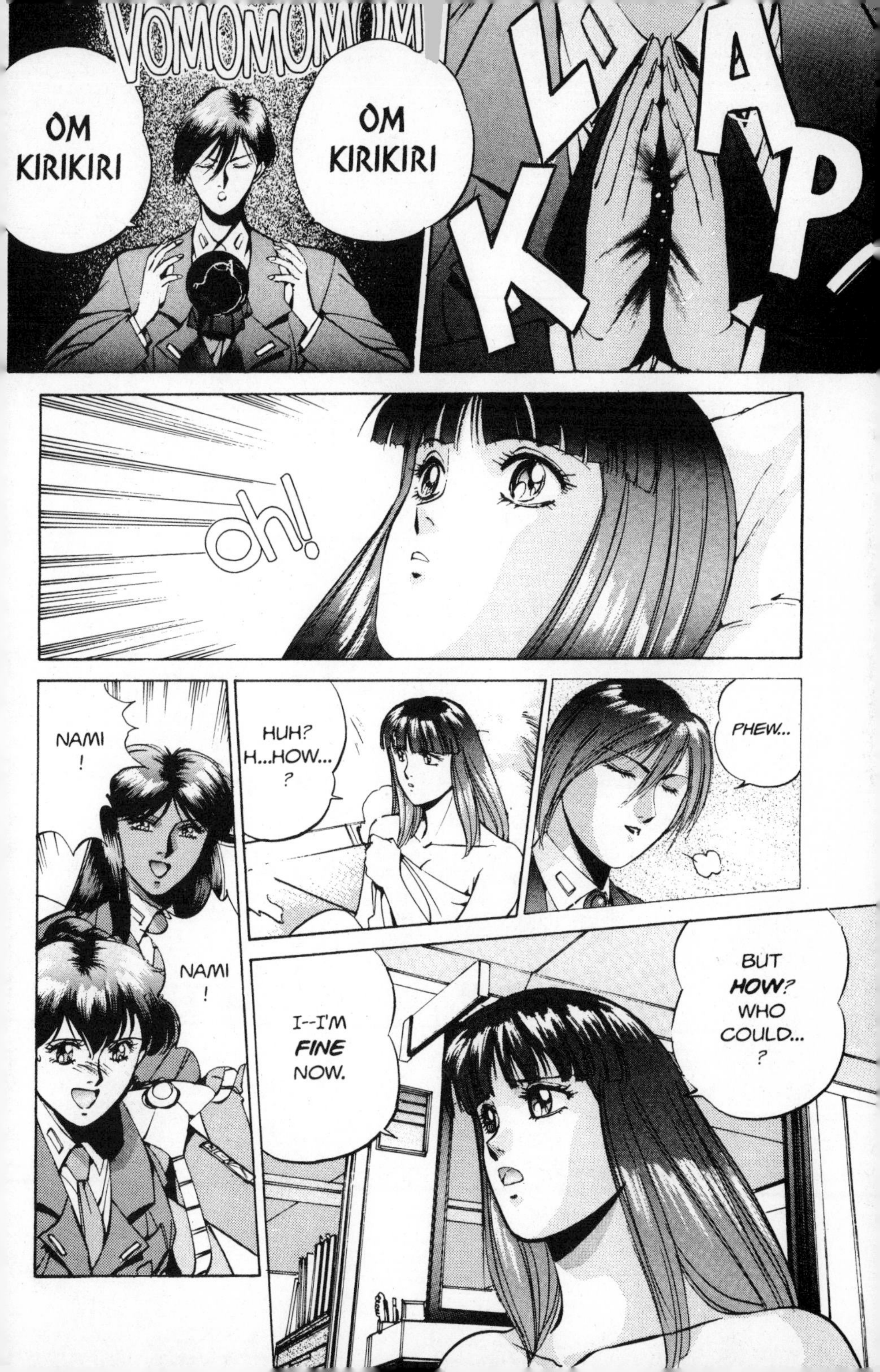
VOMOMOMOM
OM KIRIKIRI
OM KIRIKIRI
KLAP
oh!
NAMI !
NAMI !
HUH? H...HOW...?
PHEW...
I--I'M **FINE** NOW.
BUT ***HOW?*** WHO COULD...?

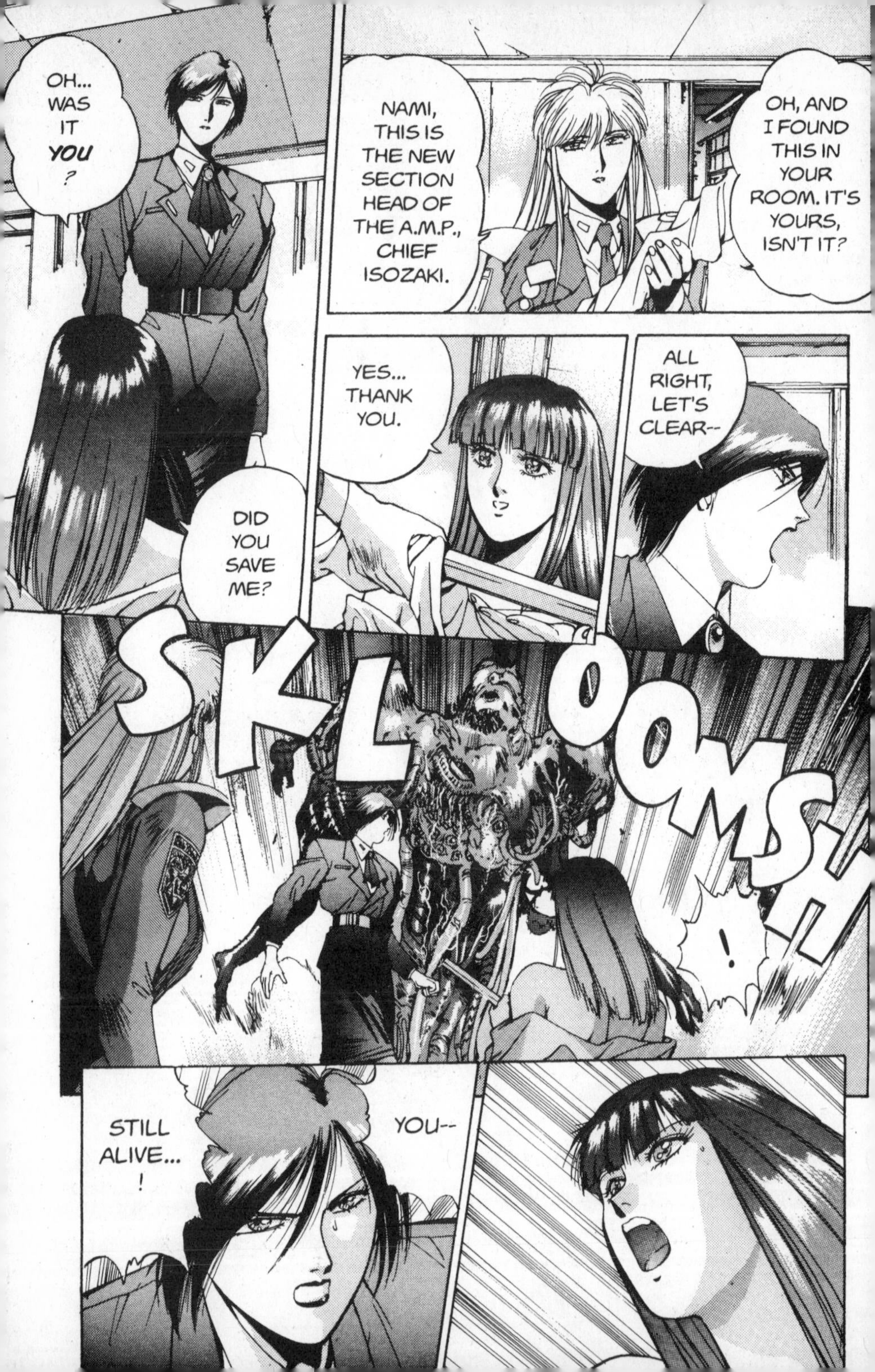
OH... WAS IT *YOU* ?
NAMI, THIS IS THE NEW SECTION HEAD OF THE A.M.P., CHIEF ISOZAKI.
OH, AND I FOUND THIS IN YOUR ROOM. IT'S YOURS, ISN'T IT?
DID YOU SAVE ME?
YES... THANK YOU.
ALL RIGHT, LET'S CLEAR--
SKLOOMSH
!
STILL ALIVE... !
YOU--

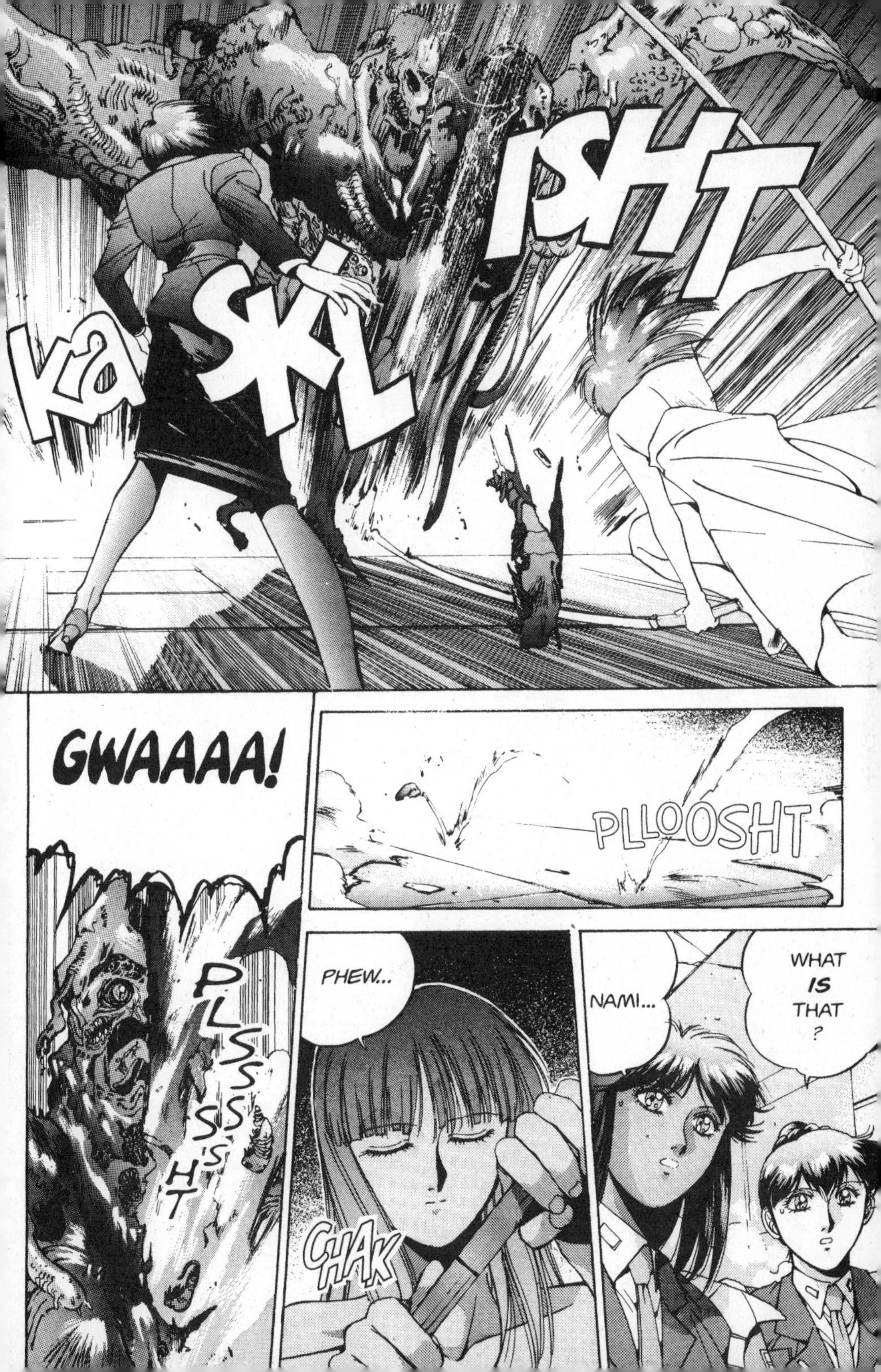
KaSKL
ISHT
GWAAAA!
PLSSSSSSHT
PLLOOSHT
PHEW...
CHAK
NAMI...
WHAT IS THAT?

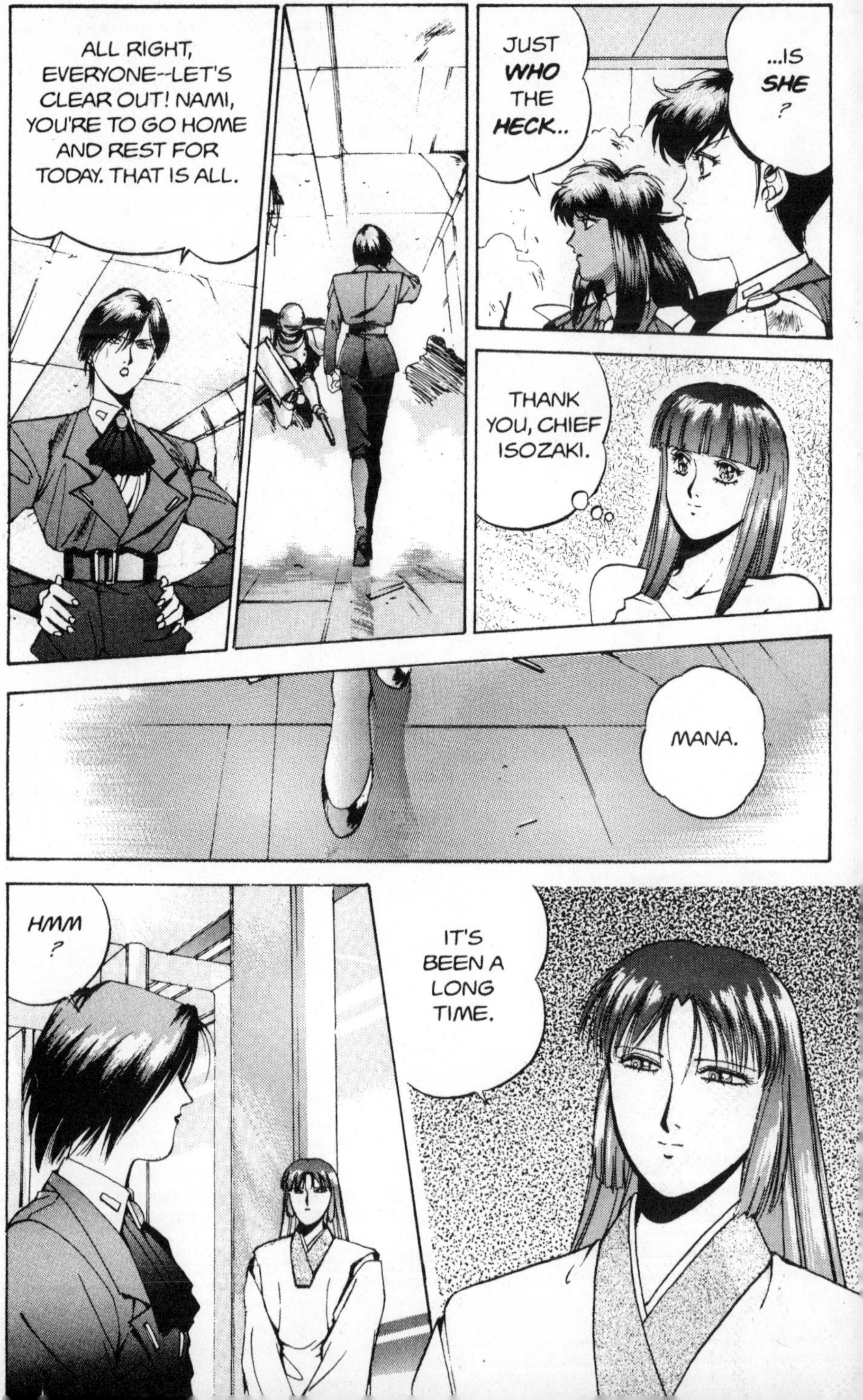
ALL RIGHT, EVERYONE--LET'S CLEAR OUT! NAMI, YOU'RE TO GO HOME AND REST FOR TODAY. THAT IS ALL.
JUST WHO THE HECK..
...IS SHE?
THANK YOU, CHIEF ISOZAKI.
MANA.
HMM?
IT'S BEEN A LONG TIME.

NANA? NANA, IT **IS** YOU!

SEVEN YEARS, ISN'T IT, MANA...?

THANK YOU, MANA, FOR SAVING NAMI... AND GIVING HER A CHANCE TO USE THE **TIGER BLADE**...

YOU SAW THAT, HUH? A POWERFUL WEAPON-- AND HER SKILLS WITH IT ARE EXCELLENT. A GOOD GIRL...

NO--I THINK **SHE'LL** BE THE ONE TAKING CARE OF **US**.

AND **YOUR** WOUNDS? HAVE THEY HEALED?

YES, MOSTLY....

PLEASE TAKE CARE OF HER, MANA.

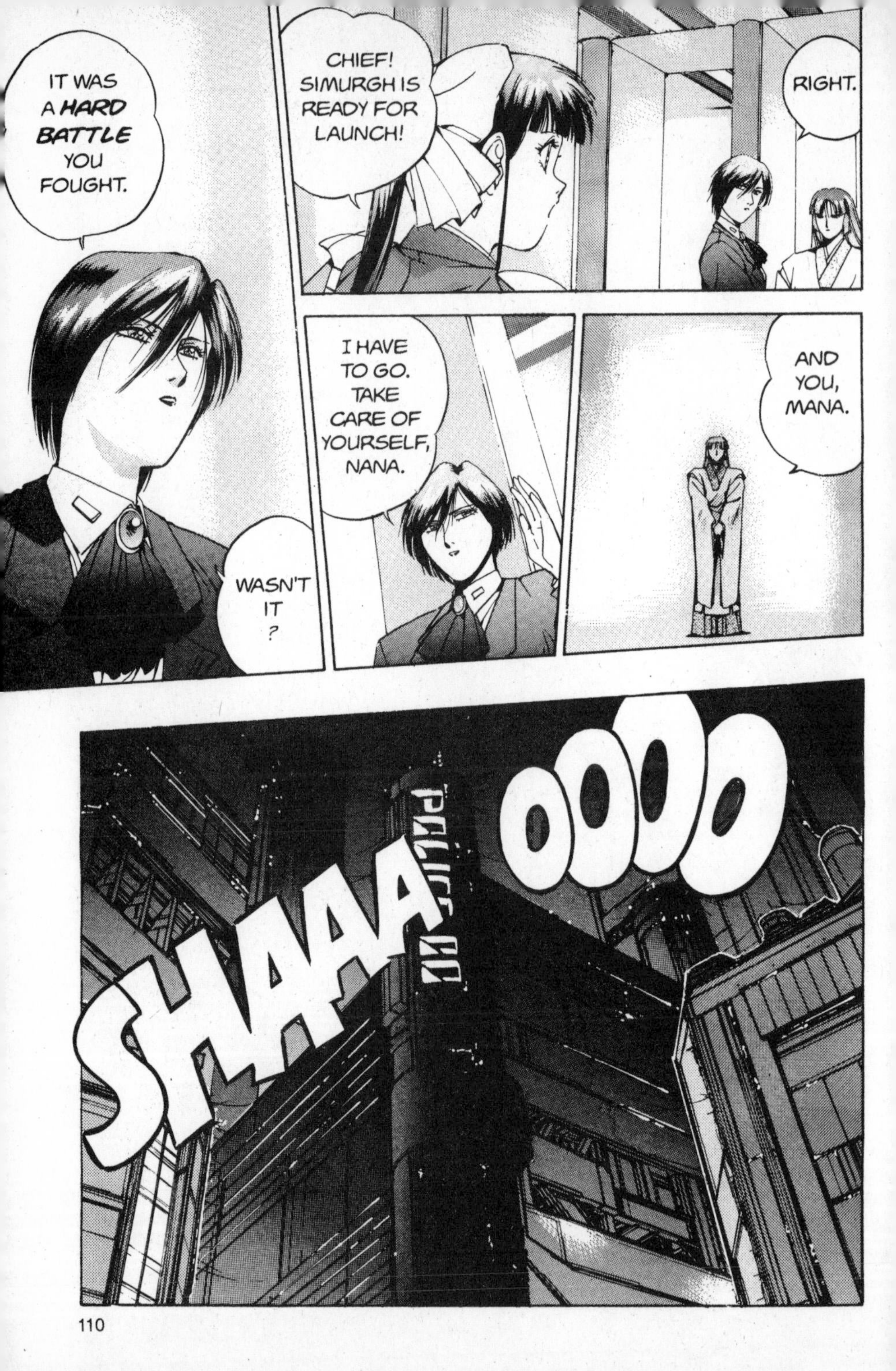
IT WAS A **HARD BATTLE** YOU FOUGHT.
WASN'T IT ?
CHIEF! SIMURGH IS READY FOR LAUNCH!
RIGHT.
I HAVE TO GO. TAKE CARE OF YOURSELF, NANA.
AND YOU, MANA.
SHAAAOOOO

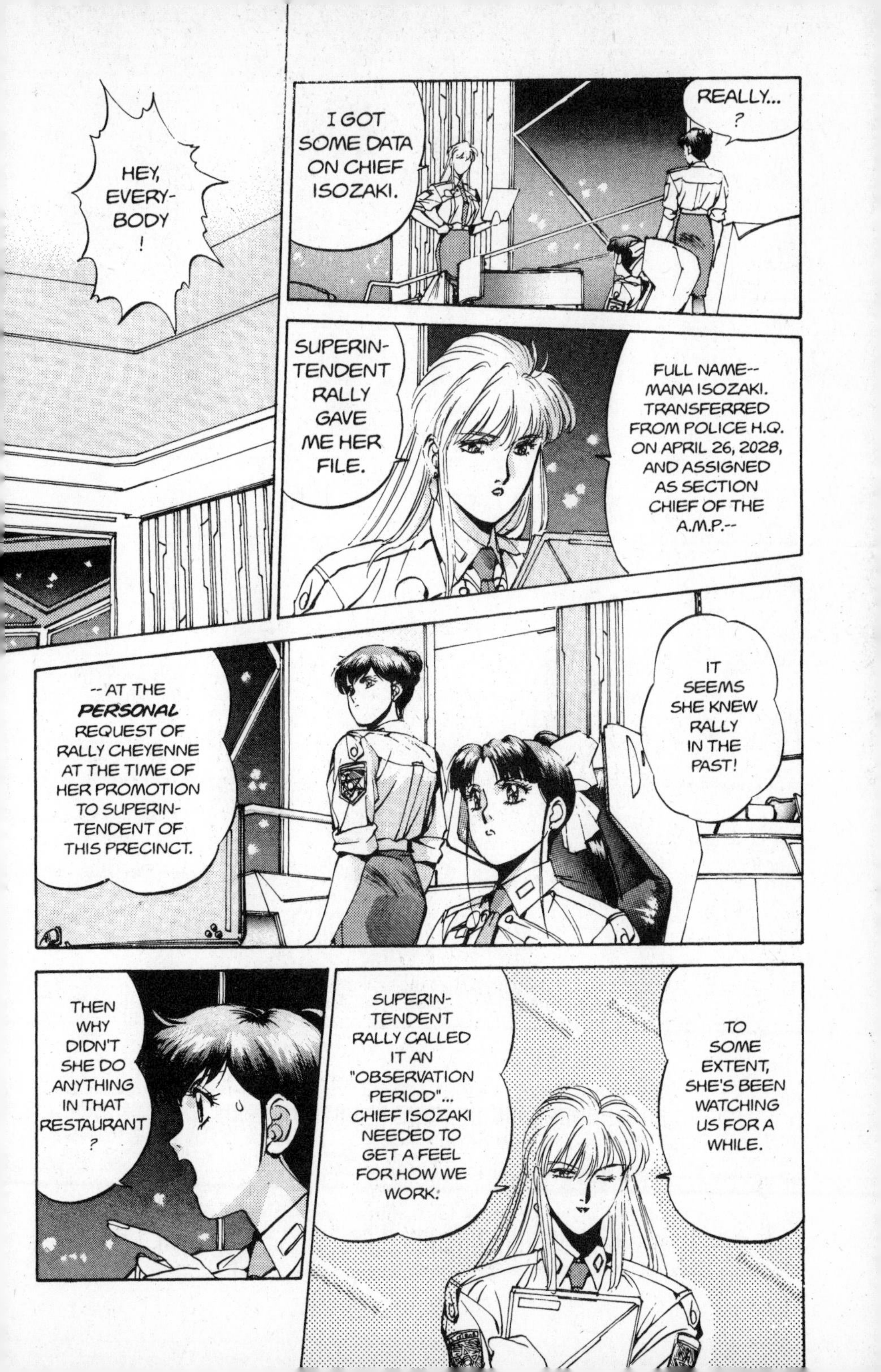
HEY, EVERY-BODY!
I GOT SOME DATA ON CHIEF ISOZAKI.
REALLY...?
SUPERIN-TENDENT RALLY GAVE ME HER FILE.
FULL NAME-- MANA ISOZAKI. TRANSFERRED FROM POLICE H.Q. ON APRIL 26, 2028, AND ASSIGNED AS SECTION CHIEF OF THE A.M.P.--
--AT THE PERSONAL REQUEST OF RALLY CHEYENNE AT THE TIME OF HER PROMOTION TO SUPERIN-TENDENT OF THIS PRECINCT.
IT SEEMS SHE KNEW RALLY IN THE PAST!
THEN WHY DIDN'T SHE DO ANYTHING IN THAT RESTAURANT?
SUPERIN-TENDENT RALLY CALLED IT AN "OBSERVATION PERIOD"... CHIEF ISOZAKI NEEDED TO GET A FEEL FOR HOW WE WORK.
TO SOME EXTENT, SHE'S BEEN WATCHING US FOR A WHILE.

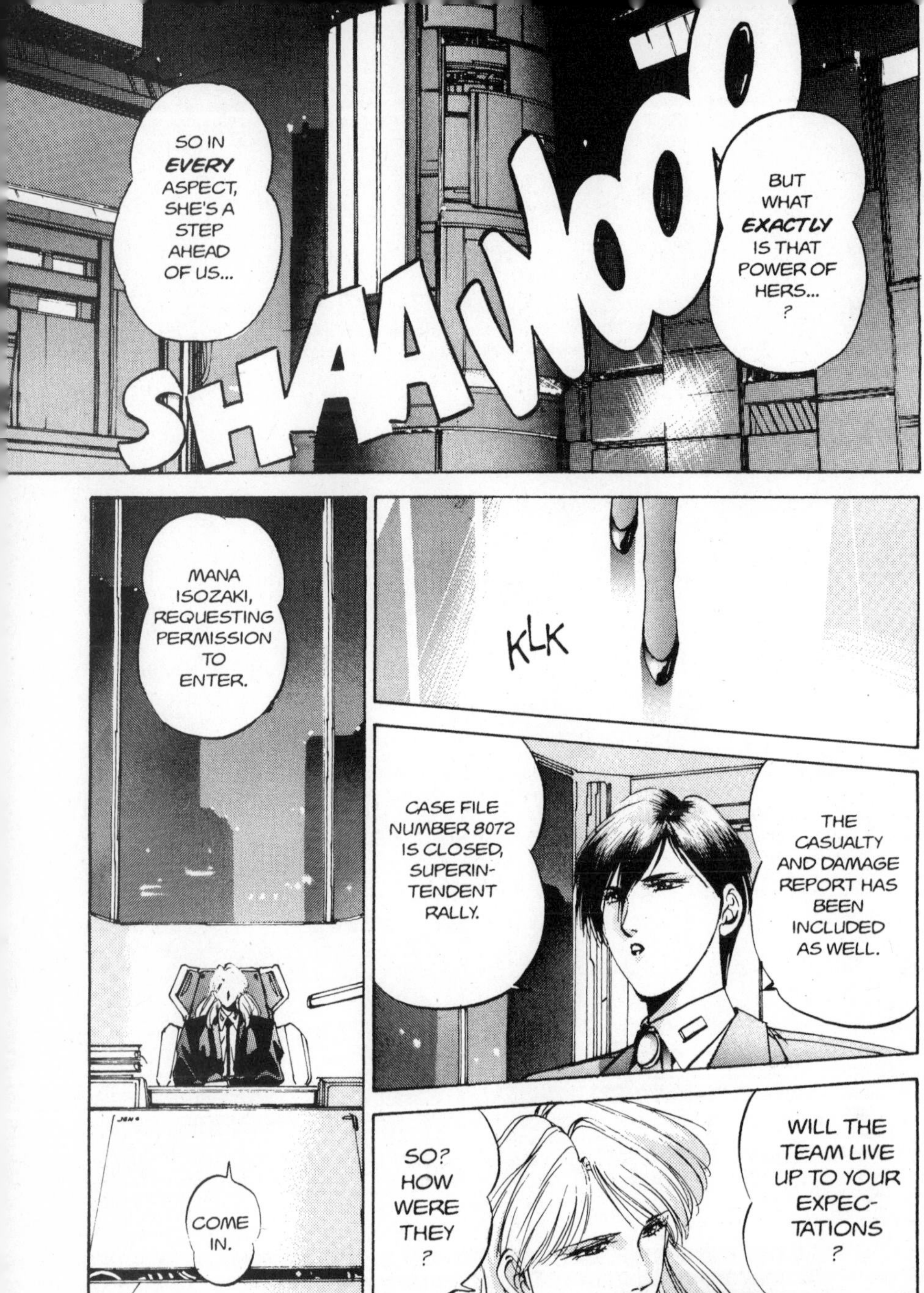
SO IN EVERY ASPECT, SHE'S A STEP AHEAD OF US...
SHAAWOOO
BUT WHAT EXACTLY IS THAT POWER OF HERS...?
MANA ISOZAKI, REQUESTING PERMISSION TO ENTER.
KLK
CASE FILE NUMBER 8072 IS CLOSED, SUPERIN-TENDENT RALLY.
THE CASUALTY AND DAMAGE REPORT HAS BEEN INCLUDED AS WELL.
COME IN.
SO? HOW WERE THEY?
WILL THE TEAM LIVE UP TO YOUR EXPEC-TATIONS?

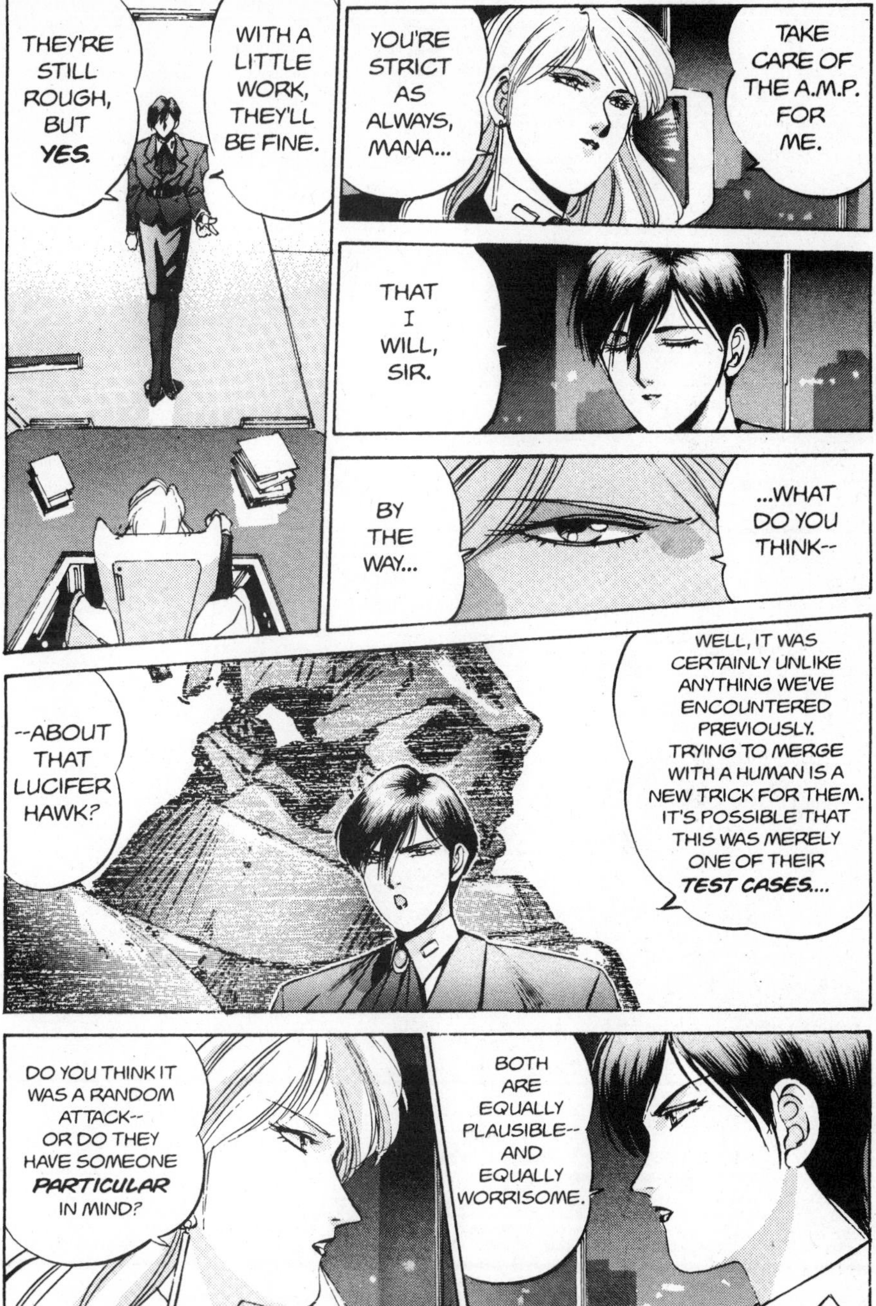

THEY'RE STILL ROUGH, BUT **YES.**
WITH A LITTLE WORK, THEY'LL BE FINE.
YOU'RE STRICT AS ALWAYS, MANA...
TAKE CARE OF THE A.M.P. FOR ME.
THAT I WILL, SIR.
BY THE WAY...
...WHAT DO YOU THINK--
--ABOUT THAT LUCIFER HAWK?
WELL, IT WAS CERTAINLY UNLIKE ANYTHING WE'VE ENCOUNTERED PREVIOUSLY. TRYING TO MERGE WITH A HUMAN IS A NEW TRICK FOR THEM. IT'S POSSIBLE THAT THIS WAS MERELY ONE OF THEIR ***TEST CASES....***
DO YOU THINK IT WAS A RANDOM ATTACK-- OR DO THEY HAVE SOMEONE ***PARTICULAR*** IN MIND?
BOTH ARE EQUALLY PLAUSIBLE-- AND EQUALLY WORRISOME.

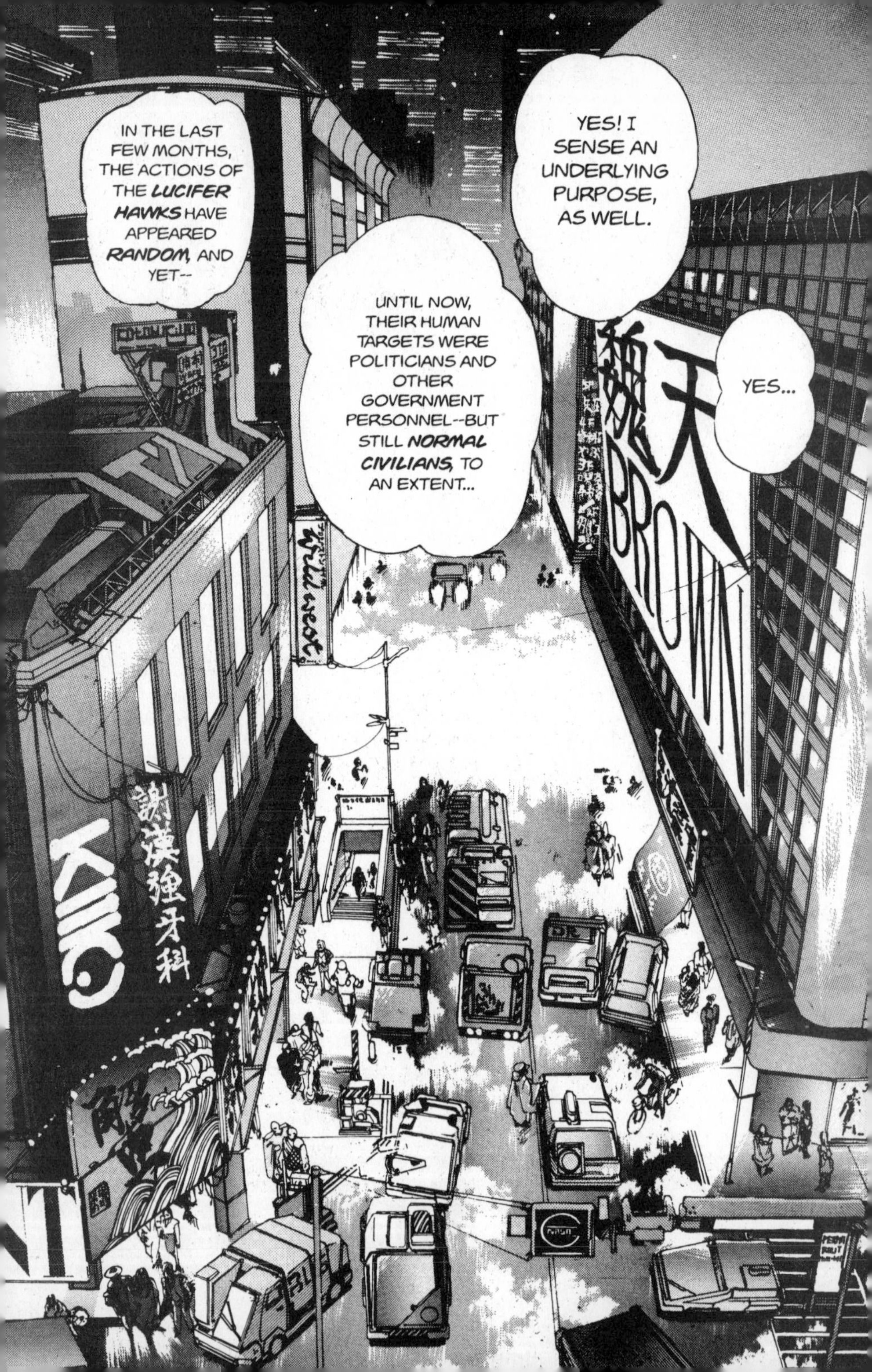
IN THE LAST FEW MONTHS, THE ACTIONS OF THE *LUCIFER HAWKS* HAVE APPEARED *RANDOM*, AND YET--
YES! I SENSE AN UNDERLYING PURPOSE, AS WELL.
UNTIL NOW, THEIR HUMAN TARGETS WERE POLITICIANS AND OTHER GOVERNMENT PERSONNEL--BUT STILL *NORMAL CIVILIANS*, TO AN EXTENT...
YES...
BROWN

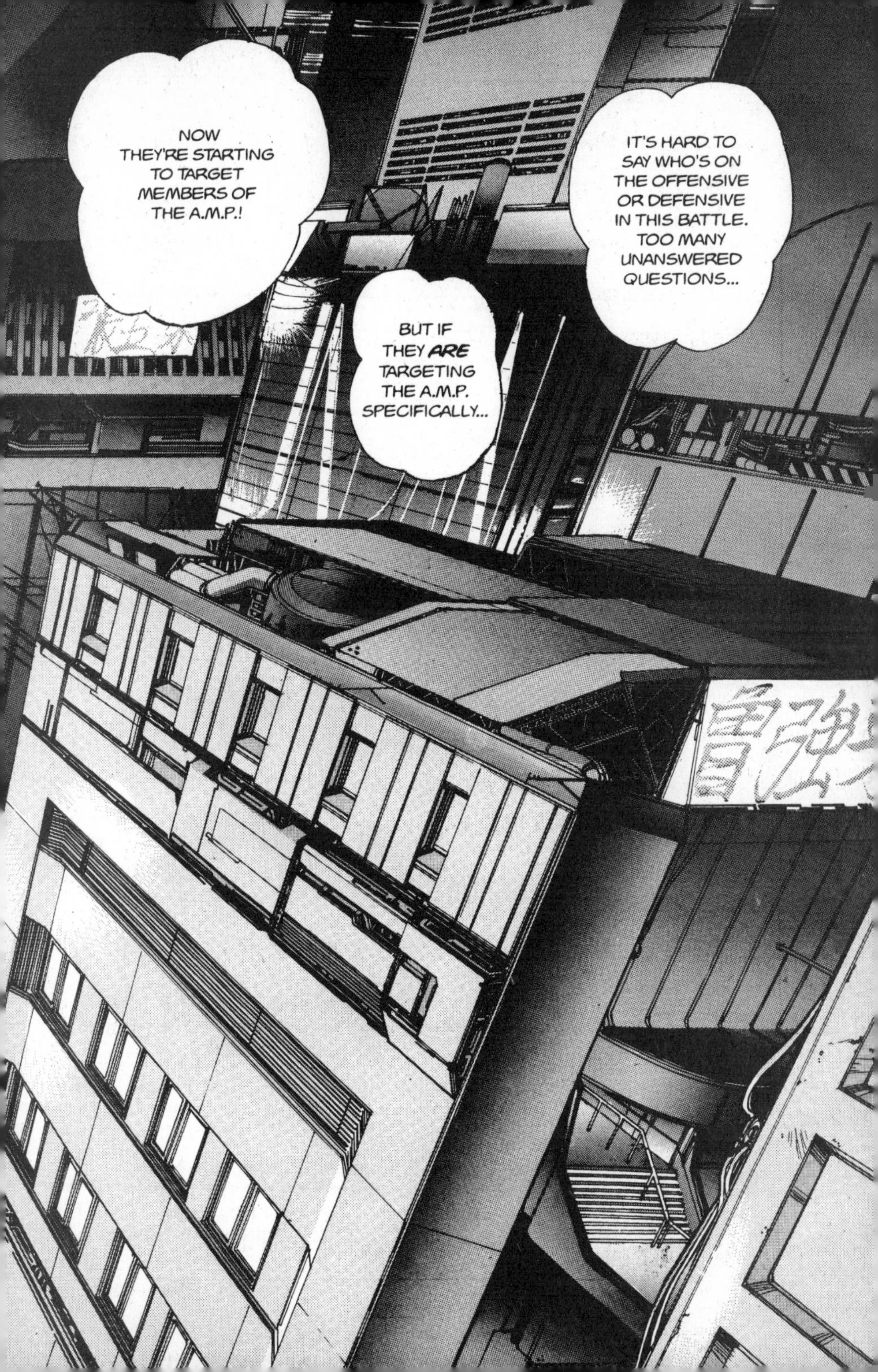
NOW THEY'RE STARTING TO TARGET MEMBERS OF THE A.M.P.!
BUT IF THEY **ARE** TARGETING THE A.M.P. SPECIFICALLY...
IT'S HARD TO SAY WHO'S ON THE OFFENSIVE OR DEFENSIVE IN THIS BATTLE. TOO MANY UNANSWERED QUESTIONS...

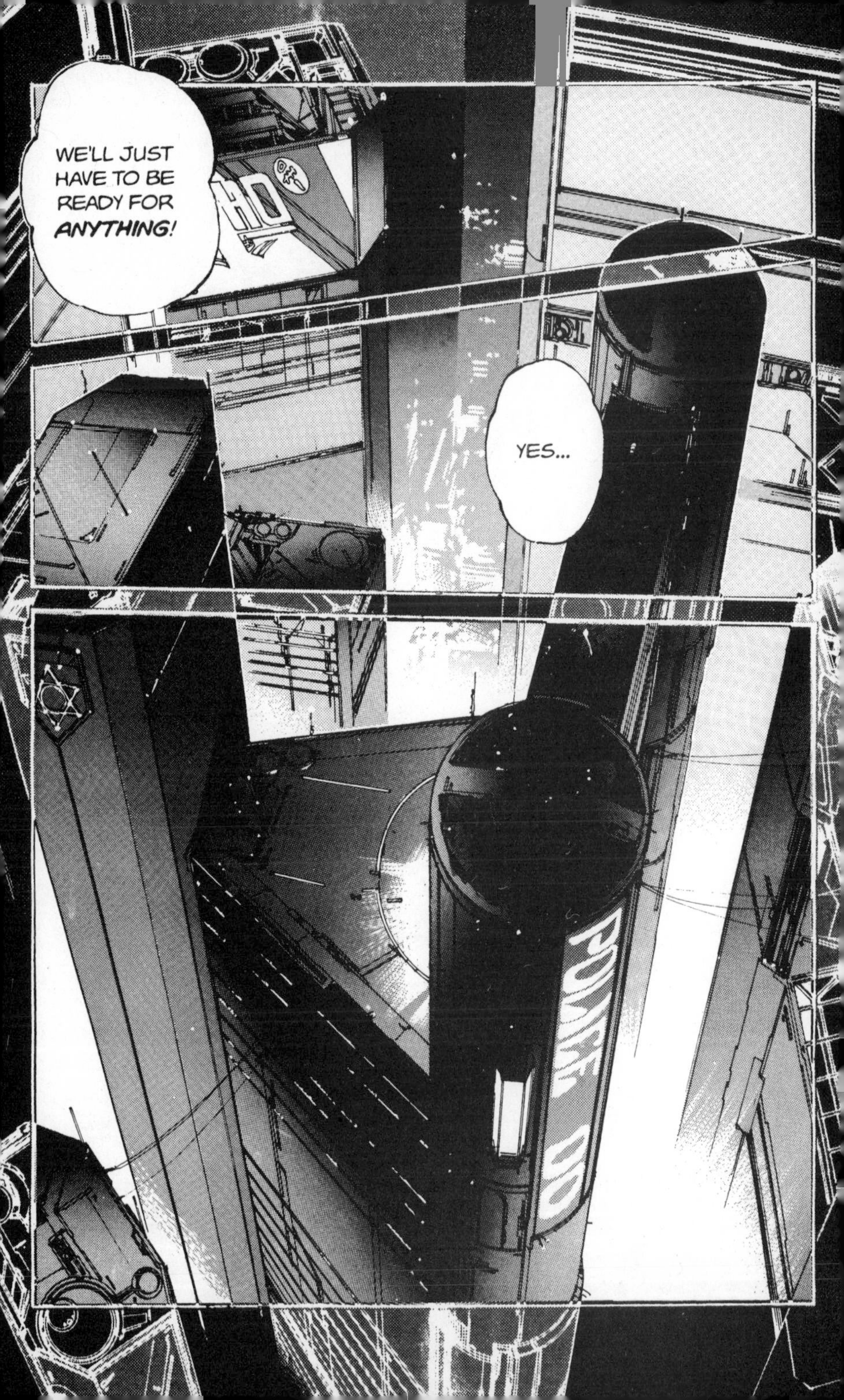
WE'LL JUST HAVE TO BE READY FOR ANYTHING!
YES...
POLICE 010

SILENT MÖBIUS

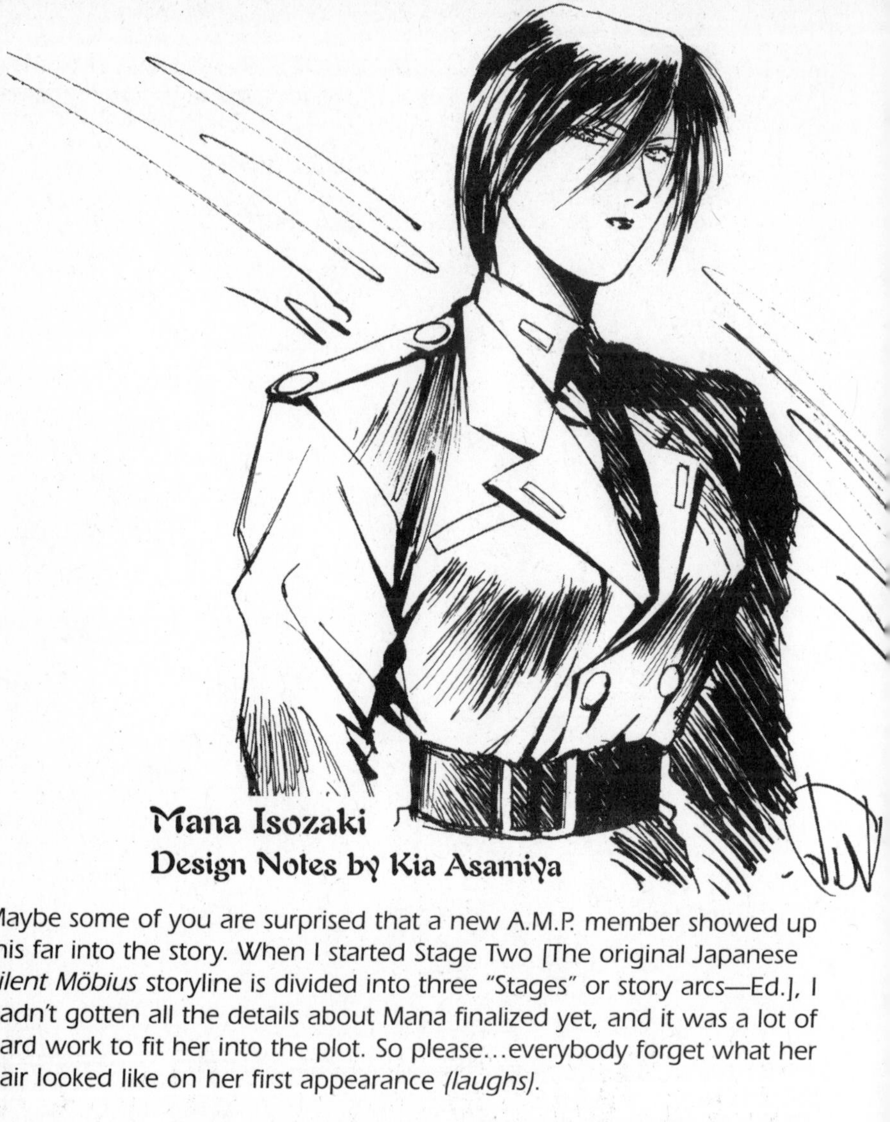

Mana Isozaki

Design Notes by Kia Asamiya

Maybe some of you are surprised that a new A.M.P. member showed up this far into the story. When I started Stage Two [The original Japanese *Silent Möbius* storyline is divided into three "Stages" or story arcs—Ed.], I hadn't gotten all the details about Mana finalized yet, and it was a lot of hard work to fit her into the plot. So please…everybody forget what her hair looked like on her first appearance *(laughs)*.

Mana has a very strict personality, but I like her a lot. From Stage Two to the beginning of Stage Three she becomes a key character.

There's a story behind Mana and Nami's sister Nana. We sort of touch on it in this current episode, but maybe one of these days I'll get to draw the story about those two. That story involves Nami's parents as well. Originally I had only meant it to be a background story, but…things happened *(laughs)*.

CHAPTER 11:

INTERMISSION: DOG DAYS OF THE A.M.P.

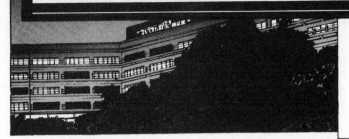

TO CELEBRATE CHIEF ISOZAKI'S JOINING THE FORCE, A PARTY WAS HELD IN KINUGAWA.

SO MUCH...

WELCOME ABOARD AND CONGRAT-ULATIONS, CHIEF!

THANKS.

BUT...

EVERY-ONE'S SO... WILD.

YEAH.

glug glug glug glug!

TIME PASSED, AND ALCOHOL FLOWED LIBERALLY.

TÁ DAA

AND SOMEHOW, THE PARTY BECAME...A TALENT SHOW!

NAMI YAMIGUMO

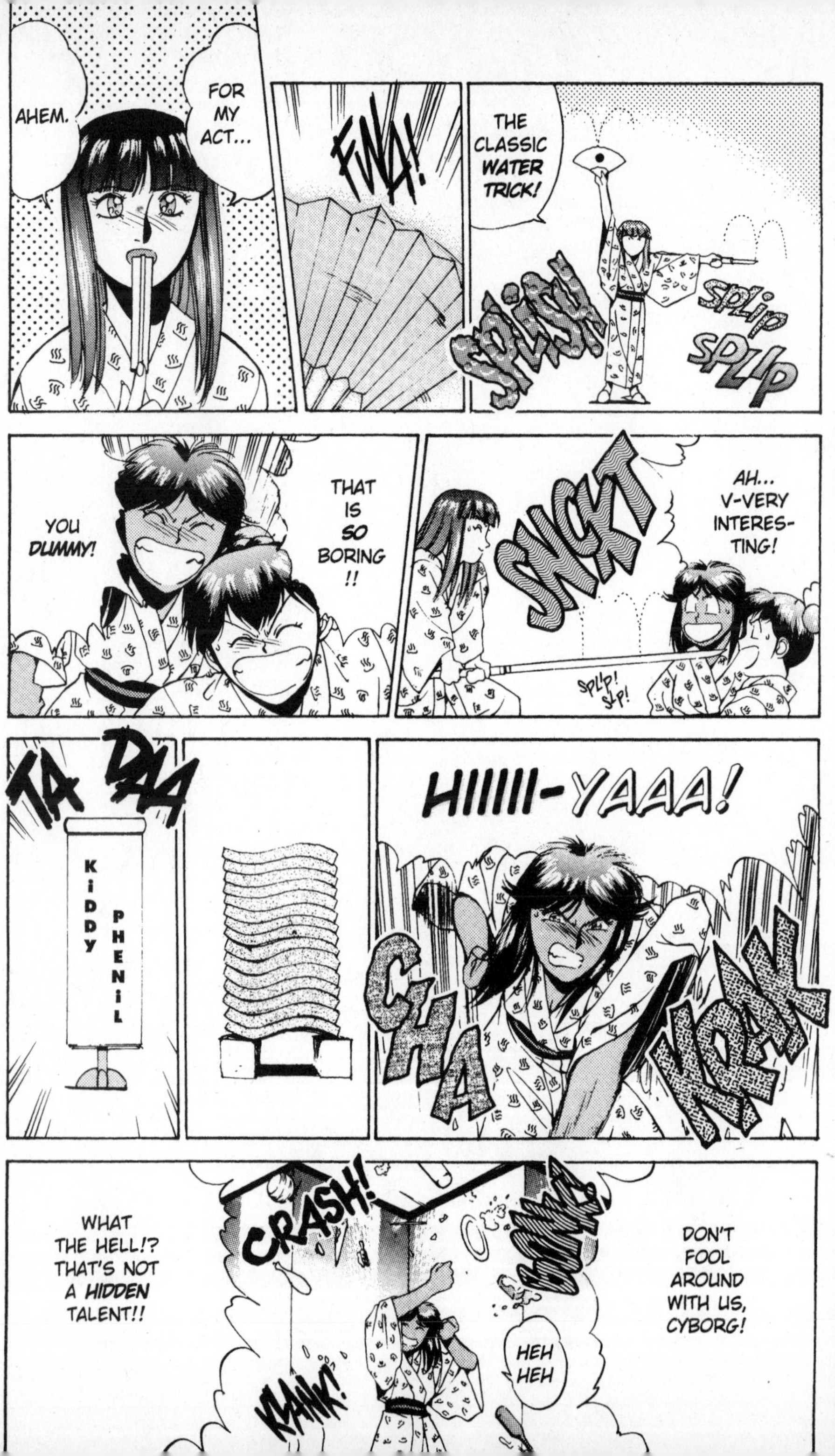
AHEM.
FOR MY ACT...
FWA!
THE CLASSIC WATER TRICK!
SPLISH
SPLIP
SPLIP
YOU DUMMY!
THAT IS SO BORING!!
SMACK
AH... V-VERY INTERES-TING!
SPLIP! SLP!
TA DAA
KIDDY PHENIL
HIIIII-YAAA!
CHA
KRAK
CRASH!
WHAT THE HELL!? THAT'S NOT A HIDDEN TALENT!!
DON'T FOOL AROUND WITH US, CYBORG!
HEH HEH
KLANK!

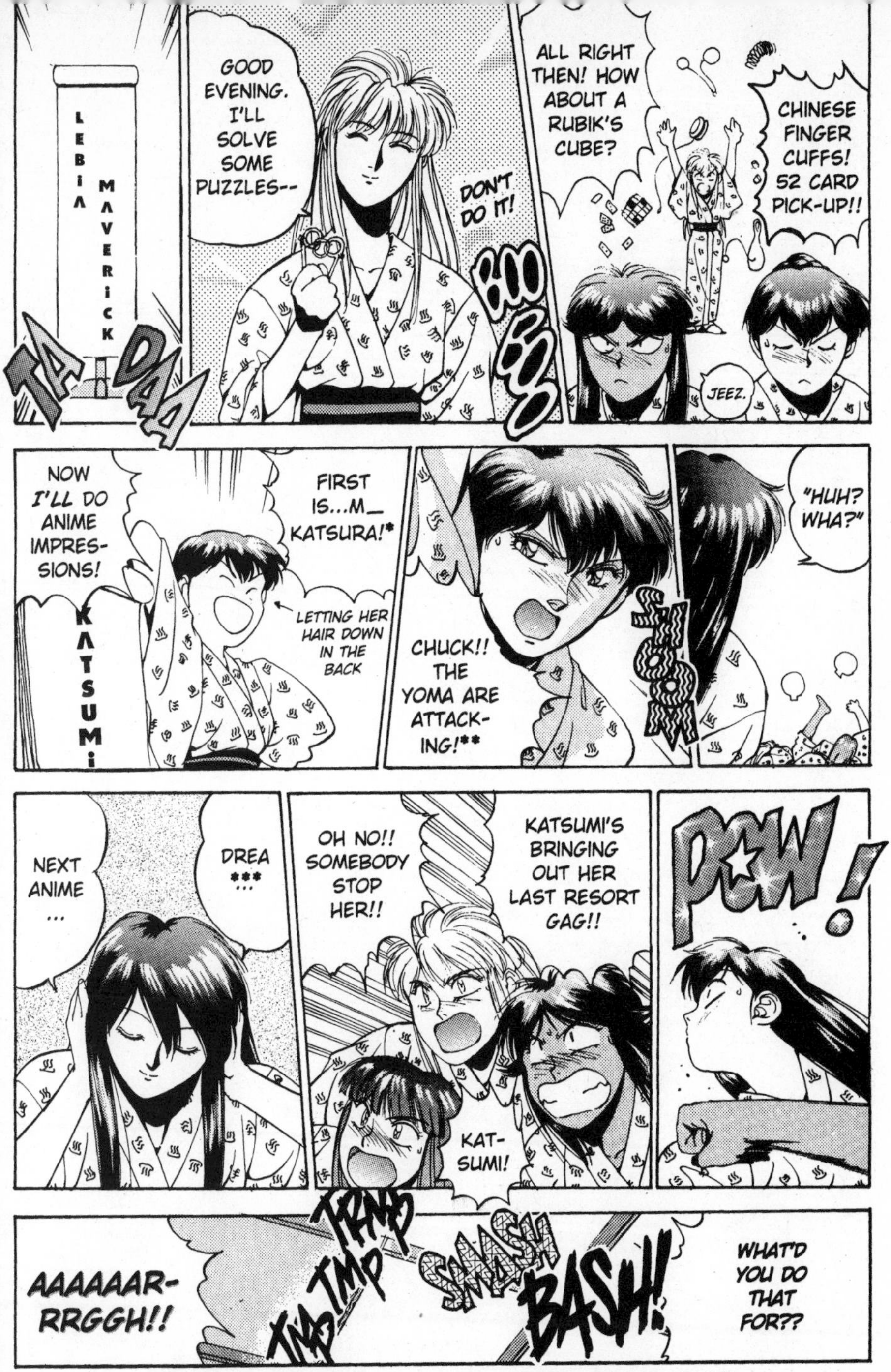
LEBIA
MAVERICK
GOOD EVENING. I'LL SOLVE SOME PUZZLES--
TA-DAA
ALL RIGHT THEN! HOW ABOUT A RUBIK'S CUBE?
CHINESE FINGER CUFFS! 52 CARD PICK-UP!!
DON'T DO IT!
BOO BOO
JEEZ.
NOW I'LL DO ANIME IMPRESSIONS!
KATSUMI
LETTING HER HAIR DOWN IN THE BACK
FIRST IS...M_ KATSURA!*
CHUCK!! THE YOMA ARE ATTACK-ING!**
"HUH? WHA?"
SHOOM
NEXT ANIME ...
DREA ***...
OH NO!! SOMEBODY STOP HER!!
KATSUMI'S BRINGING OUT HER LAST RESORT GAG!!
KAT-SUMI!
POW!
AAAAAAR-RRGGH!!
TRND TMP TMP
SMASH
BASH!
WHAT'D YOU DO THAT FOR??

*POSSIBLY MIKI KATSURA FROM MICHITAKA KIKUCHI'S ***SONIC SOLDIER BORGMAN.***

THIS COULD BE CHUCK SWAEGER, ALSO FROM ***BORGMAN.* "YOMA", THE KANJI (JAPANESE CHARACTERS) USED FOR THE MONSTERS IN BORGMAN, IS THE SAME PHRASE USED FOR THE LUCIFER HAWKS IN ***SILENT MÖBIUS.***

MAYBE A REFERENCE TO ***DREAM HUNTER REM (1985), ONE OF THE FIRST "ADULTS ONLY" OAVs. REM'S VOICE ACTRESS, NAOKO MATSUI, ALSO PLAYED KATSUMI IN THE ***SILENT MÖBIUS*** MOVIES AND MIKI IN ***BORGMAN.***

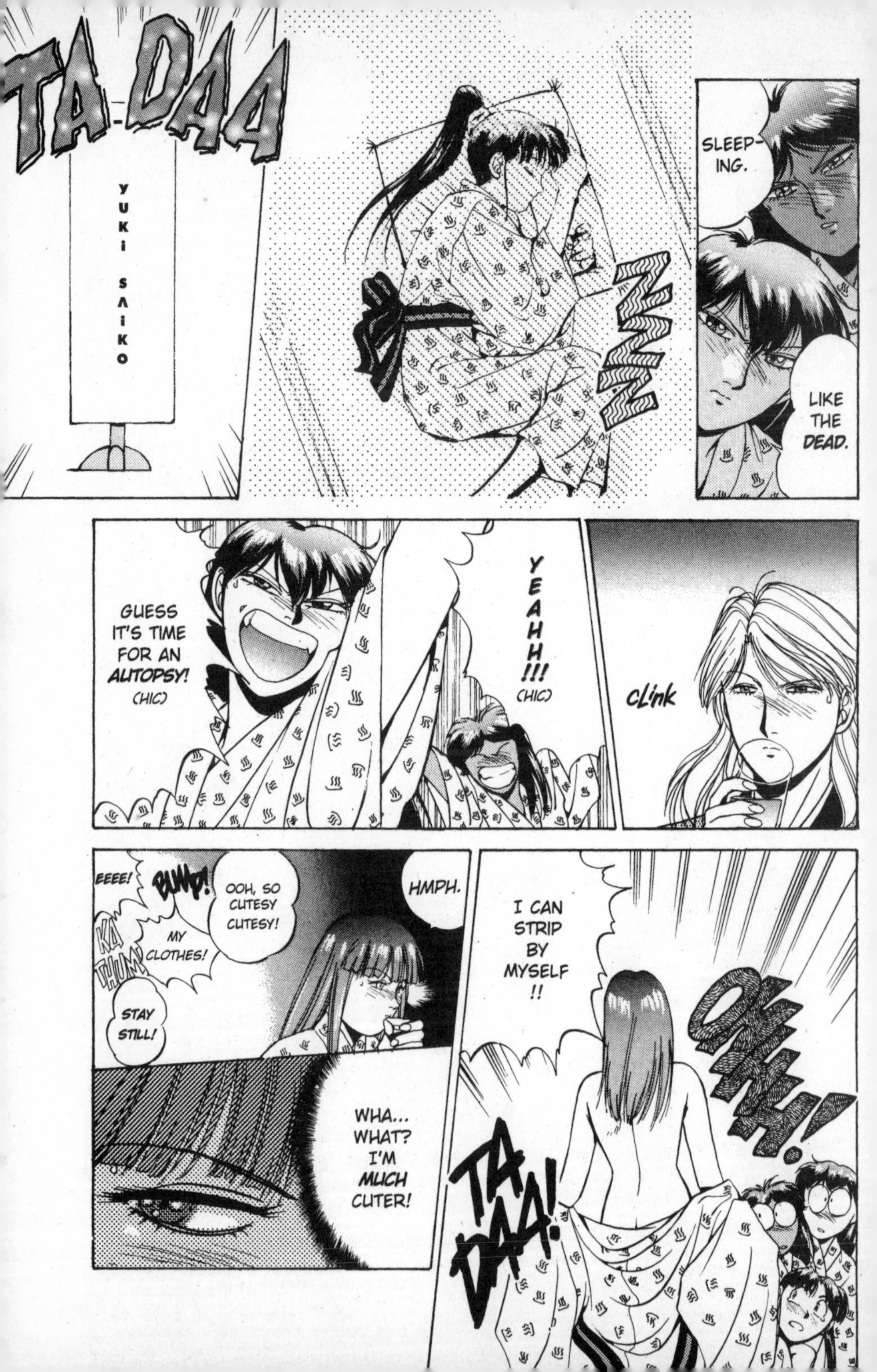
TA-DAA
YUKI SAIKO
ZWWW
SLEEP-ING.
LIKE THE DEAD.
GUESS IT'S TIME FOR AN AUTOPSY! (HIC)
YEAHHH!!! (HIC)
CLink
EEEE!
BUMP!
KA THUM
MY CLOTHES!
STAY STILL!
OOH, SO CUTESY CUTESY!
HMPH.
WHA... WHAT? I'M MUCH CUTER!
I CAN STRIP BY MYSELF !!
OHHH!!
TA DAA!

AH! WHAT'S WRONG, MANA?

MANA.

I UNDERSTAND WHY YOU'RE ANGRY...

BUT THEY'RE GOOD KIDS UNDERNEATH.

OH...SUPERINTENDENT RALLY. I'M SORRY. I DRANK TOO MUCH...

HUH?

THE PARTY CONTINUED UNTIL THE NEXT MORNING.

FIGHT ON, A.M.P.!! DON'T LOSE, A.M.P.!! A.M.P., THERE'S NO TIME TO GET DRUNK!!

SILENT MÖBIUS

CHAPTER 12:

LABYRINTH

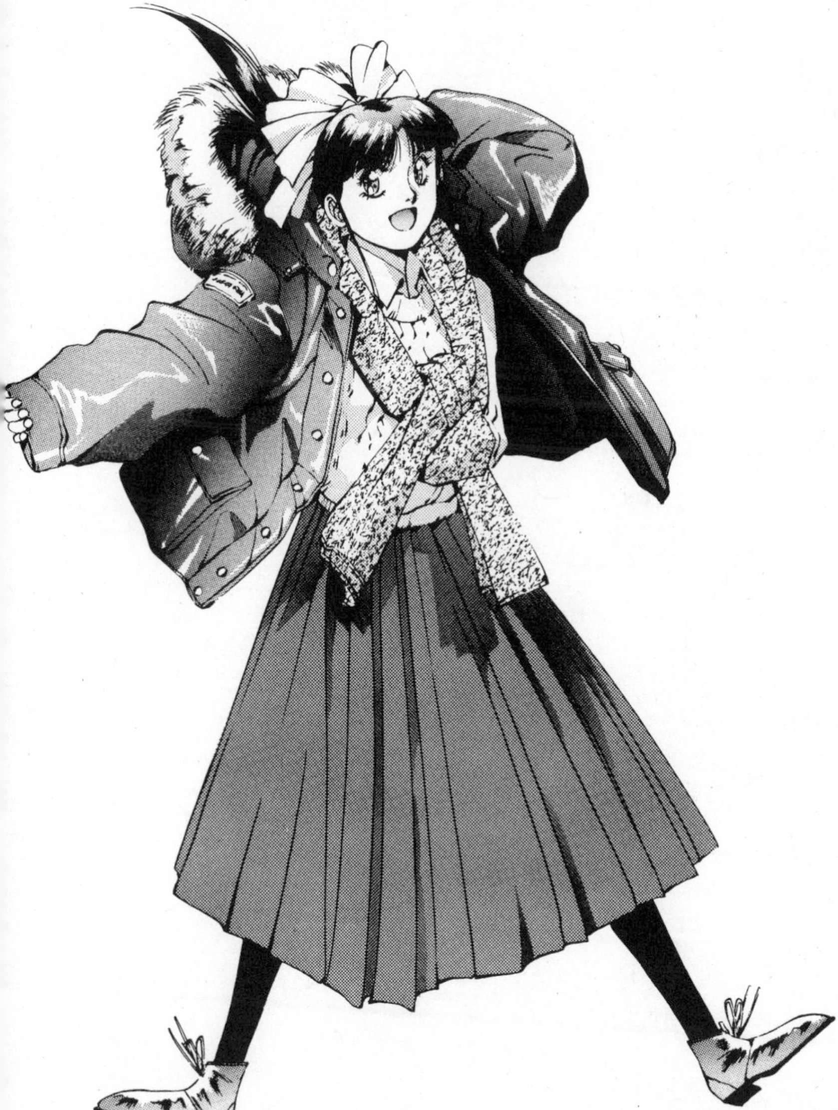

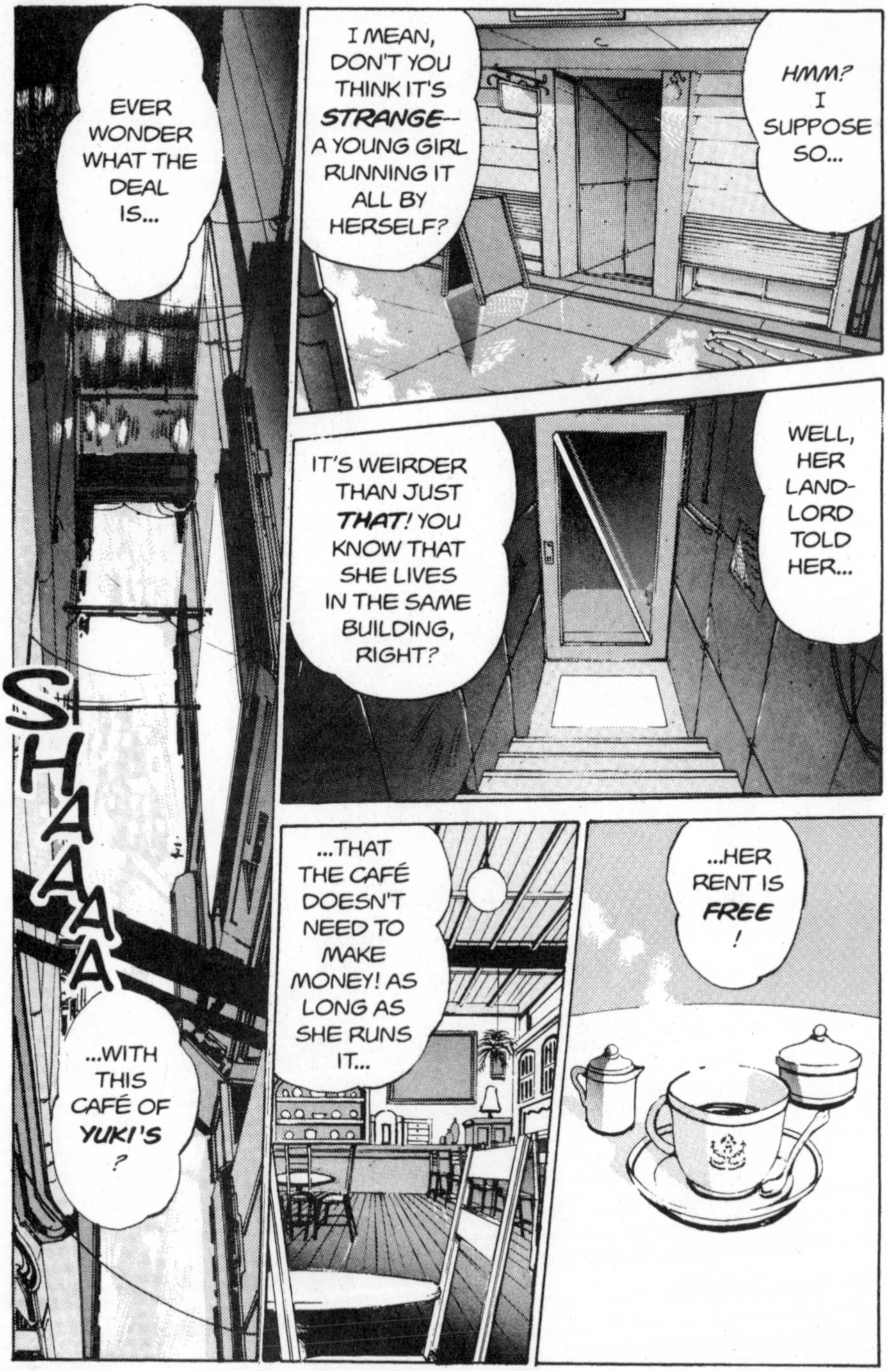
EVER WONDER WHAT THE DEAL IS...
SHAAAAA
...WITH THIS CAFÉ OF YUKI'S?
I MEAN, DON'T YOU THINK IT'S STRANGE-- A YOUNG GIRL RUNNING IT ALL BY HERSELF?
HMM? I SUPPOSE SO...
IT'S WEIRDER THAN JUST THAT! YOU KNOW THAT SHE LIVES IN THE SAME BUILDING, RIGHT?
WELL, HER LAND-LORD TOLD HER...
...THAT THE CAFÉ DOESN'T NEED TO MAKE MONEY! AS LONG AS SHE RUNS IT...
...HER RENT IS FREE!

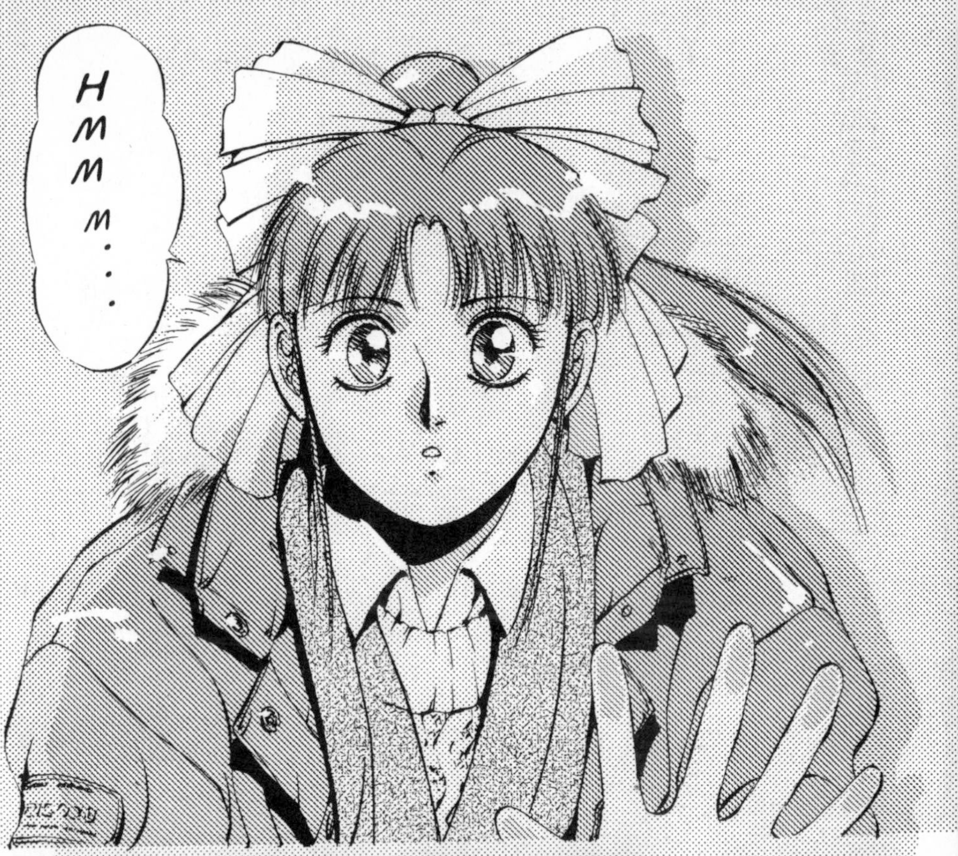
HMMM...

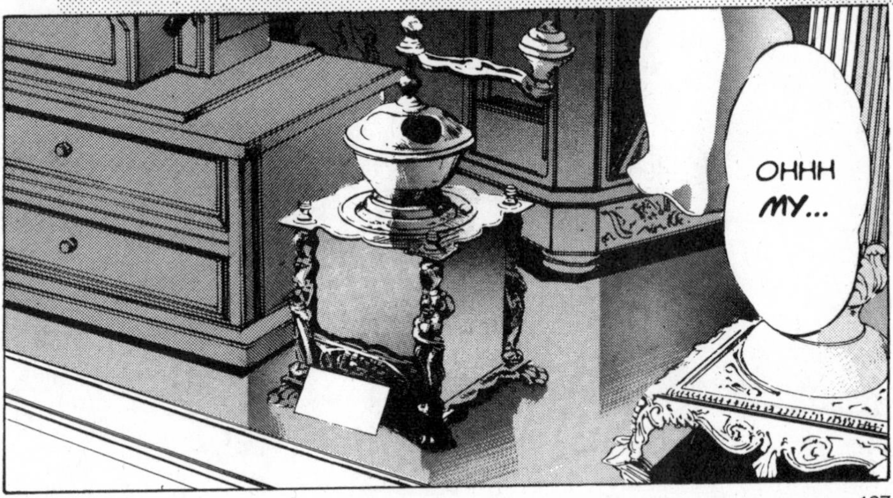
OHHH MY...

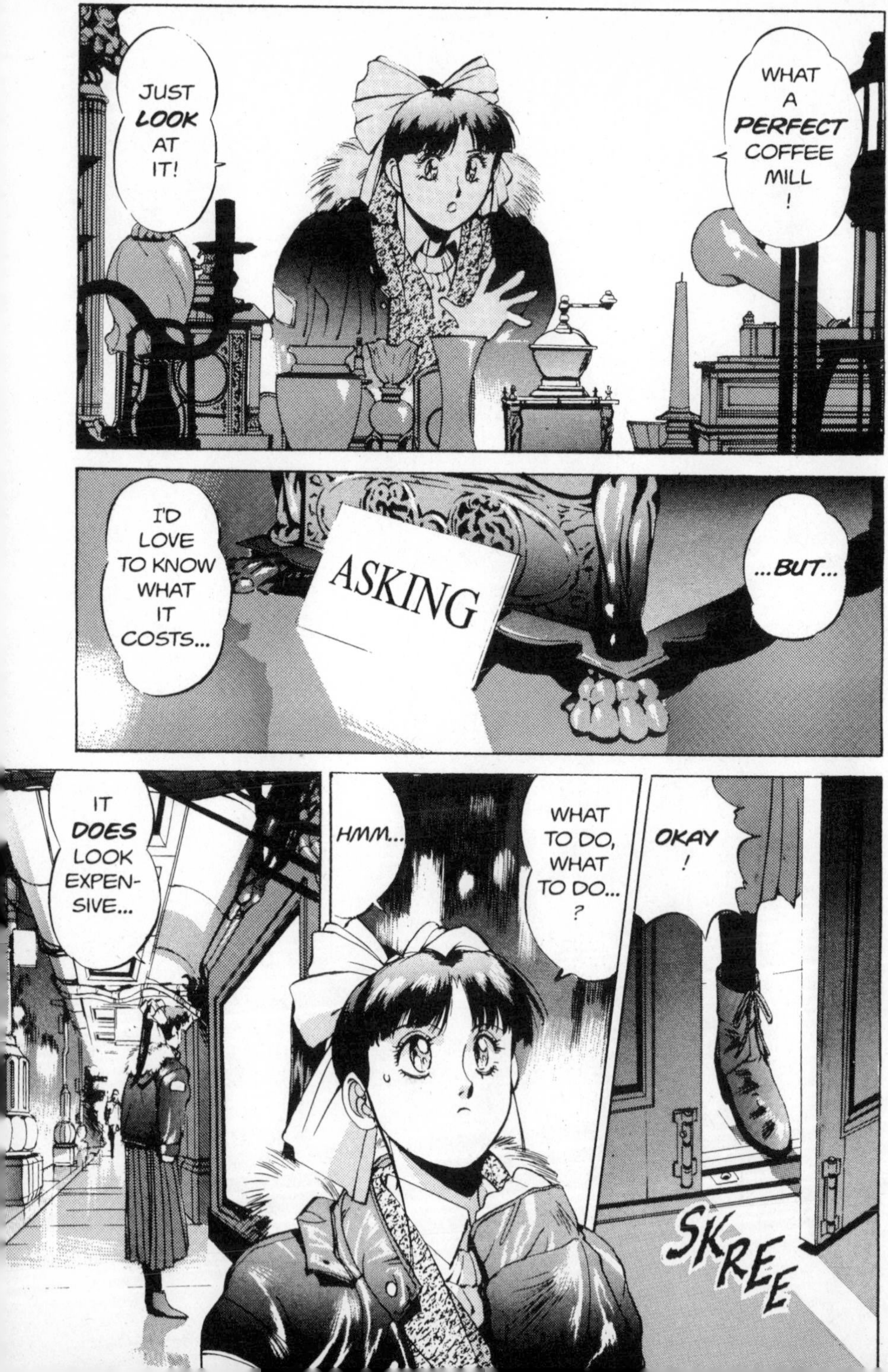
JUST LOOK AT IT!
WHAT A PERFECT COFFEE MILL!
I'D LOVE TO KNOW WHAT IT COSTS...
ASKING
...BUT...
IT DOES LOOK EXPEN-SIVE...
HMM...
WHAT TO DO, WHAT TO DO...?
OKAY!
SKREEE

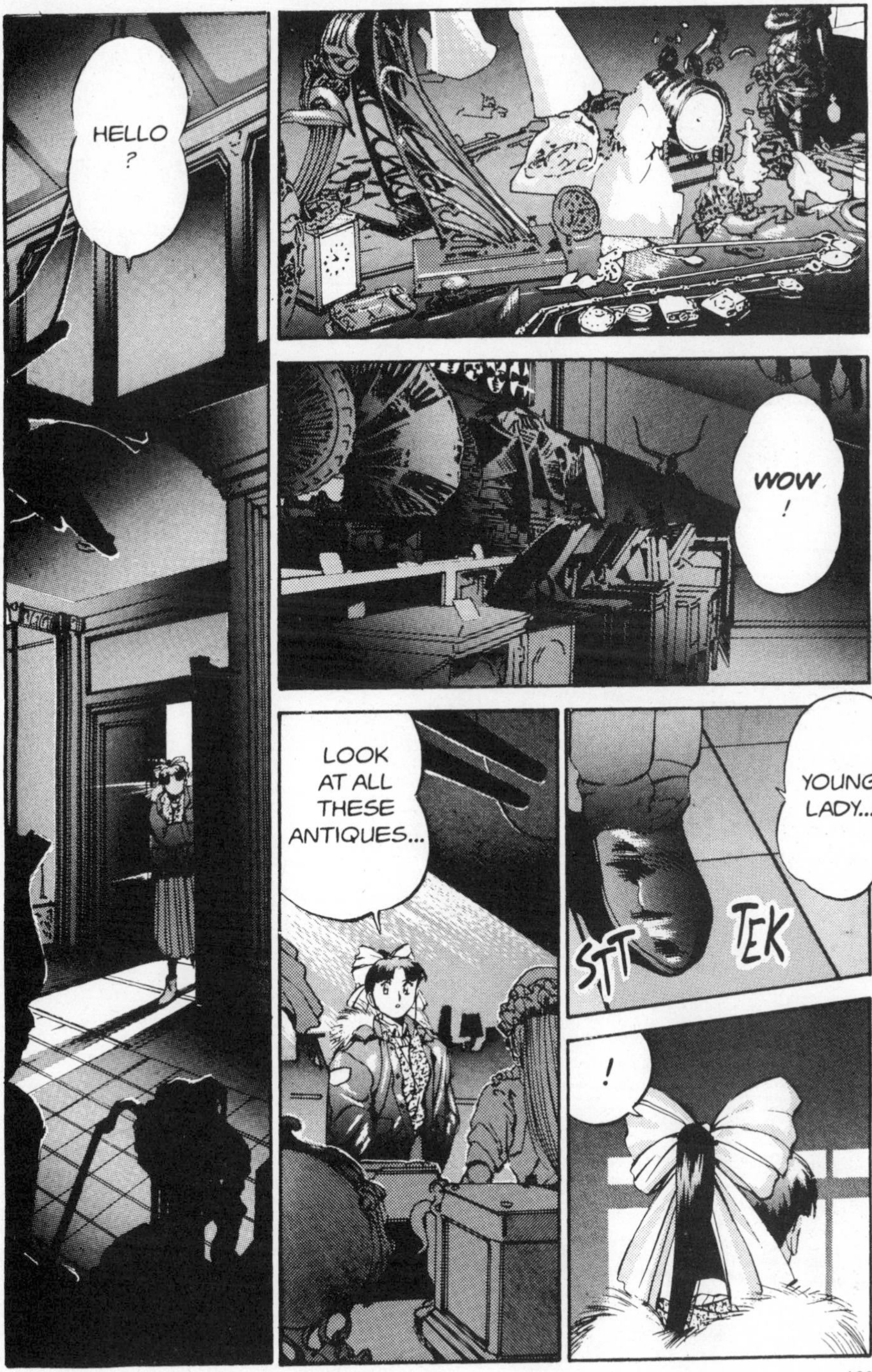
HELLO ?
WOW !
LOOK AT ALL THESE ANTIQUES...
YOUNG LADY...
STT
TEK
!

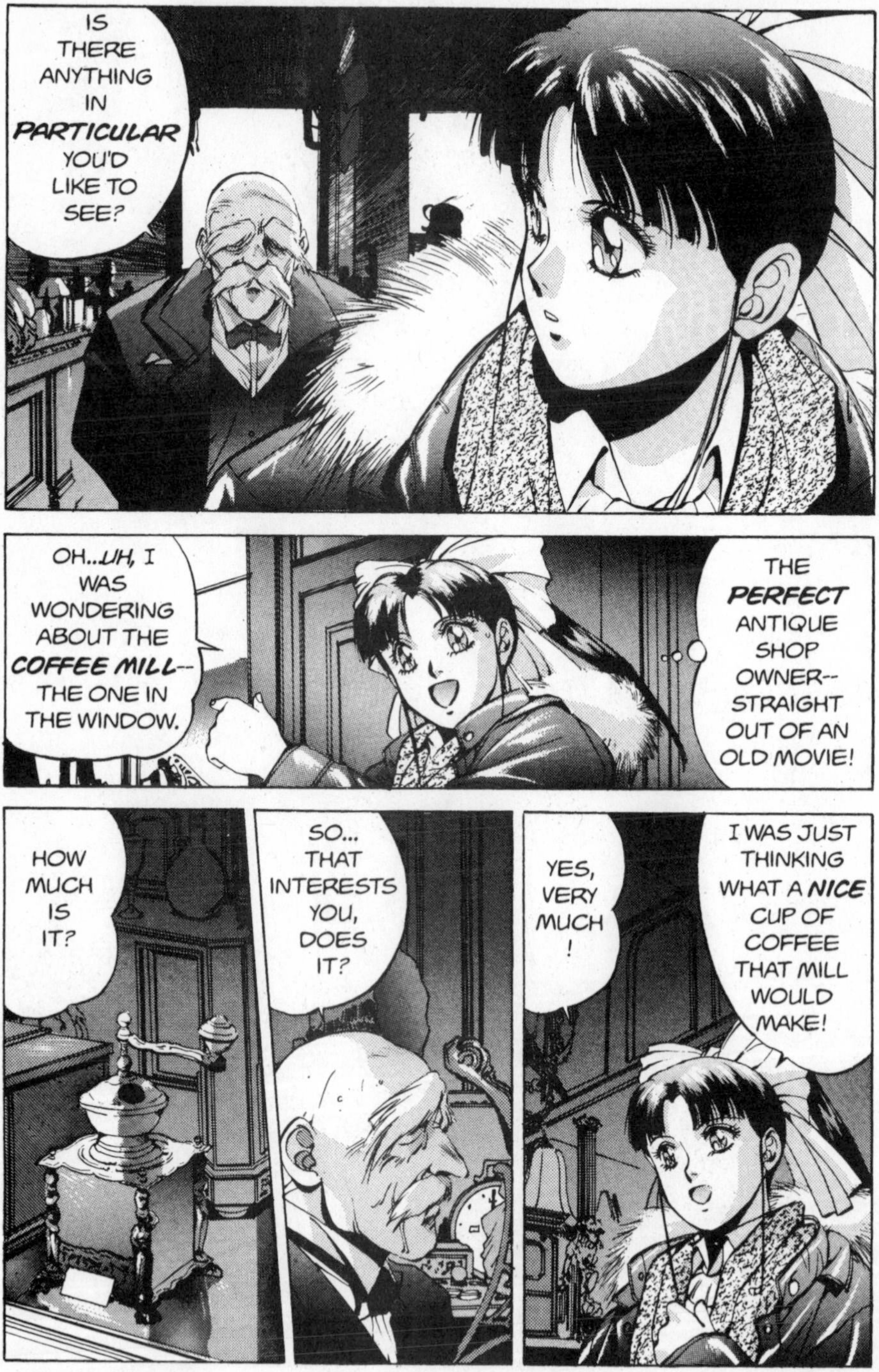
IS THERE ANYTHING IN PARTICULAR YOU'D LIKE TO SEE?
OH...UH, I WAS WONDERING ABOUT THE COFFEE MILL-- THE ONE IN THE WINDOW.
THE PERFECT ANTIQUE SHOP OWNER-- STRAIGHT OUT OF AN OLD MOVIE!
HOW MUCH IS IT?
SO... THAT INTERESTS YOU, DOES IT?
YES, VERY MUCH!
I WAS JUST THINKING WHAT A NICE CUP OF COFFEE THAT MILL WOULD MAKE!

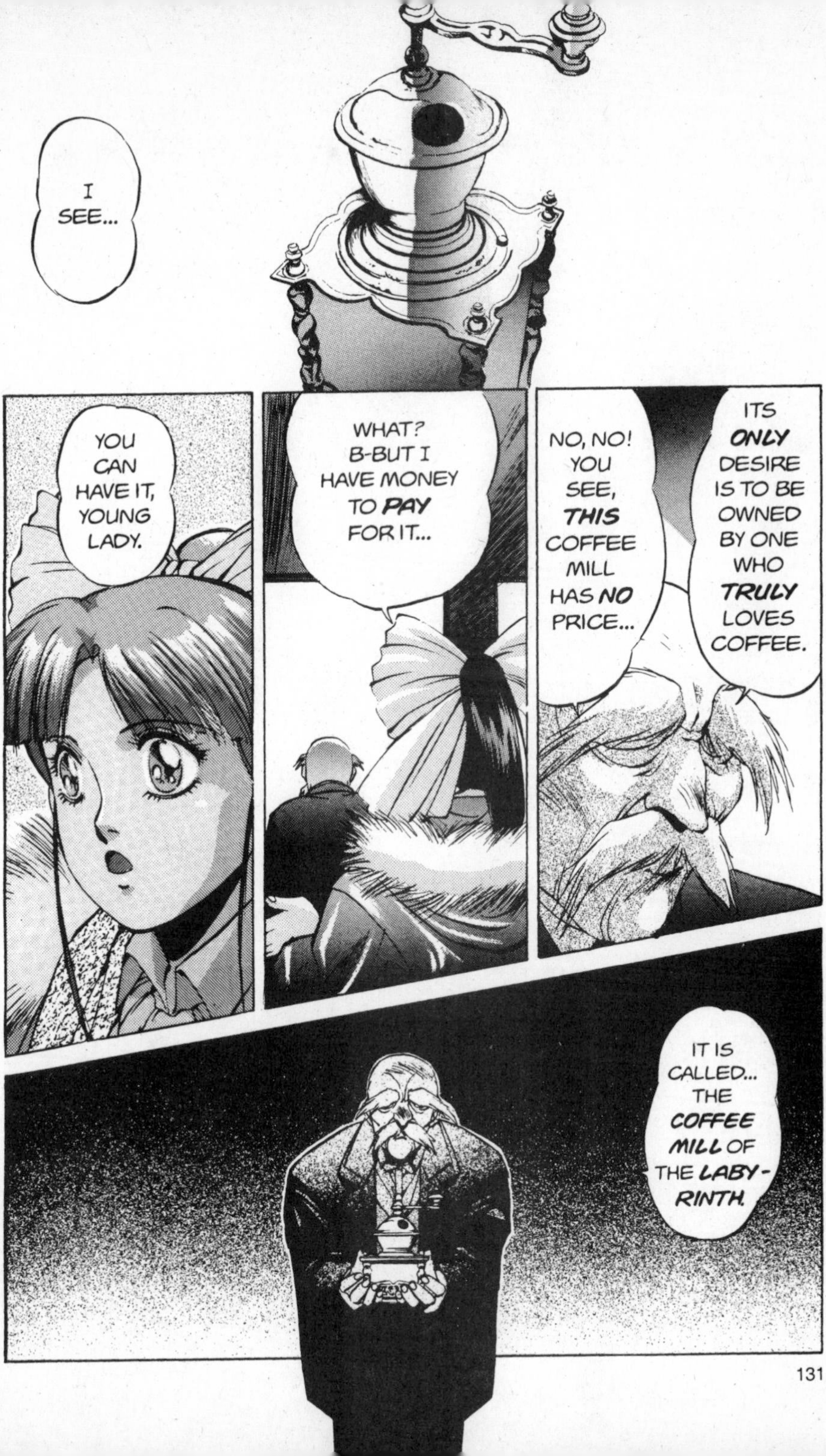
I SEE...
YOU CAN HAVE IT, YOUNG LADY.
WHAT? B-BUT I HAVE MONEY TO PAY FOR IT...
NO, NO! YOU SEE, THIS COFFEE MILL HAS NO PRICE...
ITS ONLY DESIRE IS TO BE OWNED BY ONE WHO TRULY LOVES COFFEE.
IT IS CALLED... THE COFFEE MILL OF THE LABY-RINTH.

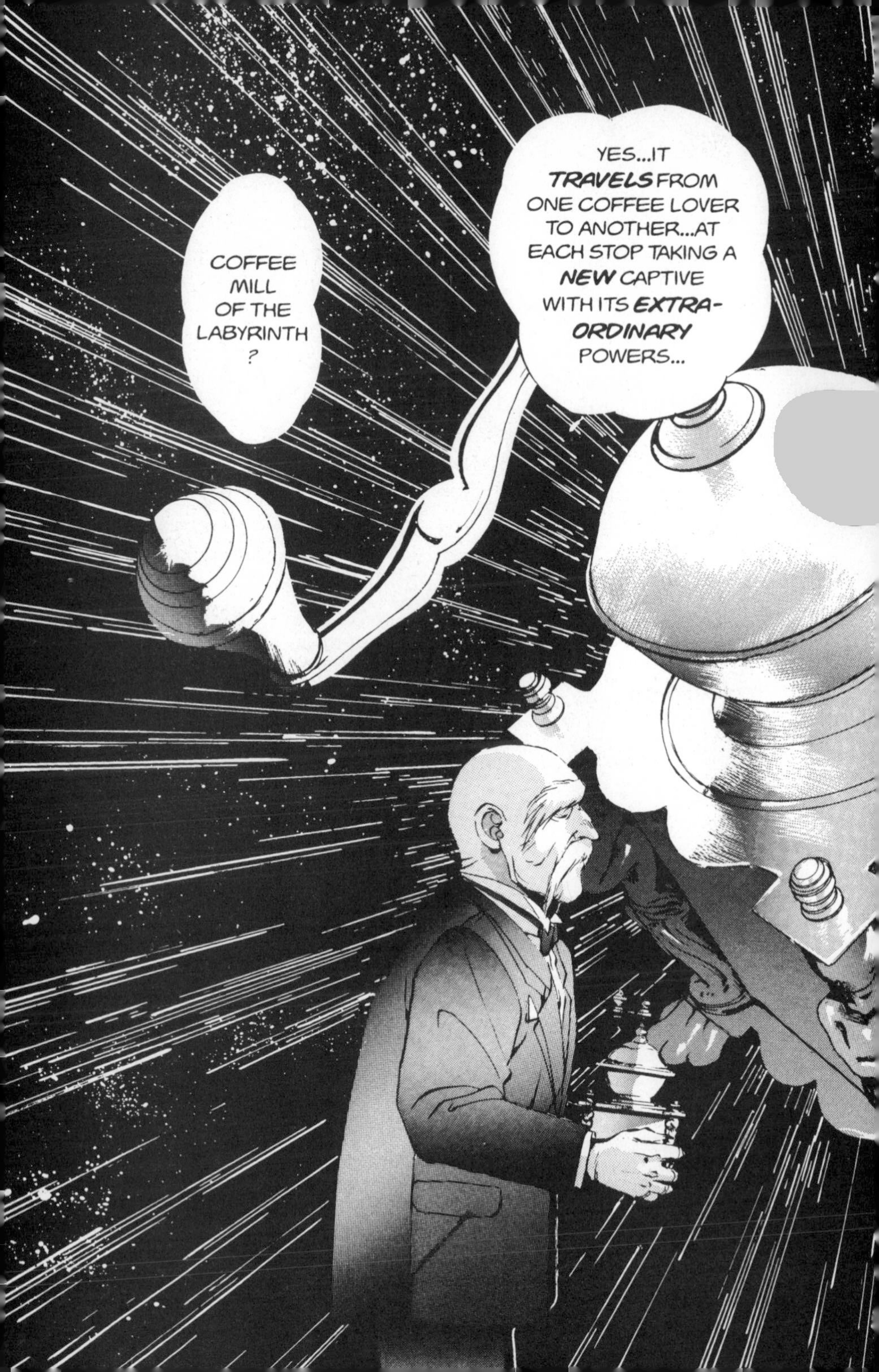
COFFEE MILL OF THE LABYRINTH ?
YES...IT TRAVELS FROM ONE COFFEE LOVER TO ANOTHER...AT EACH STOP TAKING A NEW CAPTIVE WITH ITS EXTRA-ORDINARY POWERS...

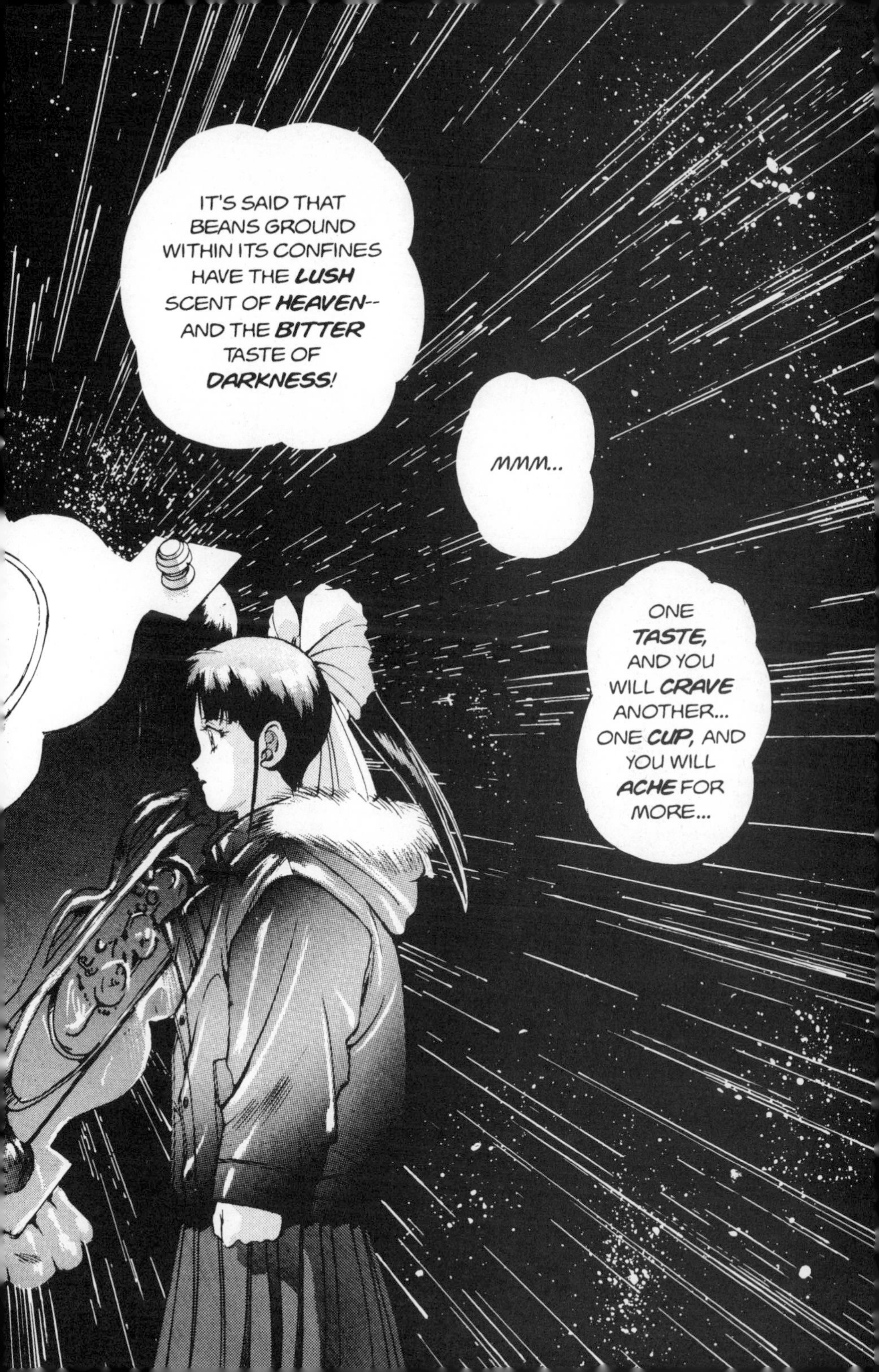
IT'S SAID THAT BEANS GROUND WITHIN ITS CONFINES HAVE THE LUSH SCENT OF HEAVEN-- AND THE BITTER TASTE OF DARKNESS!
MMM...
ONE TASTE, AND YOU WILL CRAVE ANOTHER... ONE CUP, AND YOU WILL ACHE FOR MORE...

OVER AND OVER...
SKRRNGH
OVER...
...AND OVER.
SKRRNSH
SKRNGH
AGAIN AND AGAIN...
SKRRNCH
SKRRNGH
SKRRRN

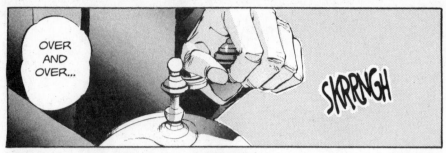

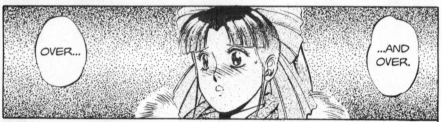

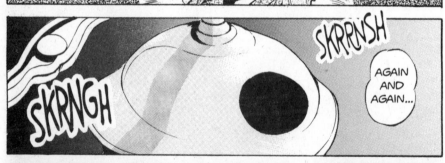

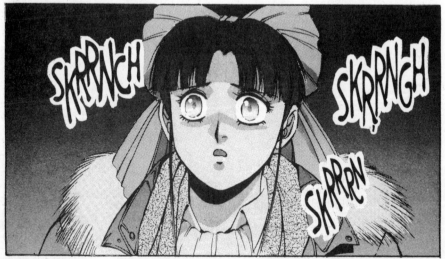

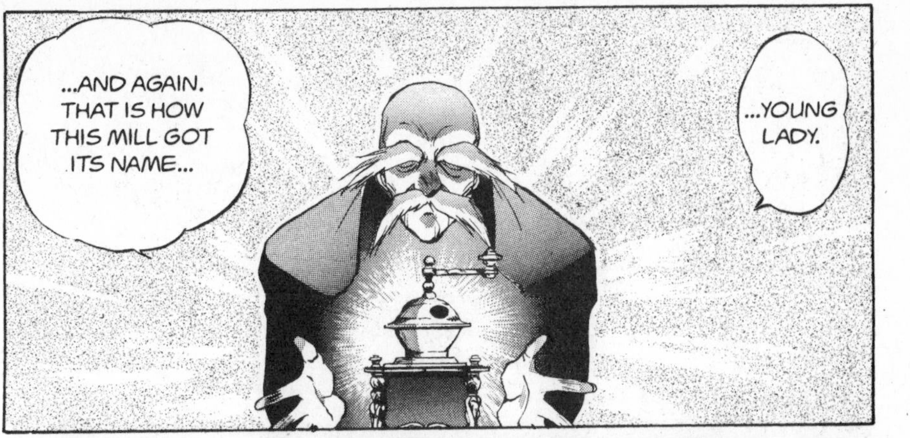
...AND AGAIN. THAT IS HOW THIS MILL GOT ITS NAME...
...YOUNG LADY.
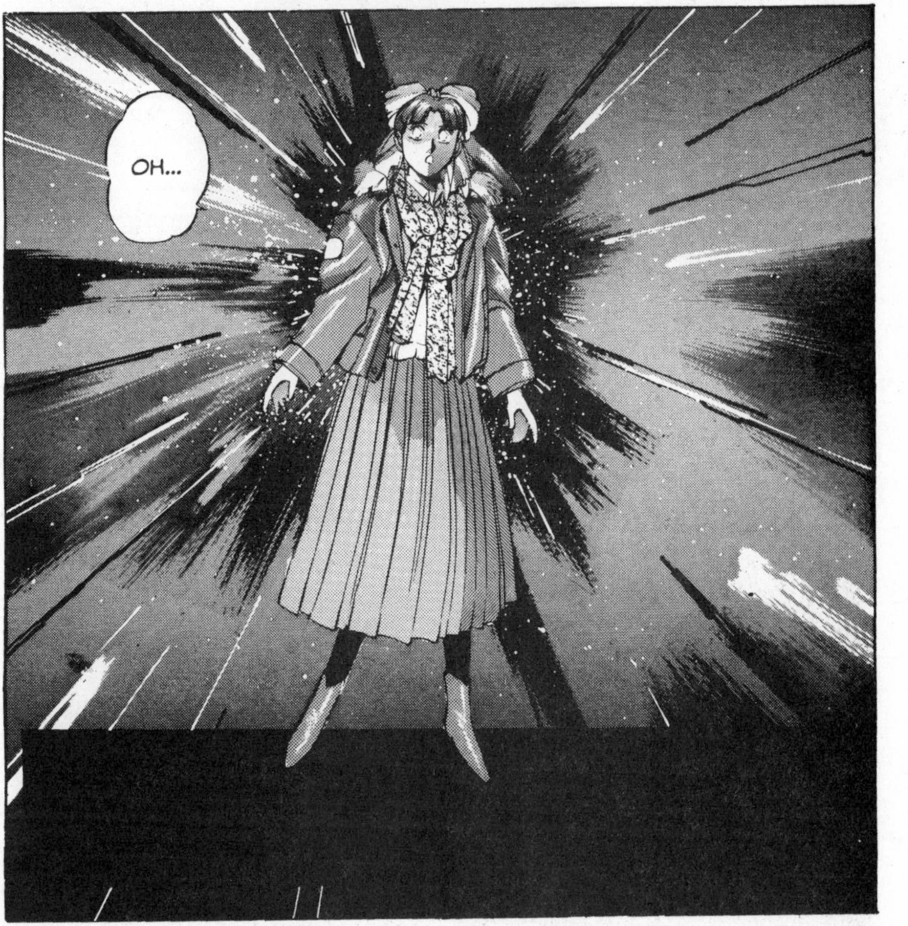
OH...

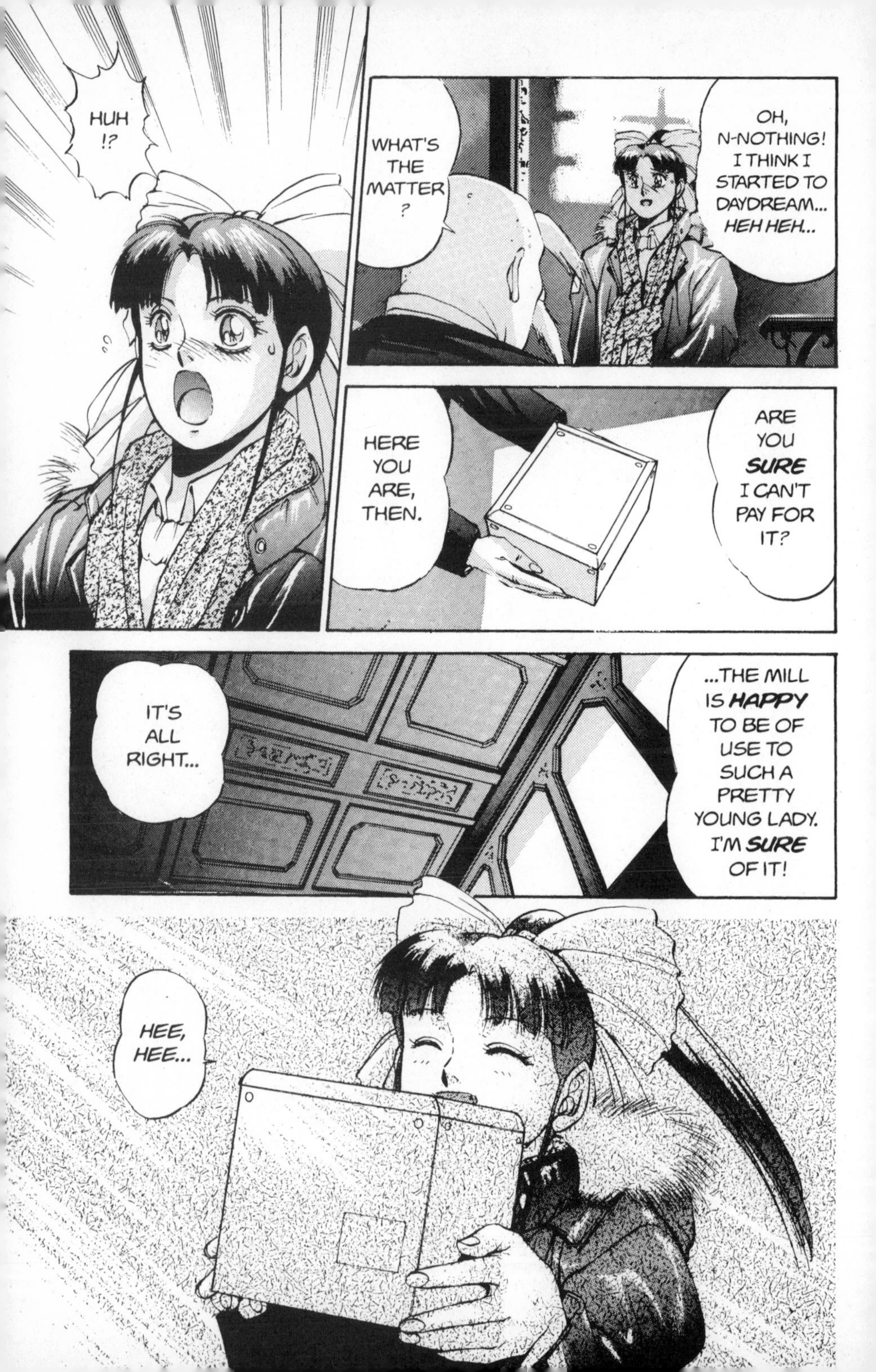
HUH !?
WHAT'S THE MATTER ?
OH, N-NOTHING! I THINK I STARTED TO DAYDREAM... HEH HEH...
HERE YOU ARE, THEN.
ARE YOU SURE I CAN'T PAY FOR IT?
IT'S ALL RIGHT...
...THE MILL IS HAPPY TO BE OF USE TO SUCH A PRETTY YOUNG LADY. I'M SURE OF IT!
HEE, HEE...

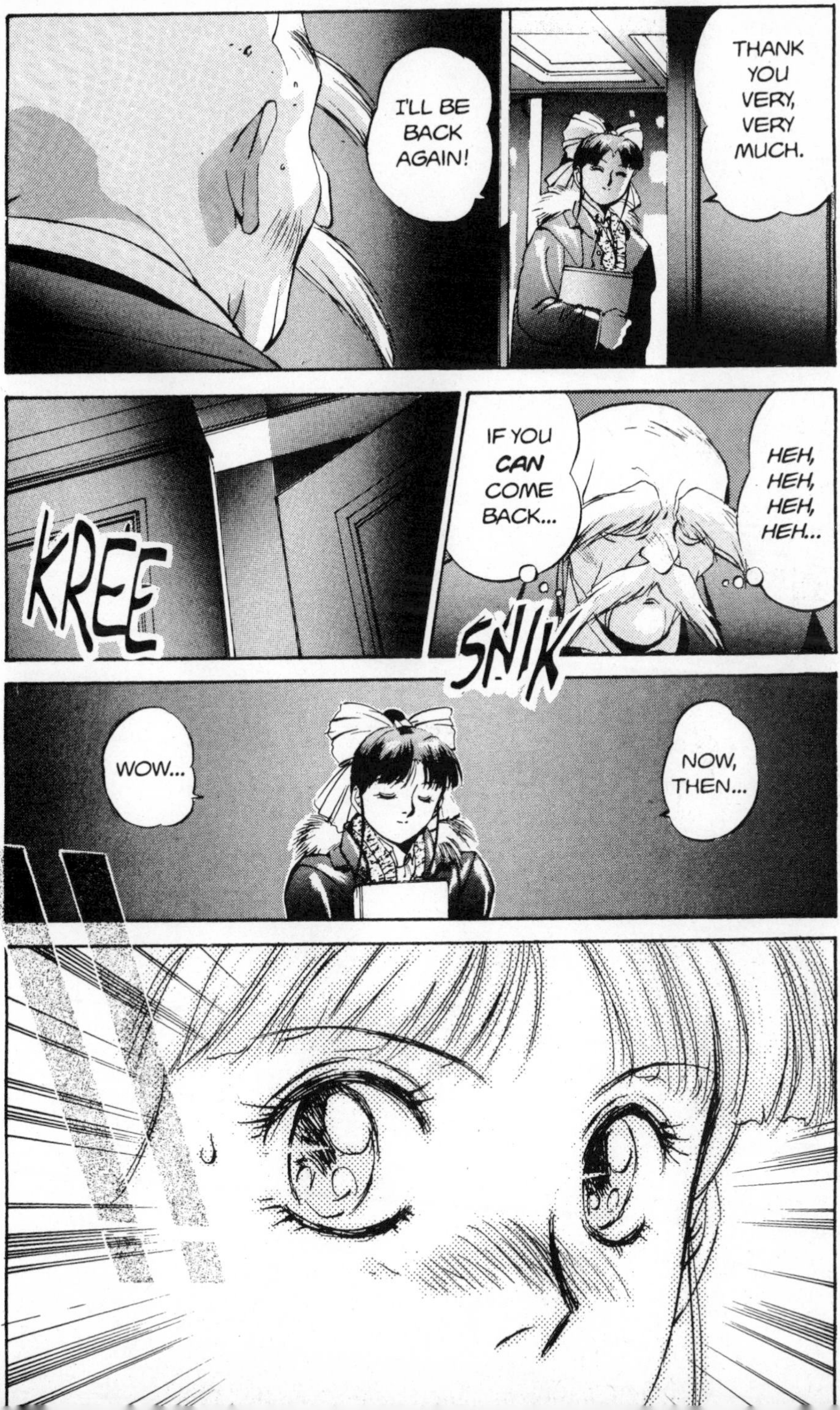
I'LL BE BACK AGAIN!
THANK YOU VERY, VERY MUCH.
KREE
IF YOU CAN COME BACK...
HEH, HEH, HEH, HEH...
SNIK
WOW...
NOW, THEN...

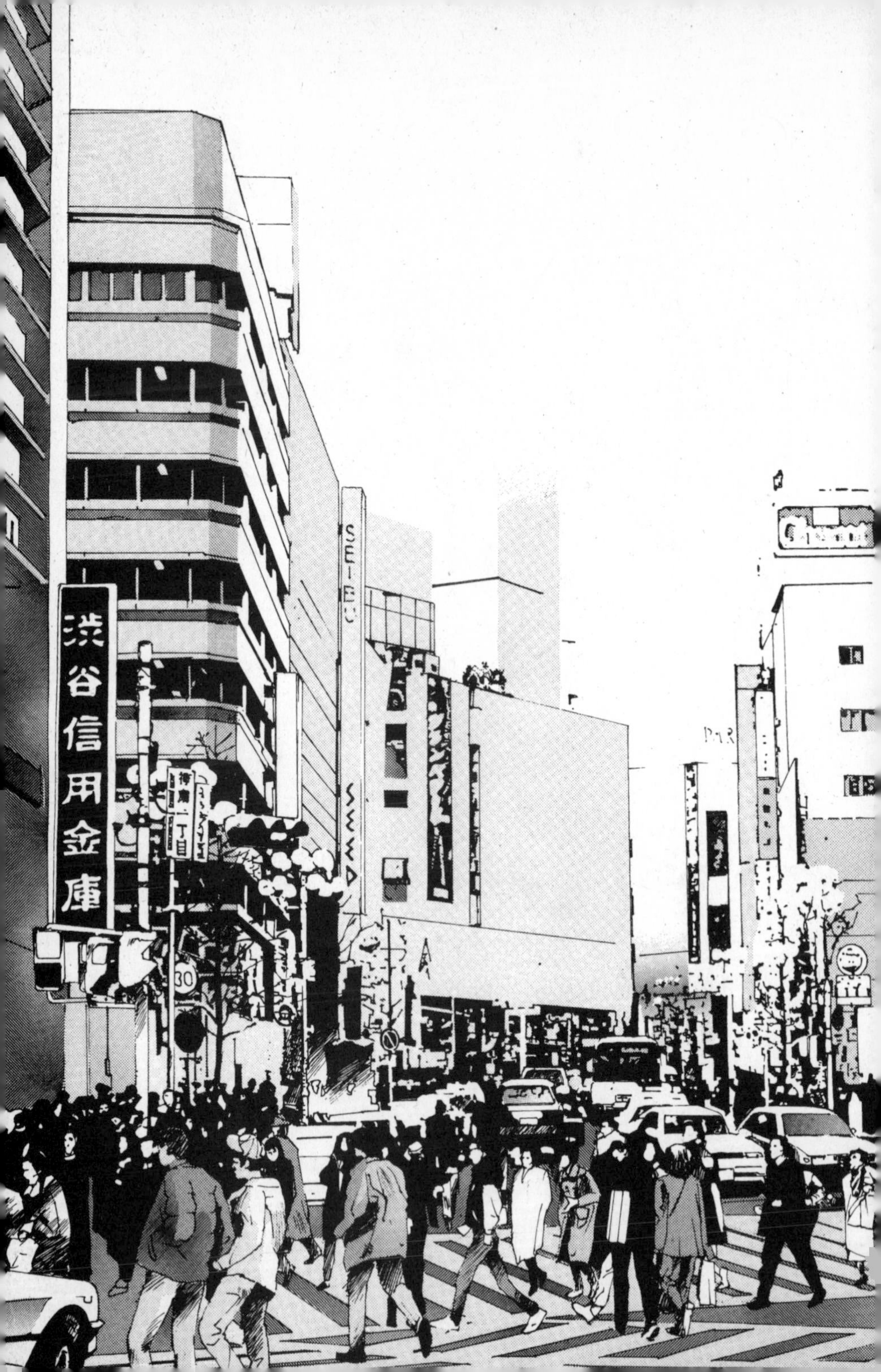
渋谷信用金庫
SEIBU
SEED
30

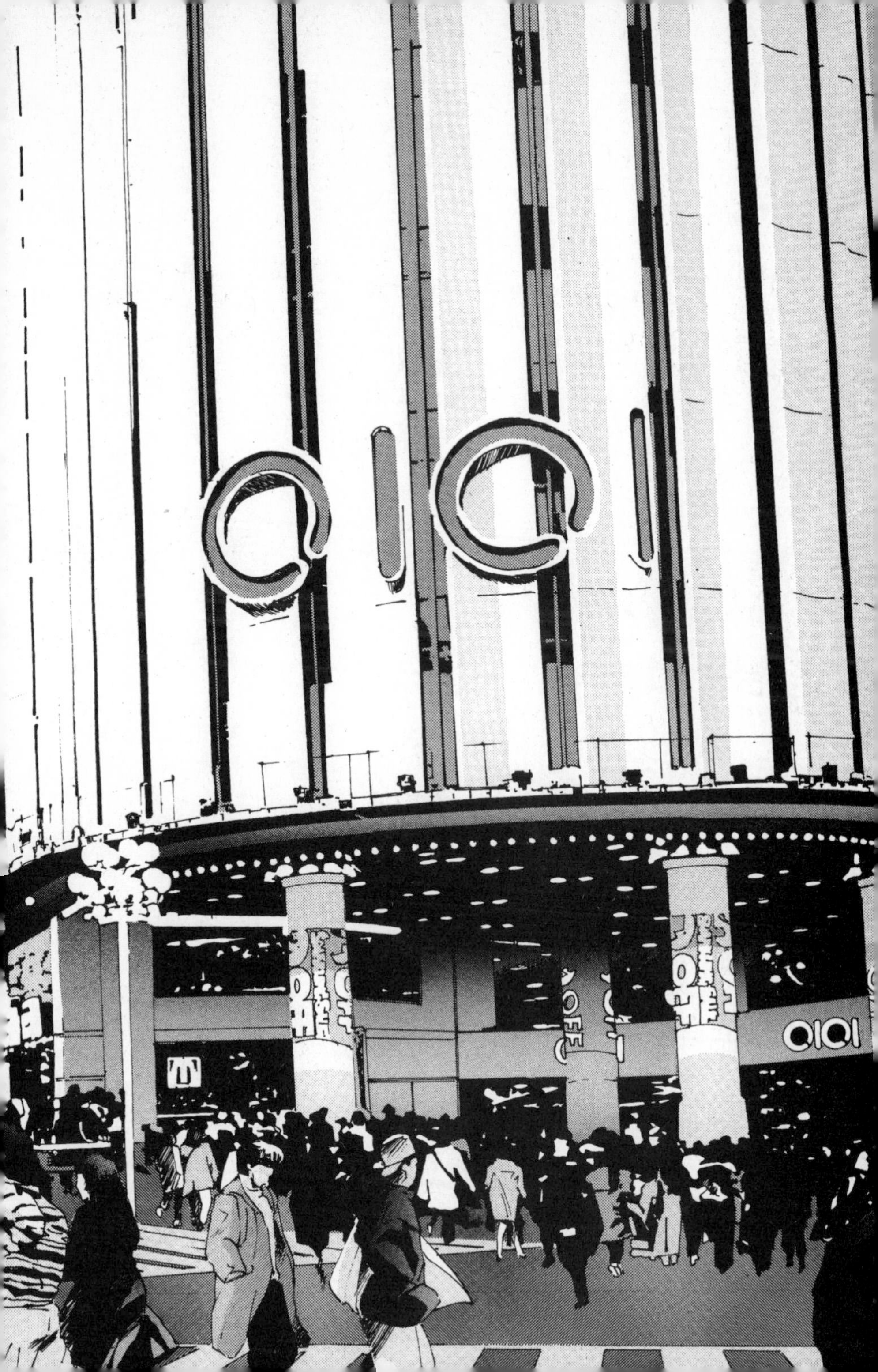
OIOI

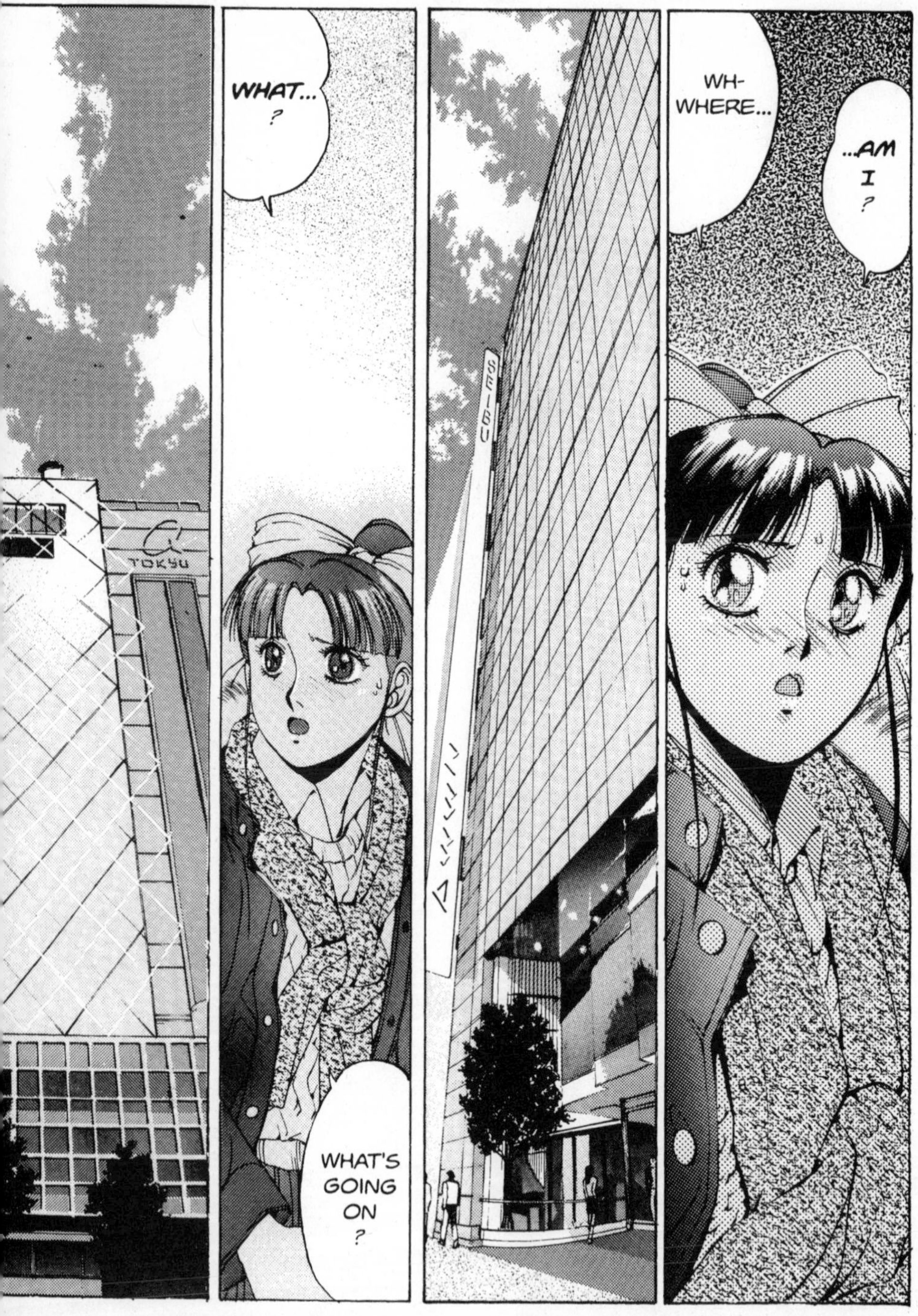
TOKYU
WHAT... ?
WHAT'S GOING ON ?
SEIBU
WH- WHERE...
...AM I ?

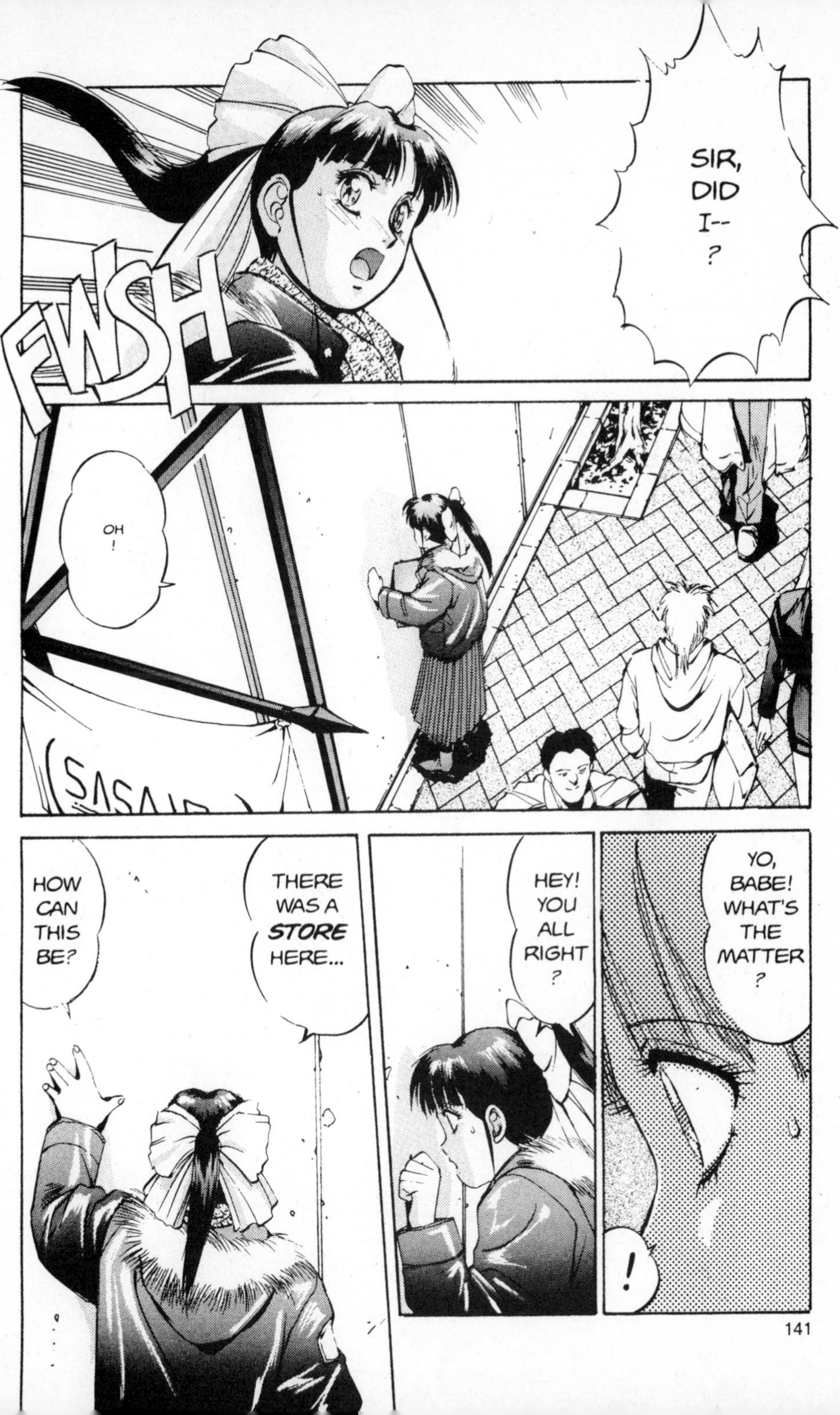
FWSH
SIR, DID I-- ?
OH !
HOW CAN THIS BE?
THERE WAS A **STORE** HERE...
HEY! YOU ALL RIGHT ?
YO, BABE! WHAT'S THE MATTER ?
!

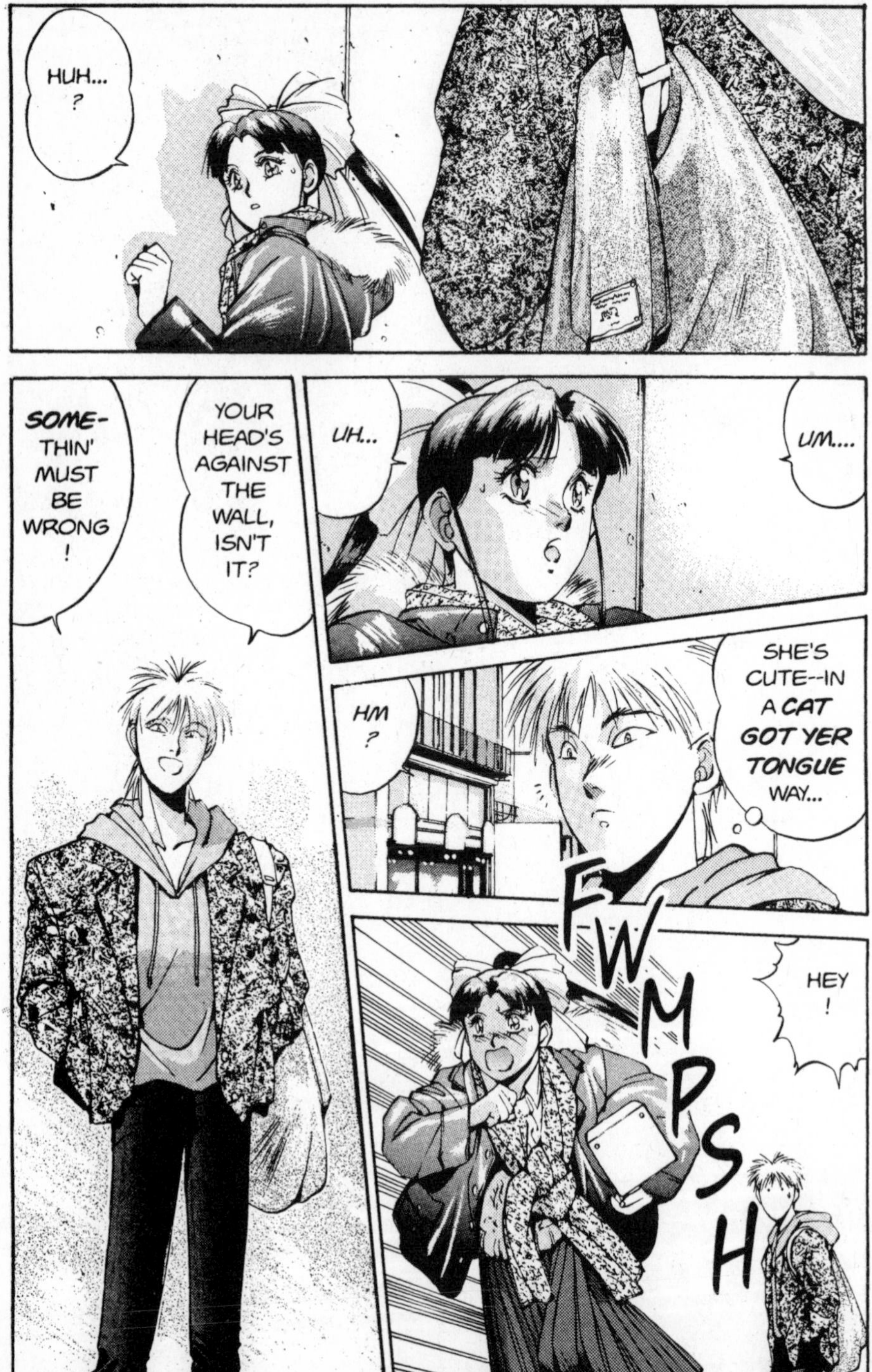
HUH... ?
SOME-THIN' MUST BE WRONG!
YOUR HEAD'S AGAINST THE WALL, ISN'T IT?
UH...
UM....
HM ?
SHE'S CUTE--IN A CAT GOT YER TONGUE WAY...
FWMPSH
HEY !

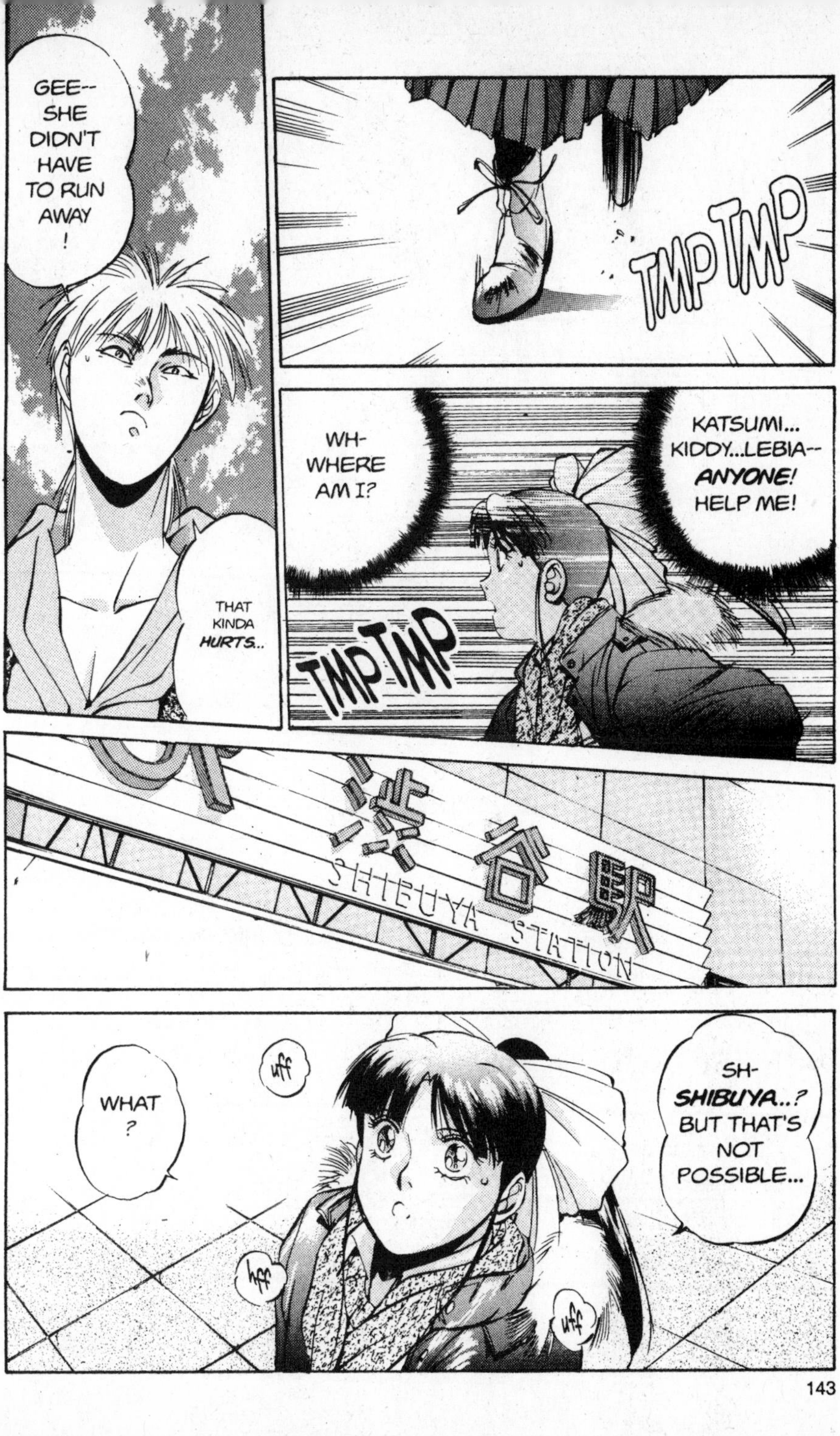
GEE-- SHE DIDN'T HAVE TO RUN AWAY !
THAT KINDA **HURTS**...
TMP TMP
WH- WHERE AM I?
KATSUMI... KIDDY...LEBIA-- **ANYONE!** HELP ME!
TMP TMP
SHIBUYA STATION
WHAT ?
uff
SH- **SHIBUYA**...? BUT THAT'S NOT POSSIBLE...
hff
uff

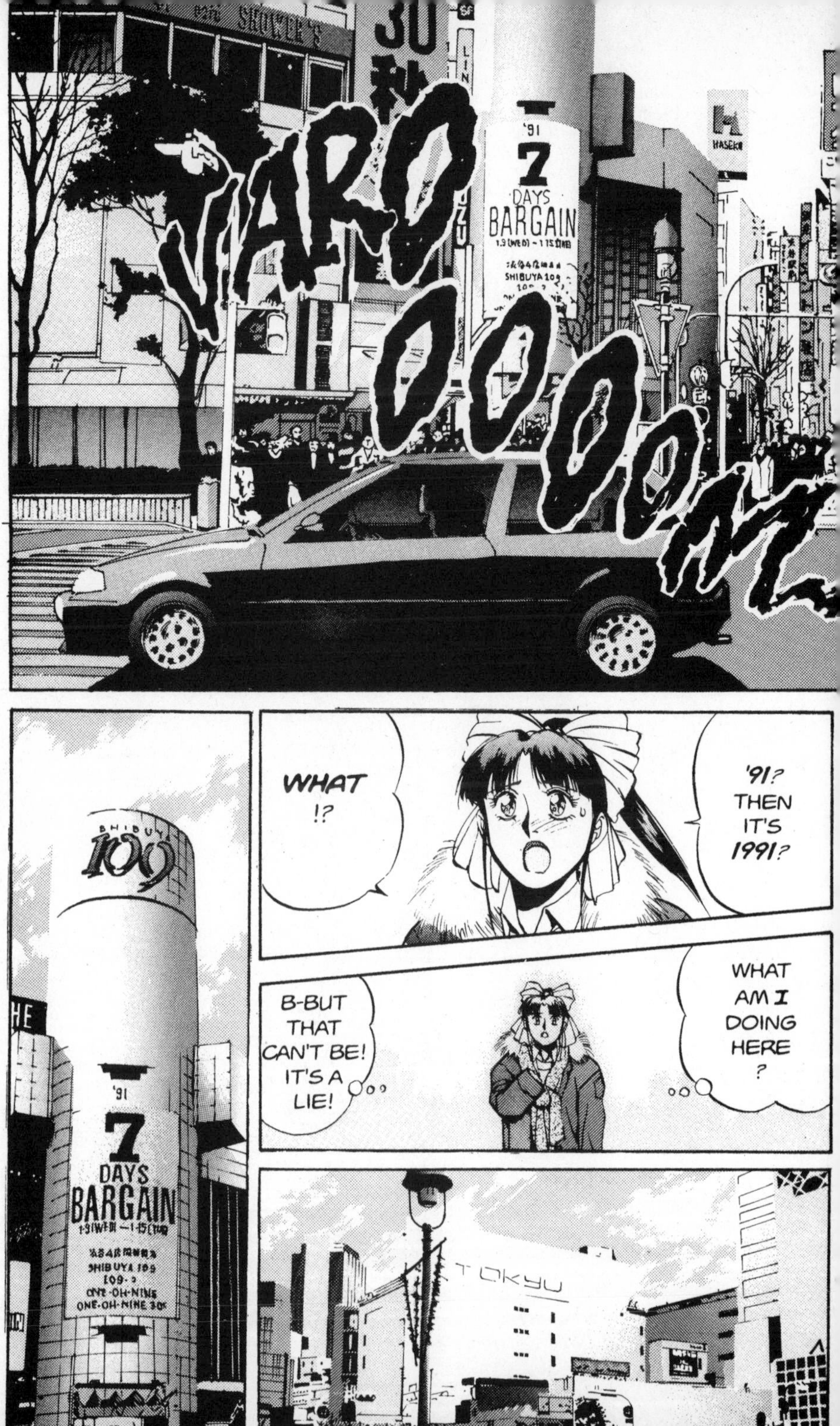
SHOWER'S
'91
7
DAYS
BARGAIN
SHIBUYA 109
VAROOOOOM
SHIBUYA
109
'91
7
DAYS
BARGAIN
SHIBUYA 109
ONE-OH-NINE
WHAT !?
'91? THEN IT'S 1991?
B-BUT THAT CAN'T BE! IT'S A LIE!
WHAT AM I DOING HERE?
TOKYU

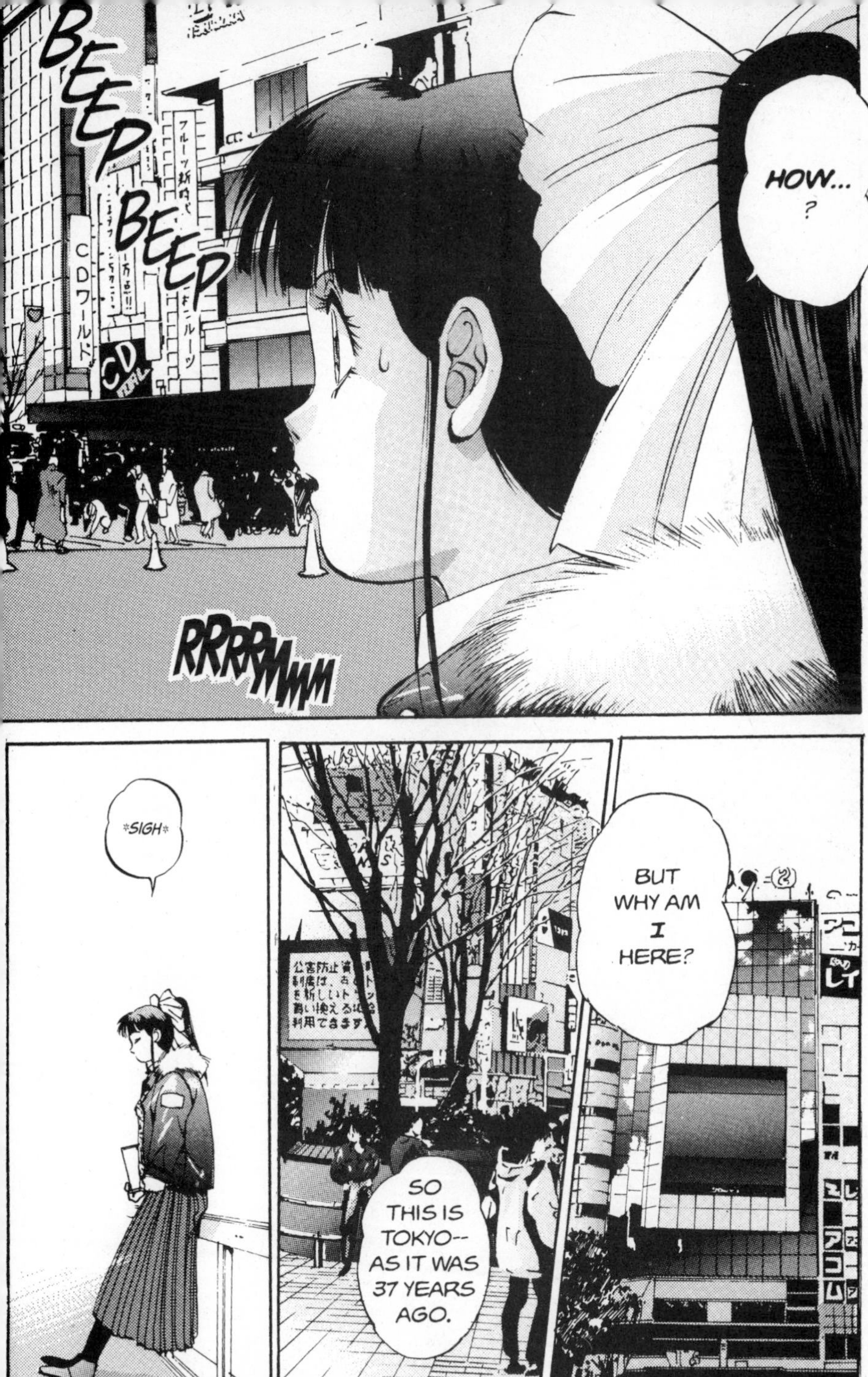
BEEP
BEEP
CDワールド
HOW...?
RRRRMMM
SIGH
SO THIS IS TOKYO-- AS IT WAS 37 YEARS AGO.
BUT WHY AM I HERE?

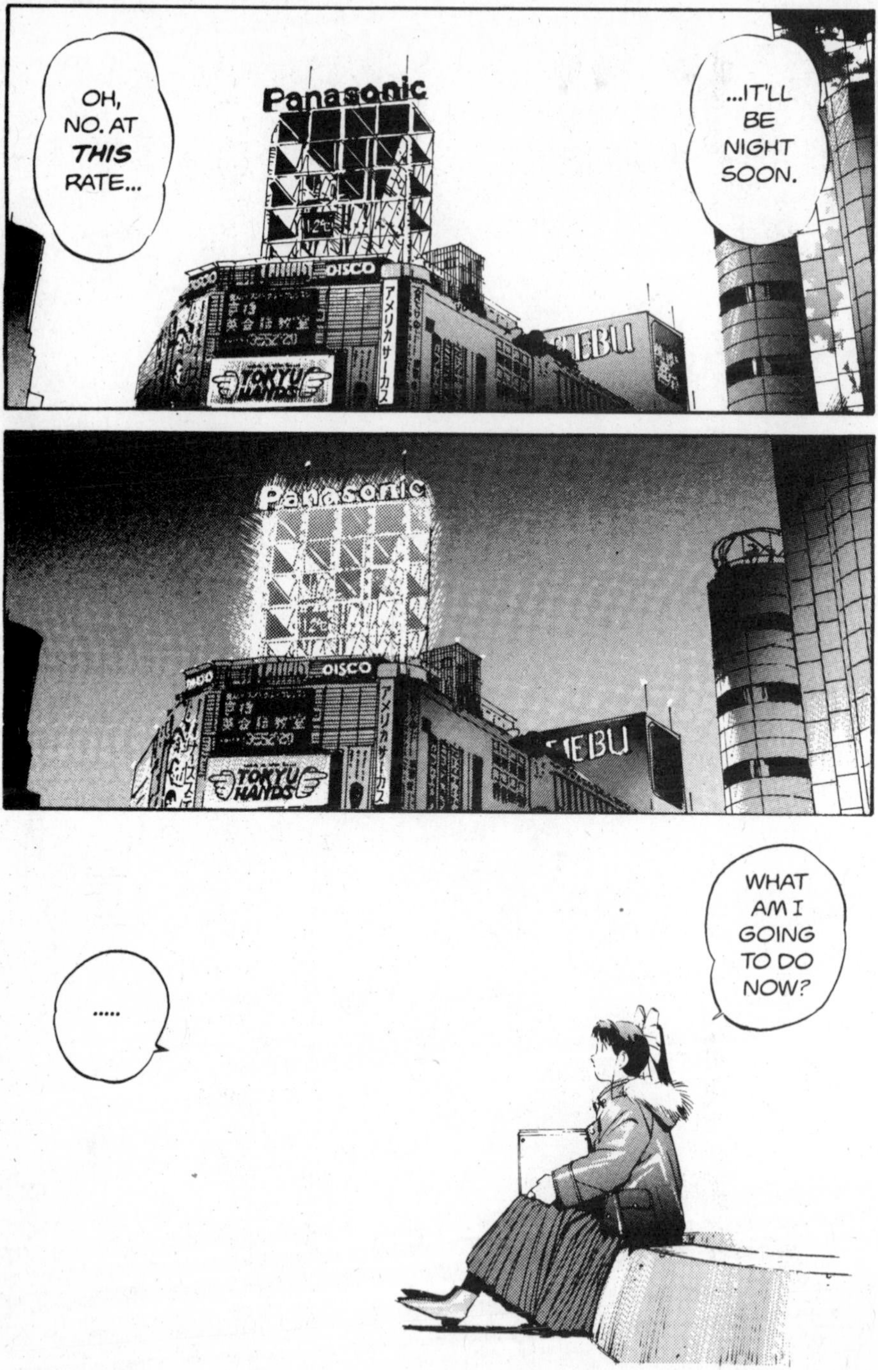
OH, NO. AT THIS RATE...
Panasonic
DISCO
TOKYU HANDS
アメリカサーカス
...IT'LL BE NIGHT SOON.
Panasonic
DISCO
TOKYU HANDS
アメリカサーカス
......
WHAT AM I GOING TO DO NOW?

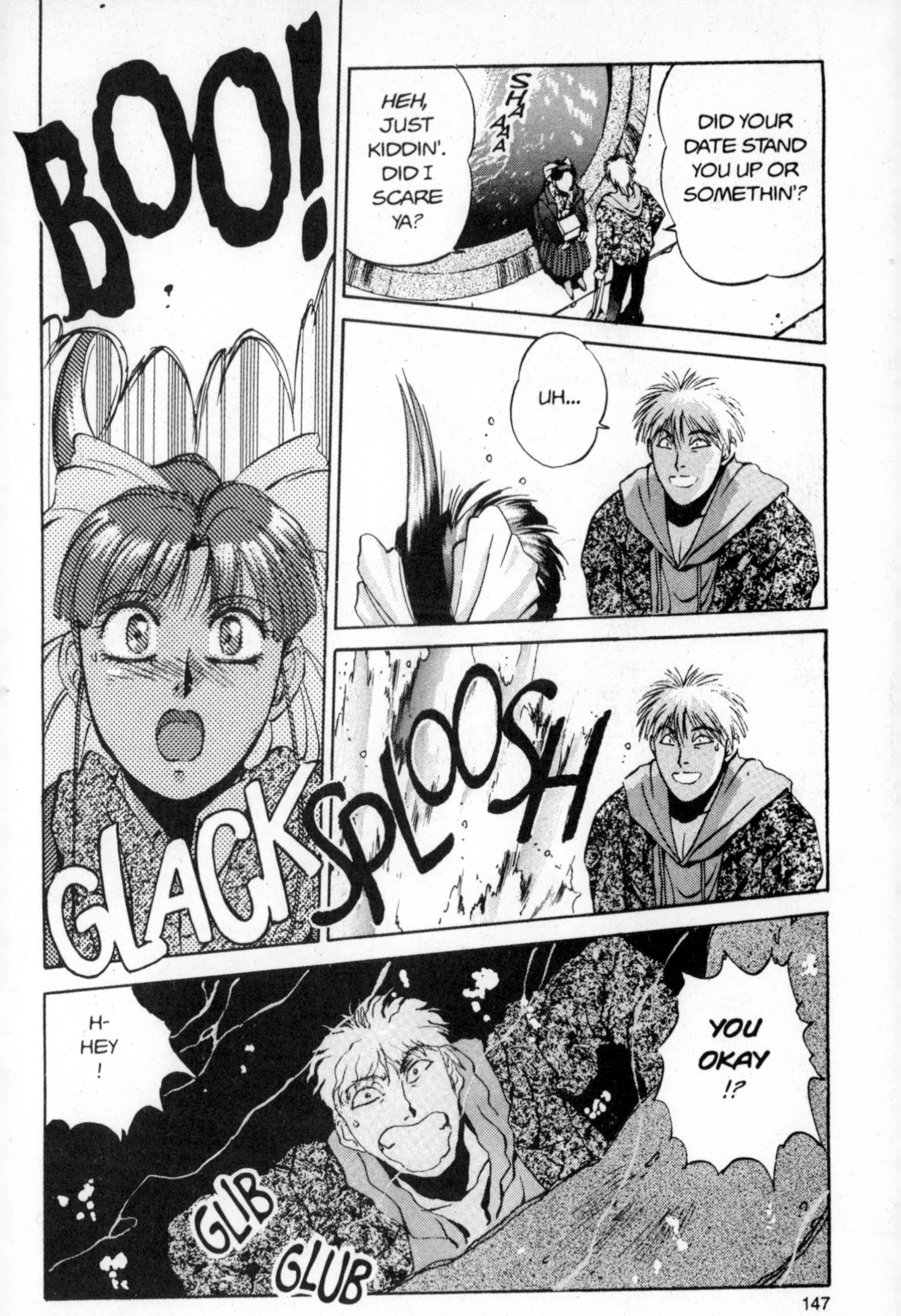
BOO!
GLACK
HEH, JUST KIDDIN'. DID I SCARE YA?
SHAAAA
DID YOUR DATE STAND YOU UP OR SOMETHIN'?
UH...
SPLOOSH
H-HEY!
YOU OKAY!?
GLUB
GLUB

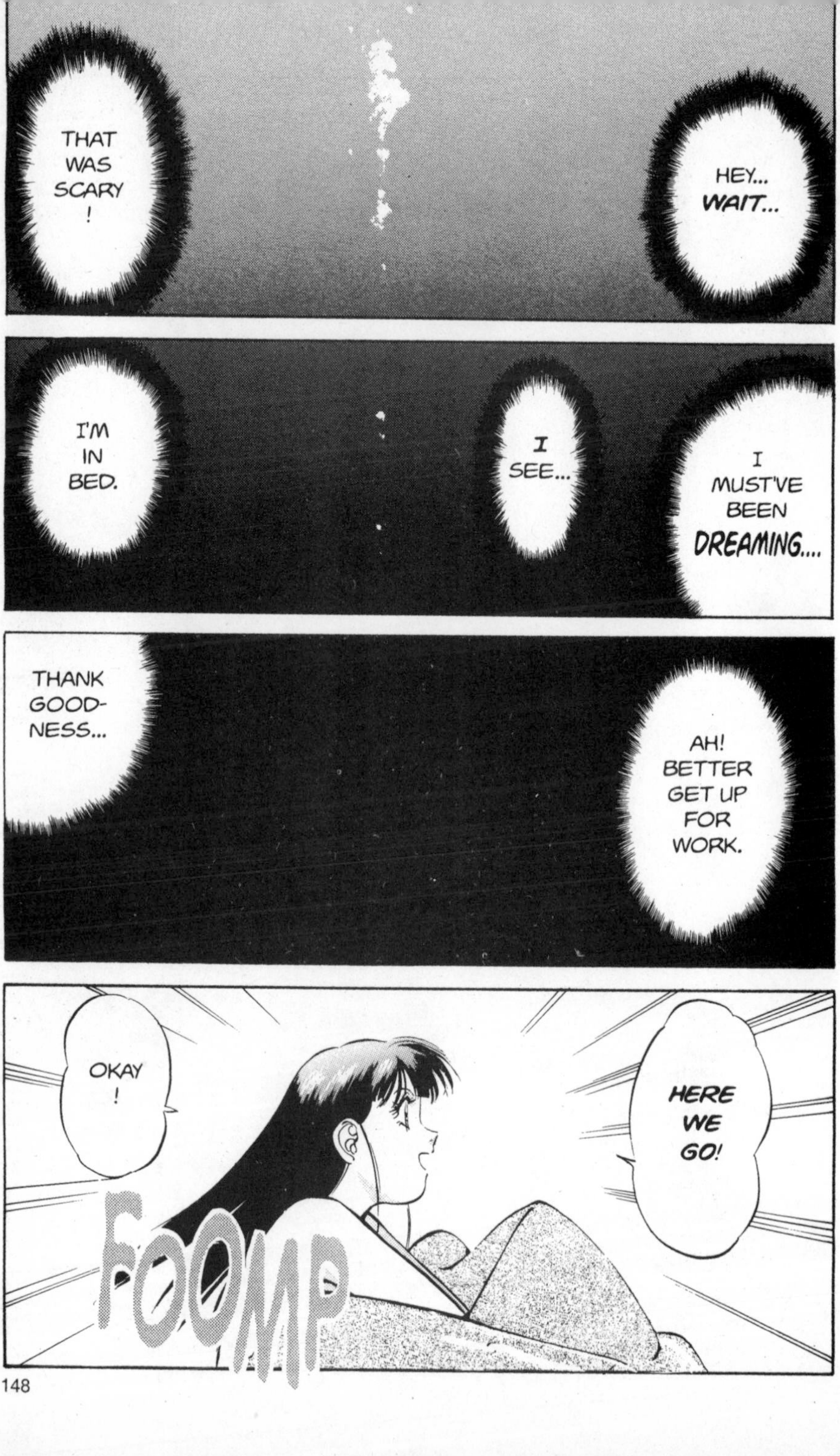
THAT WAS SCARY !
HEY... WAIT...
I'M IN BED.
I SEE...
I MUST'VE BEEN DREAMING....
THANK GOOD-NESS...
AH! BETTER GET UP FOR WORK.
OKAY !
HERE WE GO!
FOOMP

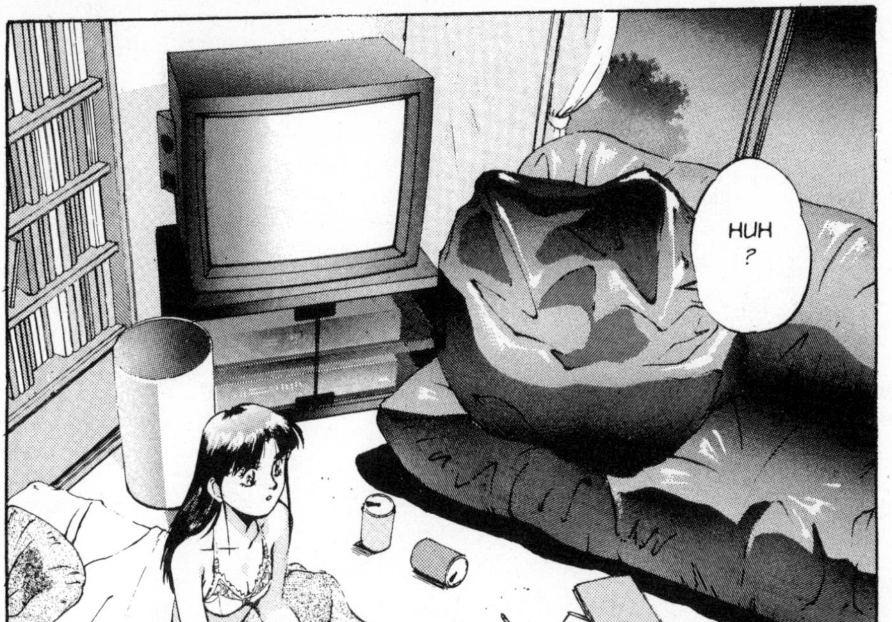
HUH
?

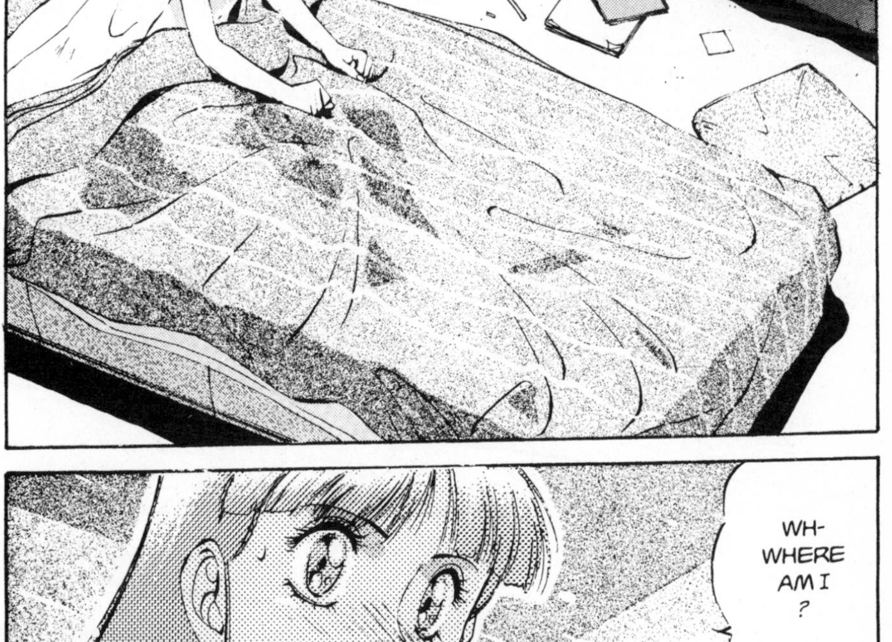
WH-
WHERE
AM I
?

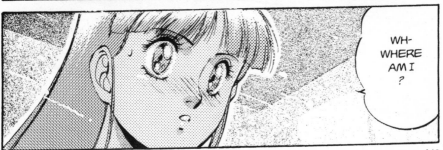

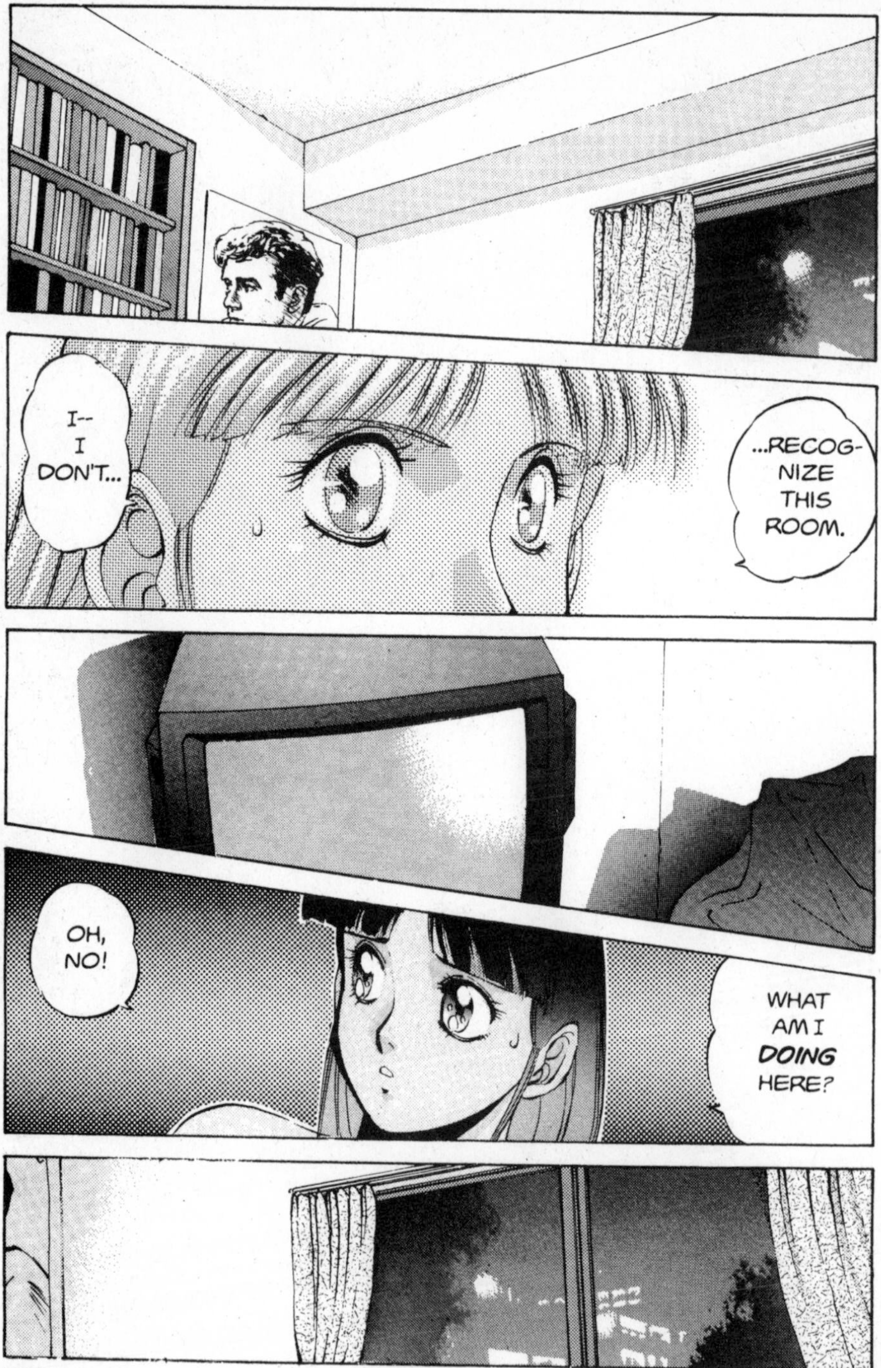
I--
I
DON'T...
...RECOG-
NIZE
THIS
ROOM.
OH,
NO!
WHAT
AM I
DOING
HERE?

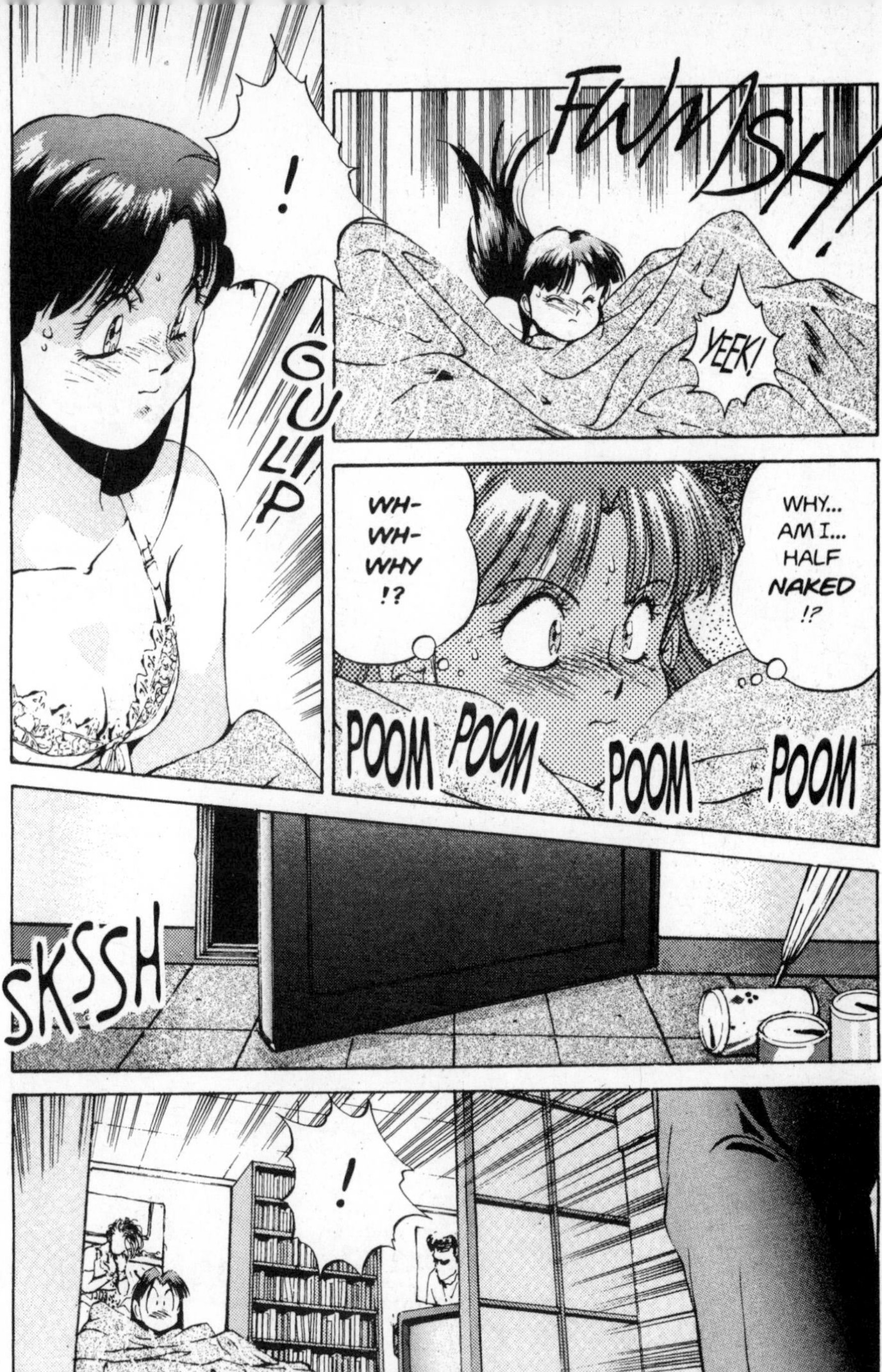
!
GULP
FWASH!
YEEK!
WH-WH-WHY!?
WHY... AM I... HALF NAKED!?
POOM POOM POOM POOM
SKSSH
!

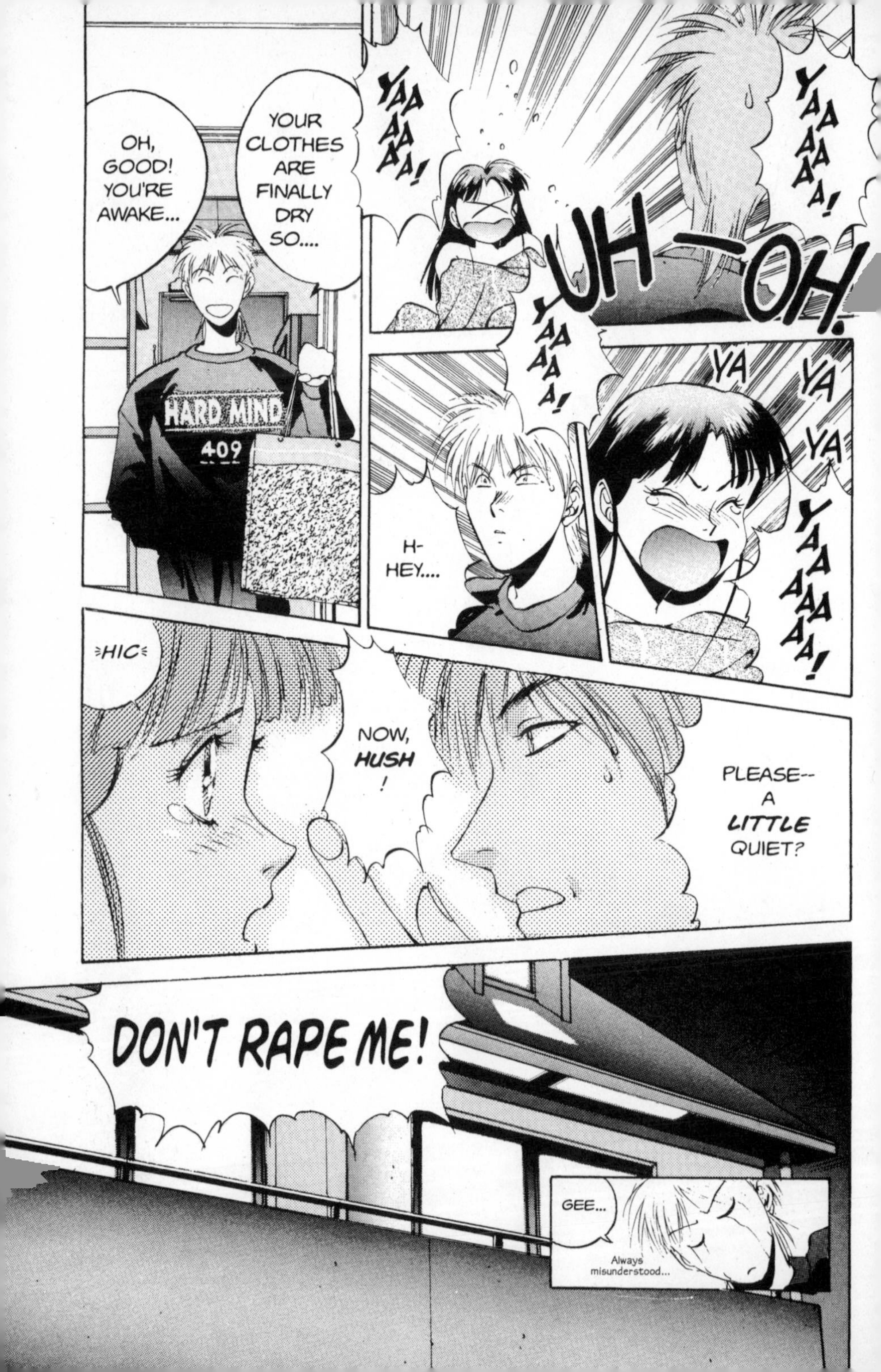
OH, GOOD! YOU'RE AWAKE...
YOUR CLOTHES ARE FINALLY DRY SO....
YAAAAA!
YAAAAA!
UH-OH.
YAAAAA!
YA YA YA
YAAAAAAA!
H-HEY....
HIC
NOW, HUSH!
PLEASE-- A LITTLE QUIET?
DON'T RAPE ME!
GEE...
Always misunderstood...

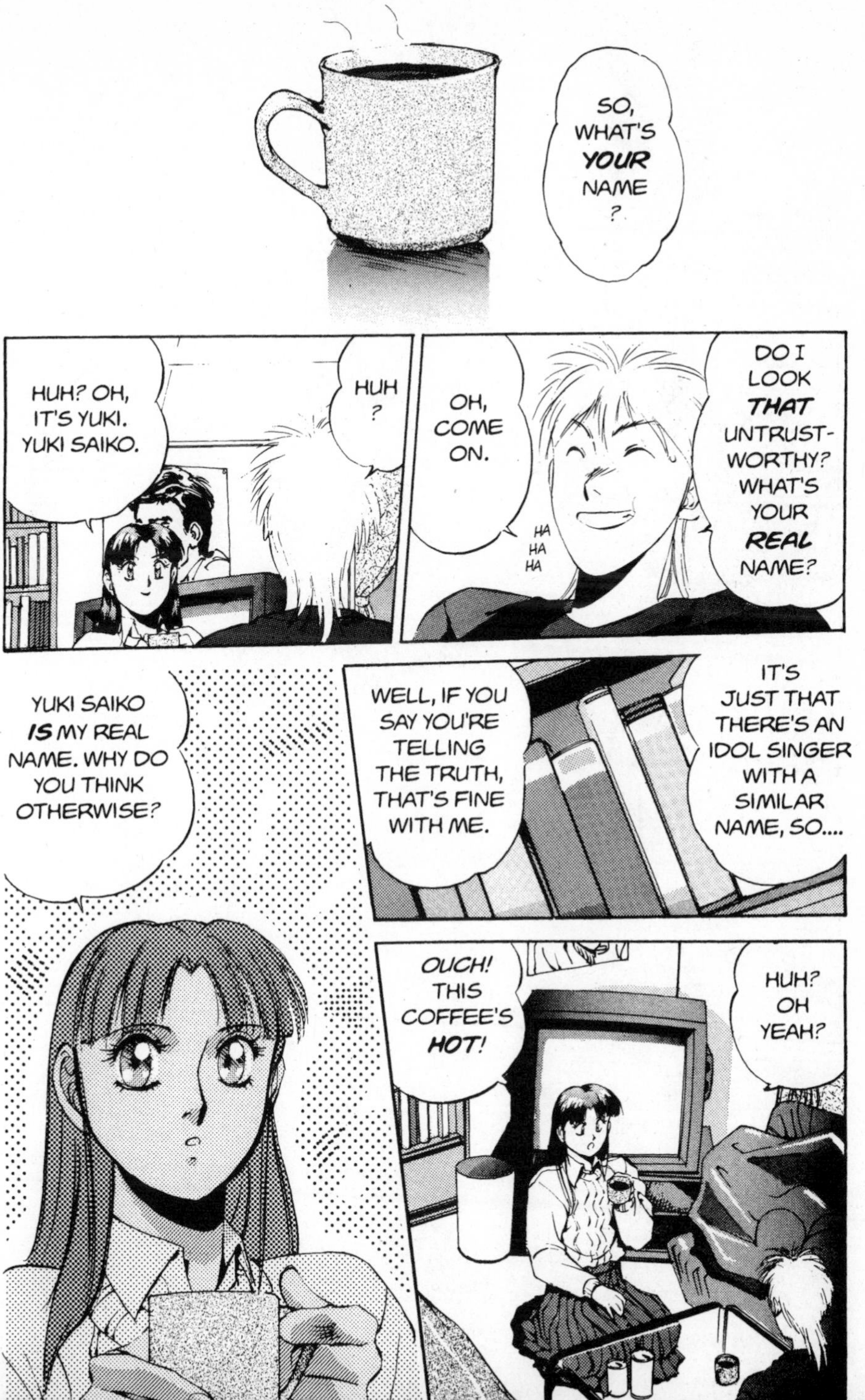
SO, WHAT'S **YOUR** NAME ?
HUH ?
HUH? OH, IT'S YUKI. YUKI SAIKO.
OH, COME ON.
HA HA HA
DO I LOOK **THAT** UNTRUST-WORTHY? WHAT'S YOUR **REAL** NAME?
YUKI SAIKO **IS** MY REAL NAME. WHY DO YOU THINK OTHERWISE?
WELL, IF YOU SAY YOU'RE TELLING THE TRUTH, THAT'S FINE WITH ME.
IT'S JUST THAT THERE'S AN IDOL SINGER WITH A SIMILAR NAME, SO....
OUCH! THIS COFFEE'S ***HOT***!
HUH? OH YEAH?

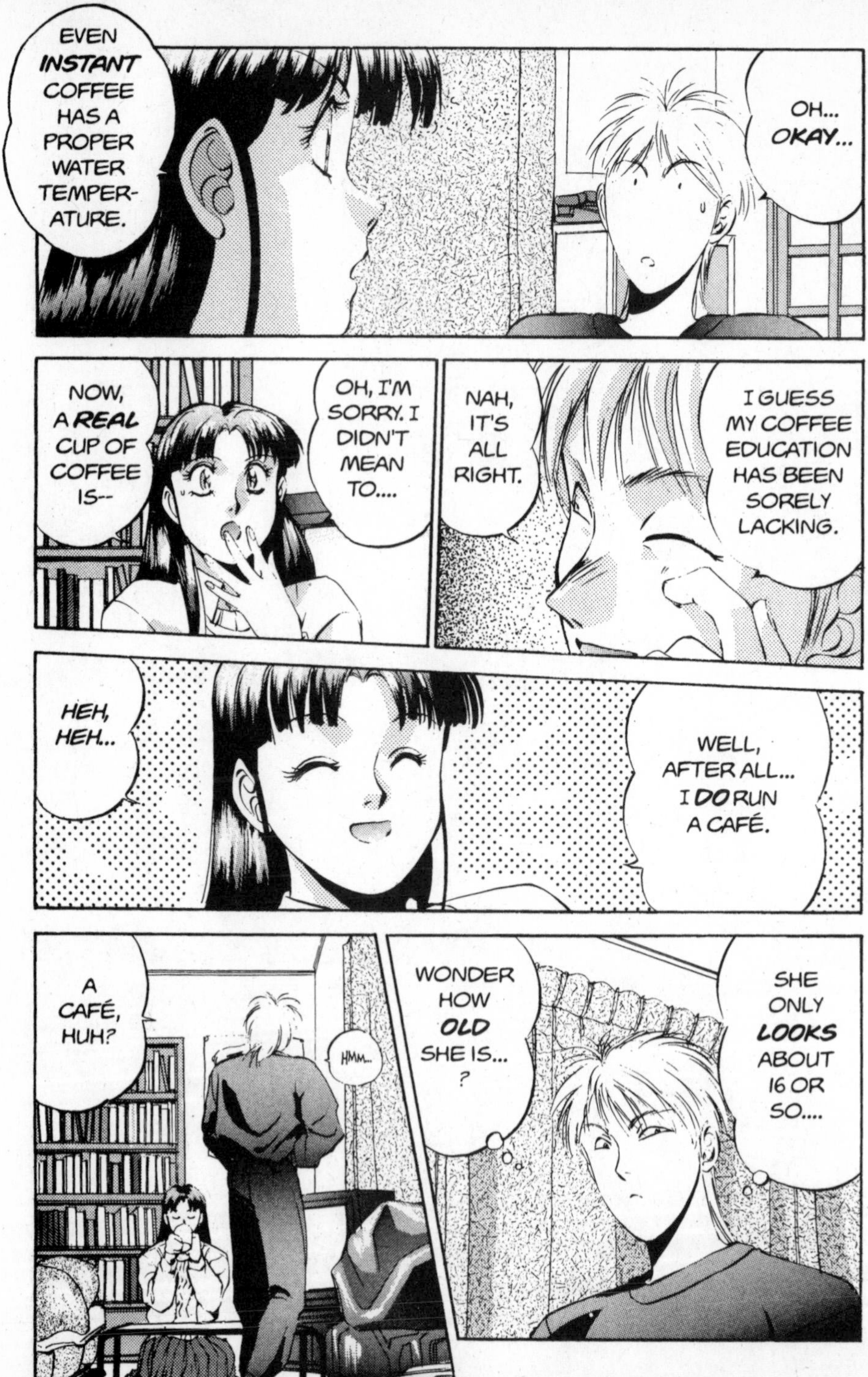
EVEN INSTANT COFFEE HAS A PROPER WATER TEMPERATURE.
OH... OKAY...
NOW, A REAL CUP OF COFFEE IS--
OH, I'M SORRY. I DIDN'T MEAN TO....
NAH, IT'S ALL RIGHT.
I GUESS MY COFFEE EDUCATION HAS BEEN SORELY LACKING.
HEH, HEH...
WELL, AFTER ALL... I DO RUN A CAFÉ.
A CAFÉ, HUH?
HMM...
WONDER HOW OLD SHE IS... ?
SHE ONLY LOOKS ABOUT 16 OR SO....

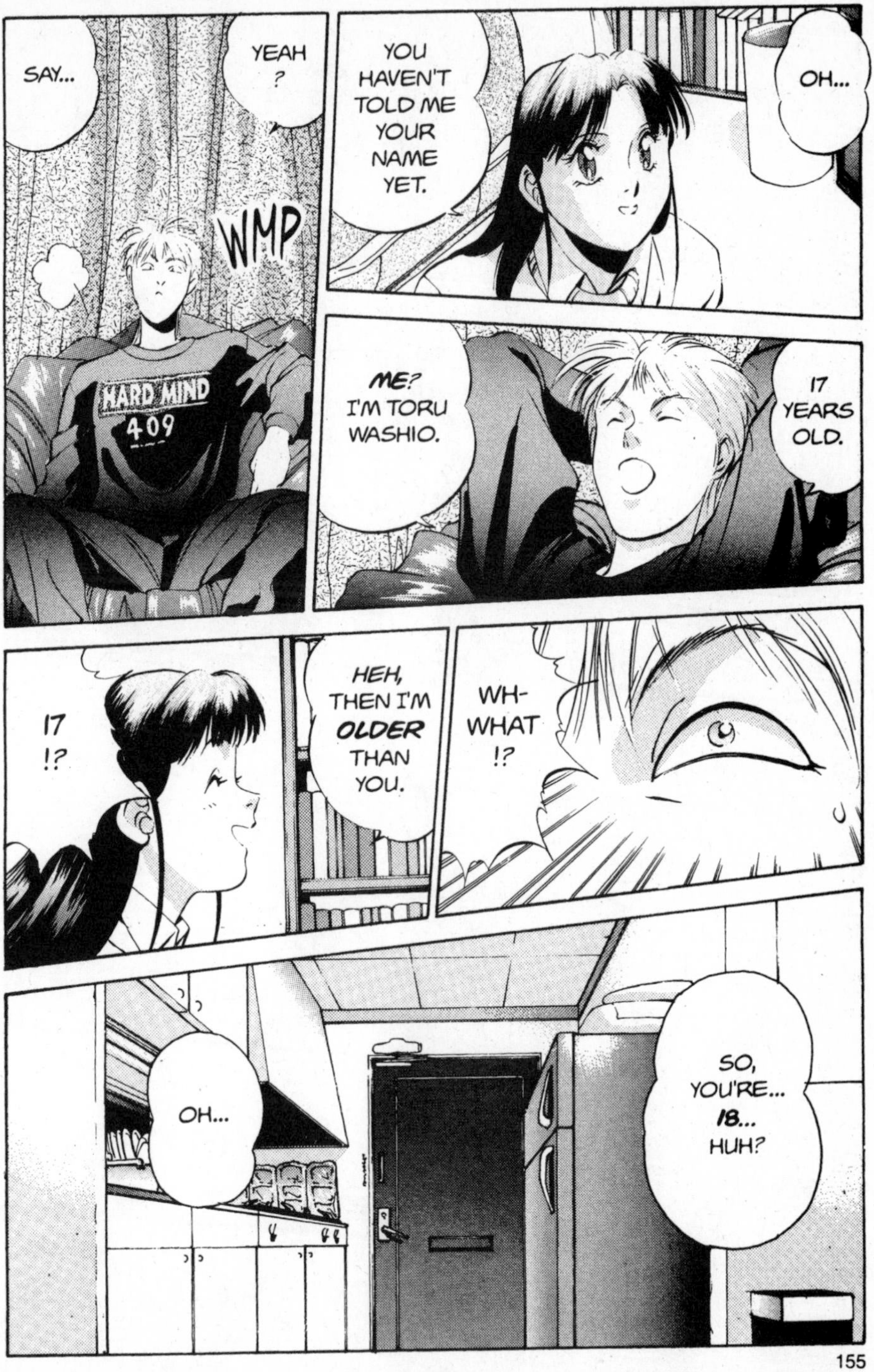
SAY...
YEAH ?
WMP
YOU HAVEN'T TOLD ME YOUR NAME YET.
OH...
ME? I'M TORU WASHIO.
17 YEARS OLD.
17 !?
HEH, THEN I'M **OLDER** THAN YOU.
WH- WHAT !?
OH...
SO, YOU'RE... **18...** HUH?

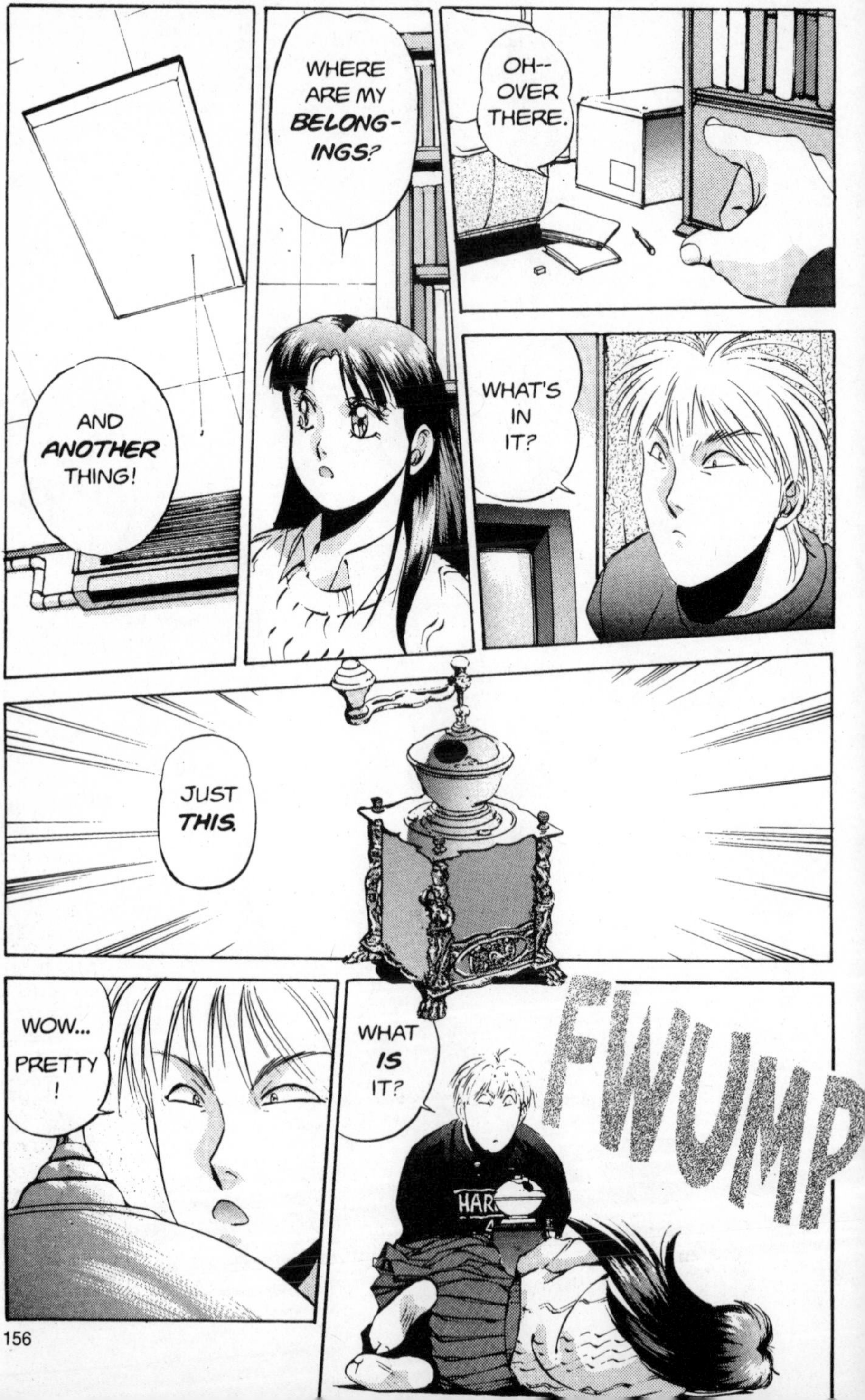
AND ANOTHER THING!
WHERE ARE MY BELONG- INGS?
OH-- OVER THERE.
WHAT'S IN IT?
JUST THIS.
WOW... PRETTY !
WHAT IS IT?
FWUMP

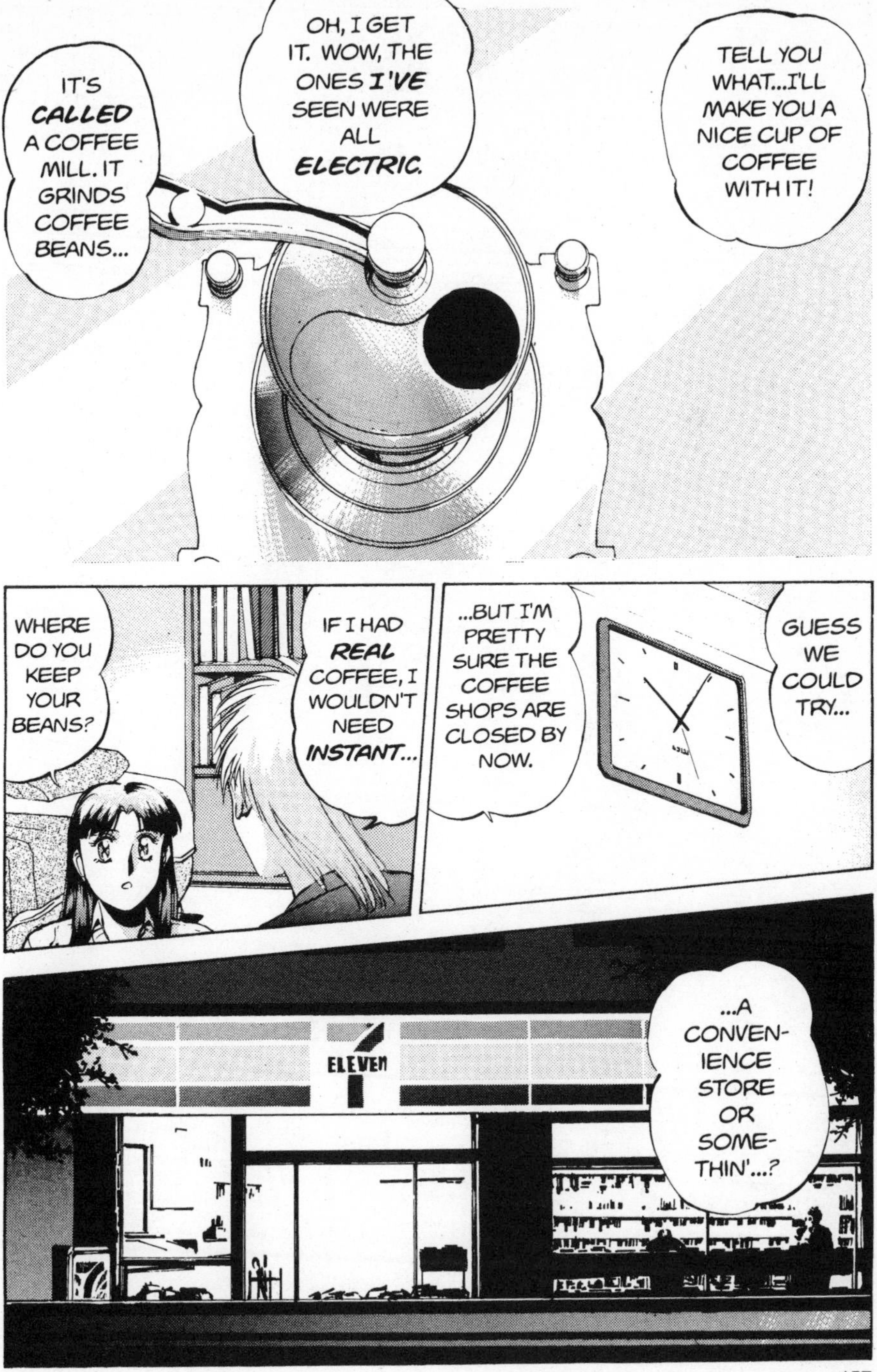
IT'S CALLED A COFFEE MILL. IT GRINDS COFFEE BEANS...
OH, I GET IT. WOW, THE ONES I'VE SEEN WERE ALL ELECTRIC.
TELL YOU WHAT...I'LL MAKE YOU A NICE CUP OF COFFEE WITH IT!
WHERE DO YOU KEEP YOUR BEANS?
IF I HAD REAL COFFEE, I WOULDN'T NEED INSTANT...
...BUT I'M PRETTY SURE THE COFFEE SHOPS ARE CLOSED BY NOW.
GUESS WE COULD TRY...
...A CONVEN-IENCE STORE OR SOME-THIN'...?

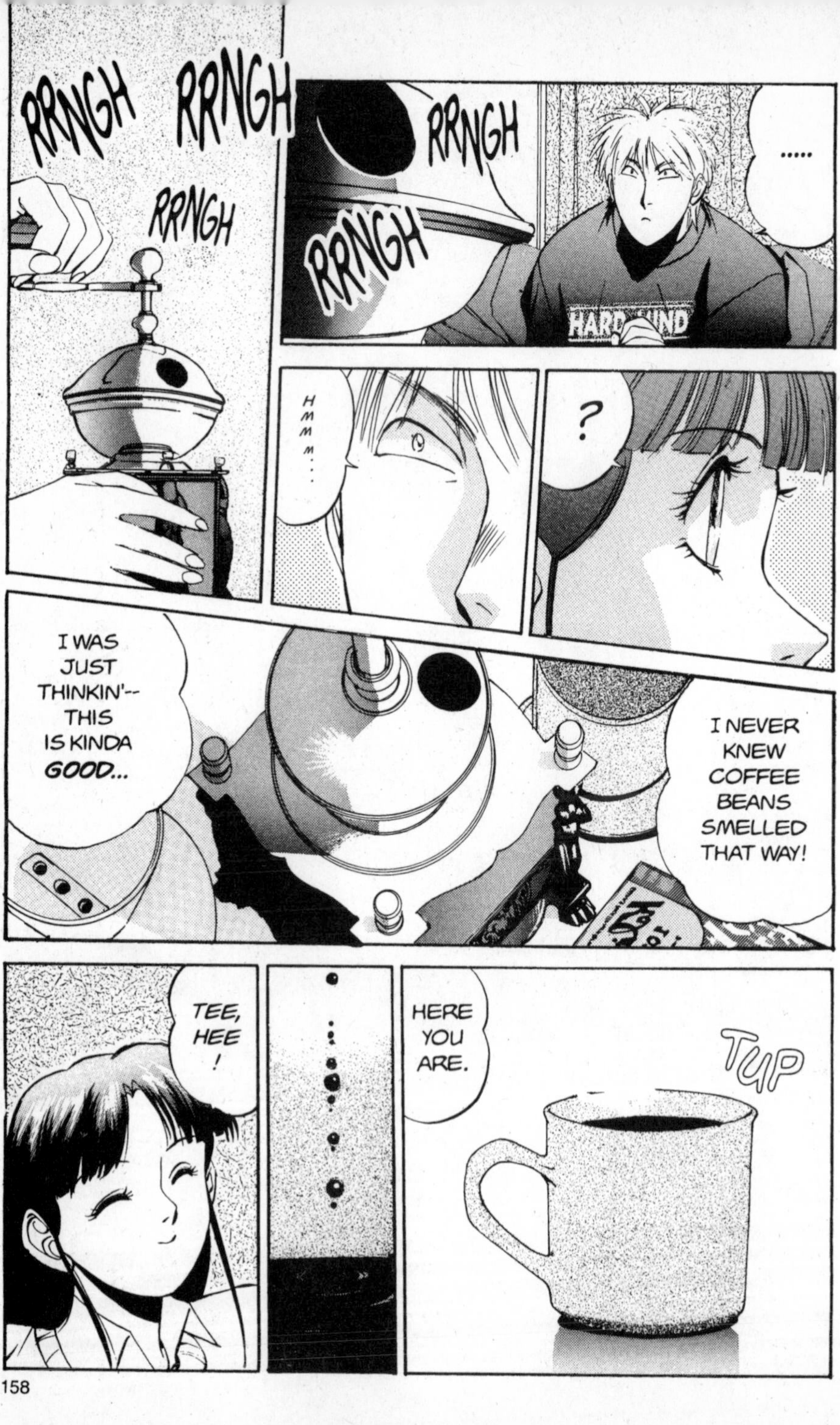
RRNGH
RRNGH
RRNGH
RRNGH
RRNGH
.....
HMMM...
?
I WAS JUST THINKIN'-- THIS IS KINDA *GOOD*...
I NEVER KNEW COFFEE BEANS SMELLED THAT WAY!
TEE, HEE!
HERE YOU ARE.
TUP

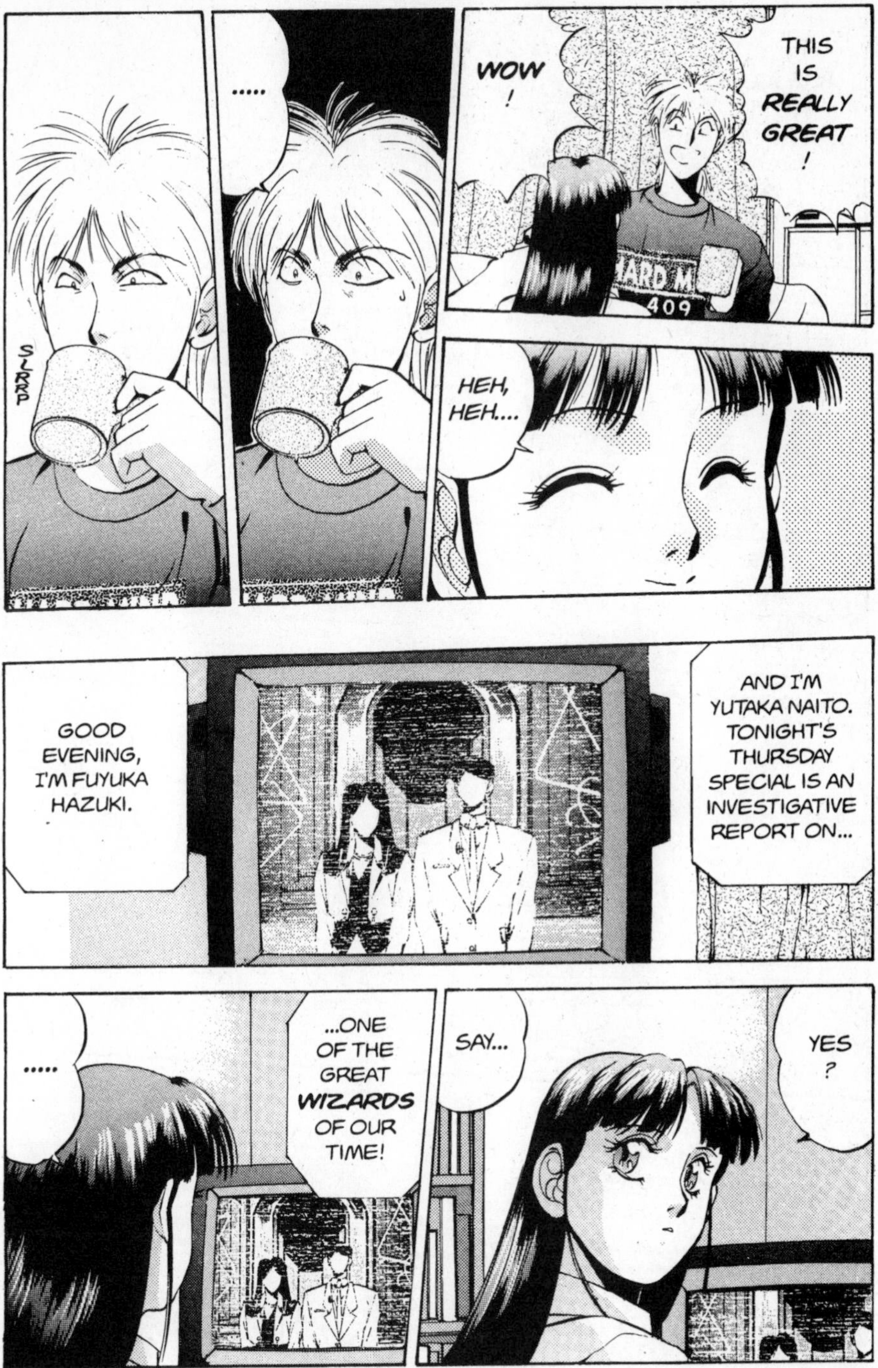
SLRRP
.....
WOW!
THIS IS REALLY GREAT!
HEH, HEH....
GOOD EVENING, I'M FUYUKA HAZUKI.
AND I'M YUTAKA NAITO. TONIGHT'S THURSDAY SPECIAL IS AN INVESTIGATIVE REPORT ON...
.....
...ONE OF THE GREAT WIZARDS OF OUR TIME!
SAY...
YES?

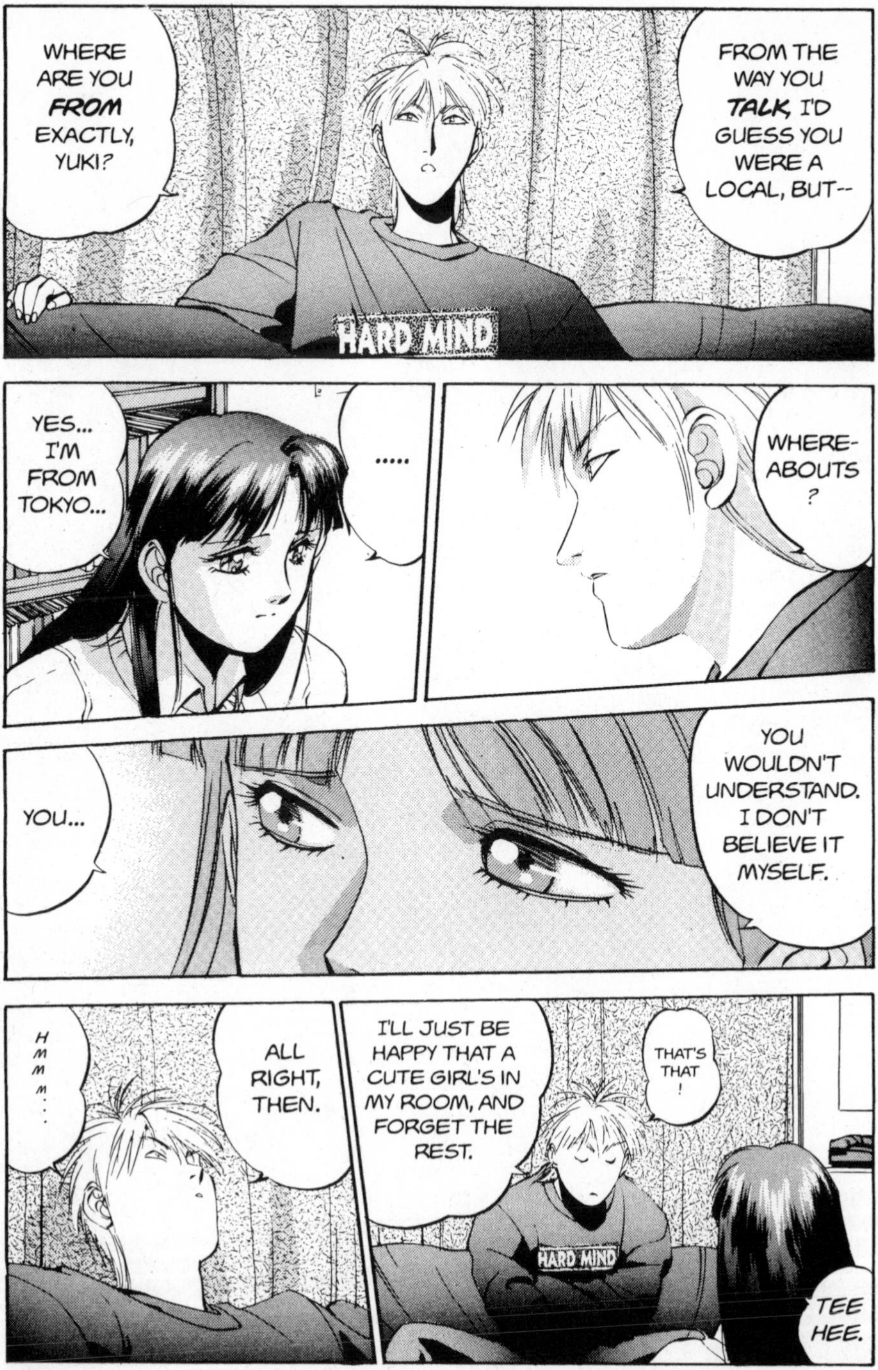
WHERE ARE YOU FROM EXACTLY, YUKI?
FROM THE WAY YOU TALK, I'D GUESS YOU WERE A LOCAL, BUT--
HARD MIND
.....
YES... I'M FROM TOKYO...
WHERE-ABOUTS?
YOU...
YOU WOULDN'T UNDERSTAND. I DON'T BELIEVE IT MYSELF.
HMMM...
ALL RIGHT, THEN.
I'LL JUST BE HAPPY THAT A CUTE GIRL'S IN MY ROOM, AND FORGET THE REST.
THAT'S THAT!
HARD MIND
TEE HEE.

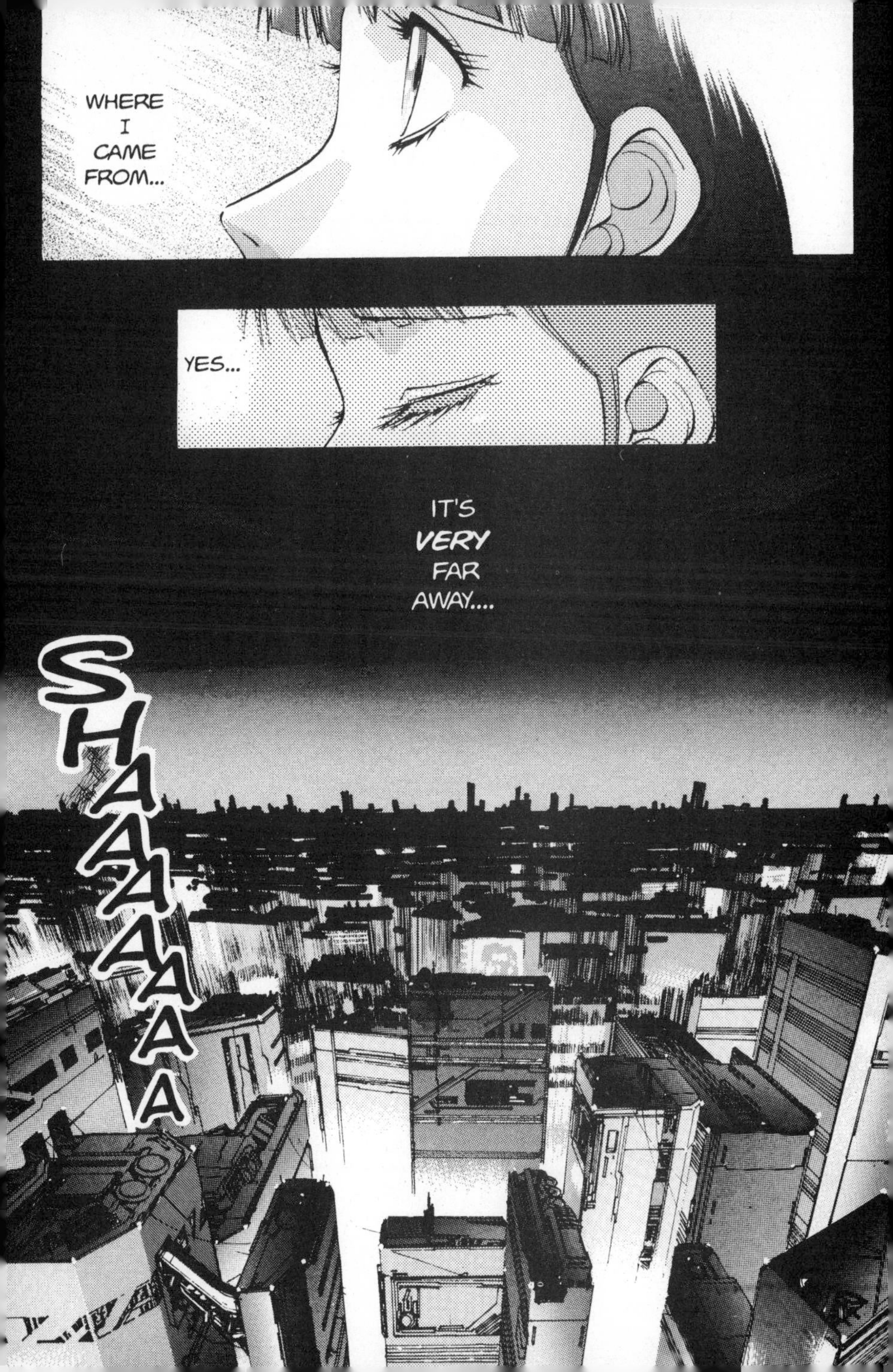
WHERE I CAME FROM...
YES...
IT'S VERY FAR AWAY....
SHAAAAAAA

WHERE...
?

I....

WH-
WHERE...

...AM
I?

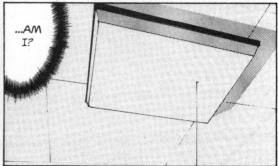

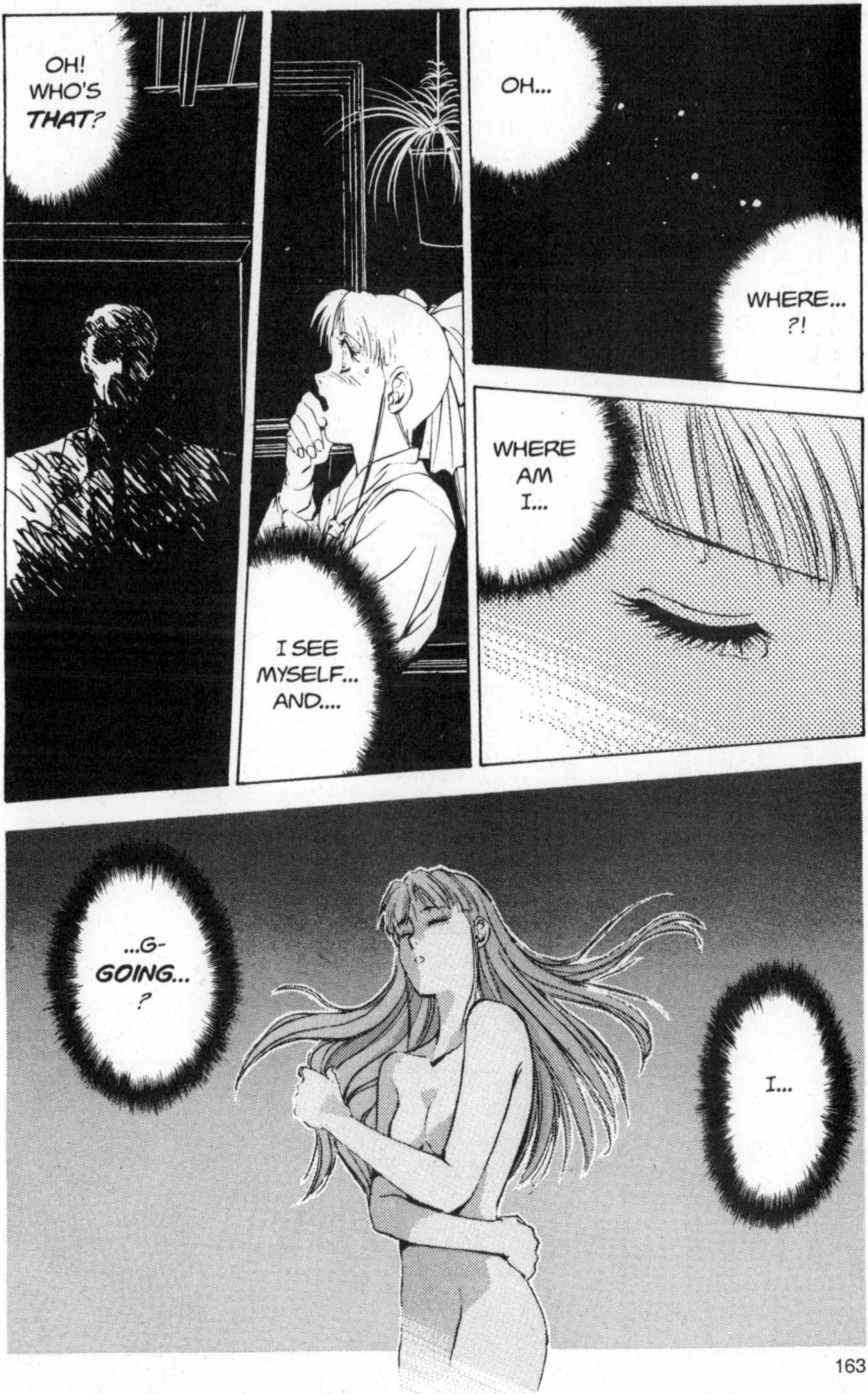
OH! WHO'S THAT?
I SEE MYSELF... AND....
OH...
WHERE... ?!
WHERE AM I...
...G- GOING... ?
I...

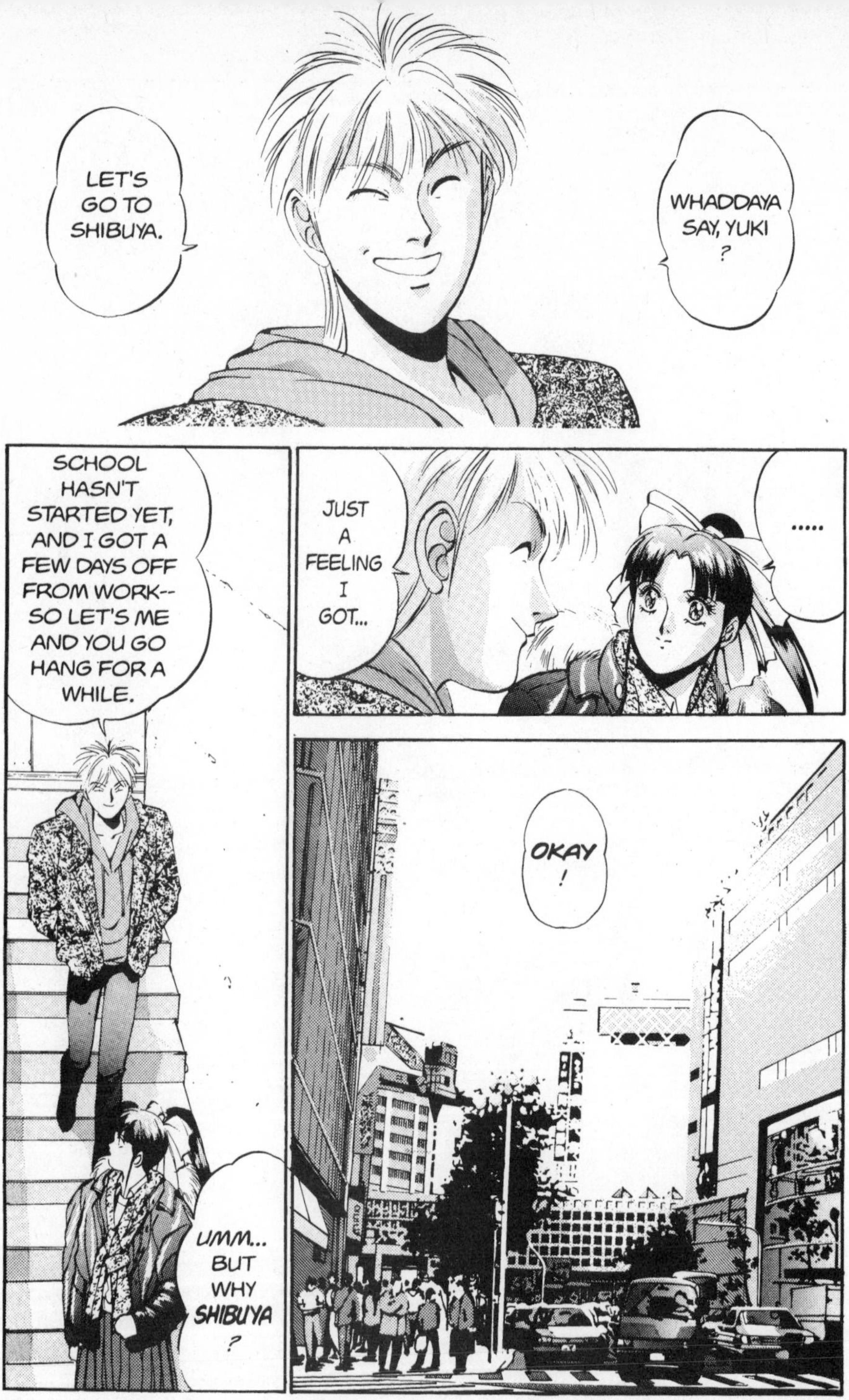
LET'S GO TO SHIBUYA.
WHADDAYA SAY, YUKI?
SCHOOL HASN'T STARTED YET, AND I GOT A FEW DAYS OFF FROM WORK-- SO LET'S ME AND YOU GO HANG FOR A WHILE.
UMM... BUT WHY SHIBUYA?
JUST A FEELING I GOT...
.....
OKAY!

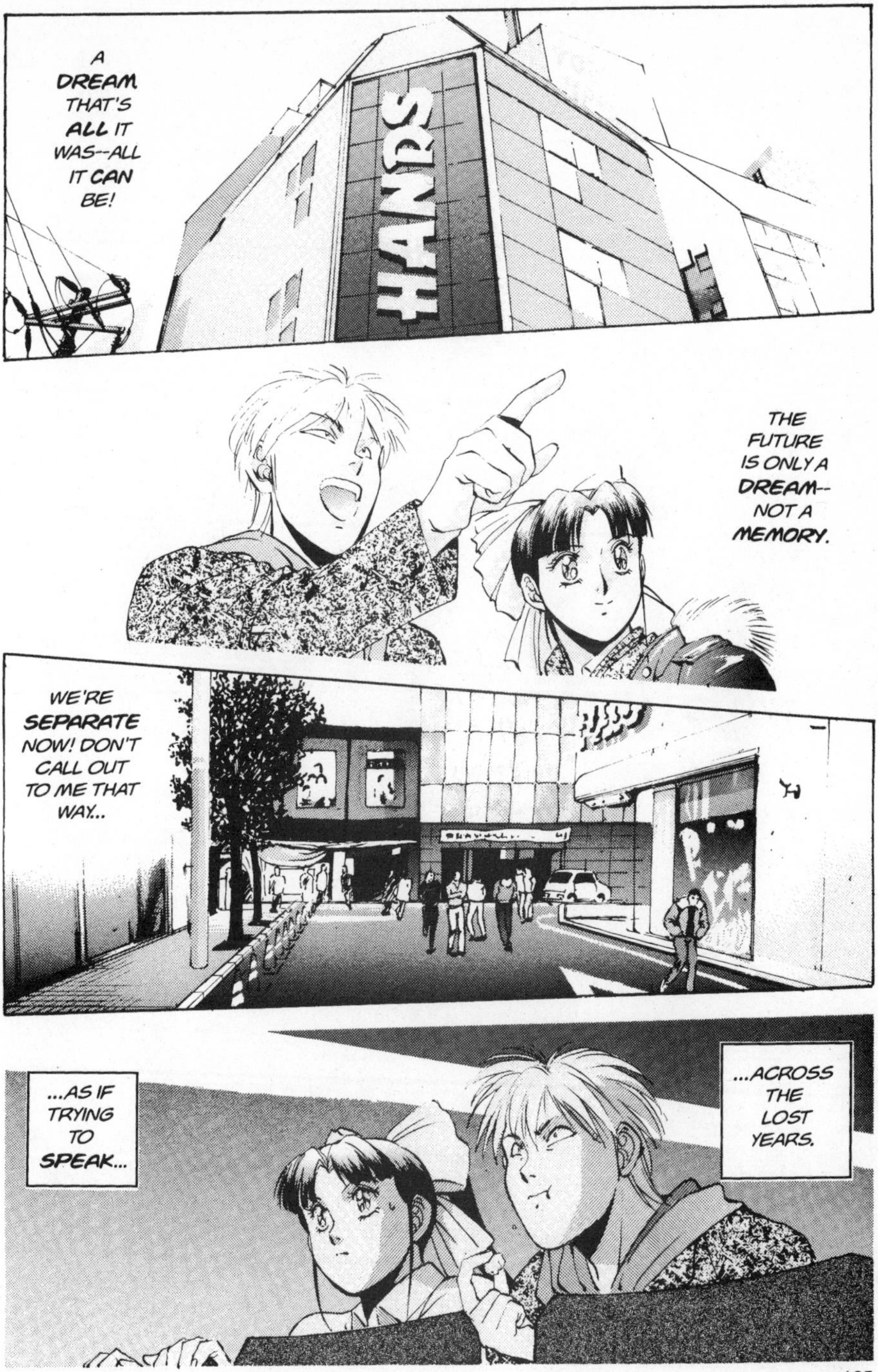
A DREAM THAT'S ALL IT WAS--ALL IT CAN BE!
HANDS
THE FUTURE IS ONLY A DREAM-- NOT A MEMORY.
WE'RE SEPARATE NOW! DON'T CALL OUT TO ME THAT WAY...
...AS IF TRYING TO SPEAK...
...ACROSS THE LOST YEARS.

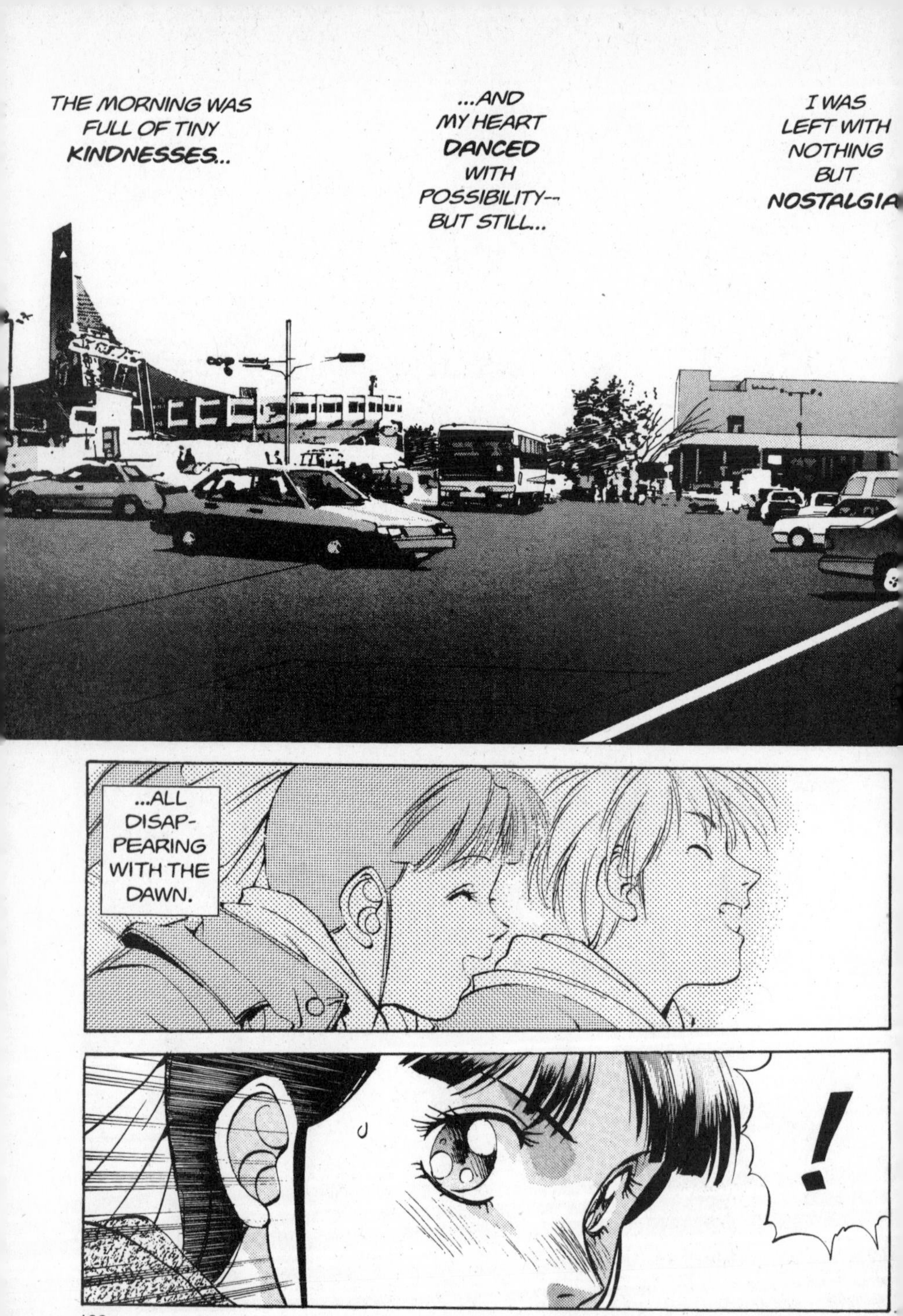
THE MORNING WAS FULL OF TINY KINDNESSES...
...AND MY HEART DANCED WITH POSSIBILITY-- BUT STILL...
I WAS LEFT WITH NOTHING BUT NOSTALGIA
...ALL DISAP-PEARING WITH THE DAWN.
!

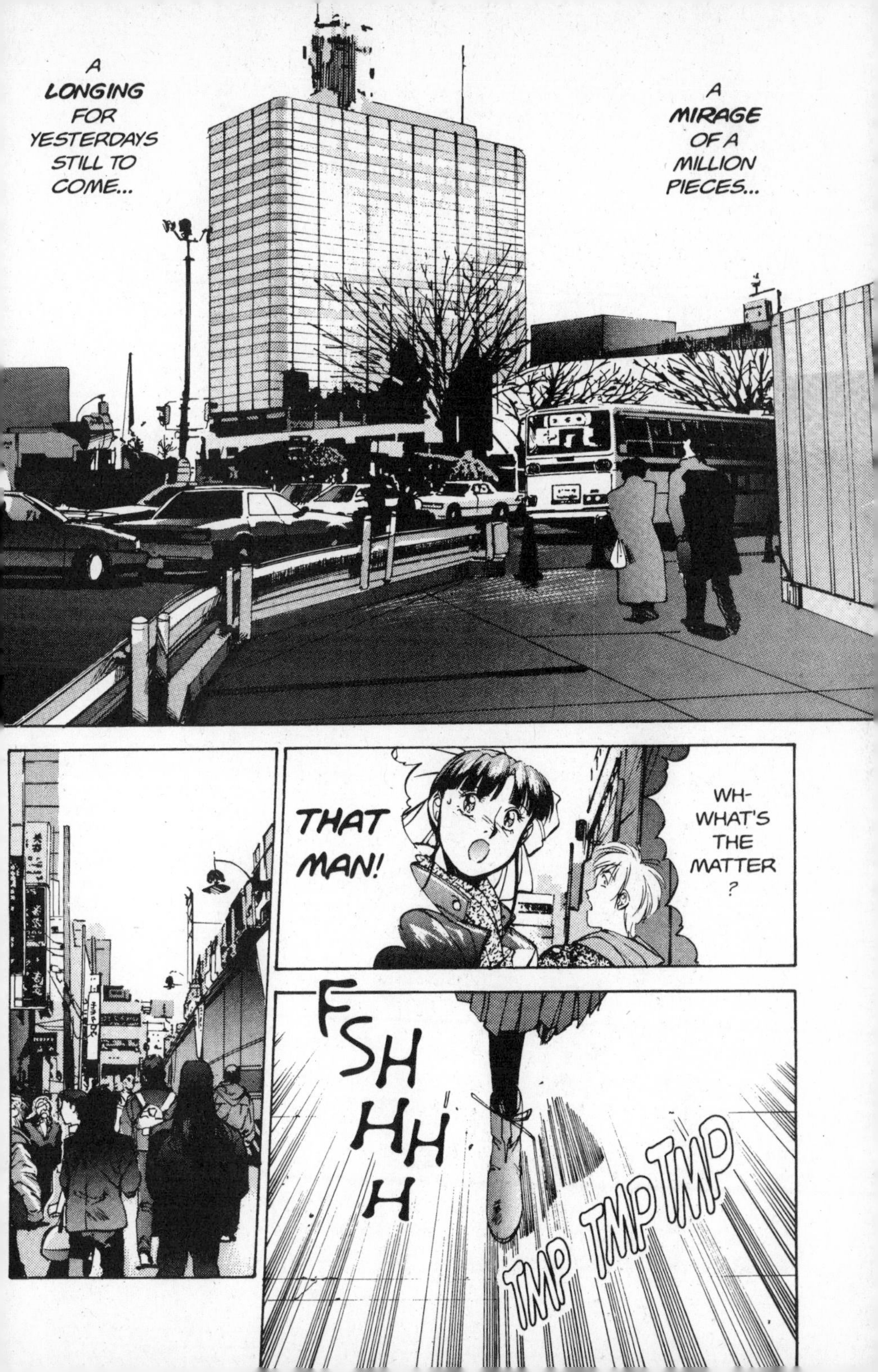
A LONGING FOR YESTERDAYS STILL TO COME...
A MIRAGE OF A MILLION PIECES...
THAT MAN!
WH- WHAT'S THE MATTER?
FSHHHH
TMP TMP TMP

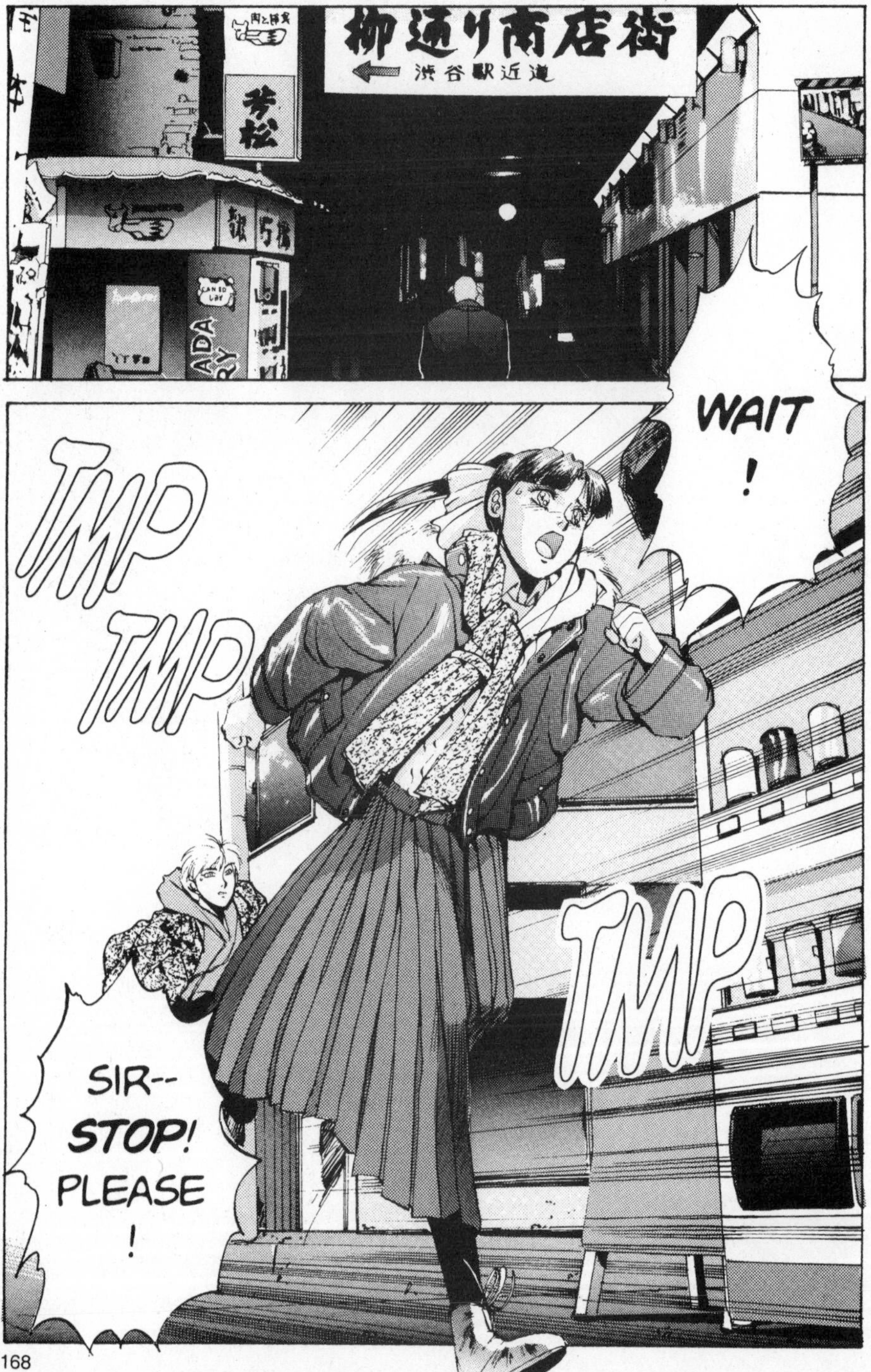
柳通り商店街
渋谷駅近道
TMP
TMP
WAIT !
TMP
SIR-- STOP! PLEASE !

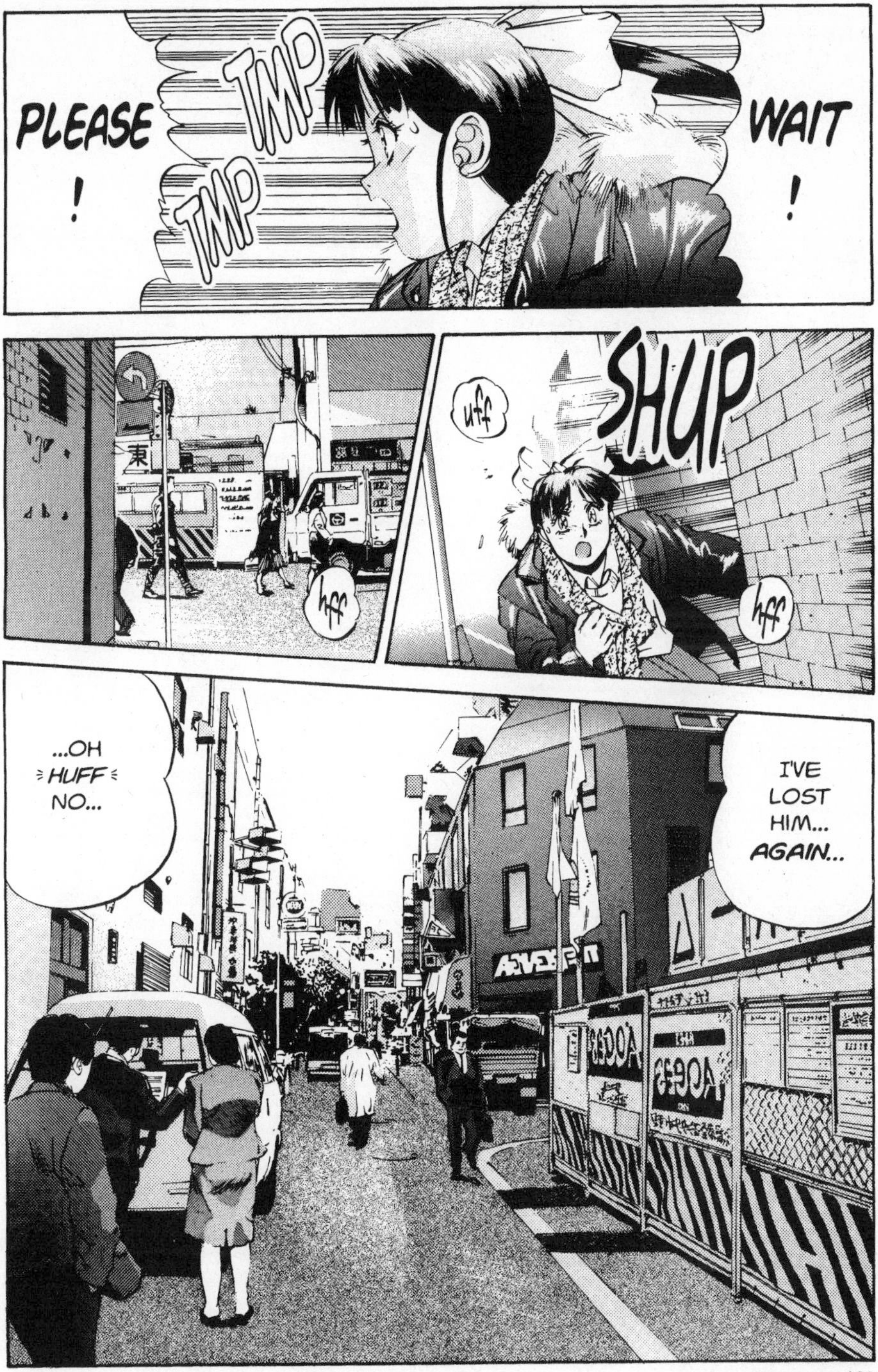
PLEASE !
TMP TMP
WAIT !
uff
hff
SHUP
hff
...OH HUFF NO...
I'VE LOST HIM... AGAIN...

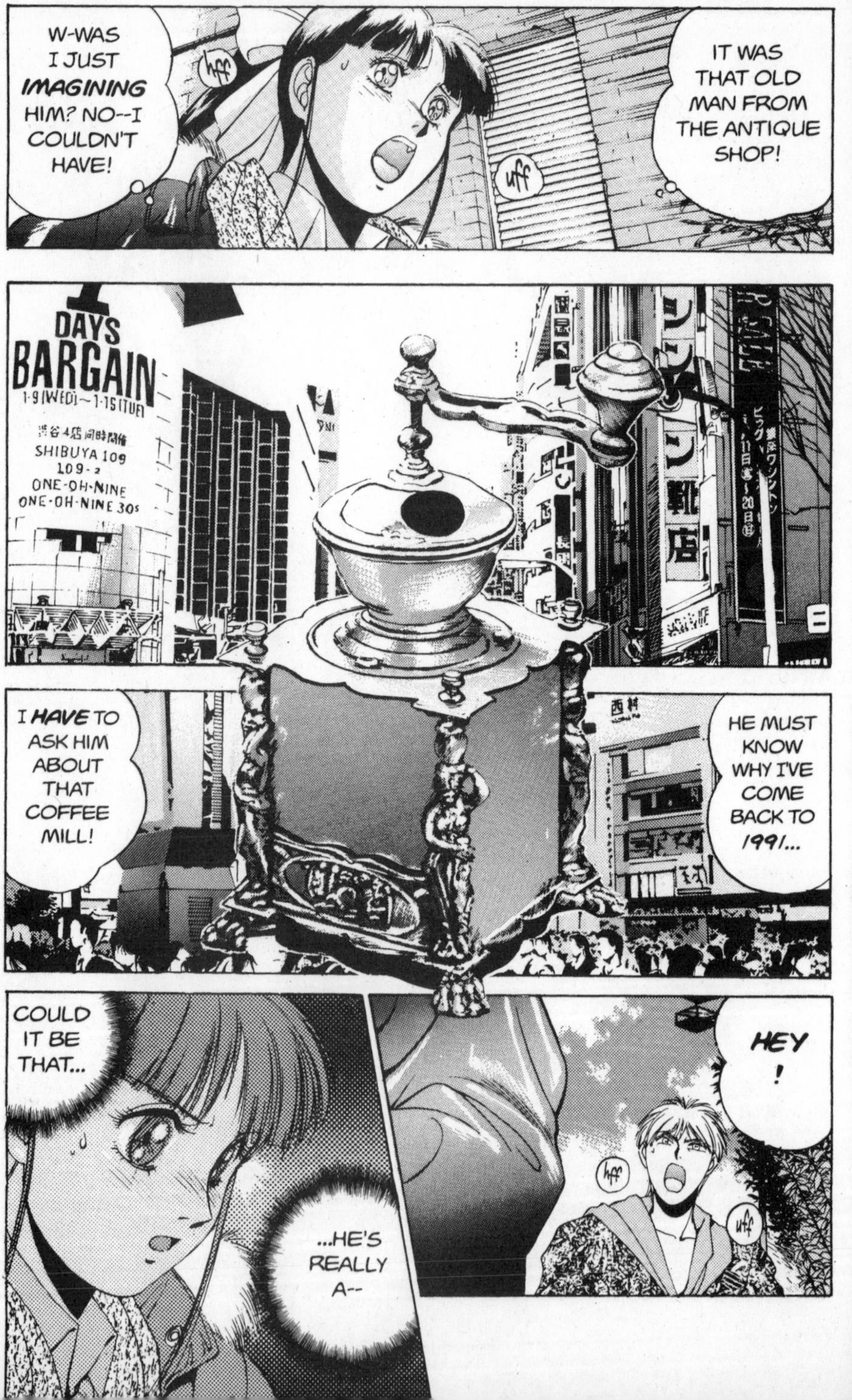
W-WAS I JUST **IMAGINING** HIM? NO--I COULDN'T HAVE!
hff
uff
IT WAS THAT OLD MAN FROM THE ANTIQUE SHOP!
DAYS
BARGAIN
1·9(WED)~1·15(TUE)
渋谷4店同時開催
SHIBUYA 109
109-2
ONE-OH-NINE
ONE-OH-NINE 30s
I **HAVE** TO ASK HIM ABOUT THAT COFFEE MILL!
西村
HE MUST KNOW WHY I'VE COME BACK TO 1991...
COULD IT BE THAT...
...HE'S REALLY A--
HEY!
hff
uff

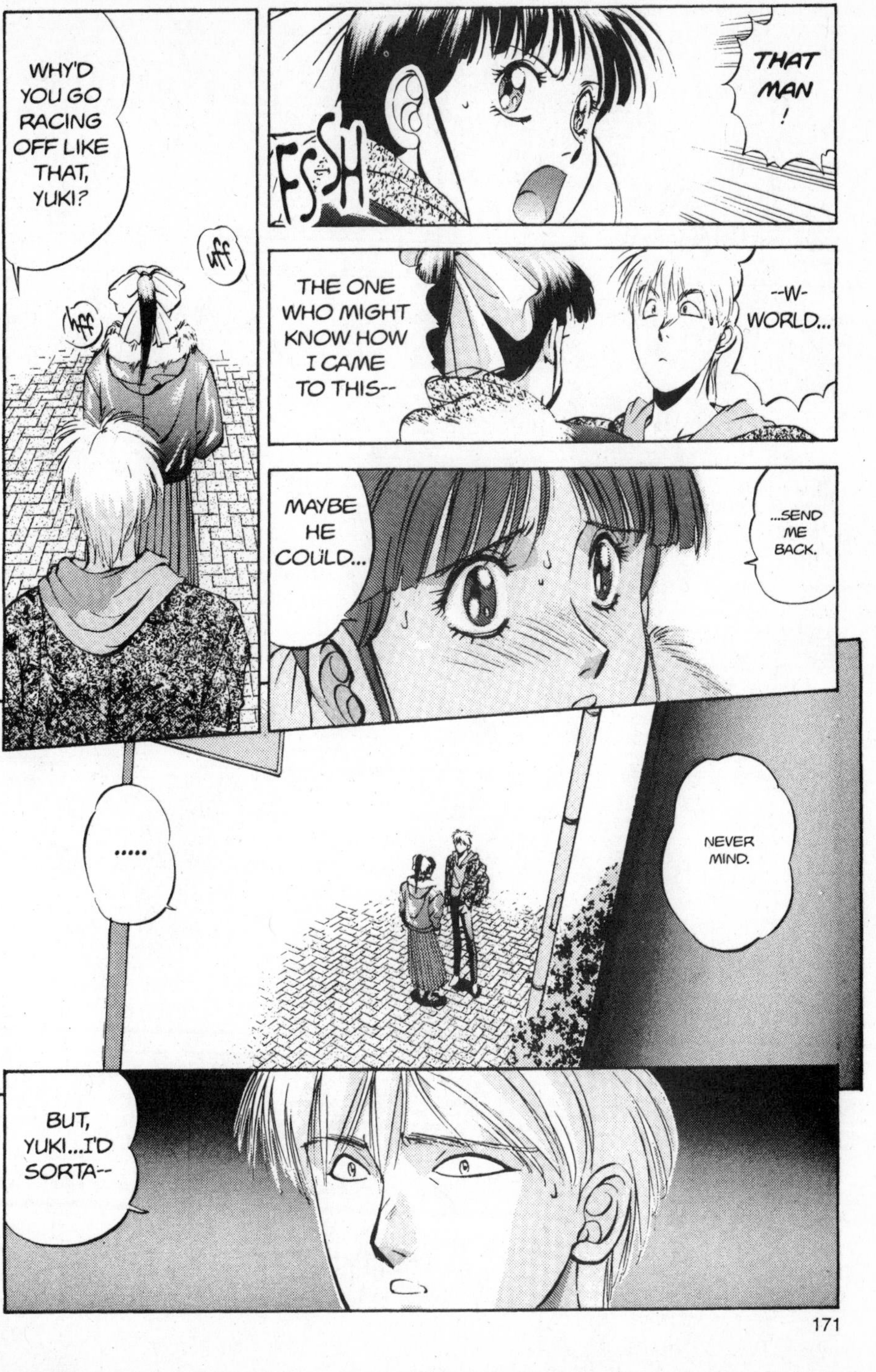
WHY'D YOU GO RACING OFF LIKE THAT, YUKI?
uff
hff
FSSH
THAT MAN!
THE ONE WHO MIGHT KNOW HOW I CAME TO THIS--
--W-WORLD...
MAYBE HE COULD...
...SEND ME BACK.
.....
NEVER MIND.
BUT, YUKI...I'D SORTA--

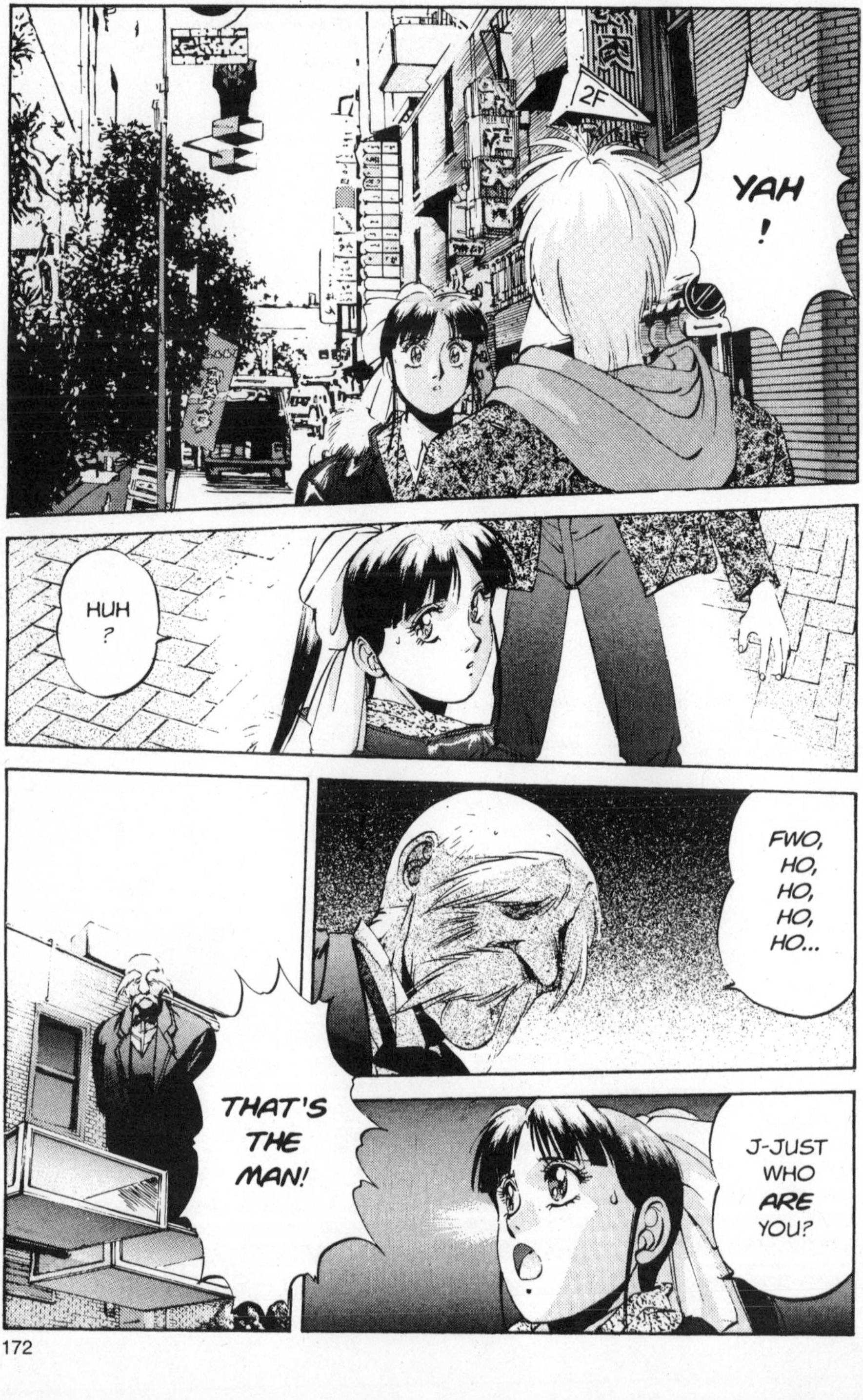
YAH !
HUH ?
THAT'S THE MAN!
FWO, HO, HO, HO, HO...
J-JUST WHO ARE YOU?

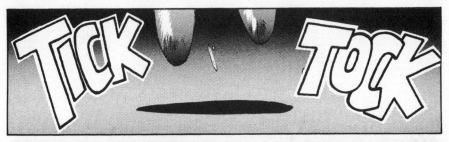

HOW DOES IT *FEEL...*

...YUKI SAIKO?

TRAPPED IN A *TIME* AND A *PLACE* WHERE YOUR *FRIENDS* CAN'T COME TO THE RESCUE?

MUST BE... *LONELY...*

C-CAN IT BE...!?

173

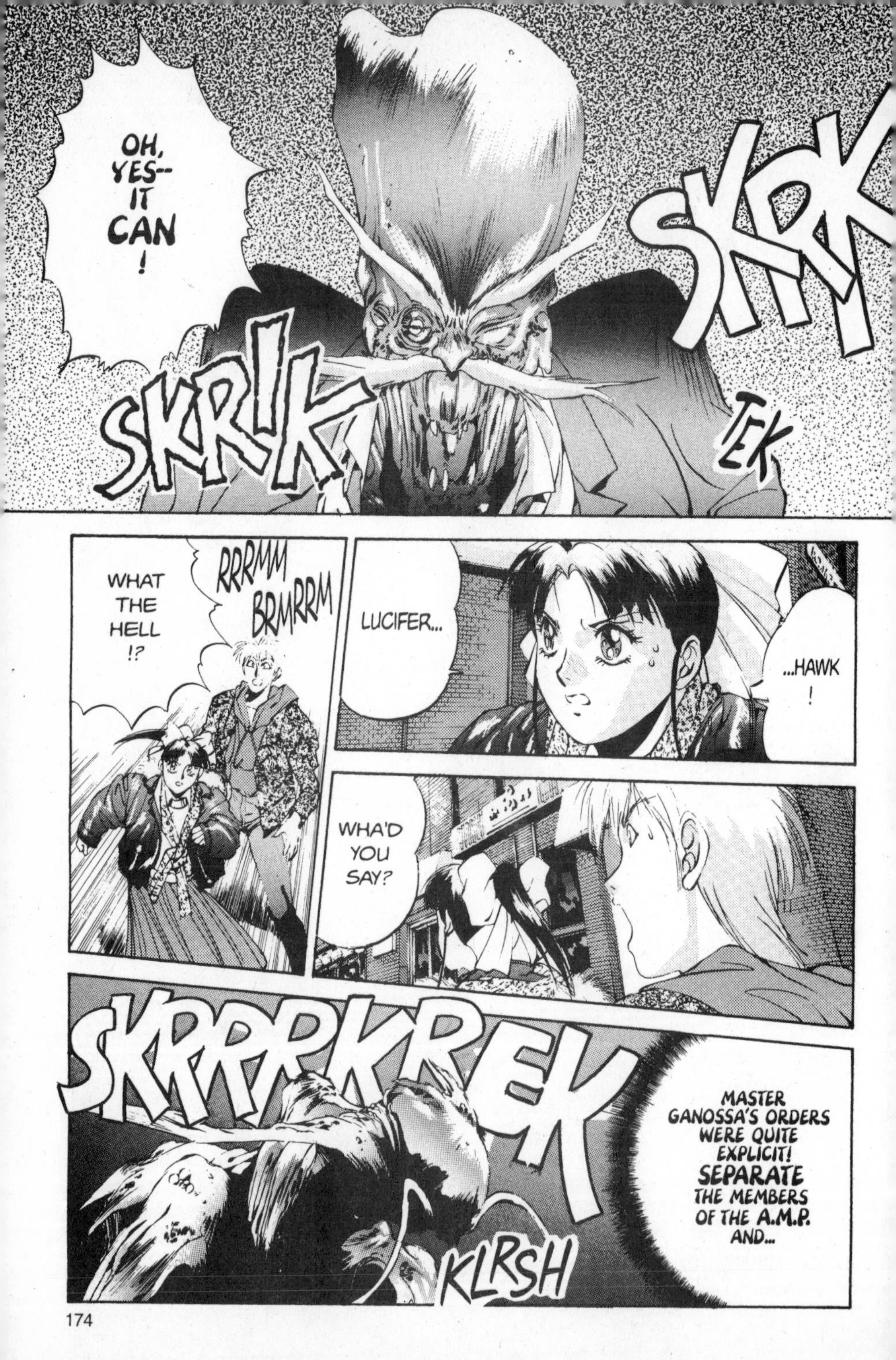
OH, YES-- IT CAN!
SKRIK
SKRK
TEK
WHAT THE HELL!?
RRRMM BRMRRM
LUCIFER...
...HAWK!
WHA'D YOU SAY?
SKRRRKREK
MASTER GANOSSA'S ORDERS WERE QUITE EXPLICIT! SEPARATE THE MEMBERS OF THE A.M.P. AND...
KLRSH

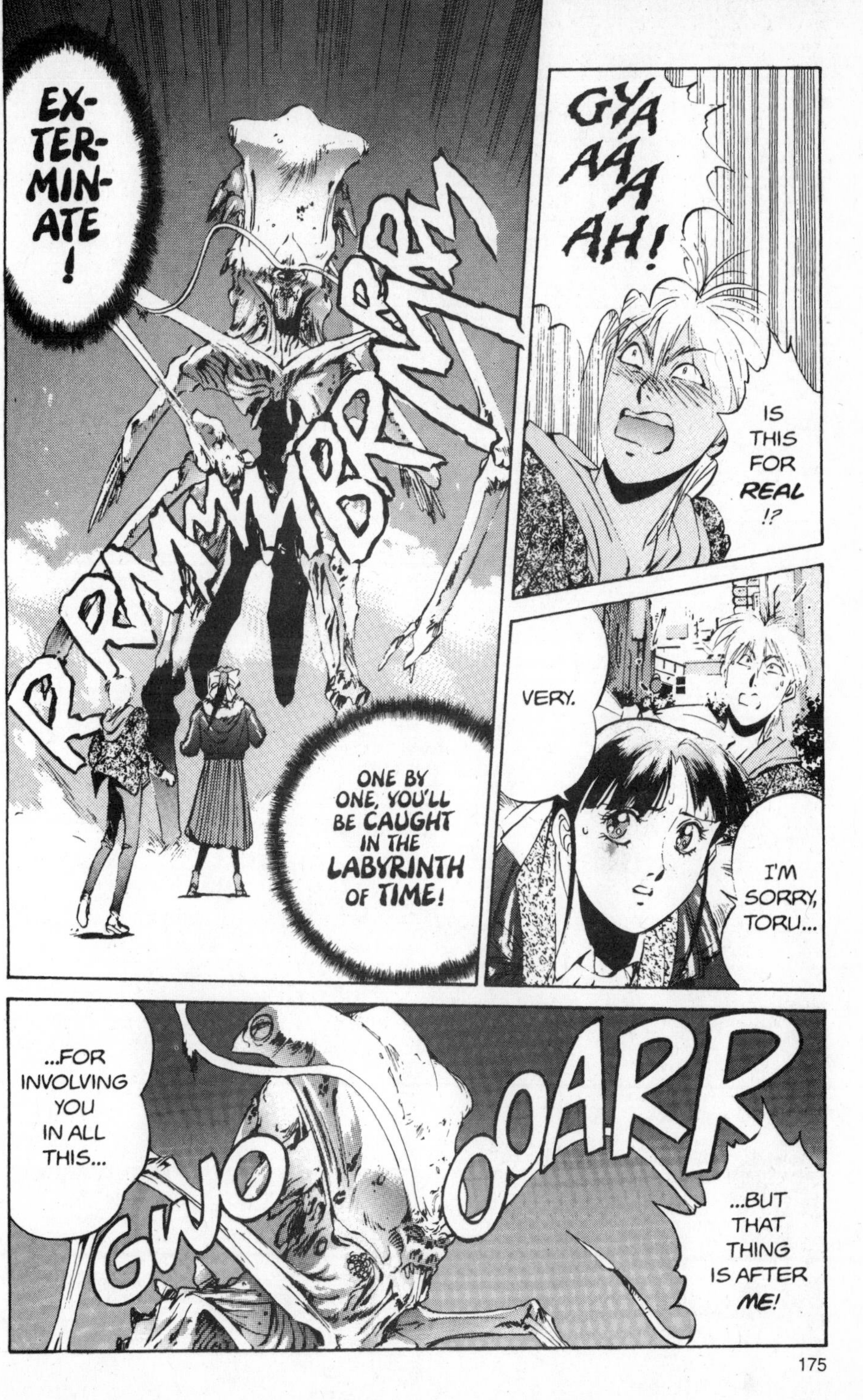
EX-TER-MIN-ATE!
ONE BY ONE, YOU'LL BE CAUGHT IN THE LABYRINTH OF TIME!
GYAAAAAAH!
IS THIS FOR REAL!?
VERY.
I'M SORRY, TORU...
...FOR INVOLVING YOU IN ALL THIS...
GWOOOARR
...BUT THAT THING IS AFTER ME!

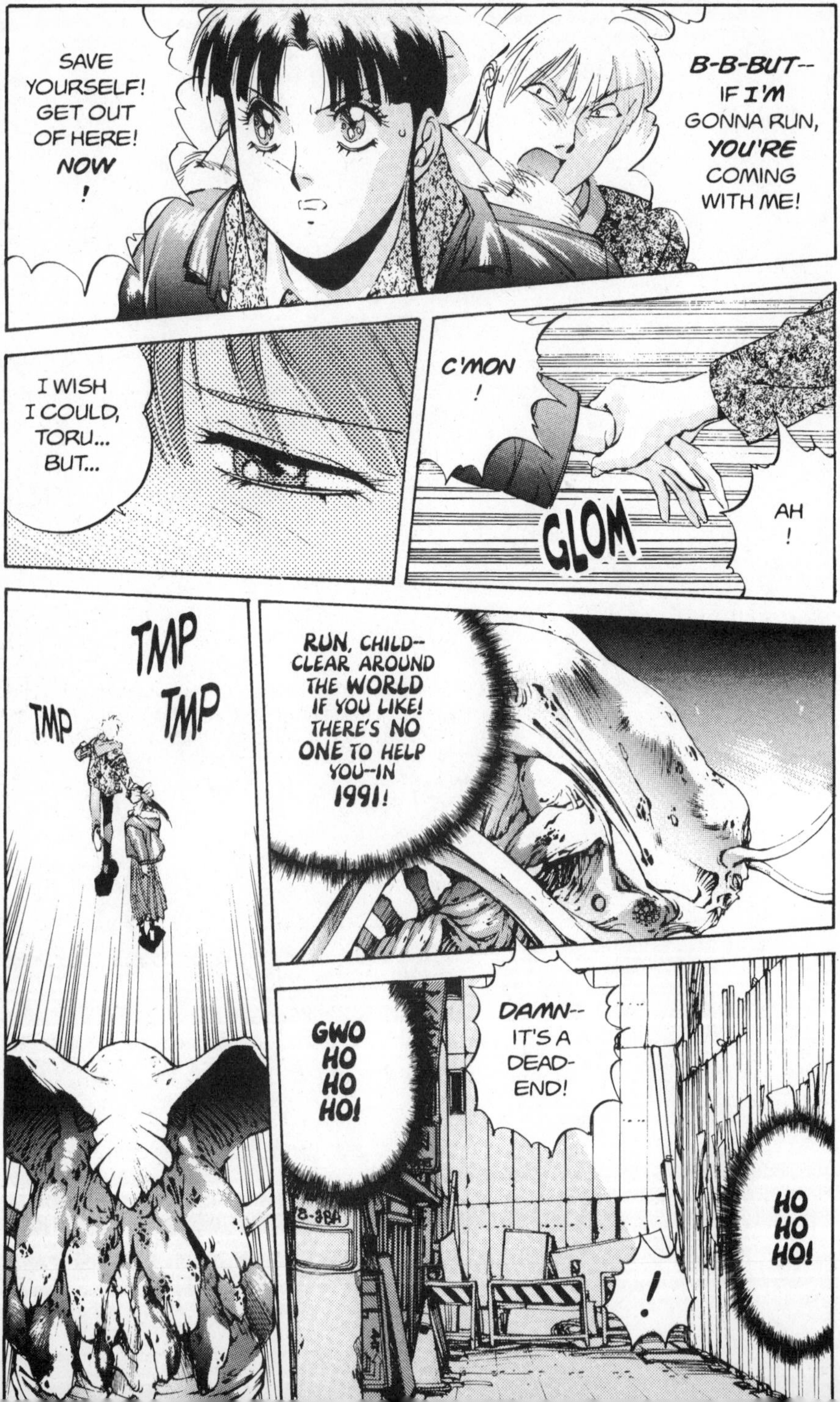

SAVE YOURSELF! GET OUT OF HERE! NOW!
B-B-BUT-- IF I'M GONNA RUN, YOU'RE COMING WITH ME!
I WISH I COULD, TORU... BUT...
C'MON!
GLOM
AH!
TMP
TMP
TMP
RUN, CHILD-- CLEAR AROUND THE WORLD IF YOU LIKE! THERE'S NO ONE TO HELP YOU--IN 1991!
GWO HO HO HO!
DAMN-- IT'S A DEAD-END!
HO HO HO!
!

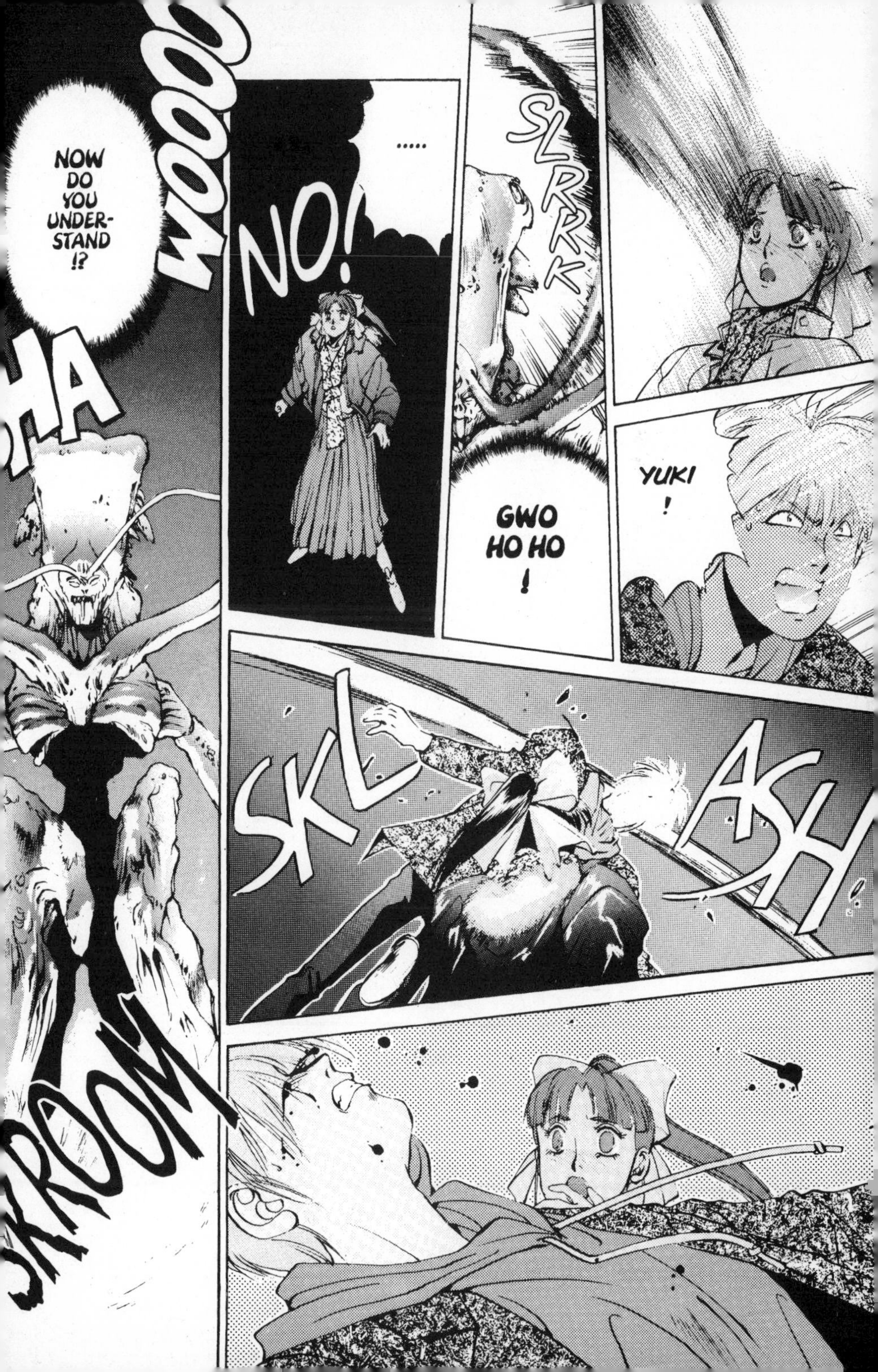
WOOOOO
NOW DO YOU UNDER-STAND!?
HA
KROOM
.....
NO!
SLRRK
GWO HO HO!
YUKI!
SKL ASH

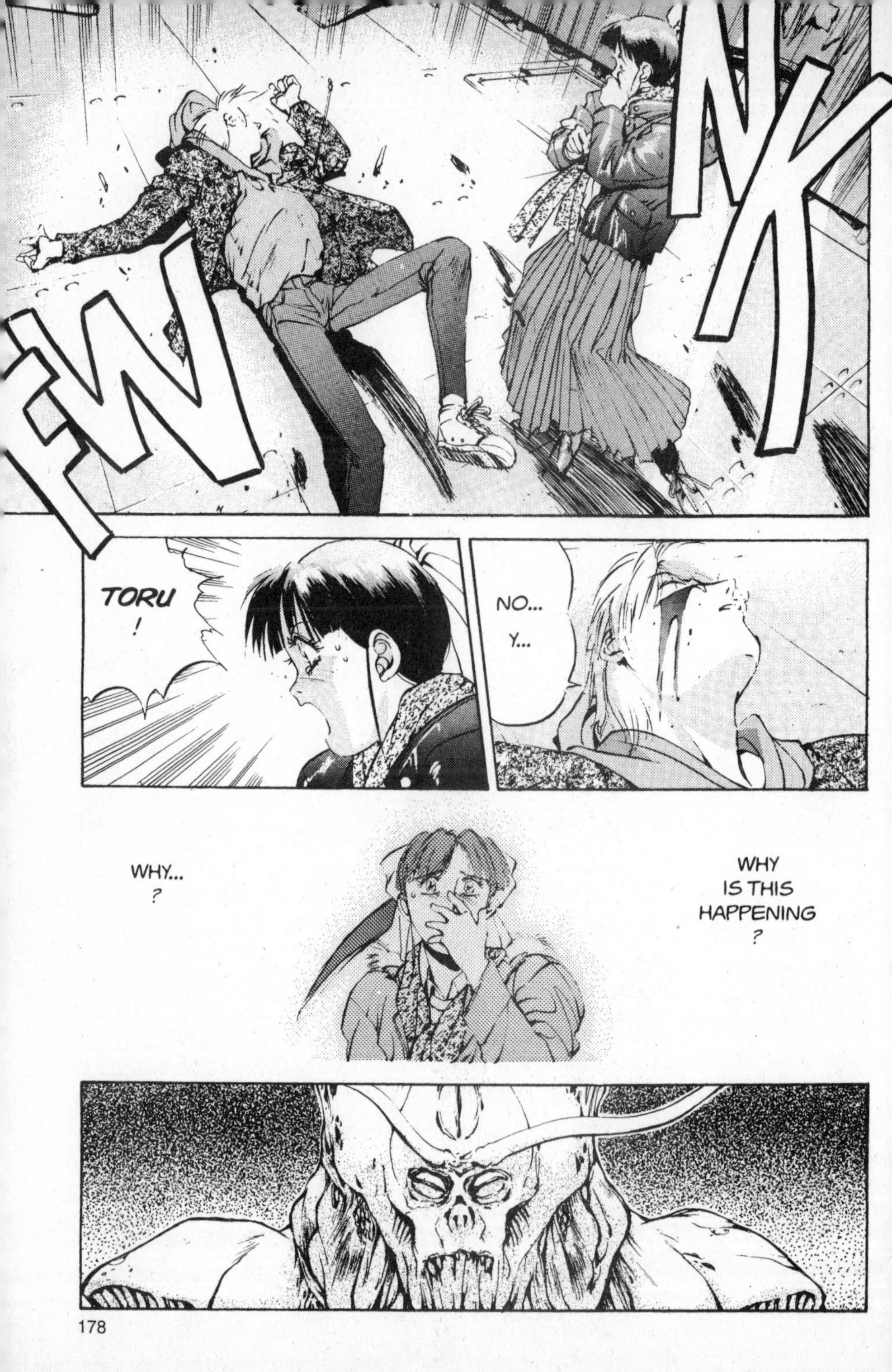
TORU!
NO... Y...
WHY...?
WHY IS THIS HAPPENING?

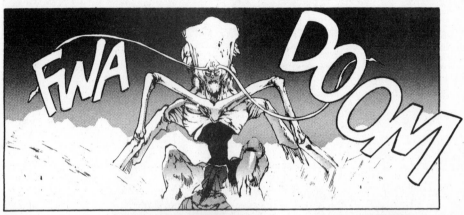

I...I **HAVE** TO FIGHT! IF I **DON'T**...

TORU AND **EVERYONE** HERE WILL **DIE**!

TORU...

BUT... I...

...I DON'T HAVE ANY **WEAPONS**!

AND THE **REST** OF THE A.M.P.--

--THEY AREN'T HERE EITHER!

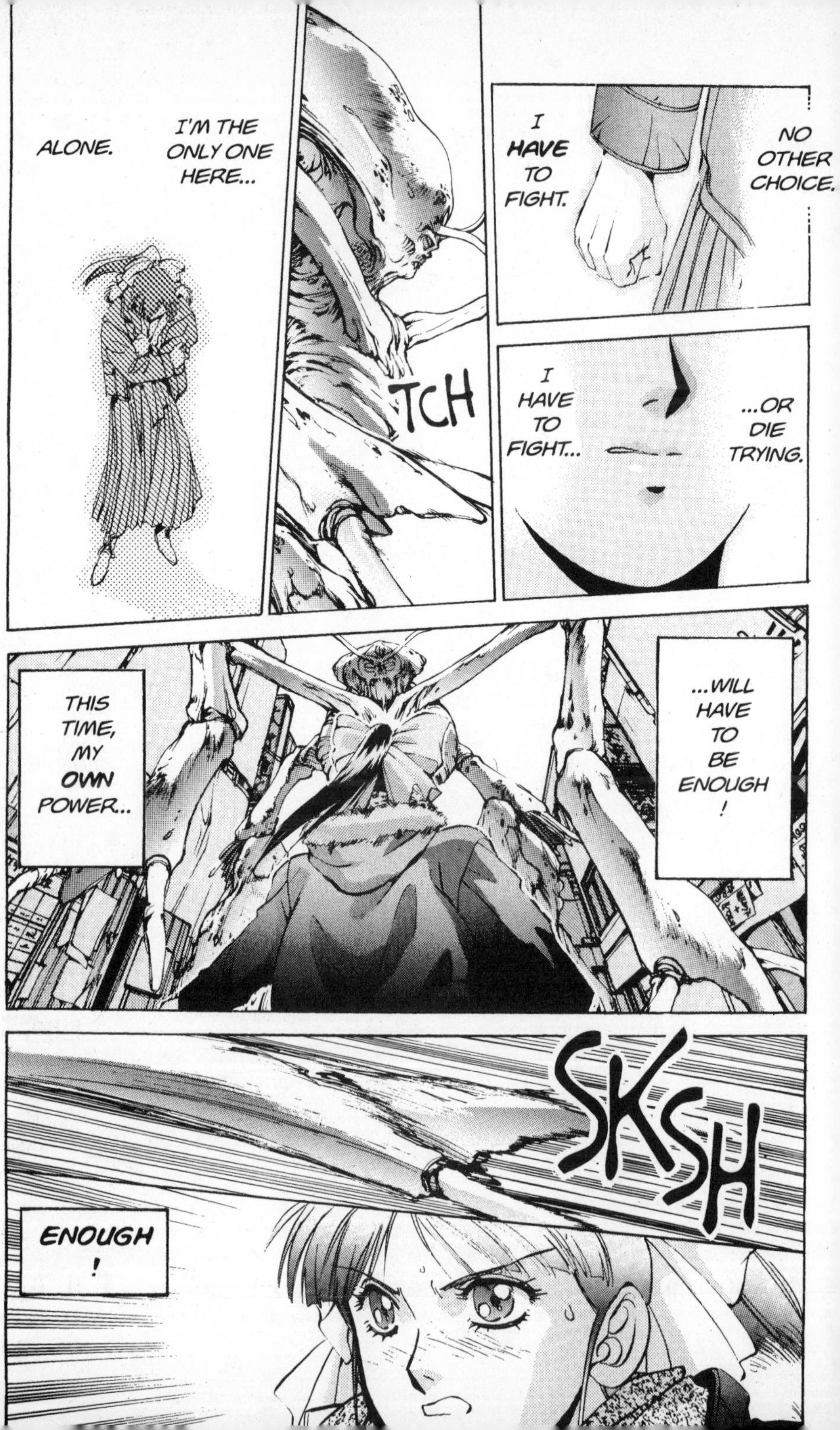
ALONE.
I'M THE ONLY ONE HERE...
TCH
I **HAVE** TO FIGHT.
NO OTHER CHOICE.
I HAVE TO FIGHT...
...OR DIE TRYING.
THIS TIME, MY **OWN** POWER...
...WILL HAVE TO BE ENOUGH!
SKSH
ENOUGH!

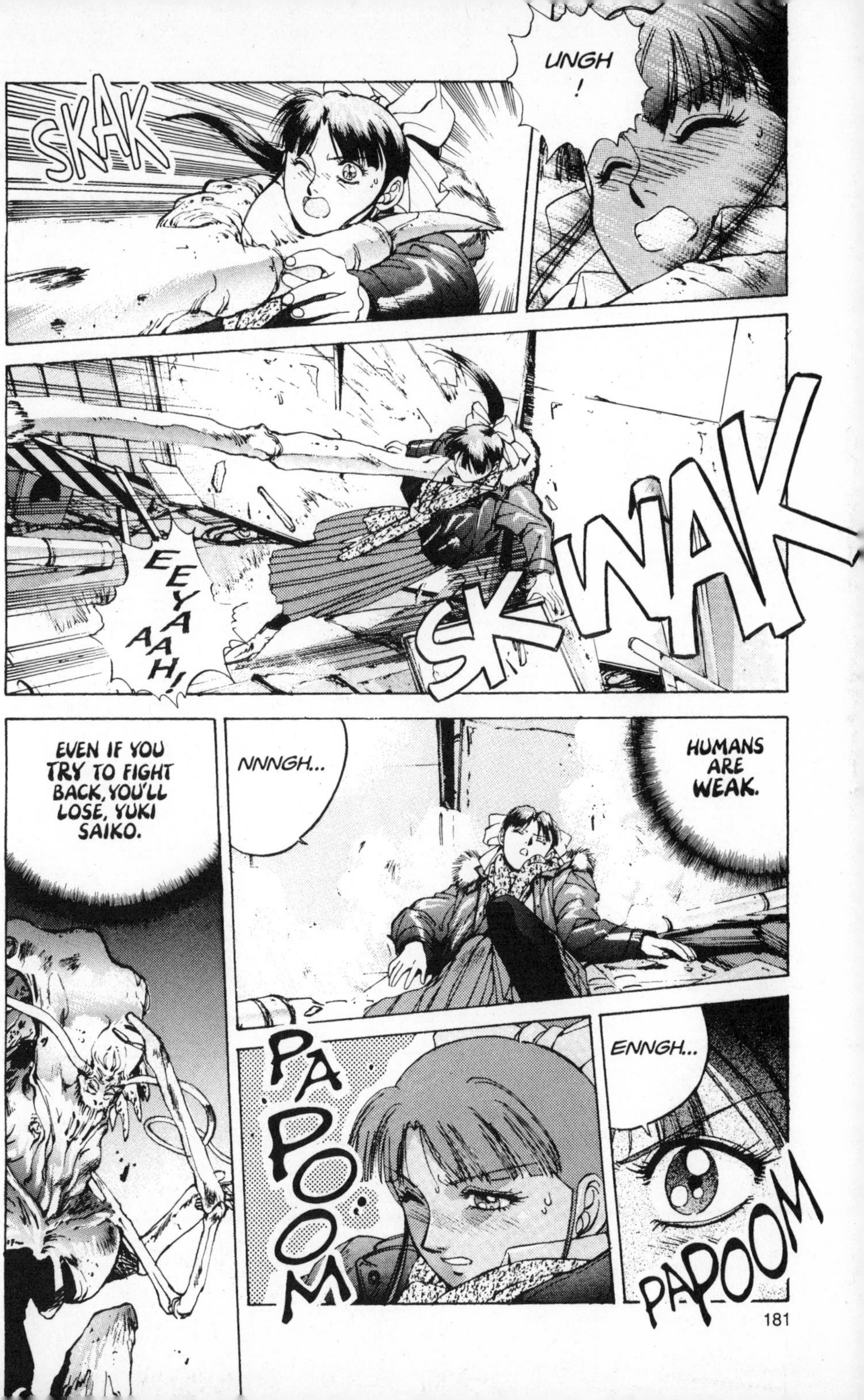
SKAK
UNGH!
EEYAAAH!
SKWAK
EVEN IF YOU TRY TO FIGHT BACK, YOU'LL LOSE, YUKI SAIKO.
NNNGH...
HUMANS ARE WEAK.
PAPOOM
ENNGH...
PAPOOM

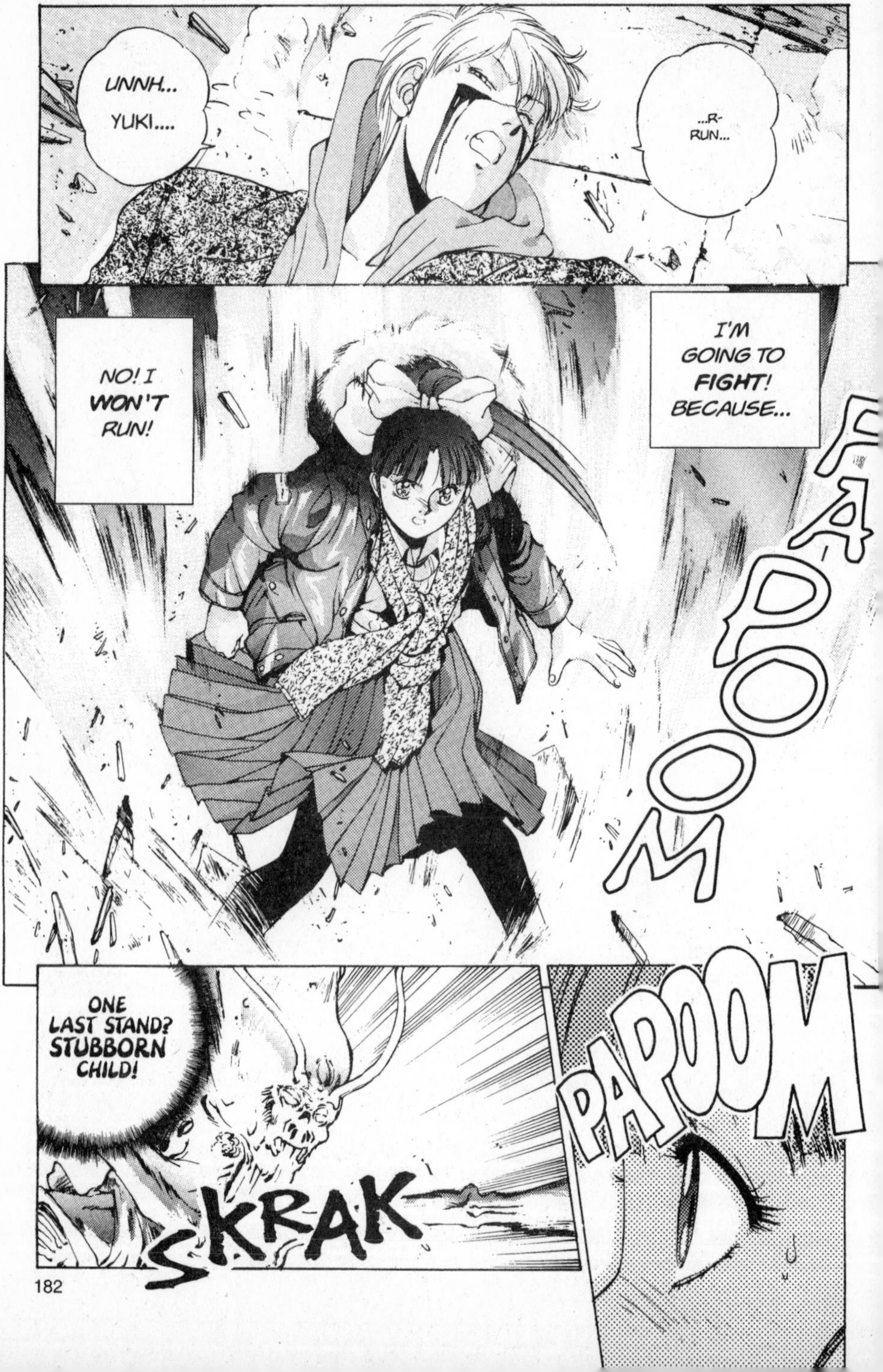
UNNH... YUKI....
...R-RUN...
NO! I WON'T RUN!
I'M GOING TO FIGHT! BECAUSE...
PAPOOM
ONE LAST STAND? STUBBORN CHILD!
SKRAK
PAPOOM

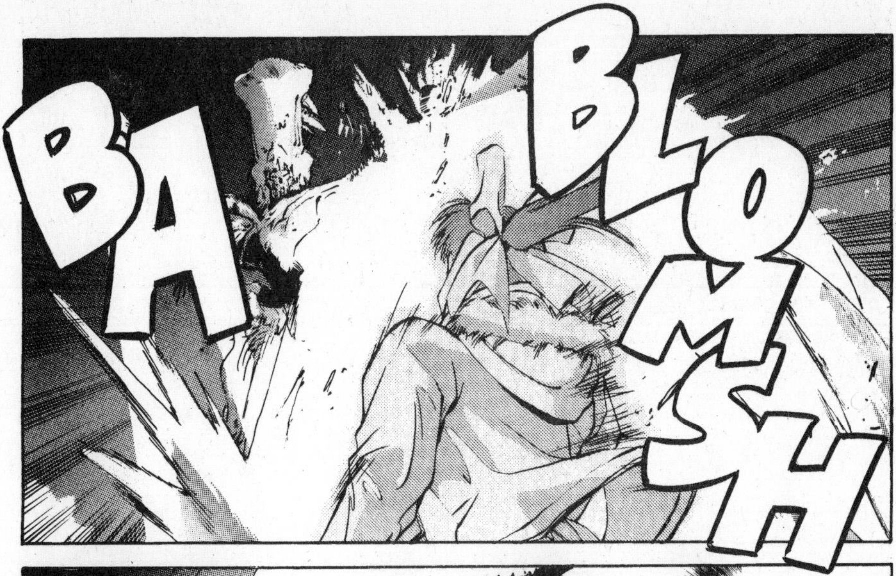
BA
BLOMSH

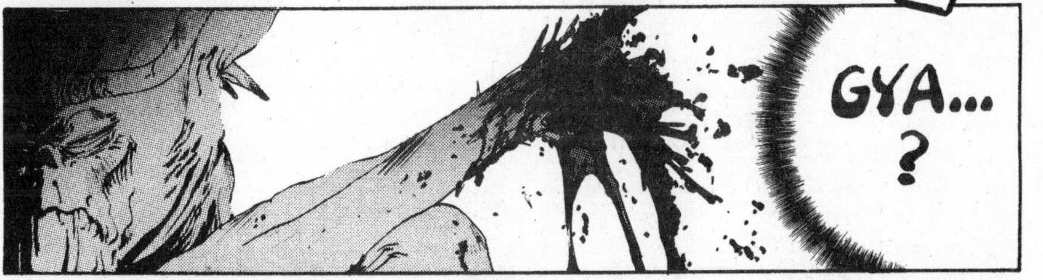
GYA...
?

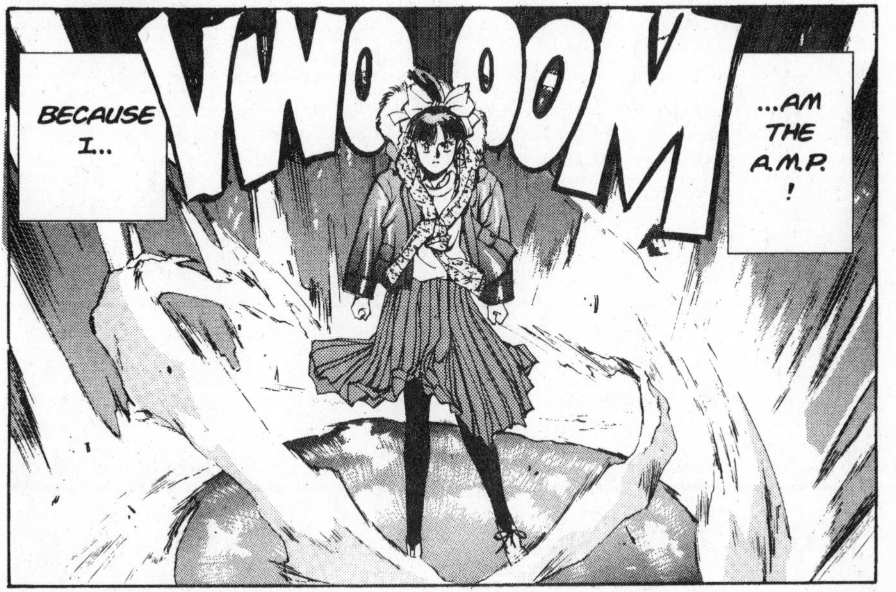
BECAUSE I...
VWO OOM
...AM THE A.M.P. !

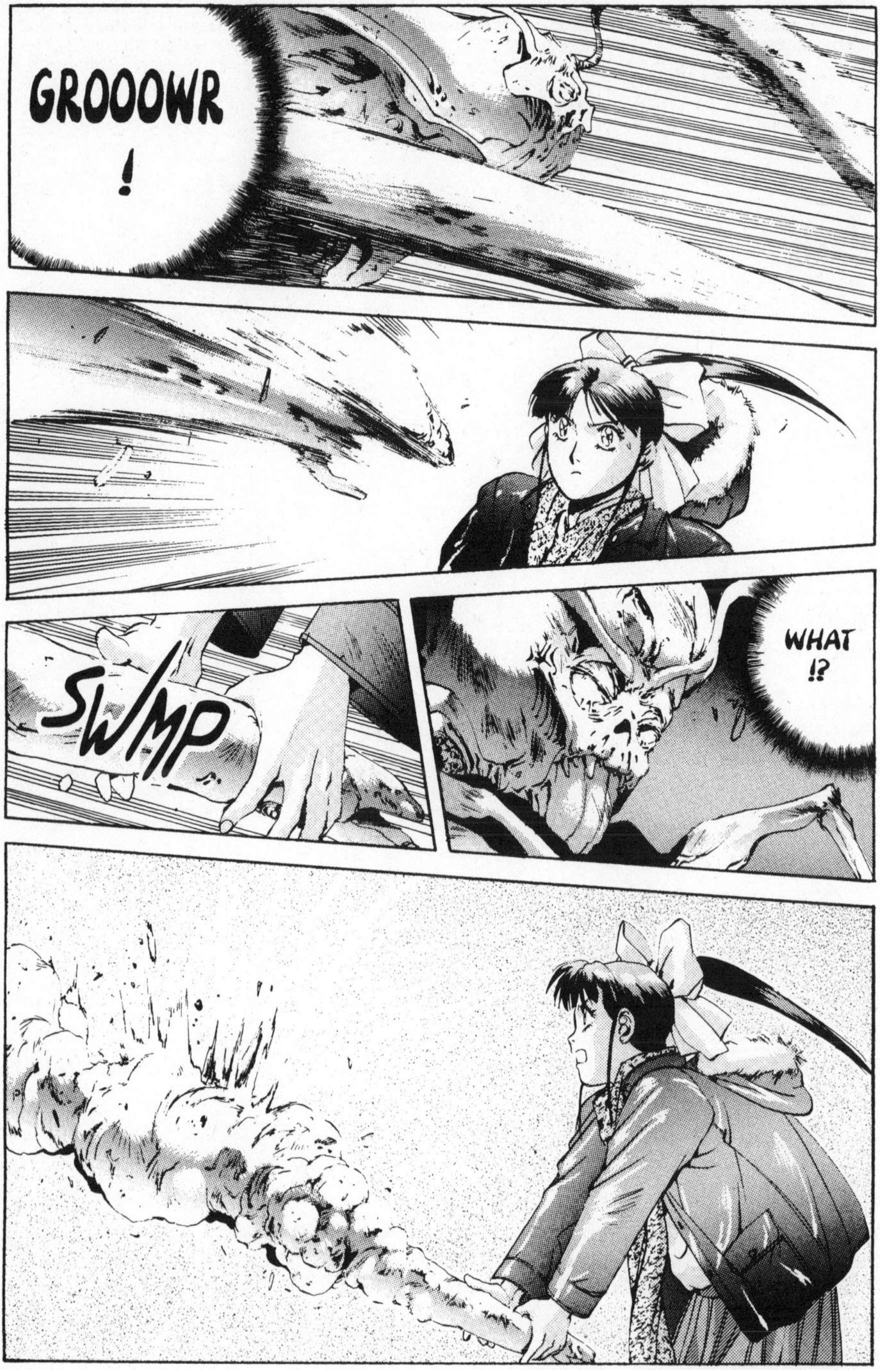
GROOOWR
!
SWMP
WHAT
!?

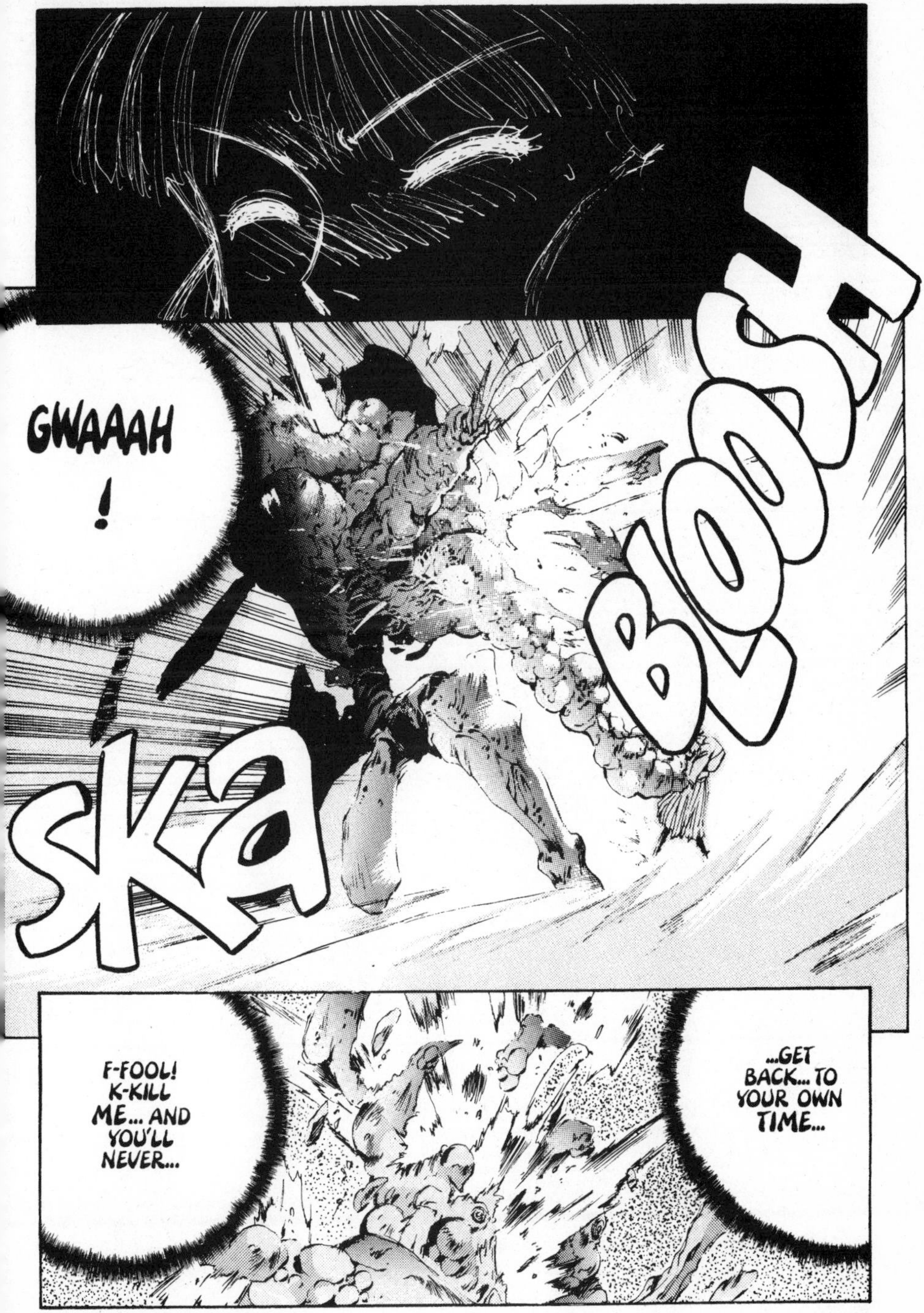
GWAAAH !
SKA
BLOOSH
F-FOOL! K-KILL ME... AND YOU'LL NEVER...
...GET BACK... TO YOUR OWN TIME...

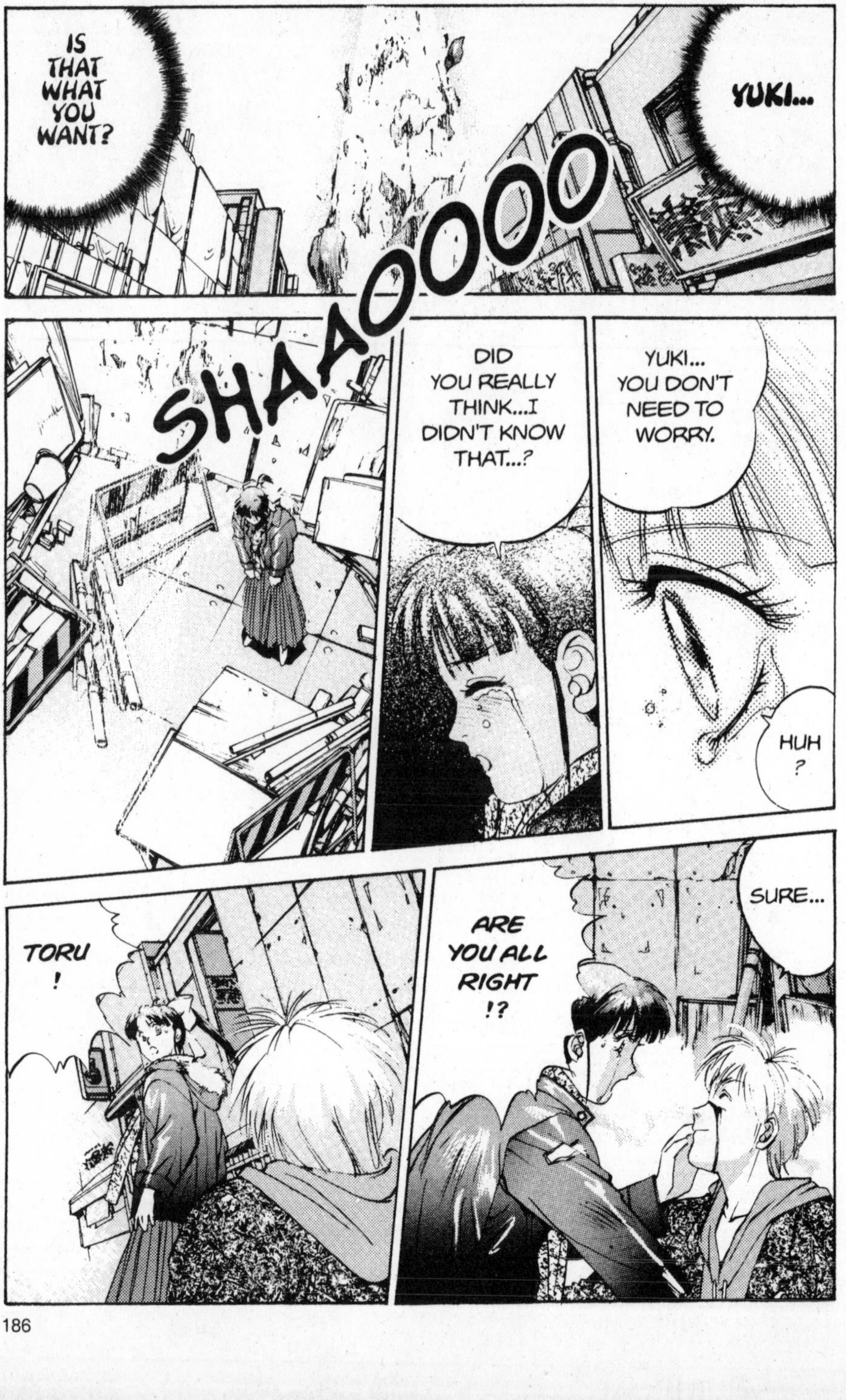
IS THAT WHAT YOU WANT?
YUKI...
SHAAOOOOO
DID YOU REALLY THINK...I DIDN'T KNOW THAT...?
YUKI... YOU DON'T NEED TO WORRY.
HUH?
TORU!
ARE YOU ALL RIGHT!?
SURE...

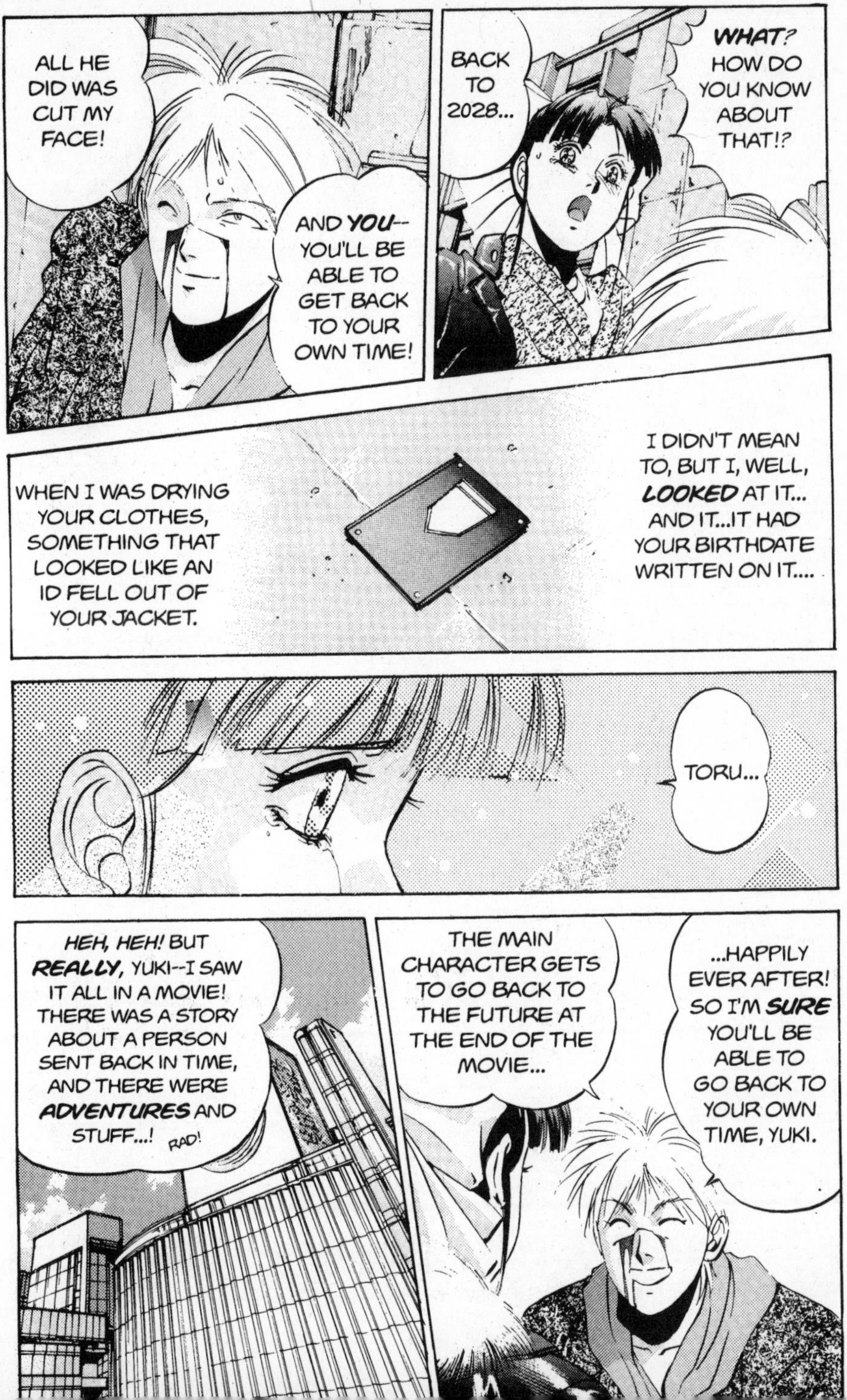
ALL HE DID WAS CUT MY FACE!
AND YOU--YOU'LL BE ABLE TO GET BACK TO YOUR OWN TIME!
BACK TO 2028...
WHAT? HOW DO YOU KNOW ABOUT THAT!?
WHEN I WAS DRYING YOUR CLOTHES, SOMETHING THAT LOOKED LIKE AN ID FELL OUT OF YOUR JACKET.
I DIDN'T MEAN TO, BUT I, WELL, LOOKED AT IT... AND IT...IT HAD YOUR BIRTHDATE WRITTEN ON IT....
TORU...
HEH, HEH! BUT REALLY, YUKI--I SAW IT ALL IN A MOVIE! THERE WAS A STORY ABOUT A PERSON SENT BACK IN TIME, AND THERE WERE ADVENTURES AND STUFF...!
RAD!
THE MAIN CHARACTER GETS TO GO BACK TO THE FUTURE AT THE END OF THE MOVIE...
...HAPPILY EVER AFTER! SO I'M SURE YOU'LL BE ABLE TO GO BACK TO YOUR OWN TIME, YUKI.

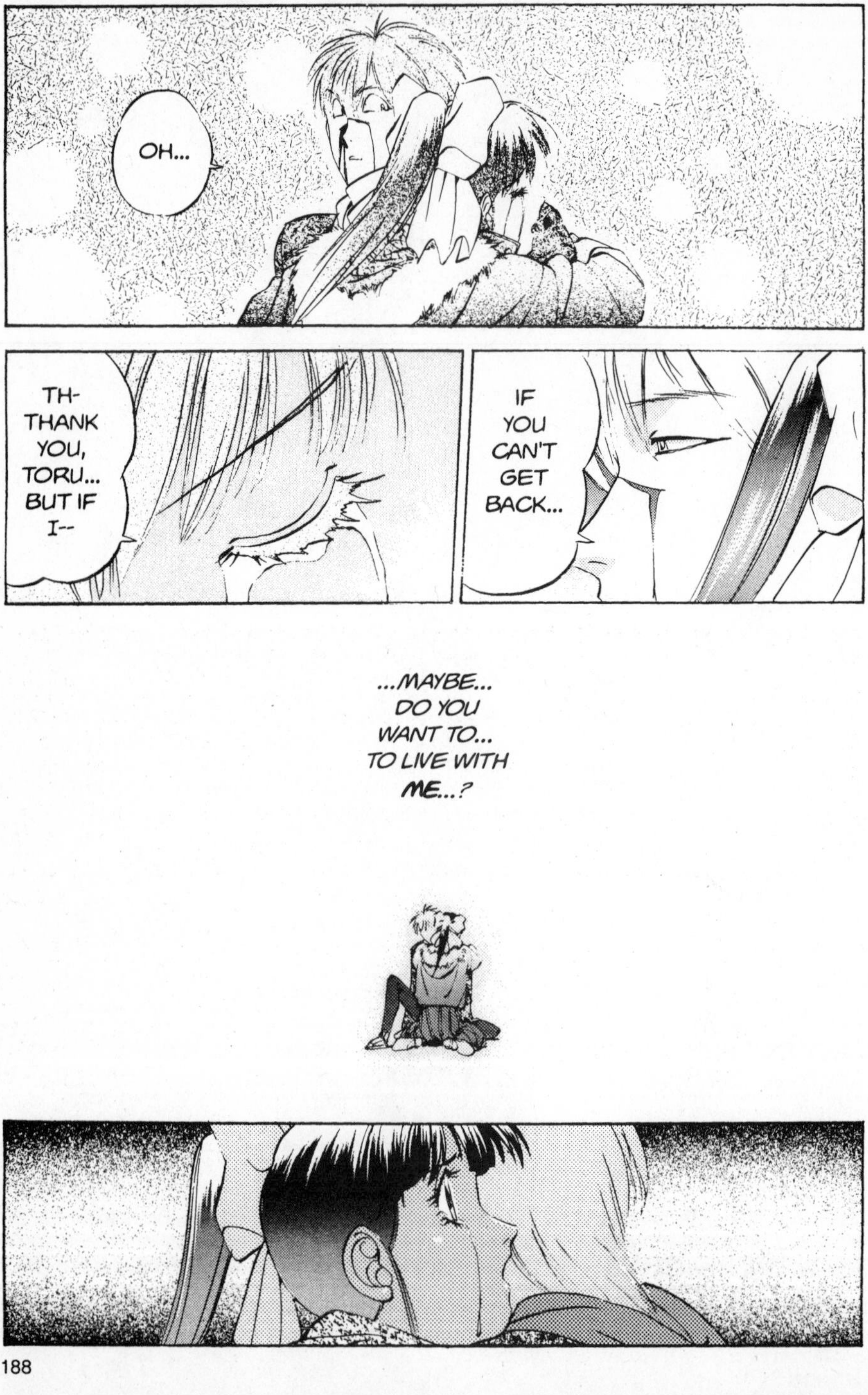
OH...
TH- THANK YOU, TORU... BUT IF I--
IF YOU CAN'T GET BACK...
...MAYBE... DO YOU WANT TO... TO LIVE WITH ME...?

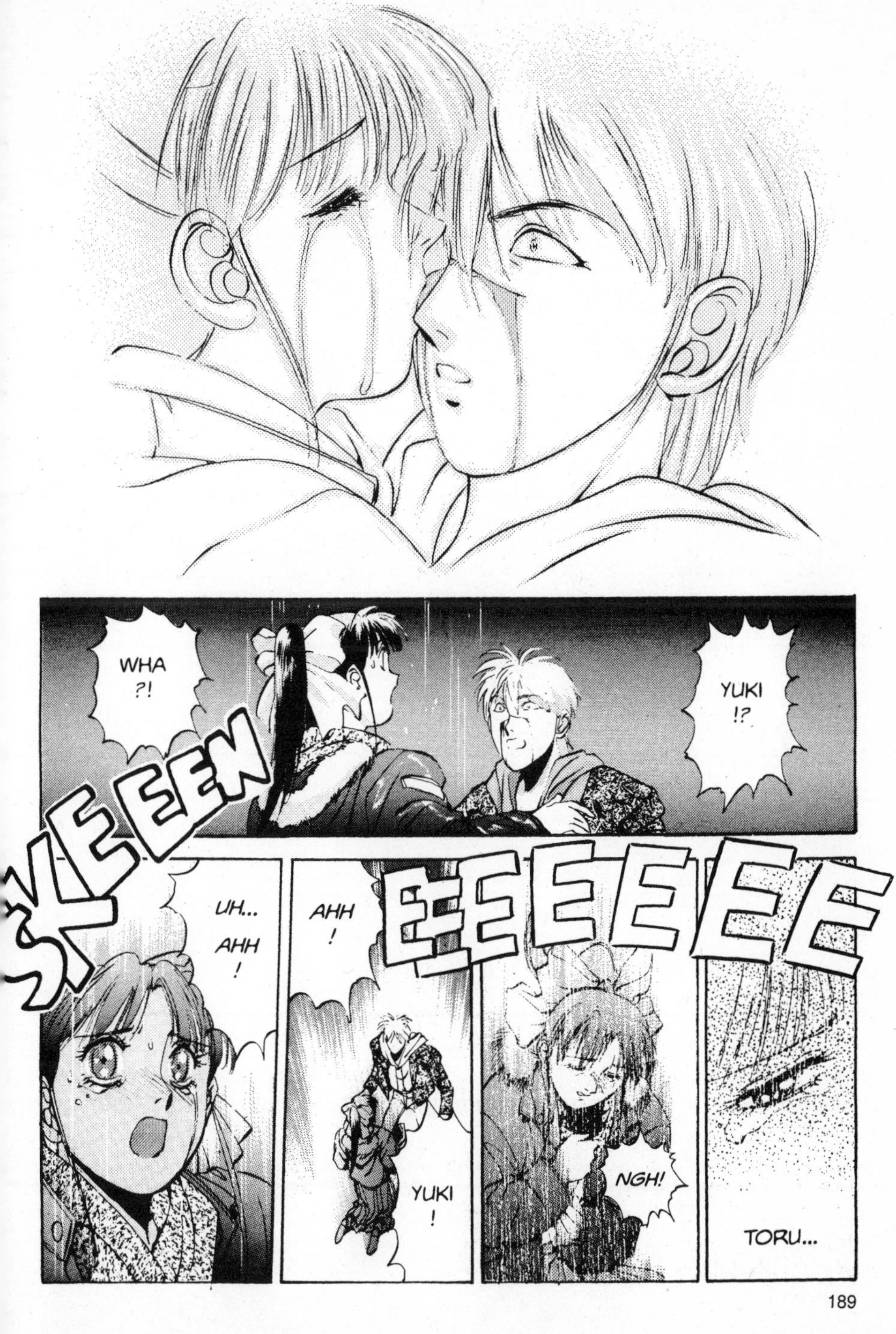
WHA ?!
SKEEEN
YUKI !?
UH... AHH !
AHH !
EEEEEEE
YUKI !
NGH!
TORU...

SHWIP
!!
YU...
YUKI....
SAAAAAAA

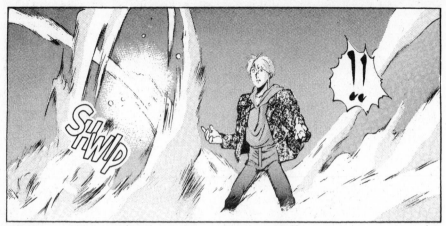

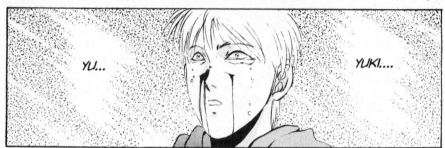

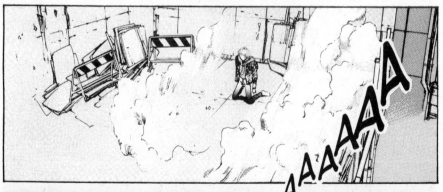

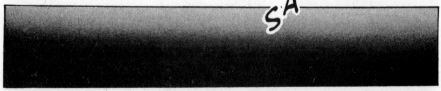

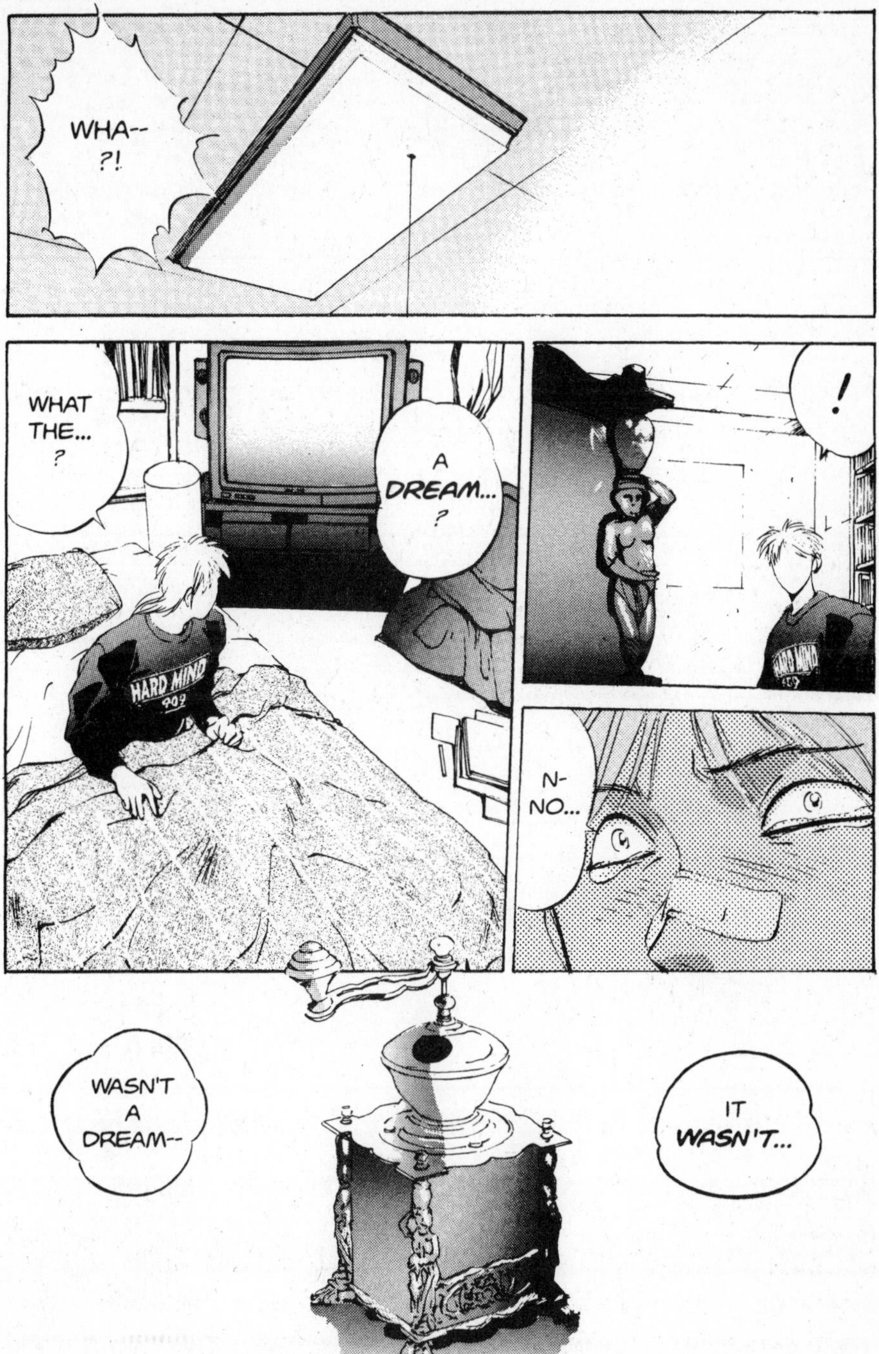
WHA-- ?!
WHAT THE... ?
A DREAM... ?
!
N-NO...
WASN'T A DREAM--
IT WASN'T...

=SIGH=

WHAT **WAS** THAT...? WAS IT A **DREAM?**

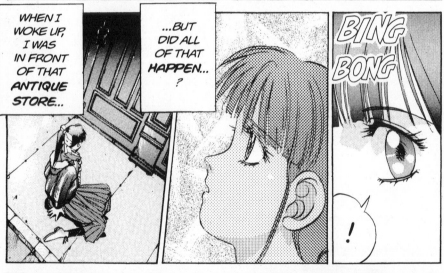

WHEN I WOKE UP, I WAS IN FRONT OF THAT **ANTIQUE STORE...**

...BUT DID ALL OF THAT **HAPPEN...**?

BING BONG

!

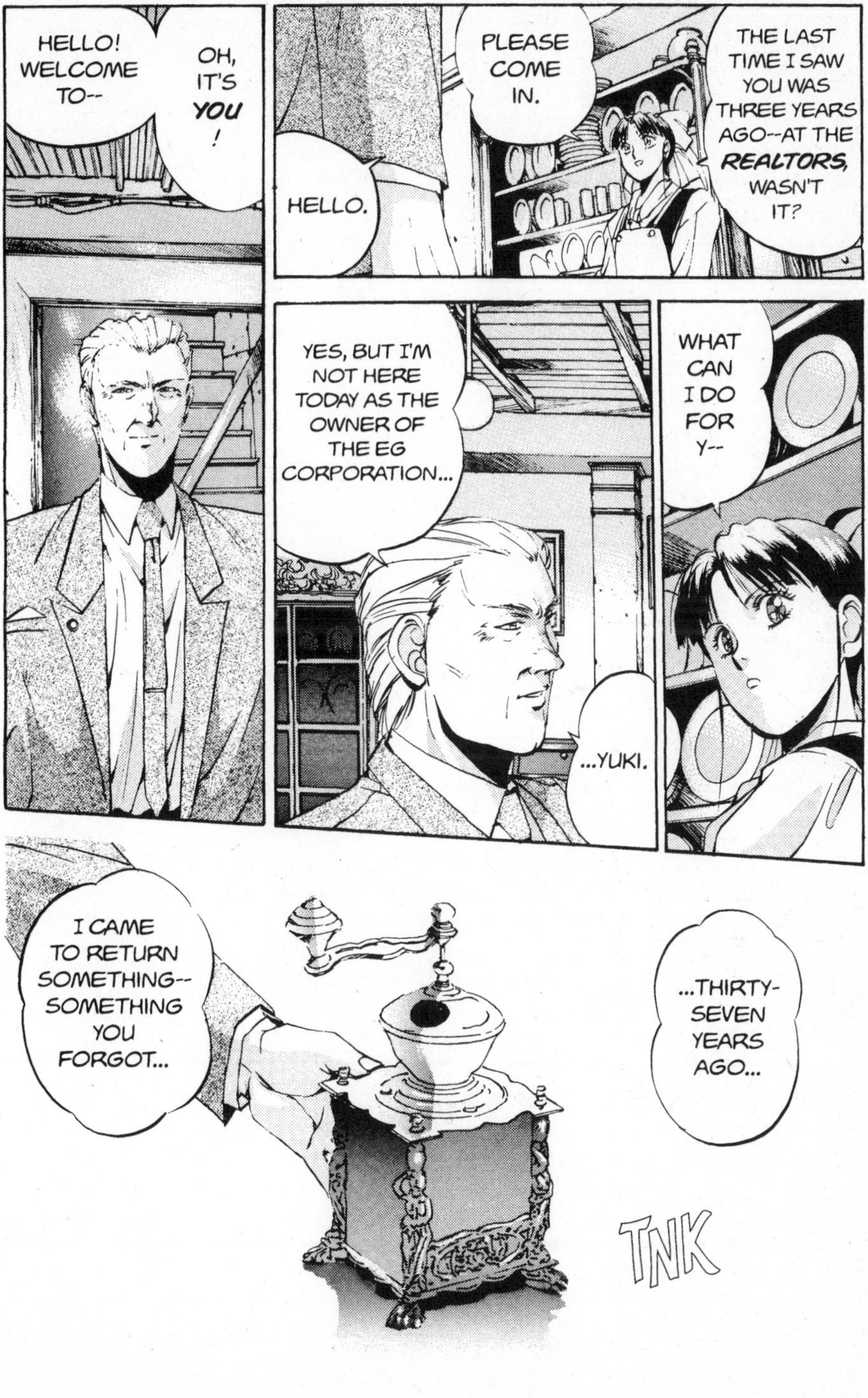
HELLO! WELCOME TO--
OH, IT'S YOU!
PLEASE COME IN.
HELLO.
THE LAST TIME I SAW YOU WAS THREE YEARS AGO--AT THE REALTORS, WASN'T IT?
YES, BUT I'M NOT HERE TODAY AS THE OWNER OF THE EG CORPORATION...
...YUKI.
WHAT CAN I DO FOR Y--
I CAME TO RETURN SOMETHING-- SOMETHING YOU FORGOT...
...THIRTY-SEVEN YEARS AGO...
TNK

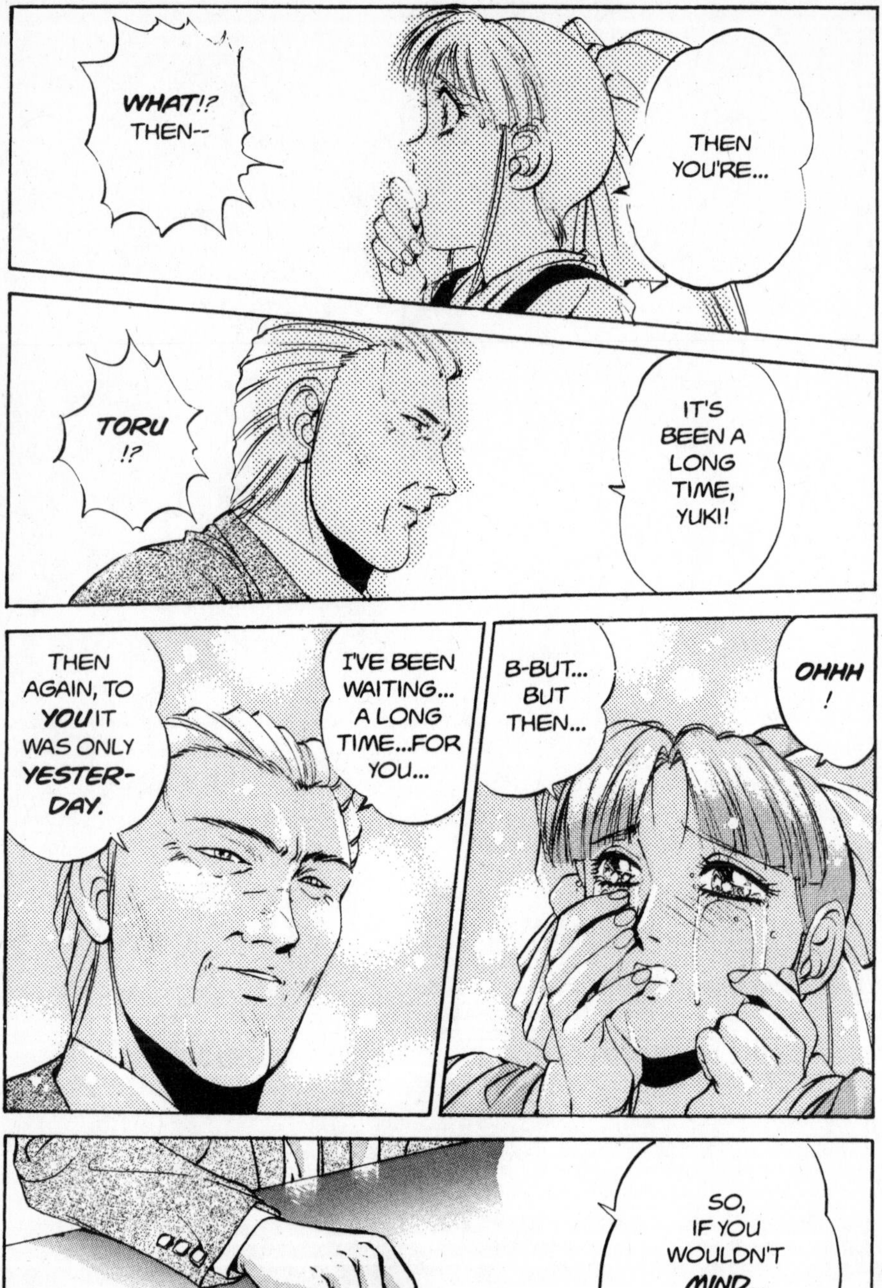
WHAT!? THEN--
THEN YOU'RE...
TORU !?
IT'S BEEN A LONG TIME, YUKI!
THEN AGAIN, TO YOU IT WAS ONLY YESTER-DAY.
I'VE BEEN WAITING... A LONG TIME...FOR YOU...
B-BUT... BUT THEN...
OHHH !
SO, IF YOU WOULDN'T MIND...

*...I'D LOVE
ONE OF
YOUR
COFFEES.*

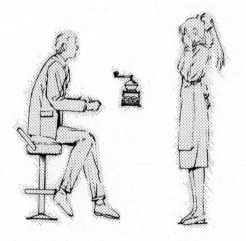

A . M . P . DATA FILE

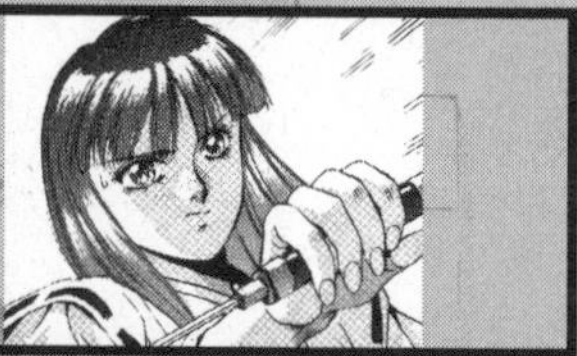

NAMI YAMIGUMO
IDENTITY: Priest
Heir to the House of Yamigumo and inheritor of its divine Ki-Rin dagger, Nami was put in the care of Rally Cheyenne at the age of 15 to develop her powers. A Shinto priestess, she can call upon many kinds of shamanic magic.

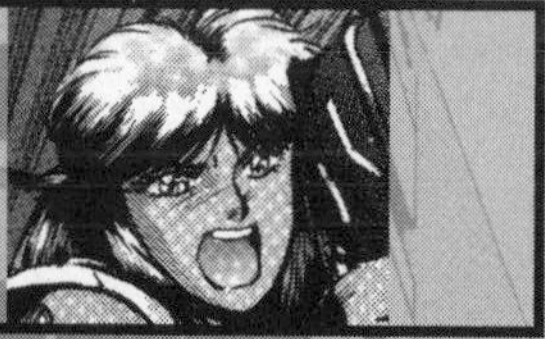

KIDDY PHENIL
IDENTITY: Cyborg
In 2023, policewoman Kiddy Phenil was nearly killed in combat with a megadyne (cyborg). She was saved by a combat-graft which gave her super strength and replaced 70% of her body with bionic parts.

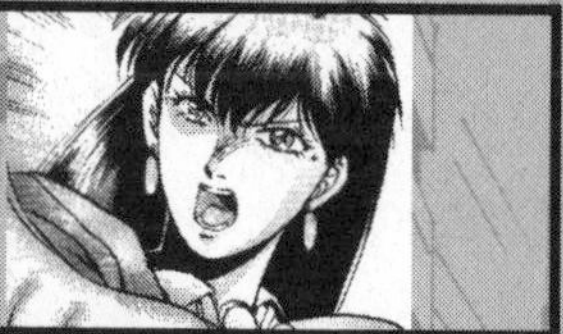

KATSUMI LIQUEUR
IDENTITY: Sorcerer
Katsumi is the daughter of the great magician Gigelf Liqueur, who was responsible for bringing the Lucifer Hawks to Earth. She has inherited many of his powers, as well as the living weapon known as Grospoliner, king of swords.

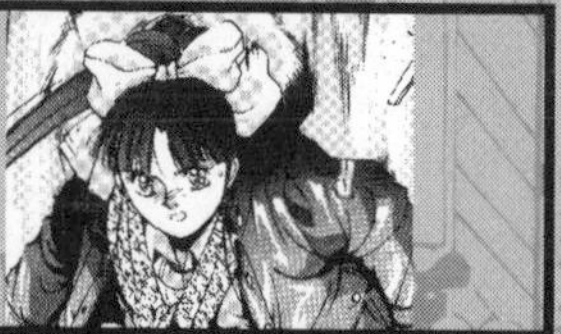

YUKI SAIKO
IDENTITY: Psychic
The youngest member of the A.M.P., Yuki was raised in a secret project to develop ESPer weapons. She has rejected the violent aspect of her training, and relies mostly on her intuition and precognitive abilities.

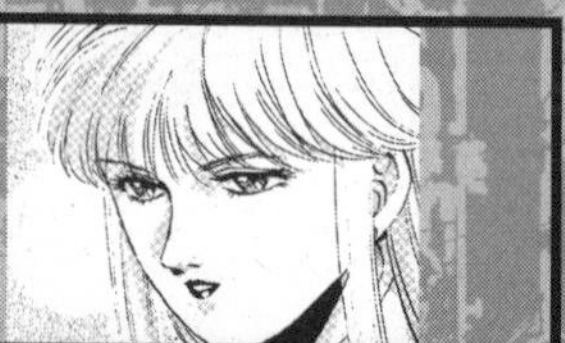

LEBIA MAVERICK
IDENTITY: Visionaire
Lebia Maverick specializes in computer operations; cybernetic systems in her body allow her to mentally enter 'computer logic space.' Her data bank is stored in an orbital satellite, giving her a memory capacity 3000 times that of an ordinary visionaire and far beyond a normal human being's.

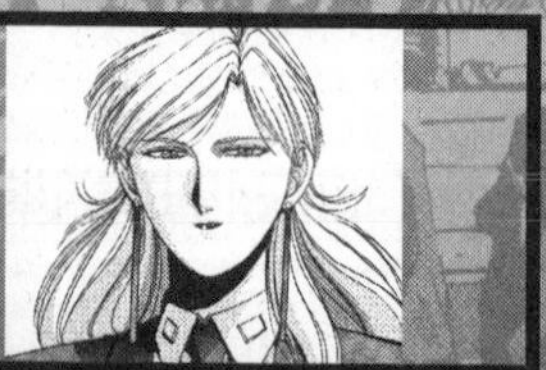

RALLY CHEYENNE
IDENTITY: Commander
The product of crossbreeding between a Lucifer Hawk and a human woman, Rally used her powers to turn the A.M.P. into the human race's strongest defense. She supervises all operations and acts as the A.M.P.'s liason to the government.

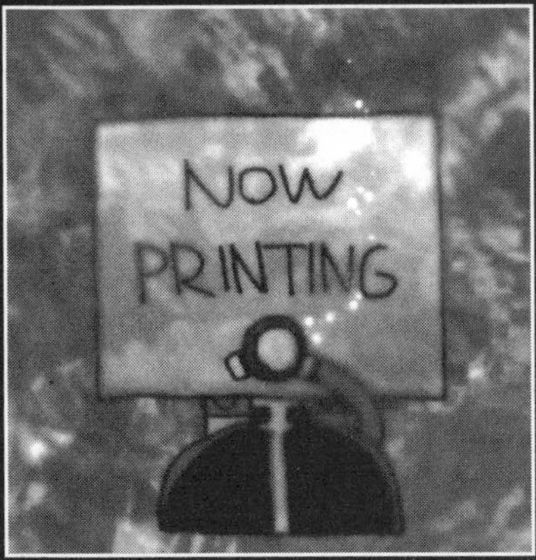
NOW
PRINTING

Kia Asamiya made his manga debut in 1986 as the artist for the fantasy series *Vagrants*. Since then, he has worked on many different stories, including *Dark Angel*, *Martian Successor Nadesico*, *Steam Detectives* and the manga adaptation of *Star Wars: The Phantom Menace*—all of which have been or are currently being translated into English, making Asamiya one of the most widely published manga artists in America. *Silent Möbius*, Asamiya's first work as both artist and writer, debuted in May 1988 in Japan in Kadokawa Shoten's monthly magazine *Comp Comics DX*.

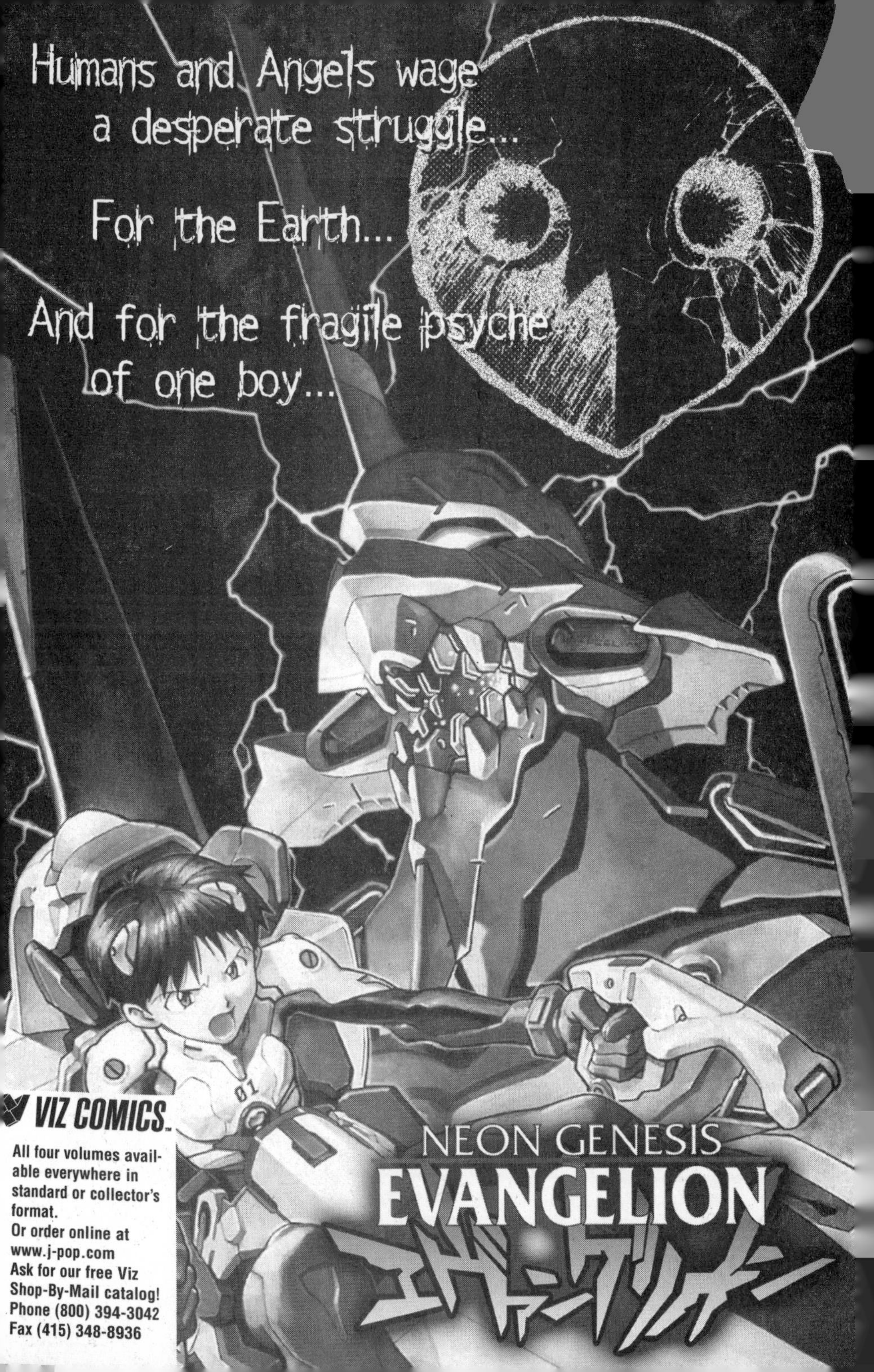
Humans and Angels wage
a desperate struggle...
For the Earth...
And for the fragile psyche
of one boy...
VIZ COMICS
All four volumes available everywhere in standard or collector's format.
Or order online at www.j-pop.com
Ask for our free Viz Shop-By-Mail catalog!
Phone (800) 394-3042
Fax (415) 348-8936
NEON GENESIS
EVANGELION

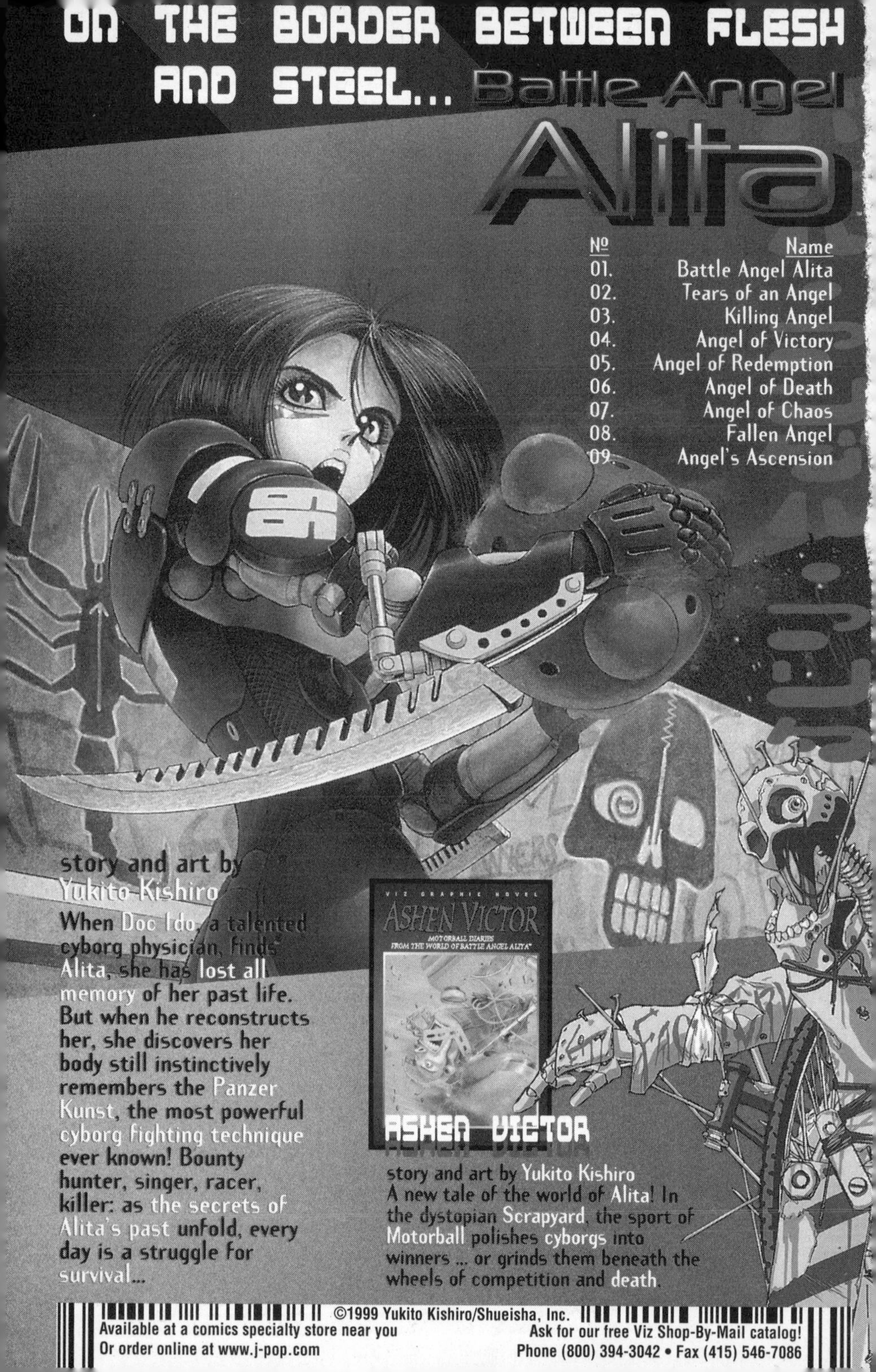
ON THE BORDER BETWEEN FLESH AND STEEL... Battle Angel Alita
№ Name
01. Battle Angel Alita
02. Tears of an Angel
03. Killing Angel
04. Angel of Victory
05. Angel of Redemption
06. Angel of Death
07. Angel of Chaos
08. Fallen Angel
09. Angel's Ascension
story and art by Yukito Kishiro
When Doc Ido, a talented cyborg physician, finds Alita, she has lost all memory of her past life. But when he reconstructs her, she discovers her body still instinctively remembers the Panzer Kunst, the most powerful cyborg fighting technique ever known! Bounty hunter, singer, racer, killer: as the secrets of Alita's past unfold, every day is a struggle for survival...
VIZ GRAPHIC NOVEL
ASHEN VICTOR
MOTORBALL DIARIES FROM THE WORLD OF BATTLE ANGEL ALITA™
ASHEN VICTOR
story and art by Yukito Kishiro
A new tale of the world of Alita! In the dystopian Scrapyard, the sport of Motorball polishes cyborgs into winners ... or grinds them beneath the wheels of competition and death.
©1999 Yukito Kishiro/Shueisha, Inc.
Available at a comics specialty store near you
Or order online at www.j-pop.com
Ask for our free Viz Shop-By-Mail catalog!
Phone (800) 394-3042 • Fax (415) 546-7086